Tolstoi: Art and Influence

Studies in Slavic Literature and Poetics

Editors

O.F. Boele (*Leiden University*)
S. Brouwer (*University of Groningen*)
J. Niżyńska (*Indiana University Bloomington*)
A. Rogatchevski (*Arctic University of Norway*)
M. Rubins (*University College London*)
G. Tihanov (*Queen Mary University of London*)
S. Vervaet (*University of Oslo*)

Founding Editors

J.J. van Baak
R. Grübel
A.G.F. van Holk
W.G. Weststeijn

VOLUME 66

The titles published in this series are listed at *brill.com/sslp*

Tolstoi: Art and Influence

Edited by

Robert Reid
Joe Andrew

BRILL

LEIDEN | BOSTON

Cover illustration: Leo Tolstoi in Iasnaia Poliana, 1908, the first colour photo portrait in Russia. Via Wikimedia Commons.

The Library of Congress Cataloging-in-Publication Data is available online at https://catalog.loc.gov
LC record available at https://lccn.loc.gov/2022050179

Typeface for the Latin, Greek, and Cyrillic scripts: "Brill". See and download: brill.com/brill-typeface.

ISSN 0169-0175
ISBN 978-90-04-51129-3 (hardback)
ISBN 978-90-04-53343-1 (e-book)

Copyright 2023 by Koninklijke Brill NV, Leiden, The Netherlands.
Koninklijke Brill NV incorporates the imprints Brill, Brill Nijhoff, Brill Hotei, Brill Schöningh, Brill Fink, Brill mentis, Vandenhoeck & Ruprecht, Böhlau, V&R unipress and Wageningen Academic.
All rights reserved. No part of this publication may be reproduced, translated, stored in a retrieval system, or transmitted in any form or by any means, electronic, mechanical, photocopying, recording or otherwise, without prior written permission from the publisher. Requests for re-use and/or translations must be addressed to Koninklijke Brill NV via brill.com or copyright.com.

This book is printed on acid-free paper and produced in a sustainable manner.

Contents

List of Figures   VII
Notes on Contributors   VIII

Tolstoi's Continuum of Influences   1
   Robert Reid

1   Does the Translation Matter?   34
   Carol Apollonio

2   Feeling and Contradiction in Tolstoi's *What Is Art?*   68
   Richard Peace

3   Tolstoi in the Work of Tolstoi   81
   Willem G. Weststeijn

4   Dostoevskii's Zosima and Tolstoi's Father Sergius: Literary Representations of *Starchestvo*   92
   Nel Grillaert

5   Tolstoi and Lidiia Veselitskaia's *Mimi at the Spa*: The *Fin de Siècle* Tourist Adulteress   111
   Susan Layton

6   Legitimate and Illegitimate Children: Rozanov's 'Indecent Proposal' to Tolstoi   133
   Henrietta Mondry

7   Tolstoi's *Resurrection* on the Russian Stage   148
   Olga Sobolev

8   The Dreamer and the Destroyer: Two Unconventional Tolstoians and Their Impact in Australia   161
   Elena Govor and Kevin Windle

9   Reconfiguring the Empire through Performance: Petr Fomenko's 2001 Production of Tolstoi's *War and Peace*   179
   Alexandra Smith

10 Bridging Cultures? John McGahern's *The Power of Darkness*   208
    Cynthia Marsh

11 Elizabeth Gaskell, Tolstoi and Dostoevskii   220
    Katherine Jane Briggs

    Index   237

Figures

1 Nicholas Illin. Reproduced by kind permission of the Illin family. 163
2 Nikolai Ge by Nikolai (Mykola) Iaroshenko. State Russian Museum. Public domain. 165
3 Nikolai Ge's What is Truth? Tretiakov Gallery, Moscow. Public domain. 166
4 The Illin family (1929). Reproduced by kind permission of the Illin family. 167
5 The Illins' family farm. Reproduced by kind permission of the Illin family. 168
6 Alexander Zuzenko c. 1905. Reproduced by kind permission of Ksenia Zuzenko. 169
7 Alexander Zuzenko in 1921. Reproduced by kind permission of Ksenia Zuzenko. 170
8 Cane-cutting. Reproduced by kind permission of Ksenia Zuzenko. 171

Notes on Contributors

Joe Andrew
Educated at Oxford, Joe Andrew was appointed to a Lectureship at Keele University in 1972 where he remained until retirement in 2018; he is now Professor Emeritus. He taught Russian literature and language for many years, before setting up a degree in Film Studies. He has published extensively, with over 25 books, most recently *Tolstoi and the Evolution of His Artistic World*, edited with Robert Reid (Brill, 2021). Most of his publications are on nineteenth-century Russian literature, but he has also written on twentieth-century Russian literature, as well as Russian and British film.

Carol Apollonio
Carol Apollonio is Professor of the Practice of Slavic and Eurasian Studies at Duke University. She is author and editor or co-editor of books and articles about Russian literature, including *Dostoevsky's Secrets*, *Simply Chekhov*, *Chekhov's Letters* (with Radislav Lapushin) and *The New Russian Dostoevsky*. She is also a literary translator from the Russian and Japanese. Her current projects include a translation of Alisa Ganieva's novel, *Offended Sensibilities*, for Deep Vellum, and the ongoing blog, 'Chekhov's Footprints', (https://sites.duke.edu/chekhovsfootprints/) tracking Russian writers across Siberia. In years past, Carol worked as a Russian interpreter and translator at nuclear arms control negotiations. She currently serves as President of the International Dostoevsky Society.

Katherine Jane Briggs
Katherine Jane Briggs was awarded a PhD in Theology from the University of Birmingham in 2007. Her thesis on 'Dostoevsky, Women and the Gospel: a Feminist Theological Perspective', was published by the Edwin Mellen Press in 2009, as *How Dostoevsky Portrays Women in His Novels: A Feminist Analysis*. Dr Briggs is a Licensed Lay Minister (Reader) in the Church of England, and the present focus of her research is on writing and teaching about Theology and Biblical Studies, and the works of Dostoevskii, which have recently attained new prominence in the instability of our times.

Elena Govor
Elena Govor, PhD (History), is a research fellow in the College of Arts and Social Sciences at the Australian National University. Her interests are early Russian-Australian and Russian-South Pacific contacts. Her publica-

tions include *Australia in the Russian Mirror: Changing Perceptions, 1770–1919* (MUP, Melbourne, 1997); *My Dark Brother: the Story of the Illins, a Russian-Aboriginal Family* (UNSW Press, Sydney, 2000); *Russian Anzacs in Australian History* (UNSW Press and NAA, Sydney, 2005); *Twelve Days at Nuku Hiva: Russian Encounters and Mutiny in the South Pacific* (UHP, Honolulu, 2010); *Tiki: Marquesan Art and the Krusenstern Expedition*, edited with N. Thomas (Sidestone Press, Leiden, 2019).

Nel Grillaert

Nel Grillaert worked as a doctoral and postdoctoral researcher at Ghent University (Belgium). Her main research topics were nineteenth-century Russian literature and philosophy, with a strong focus on Dostoevsky's and Tolstoi's embedding of religious, ethical and philosophical themes in their literary works. A list of publications can be found at https://biblio.ugent.be/person/801001475669. She moved from research to supporting researchers in their career and now works as career coach and career policy advisor for researchers at Ghent University. Research for her chapter was financed by the research foundation Flanders (FWO).

Susan Layton

Susan Layton is a research associate at Centre d'études des mondes russe, caucasien et centre-européen (CERCEC) in Paris. She has recently published *Contested Russian Tourism: Cosmopolitanism, Nation and Empire in the Nineteenth-Century* (Academic Studies Press, Boston, 2021). In addition to numerous articles, her previous work includes *Russian Literature and Empire: Conquest of the Caucasus from Pushkin to Tolstoy* (Cambridge University Press, Cambridge, 1994; ebook 2009). Her current projects concern Tolstoi: the development of his aesthetics, his relation to military memoirs of 1812, and his position vis-à-vis Russia's poetry of war in the Romantic era.

Cynthia Marsh

Cynthia Marsh is Emeritus Professor of Russian Drama and Literature, University of Nottingham, UK. She has written extensively on Chekhov and Gorkii as dramatists and on Russian theatre translated and performed in English (2020). She has directed her own translations from Chekhov, Gorkii and Ostrovskii, most recently *A Virtual Vanya* (2021). She curated the 2014 Nottingham University exhibition *Chekhoviana: Marketing a Foreign Classic to British Audiences*. She is currently working on new approaches to Chekhov's *The Cherry Orchard*.

Henrietta Mondry

Henrietta Mondry is Professor in the Department of Global, Cultural and Languages Studies at the University of Canterbury, New Zealand. She is a Fellow of the Royal Society of New Zealand and has published widely on literature and cultural history. Her recent research interests relate to representations of posthumanist thinking in literature. Her latest books are *Embodied Differences: The Jew's Body and Materiality in Russian Literature and Culture* (Academic Studies Press, Boston, 2021) and a co-authored *Dostoevskii i evrei* (Aletheia, St Petersburg, 2021).

Richard Peace

The late Richard Peace was Professor of Russian at Hull from 1975–84 and at Bristol from 1984–94. He had an international reputation as a specialist in nineteenth-century Russian literature. He wrote authoritative monographs on Gogol, Dostoevskii, and Chekhov, publishing with Cambridge and Yale University Presses. He also served as Vice-president of the International Dostoevsky Society and as President of the British Universities Association of Slavists.

Robert Reid

Robert Reid is an honorary fellow of Keele University and specializes in nineteenth-century Russian literature. As well as a number of articles and essays his publications include *Problems of Russian Romanticism* (Gower, 1983), *Pushkin's Mozart and Salieri: Themes and Structure* (Rodopi, 1995) and *Lermontov's A Hero of Our Time* (Bristol Classical Press, 1997). He has collaborated with Joe Andrew on several edited works, including *Aspects of Dostoevskii: Art, Ethics and Faith* (Rodopi, 2012) and *Tolstoi and the Evolution of His Artistic World* (Brill, 2021). He has also translated Russian poetry and contributed to collections by Prigov, Prokofiev, Rein and Sedakova.

Alexandra Smith

Alexandra Smith (PhD, SSEES, UCL, 1993) is Reader in Russian Studies at the University of Edinburgh. She has published extensively on Russian literature and culture and authored the following books: *Poetic Canons, Cultural Memory and Russian National Identity after 1991* (co-authored with Katharine Hodgson [2020]); *Twentieth-Century Russian Poetry: Reinventing the Canon* (co-edited with Katharine Hodgson and Joanne Shelton [2017]); *Montaging Pushkin: Pushkin and Visions of Modernity in Russian 20th-century Poetry* (2006); *Pesn' peresmeshnika: Pushkin v tvorchestve Mariny Tsvetaevoi* (1998); and *The Song of the Mockingbird: Pushkin in the Work of Marina Tsvetaeva* (1994).

Olga Sobolev

Olga Sobolev is Director of the Language, Culture and Society Programme at the London School of Economics and Political Science. Her research interests lie in comparative studies and concern nineteenth- and twentieth-century Russian and European culture. Her recent publications include: 'Anna Karenina: The Ways of Seeing' in *Critical Insights: Anna Karenina* (2021); 'A Collective Analysis of *The Kreutzer Sonata*' (co-authored with Robin Milner-Gulland) in *Tolstoi and the Evolution of his Artistic World* (2021); *From Orientalism to Cultural Capital: The Myth of Russia in British Literature of the 1920s* (co-authored with Angus Wrenn, 2017); 'The Reception of Alfred Tennyson in Russia' in *The Reception of Tennyson in Europe* (2016); *The Only Hope of the World: G. B. Shaw and Russia* (with Angus Wrenn, 2012).

Willem G. Weststeijn

Willem G. Weststeijn is Emeritus Professor of Slavic Literatures at the University of Amsterdam. He wrote his dissertation on the Futurist poet Velimir Khlebnikov (1983) and has published much on Russian literature of the nineteenth and twentieth century, particularly the avant-garde. For a long period he was the editor-in-chief of the journal *Russian Literature*. Recent publications include a two-volume edition on the history of Russian literature (in Dutch) and a bilingual (Russian-Dutch) edition of Russian poetry from its beginnings to the present day. He is currently translating Khlebnikov's poetry into Dutch.

Kevin Windle

Kevin Windle is an Emeritus Professor in the School of Literature, Languages and Linguistics at the Australian National University. His major publications include the biography *Undesirable: Captain Zuzenko and the Workers of Australia and the World*; *From St Petersburg to Port Jackson: Russian Travellers' Tales of Australia 1807–1912* (co-edited with Elena Govor and Alexander Massov), and *A New Rival State: Australia in Tsarist Diplomatic Communications 1857–1917* (co-edited with Alexander Massov and Marina Pollard). For his translations from various languages he has been awarded several prizes, including the Fédération Internationale des Traducteurs (FIT) Aurora Borealis Prize for the translation of non-fiction.

INTRODUCTION

Tolstoi's Continuum of Influences

Robert Reid

Abstract

This introduction locates Tolstoi's artistic achievements within a continuum of influences: those which helped him mature as a writer and those he exerted on other writers and thinkers. Section 1 considers the impact on Tolstoi of two figures who are generally claimed to have been formative influences on him: Rousseau and Schopenhauer. Rousseau's influence is particularly evident in the confessional component in Tolstoi's work, while Rousseau's craving for authenticity in social relationships is detectable in the views and lifestyle of the later Tolstoi. Schopenhauer emphasized the power of art in his philosophy, a subject Tolstoi wrestled with in his *What Is Art?*. Section 2 examines Tolstoi's debt to Pushkin in the provision of themes he elaborated at length; though in his later years Tolstoi repudiated his predecessor's work along with that of many other major writers. Section 3 traces the evolution of Tolstoi's popularity in England, from his early acclaim by Matthew Arnold to later polemics centring on *Anna Karenina*. Section 4 examines aspects of Tolstoi's philosophical thought, and contemporary thinkers' reactions to it. Tolstoi's legacy in post-revolutionary Russia is the theme of Section 5, while Section 6 assesses Tolstoi's popularity today. Section 7 reviews the chapters of the collection.

Keywords

Influences on Tolstoi – Tolstoi as influencer – Tolstoi today

Tolstoi's status as a major figure of world literature is generally acknowledged, even if not everyone would subscribe to Marc Slonim's view that he is 'unquestionably and universally recognised as Russia's greatest novelist'.[1] However, his combined impact as moralist and artist has guaranteed him an international

---

1 Marc Slonim, 'Four Western Writers on Tolstoy', *Russian Review*, XIX, 2, 1960, pp. 187–204 (187).

status unrivalled by any other Russian writer. Moreover, no other Russian author has inspired in their readers such a wide range of responses from enthusiasm to outrage. It is instructive to note, in their efforts to encompass the phenomenon of Tolstoi, the kind of superlatives that commentators resort to. D.S. Mirsky felt that it was 'impossible to deny that he was the biggest man (not the best, nor perhaps even the greatest, but just morally the bulkiest) that trod the Russian soil within the last few lifetimes ...).[2] G.K. Chesterton speaks of his 'immense genius ... colossal faith ...vast fearlessness and vast knowledge of life',[3] while subscribing to the 'two Tolstois' approach to the writer: ... 'a small and noisy moralist ... inhabiting one corner of a great and good man'.[4] Henry James famously numbers Tolstoi's longer works alongside those of Dumas and Thackeray as 'loose, baggy monsters' and Tolstoi himself 'is a monster harnessed to his great subject ... as an elephant might be harnessed, for purposes of traction...'.[5]

Such figurative language attempts to capture not only the international stature of Tolstoi as perceived by its users but also the varied cultural channels by which that stature has been attained. Tolstoi's social and religious views reached audiences far beyond Russia while at the same time he was a novelist of international renown. The novels themselves, particularly *War and Peace*, are indeed famed for their proverbial 'vastness', and despite the truism, this was a real aesthetic issue for novelists like James who argued the case for conciseness and those who, like George Steiner, advanced the 'law of necessary amplitude' in defence of Tolstoi.[6] As for Chesterton's parasitic homunculus, it personifies an issue central to Tolstoi studies: the relation of Tolstoi the artist to Tolstoi the preacher and dogmatist.

Daniel Moulin notes that 'Tolstoy's fame and literary talent make it possible to trace the complex reception of his ideas in the social, artistic, intellectual and political context of his time'.[7] These and related issues bear upon the contents of the present volume, and the purpose of this introduction is to provide

---

2 D.S. Mirsky, *A History of Russian Literature from Its Beginnings to 1900*, Francis J. Whitfield, ed., Northwestern University Press, Evanston, 1999 (first published 1926), p. 257. Mirsky goes on to tell us that the 'bigness of Tolstoi' required that he 'cut him in two' allotting him two sections: 'Before 1880' and 'After 1880' (loc. cit.).
3 'G.K. Chesterton on Tolstoy's Fanaticism', in *Leo Tolstoy: The Critical Heritage*, A.V. Knowles, ed., Routledge, London and New York, 1997 (first published 1978), pp. 481–9 (489).
4 Quoted by Slonim, p. 190.
5 Henry James, 'Turgenev and Tolstoy' in *Leo Tolstoy*, Henry Gifford, ed., Penguin, Harmondsworth, 1971, pp. 103–4 (104).
6 George Steiner, *Tolstoy or Dostoevsky*, Penguin, Harmondsworth, 1967, p. 258.
7 Daniel Moulin 'Tolstoy, Universalism and the World Religions', *Journal of Ecclesiastical History*, LXVIII, 3, 2017, pp, 570–87 (585). Hereafter Moulin (a).

an overview of the principal cultural influences that shaped Tolstoi's work, as well as the impact it had on later writers, critics and commentators. Section 1 considers the impact on Tolstoi of two thinkers who are generally claimed to have been formative influences on him: Rousseau for his social thought and aesthetics, and Schopenhauer for his quietism and the central role allotted to art in his philosophy. Section 2 examines Tolstoi's debt to Pushkin; Section 3 traces the evolution of Tolstoi's popularity in England. Aspects of Tolstoi's philosophical thought, and philosophers' reactions to Tolstoi are the theme of Section 4. Section 5 discusses Tolstoi's legacy in post-revolutionary Russia and Section 6 assesses Tolstoi's popularity today. Section 7 reviews the chapters of the collection.

1   Tolstoi, Rousseau and Schopenhauer

It has been said that, just as Goethe, a product of the eighteenth century, anticipated the nineteenth century in his works, 'much of the eighteenth [...] survived in Tolstoy' who was born and lived most of his life in the nineteenth.[8] The reasons for this lie partly in Tolstoi's aristocratic background with an upbringing that heavily emphasized French language and culture, but also in his resistance to the sort of radical social and political thought espoused by many influential Russian intellectuals in the aftermath of the Crimean War when Tolstoi was trying to establish himself as a writer. The eighteenth century 'survived' in Tolstoi largely thanks to Rousseau who, according to Rosamund Bartlett, exercised 'more influence on Tolstoy than any other thinker over the course of his lifetime'.[9] It is interesting that Bartlett sees Tolstoi's formative reading as 'inevitably' inducting him into the intelligentsia with its implications:[10] a social conscience as a privileged serf owner, a recognition of the unjustness of a regime (and a church) which permitted this, idealization of the peasant class, its attitudes and culture, and an awareness of the intellectual responsibility that rested on the intelligentsia. Yet at the same time, the intelligentsia itself was riven by factionalism and Tolstoi the individualist managed to alienate many of the key gatekeepers of contemporary Russian culture. Liberal ideas could, of course, be acquired by osmosis from a liberal background without direct reference to Rousseau, while some tendencies in Tolstoi's life

---

8   Thomas Mann, 'Goethe and Tolstoy' in Gifford, ed., pp. 180–7 (180).
9   Rosamund Bartlett, *Tolstoy: A Russian Life*, Houghton Mifflin Harcourt, Boston and New York, 2011, p. 76.
10 Ibid., p. 3.

and work – 'a *penchant* for utopias', a 'hatred of civilization', a 'passion for rusticity' (retiring to one's estate) might be seen as symptoms of a more generalized aristocratic habitus.[11] Tolstoi, however, was an avowed devotee of Rousseau to a degree not evident in other Russian nineteenth-century writers.

His Rousseauism is manifest in a number of ways. One is in the autobiographical works, particularly *Childhood*, where we find it both in the idealization of childhood for its authentic mode of perception, as well as in the character of Grisha, the holy fool, who not only embodies a uniquely peasant tradition, but is presented as a primitive being with strange and incoherent speech.[12] We further see the influence of Rousseauism in the strong confessional tendency in Tolstoi's oeuvre: his diaries, his *Confession*, as well as fictional works (*Resurrection*, *The Kreutzer Sonata*) have this component.[13] Merezhkovskii went so far as to suggest that all of Tolstoi's artistic work 'is at bottom nothing else but one tremendous diary [...] one endless explicit confession,'[14] but one may equally argue that his works also expose the limits of adequate confession. As J.M. Coetze points out, it requires a postscript to elucidate what Pozdnyshev confesses in the body of *The Kreutzer Sonata*, which raises the interesting question of whether a confession can be made full by another's elucidation.[15] Lermontov's framing narrator writes in the introduction to *Pechorin's Journal* 'One of the defects of Rousseau's *Confessions* is that he reads them to his friends';[16] however Rousseau himself thought that genuine confession, speaking truth about oneself, one's inner feelings, was entirely possible, even though the factual details of the account might be inaccurate.[17]

---

11   On this see Mann, p. 181. More negative fictional representations of rusticity are provided by Gogol (Manilov in *Dead Souls*) and Goncharov (Oblomov).

12   See Liza Knapp, 'Language and Death in Tolstoy's *Childhood* and *Boyhood*: Rousseau and the Holy Fool', *Tolstoy Studies Journal* (hereafter *TSJ*), X, 1998, pp. 50–62 (passim).

13   According to Kristina Toland, 'the regulatory dogmatic element of his diaries became the overall controlling tone of Tolstoy's autobiographical discourse and in his writing in general; it was the dominant form of self-reflection in his late life-guide books': Kristina Toland, 'Path of Life: Lev Tolstoy's Prescriptive Spiritual Diaries', *TSJ*, XXIV, 2012, pp. 15–25 (20).

14   Quoted in Mann, p. 183.

15   J.M. Coetze, 'Confession and Double Thoughts: Tolstoy, Rousseau, Dostoevsky', *Comparative Literature*, III, 37, 1985, pp. 193–232.

16   Mikhail Lermontov, *A Hero of Our Time* and *Princess Ligovskaya*, translated by Martin Parker and Neil Cornwell, Oneworld Classics Ltd., 2009, p. 51.

17   Coetze, p. 208. An inevitable confessional 'triangulation' is that of Augustine, Rousseau and Tolstoi. In this context it is worth noting that 'Rousseau took the [confessional] genre in a direction away from God [contrary to Augustine] and Tolstoy reversed it back again'. See Steve Hickey, *Second Tolstoy: The Sermon on the Mount as Theo-tactics*, Wipf and Stock Publishers, Eugene, Oregon, 2021, p. 22.

From this it is a short step to saying that it is the 'inner truth' of discourse that matters and its veridical status, whether fact or fiction, is non-essential. This is a distinguishing feature of Romanticism's vision of personal artistic development which replaces the classical notion of artistic 'apprenticeship' with 'sincerity [...] a truthful relation of the writer to himself' but culminating in Keats' dictum that 'truth entails beauty' and 'beauty entails truth'.[18]

This Romantic aesthetic cascades down to writers of the realist era. In the case of Tolstoi it manifests itself in a growing desire to dispense with artifice, with any superfluous barriers to the reader's immediate contact with the pure message of the author. This is the central theme of Tolstoi's *What Is Art?* and it is what Tolstoi seeks to enact in his late moralizing stories. It is also in this desire for immediacy that we see the social influence of Rousseau coming into play: both Rousseau and Tolstoi remove 'what they consider to be the artifices and conventions separating humanity from itself. Their utopian projects call for the restoration of an activity they consider to be essentially and naturally human – the flight from the isolation of the self and the striving toward communality'.[19] Thus, despite an apparent distinction between Tolstoi the artist and Tolstoi the social reformer and moralist they stand on a common foundation: the sage in peasant garb and the writer striving to move the reader are engaged in a consistent endeavour.

It is here that the influence of Schopenhauer is of relevance. Schopenhauer, whom Tolstoi read with enthusiasm after the completion of *War and Peace*, was the conduit through which he accessed the Eastern writings which influenced his later philosophy.[20] There is an argument, too, that Schopenhauer's own thought directly influenced Tolstoi's philosophy and life-style, that Tolstoi followed his 'ethics of extreme abnegation and abstinence'.[21] A more measured assessment would be that 'Tolstoy found an antidote to his own miseries, and hope for the redemption of humankind in Schopenhauer's prescription of art and Christian, quietistic oblivion as the only means to achieve victory over the

---

18   Coetze, loc. cit.
19   On this see Thomas Barran, 'Rousseau's Political Vision and Tolstoy's *What Is Art?*', *TSJ*, V, 1992 1–13 (9). Colm McKeogh argues that the most tangible influence of Rousseau on Tolstoi was in land reform which Tolstoi, like Rousseau, invested with a moral value, in that it freed not only the labourer but also the landowner from the sin of exploiting others: Colm McKeogh, *Tolstoy's Pacifism*, Cambria Press, Amherst, New York, 2009, p. 164.
20   See James Scanlan, 'From William James to Karl Marx: David Kvitko's Studies of Tolstoy the Thinker', *TSJ*, XV, pp. 67–78 (68).
21   Maurice Adams, 'The Ethics of Tolstoy and Nietzsche', *International Journal of Ethics*, XI, 1, 1900, pp. 82–105 (88).

will'.[22] Not only this, but for Schopenhauer '[A]rt, or rather the contemplation of a work of art has the power to free the intellect from its original subservience to the will, so that it rises above the trammels of everyday existence and beyond the illusory satisfactions of the world of appearances'.[23] This privileging of art makes Schopenhauer unique among philosophers and is thrown into relief by the bleak pessimism which pervades the rest of his philosophy. Through art alone humankind is granted a true perception of how things are in themselves while all other forms of human experience are at the mercy of the blind force of the will to be. It is this aesthetic aspect of Schopenhauer's thought which made it so congenial to artists in the latter half of the nineteenth century and beyond. Although Tolstoi had repudiated Schopenhauer's pessimism by the time he wrote *What Is Art?* the aesthetic component clearly left an impact.[24] While critical of many established classics the work is imbued with a fervent belief in the value of art. Works of art can be bad precisely because of art's ability to change minds, to generate powerful emotions, and they can be good for the same reason. In his diary Tolstoi expressed the view that

> [...] it's impossible to prove anything to people – impossible, that is, really to refute people's delusions. Every deluded person has his own special delusion. And when you want to refute them, you lump them all together into one typical delusion. But every person is unique, and because he has his own special delusion, he thinks that you have not refuted him. To him, you seem to be talking about someone else ...Thus refutation and polemics are never what is needed. [...]
>
> Only through art can you act on people who are deluded, can you do what you would like to do through polemics. With art you capture the deluded person completely and carry him away as needed. New conclu-

---

22 Gregory Maertz, 'Elective Affinities: Tolstoy and Schopenhauer', *Wiener Slavistisches Jahrbuch*, XL, 1994, pp. 53–62 (57). Bunin's interesting variation on this theme is that 'Schopenhauer's "systematized" sense of pessimism helped to explain his [Tolstoi's] own "chaotic" sense of the futility and terribleness of life'. Ivan Alekseevich Bunin, *The Liberation of Tolstoy: A Tale of Two Writers*, Thomas Gaiton Marullo and Vladimir T. Khmelkov, eds and trans., Northwestern University Press, Evanston, Illinois, 2001 (first published as *Osvobozhdenie Tolstogo*, 1937), p. 295, n. 32.

23 Maertz, loc.cit.

24 Tolstoi had become disillusioned with Schopenhauer's pessimism by the 1880s. See Henri Troyat, *Tolstoy*, Nancy Amphoux, trans., Doubleday and Co., New York, 1968, p. 316n.

sions of thought can be laid out by logical reasoning; but to contest them, you can't engage in refutation: you must take hold of people.[25]

In short, it is impossible to refute a person's fixed belief because, even though the argument you make to them may seem valid in general, the person concerned may refuse to apply it to their own subjective condition. An example of this is the syllogism which the ailing hero of *The Death of Ivan Ilich* recalls learning at school: All men are mortal; Caius is a man; therefore Caius is mortal. Ivan Ilich can see how this deduction might apply to Caius, but resists applying it to himself. It is an interesting question whether Tolstoi's artistic skill at this point allows the reader to apply the syllogism to him or herself, or whether it leaves them in the same situation as Ivan Ilich.

Schopenhauer particularly privileged music in his aesthetics because it is unmediated and unrepresentational.[26] It excites feelings directly, as a force in itself, rather than with accompanying context (words or images) and examinable causality. *The Kreutzer Sonata* seems to illustrate this view particularly well, though it is really a perversion of the Schopenhauerian view of music.[27] In the story music leads to a *crime passionel*: the protagonist becomes uncontrollably jealous of his wife's playing the piano with her music instructor and murders her. The music is what in the Catholic Church was traditionally called 'an occasion of sin': it brings the man and woman into close proximity, at the same time causing them to share together the moving experience of playing it. In this instance, though, aesthetic experience does not produce the Schopenhauerian relief from the 'will to existence' which is our customary experience of the world. Indeed, it is probably true to say that by this stage in his creative career Tolstoi had evolved his own version of Schopenhauer's all-powerful will: emphasizing 'the will's primacy over the intellect [...] the superiority of man's savage instincts over his civilising urge'.[28]

---

[25] Diary entry for November 4, 1889, quoted by James P. Scanlan, 'Tolstoy among the Philosophers: His Book on Life and Its Critical Reception', *TSJ*, XVIII, 2006, pp. 52–69 (66).

[26] On this see Henry H. Pickford, 'Of Rules and Rails: On a Motif in Tolstoy and Wittgenstein', *TSJ*, XXII, 2010, pp. 40–53.

[27] For a wide-ranging discussion on the role of music in *The Kreutzer Sonata* see Robin Milner-Gulland and Olga Sobolev, '"What Is Music? What Does It Do?" A Collective Analysis of *The Kreutzer Sonata*', in *Tolstoi and the Evolution of His Artistic World*, Joe Andrew and Robert Reid, eds, Brilll, Leiden and Boston, 2021, pp. 265–86.

[28] Maertz, pp. 56–7.

2   Tolstoi and Pushkin

Tolstoi's relationship to his Russian literary predecessors is one of both influence and resistance. Certain fictional themes that would have been congenial to Tolstoi such as the 'southern tale', 'the soldier's tale' and the 'society tale' were well established in uniquely Russian form by the time Tolstoi began to publish. Also, in Pushkin, Russia already had a universally recognized national poet from whose style, themes and experimental works his successors frequently drew inspiration. At first glance there might seem to be little affinity between a writer known for his substantial prose works and a lyric poet who also produced some narrative poems, short stories and a novel in verse.[29] However, as is often the case with Pushkin, it is precisely what he etches out *in parvo* which is taken up and developed by his successors. As Richard Freeborn puts it, he 'set in motion all manner of themes' among which he lists 'the contrast between Russian town and country' the prototype of the 'moral' Russian heroine, the egoistic hero and the 'nature of political power'.[30] With regard to the latter we find the theory of history elaborated in *War and Peace* already adumbrated by Pushkin. The 'great man' who, according to Hegel, is the motor of history, and for him was exemplified by Napoleon, is parodied in chapter two, stanza 14 of *Eugene Onegin*: 'We consider all people to be nonentities, but ourselves to be the entities. We all strive to become Napoleons. The millions of two-legged creatures are for us just a weapon'.[31] In *The Queen of Spades*, too, the ruthless and obsessive hero is described as bearing a striking physical resemblance to Napoleon. Both Tolstoi and Pushkin seek to refute the great-man theory as it pertains to Napoleon. Tolstoi presents a Napoleon who is at the mercy of historical forces rather than embodying or harnessing them. He is merely a symptom of great popular upheavals that manifest themselves in war. Pushkin implies a Kantian maxim as a means of refutation: what if everybody decided to declare themselves a great man (a 'unit'), and everybody else a 'nought'? This, of course, is the central question posed by Dostoevskii's *Crime and Punishment* but in the latter case it is not posed in a historical context. For Tolstoi the historical dimension *is* central. We do find in Pushkin, however, an anticipation of the historical issue (which comes to full fruition in Tolstoi),

---

29   On this see A.D.P. Briggs, *Alexander Pushkin: A Critical Study*, Croom Helm, London, 1983, p. 216.
30   Richard Freeborn, *Russian Literary Attitudes from Pushkin to Solzhenitsyn*, Macmillan, London, 1976, p. 5.
31   *Pushkin*, John Fennell, ed. and trans., Penguin, Harmondsworth, 1964, p. 150.

namely in *The Bronze Horseman*. Here Peter the Great (the *great* man) successfully imposes his will on the forces of nature, by building his capital, at considerable human cost, on the banks of the Neva. Though he would appear to embody the Hegelian theory, Pushkin's message is more nuanced: Peter cannot control his legacy – his successor, Alexander I, is like Tolstoi's great man, impotent in the face of a stronger force, in this case a flood: 'In that dread year the late Tsar still ruled Russia with glory. He came out on to the balcony, sad, troubled and said, "Tsars cannot master the divine elements"'.[32]

Konstantin Leontiev conducted an interesting thought experiment whereby he imagined Pushkin dodging D'Anthes' bullet and surviving to write, in the 1840s, 'a long novel about the year 1812'. 'Would he have written it as Tolstoy did? No, he would not! [...] Pushkin's novel would probably be less original, less subjective, less overburdened, perhaps less pithy, than *War and Peace* [...] Pushkin would write of 1812 in the way he wrote his *Dubrovsky*, *Captain's Daughter* and *Blackamoor of Peter the Great*'.[33] Leontiev is, of course, basing his projection on the few relatively short prose works which Pushkin embarked on towards the end of his truncated literary career, but it does force us to consider those features of Tolstoi's work which are entirely his own, entirely original additions to the Russian literary repertoire, rather than elaborations of his predecessors. In the case of *War and Peace* this does include the ability to cope with the 'amplitude' necessitated by the historical scope of the work, the ability to sustain parallel plots and create the grandeur of historical events. For this reason among others, Steiner defines *War and Peace* as an epic – in the modern sense of the term: having shed its strict formal and thematic prescriptions in the seventeenth century, it now connotes 'immensity and seriousness'.[34] However, while his extension of the term to include *Anna Karenina* may be acceptable, it is hard to see how it can also be applied, as he does, to *The Cossacks* and *The Death of Ivan Ilich*, without expanding its denotation beyond usefulness.[35]

Anna Karenina also bears the imprint of its Russian literary antecedents, again of Pushkin in particular. In David Sloane's view the novel 'continually mediates Pushkin's legacy in very significant ways'.[36] In particular, '[t]he tri-

---

32 Ibid., pp. 242–3.
33 Konstantin Leontiev, extract from his *Analiz, stil' i veianie: O romanakh Gr. L.N. Tolstogo. Kriticheskii etiud* (1890), translated by Spencer E. Roberts, in Gifford, ed., pp. 80–96 (92–3).
34 Steiner, p. 49.
35 Loc. cit.
36 David A. Sloane, 'Pushkin's Legacy in Anna Karenina', *TSJ*, IV, 1991, pp. 1–23 (4). Hereafter Sloane (a).

angle of Anna's relationship with Karenin and Vronsky is [...] a direct analogue to the relationship between Tatiana, her husband (who is wounded in the war of 1812 and presumably a much older man) and Onegin' in Pushkin's *Eugene Onegin*.[37] Sloane notes that the influence takes the form of an inversion and is directly related to the novels they model themselves on. Whereas Tatiana reads sentimentalist novels and, in the course of the plot, emancipates herself from them and the ideas they contain, Anna at the end of her life is shown reading a novel which reinforces her tragic view of life.[38] In crude terms, though, the influence of a novel of modest size on a substantial work like *Anna Karenina* is bound to be limited. We can compare Levin's lifestyle with that of the rusticating Onegin and Lenskii, but the comparison is entirely negative in that Levin seeks to engage positively with his environment, whereas Pushkin's male protagonists merely share a mutual alienation from it. Another area of influence noted by Sloane is the image of the artist, in the person of the painter Mikhailov. As a fellow artist – a poet – Lenskii invites comparison. However, through Onegin and his own digressions Pushkin distances himself from Lenskii's sentimentalist aesthetics, whereas Mikhailov, for all his eccentricity, is held up as an exemplar of artistic integrity, an effect enhanced by Vronskii's unsuccessful attempts at painting. As Sloane notes, '[t]he paradigm of Mikhailov's creative method is the open text'[39] and his studio is littered with works in various stages of non-completion, itself reminiscent of Pushkin's many unfinished and schematic works.

Moving away from Pushkin's influence on Tolstoi, we can see other recurrent themes from Russian literature manifesting themselves in his works. The 'soldier's tale', probably best authored by those who have actually see military service is, of course, congenial to Tolstoi. *The Cossacks*, for instance, may resonate with Lermontov's antecedent, *A Hero of Our Time*, but it draws upon Tolstoi's personal experience of a military posting among the Cossacks.[40] This produces an ambiguous ethnographic: these are not the aboriginal 'other' of

---

37 Ibid., p. 2.
38 Ibid., p. 14.
39 Ibid., p. 18.
40 Tolstoi read Lermontov 'incessantly throughout 1853 and 1854' and, while in Sevastopol in 1854, wrote verses reminiscent of Lermontov. Inessa Medzhibovskaya, *Tolstoy and the Religious Culture of His Time: A Biography of a Long Conversion, 1845–1885*, Lexington Books, Washington, 2009, p. 47. Tolstoi's *Sevastopol Stories* clearly follow in the tradition of Lermontov's novel, not only in their military theme, but in their structural interrelationship. On this see 'Tolstoy's Sevastopol Tales: Pathos, Sermon, Protest, and Stowe' in *Before They Were Titans: Essays on the Early Works of Dostoevsky and Tolstoy*, Elizabeth Cheresh Allen, ed., Academic Studies Press, Boston, 2019, pp. 211–66 (214).

Lermontov's novel, nor the contemporary Russian peasants who would preoccupy Tolstoi later. They were, however, something in between, descendants of Russian peasants who had eluded serfdom by migrating to the borderlands of empire, where they 'went native', or partially so. Jostein Børtnes notes that Pushkin's *Gypsies* had already suggested the impossibility of Rousseau's idea of 'becoming "natural" by casting aside the vestments of civilization'.[41] However, Pushkin's poem, whatever its virtues, is a work based on romanticized ethnic preconceptions, whereas Tolstoi's story, while it may point to the same conclusions, does so more convincingly. In *Anna Karenina* Vronskii embodies the officer ethos that would have been very familiar to Tolstoi, although, as Sloane points out, he is 'an anachronism, a gallant hussar in an age of railroad magnates and nihilists' who 'fits [Anna's] image of a mythical romantic hero'.[42] As such he would have represented a type already well-known to Tolstoi's Russian readers, somewhat unremarkable, alongside Tolstoi's more original creation, Levin. By the time Tolstoi unveils the character of Nekhliudov in *Resurrection*, it perhaps becomes difficult to talk about 'influence' as it pertains to earlier works. If anything, his character is most reminiscent of his predecessor Levin, whose social and moral attitudes he comes to share and develop. Here we reach the horizon of influence and enter the territory of originality.

3   Tolstoi in England

Matthew Arnold was the first English critic of note to make a positive case for Tolstoi and, in so doing, began a process whereby he would supplant Turgenev, Henry James' 'novelist's novelist' in British readers' affections. Steiner states, somewhat ambiguously, that Arnold's enthusiasm for Tolstoi contributed to the Russian novel casting a 'tremendous and accepted shadow over our sense of literary values'.[43] Arnold's influence was certainly considerable: 'From the late 1880s until his death in 1910 he was not only a prominent author but also a well-known public figure whose religious pronouncements and arguments with the church and the government were detailed in articles in the Times'.[44]

---

41   Jostein Børtnes, 'Religion' in *The Cambridge Companion to the Classic Russian Novel*, Malcolm Jones and Robin Feuer Miller, eds, Cambridge University Press, Cambridge, 1998, pp. 104–29 (106).
42   Sloane (a), pp. 18–19.
43   Steiner, p. 57.
44   Gwendolyn J. Blume, 'The Reader-Brand: Tolstoy in England at the Turn of the Century', *Texas Studies in Literature and Language*, LIII, 3, 2011, pp. 320–37 (320).

With his review of *Anna Karenina* in 1887 Arnold 'inaugurated a fashion for Russian realism over French'. He stressed that 'Anna's passion for Vronsky' had 'a disastrous effect on her physical and spiritual health' which distinguished *Anna* from contemporary French novels in which the passions were vindicated.[45] He was voicing a general turn against what was seen as decadence in French literature as against a Goethe-like 'determination' in Russian literature, Tolstoi in particular, 'to see life truthfully, to shirk none of its enigmas, to explain where he can, and where he cannot, to reflect its glittering facets in their cold and hard reality'.[46] Importantly, at Arnold's time of writing, Russian literature would have been largely consumed in French translation by a British cultural elite fluent in the language. However, by the 1920s not only was there greater availability of English translations but the earlier 'biographical craze over Tolstoy' which had been in much evidence outside Russia had begun to give way to the establishment of his principal novels as 'literary classics' aimed at those who wished to read 'masterpieces'.[47]

In England the Bloomsbury group took a particular interest in Tolstoi as a novelist outside the literary tradition from which they were seeking to distance themselves. However, there was no unanimity of attitude. 'Forster admired not only the epic scope of *War and Peace* but also the epic omniscience of its author' whereas Woolf, though she admired Tolstoi, found his preaching off-putting.[48] Forster was impressed by the relationship between 'place' and 'space' in Tolstoi, particularly *War and Peace*, where the latter, in his view, prevails over the former.[49] This, perhaps, is a more subtle version of 'necessary amplitude' mentioned above, for it is the case that the plurality of settings and plots in Tolstoi's novels makes its impact by contrast rather than by a granular analysis of a single setting.

Literary methodology in the years after Tolstoi's death did not exactly correspond to 'the art of the future', that he believed he was predicting in *What Is Art?*. Harold Bloom expressed his relief that such a vision never materialized in the age of Proust and Joyce and yet acknowledged its attraction: 'Tolstoy seems at moments to have found his way back to an art that never quite was, even in the remote past, and yet something in us wants it to have existed'.[50] It

---

45 Ibid., p. 322.
46 Clarence Decker, 'Victorian Comment on Russian Realism', PMLA, LII, 1937, pp. 542–9 (545).
47 Blume, pp. 331–2.
48 Galya Diment, 'Tolstoy and Bloomsbury', TSJ, V, 1992, pp. 39–53 (50–1).
49 E.M. Forster, *Aspects of the Novel*, 1927 (reprinted 1962), pp. 46–7, in Gifford, ed., p. 193.
50 Harold Bloom, ed., *Leo Tolstoy*, Chelsea house Publishers, Broomhall, 2003, p. 5.

was common for prominent English writers of whatever stripe to take the attitude that Tolstoi was, like the proverbial curate's egg, 'good in parts'. Some were put off Tolstoi by his moral or religious views, either those that were expressed didactically or those embodied in his fiction. G.K. Chesterton, though a religious believer, took this line, arguing that writers teach inadvertently by their mere 'background and properties' as well as 'landscape' 'costume' 'idiom and technique'.[51] Presumably this was his intended approach in the *Father Brown* stories. Shaw was quite the opposite: not only did many of his social and political ideas coincide with those of Tolstoi but he also thought highly of Tolstoi's later stories.[52] Shaw applauded *The Kreutzer Sonata* and *Resurrection* for their exposure of the hypocrisy of family values and social hypocrisy more generally but disagreed with Tolstoi about sexual issues.[53] He felt that Tolstoi had offered a solution to social ills, unlike Chekhov, for instance, and regarded him as a herald of the Revolution (of which he approved).[54] However, he accuses Tolstoi and, those who think like him, of assuming that the 'labouring classes [...] have entirely escaped the class vices [...] of the bourgeoisie' and of entertaining the view, 'highly characteristic of the Russian aristocrat' that a 'true work of art...will always be recognized by the unsophisticated perception of the peasant folk'.[55]

Much of the most memorable discussion of Tolstoi in English has revolved around *Anna Karenina*. As already mentioned, Arnold had singled it out for praise, but critics were divided on the moral message of the novel. Lawrence's argument is that Tolstoi, along with many novelists, has replaced the divine law (or fate), of the Greek tragedians with the petty prejudices of society. Whereas the furies once pursued and destroyed the tragic heroes who offended the eternal law of the Gods, now the offending (often female) protagonist is shamed or ostracized by the social milieu.[56] Raymond Williams' response to this is to regard the novel as an organic whole in which, as he notes, 'the Anna-Vronsky-Karenin story [...] occupies rather less than half the narrative'. This approach rests on the view that 'Anna-Vronsky is the real story, and that the story of Levin [...] is simply the result of Tolstoy's incurable autobiographical itch: he had to record his discursive observations on work and

---

51 Slonim, p. 189.
52 Ibid, p. 190.
53 Ibid., p. 191.
54 Ibid., p. 192.
55 George Bernard Shaw, 'Tolstoy on Art' (1898) in Gifford, ed., pp. 105–11 (106–7).
56 D.H. Lawrence, *Study of Thomas Hardy* ([1914] extract) in Gifford, ed., pp. 149–51 (149).

faith even though the real story was about the lovers'.[57] Leavis also takes issue with Lawrence's view that Anna and Vronskii's tragedy was that they failed to stand up to the social prejudices from which they suffered. The causes of their tragedy are more subtle and involve personal issues. Social prejudice cannot explain why Anna and Vronskii 'with no money troubles and plenty of friends' cannot make a success of things in Italy.[58] Mention should be made here of Shestov's assessment: for Tolstoi the good is on Levin's side and all the rest must suffer in some degree because they are not 'good' in the way Levin is. Because of this 'many readers accuse him of being cold' of not shedding tears over his tragic figures.[59]

4 Tolstoi and Philosophy

As well as literary critics, Tolstoi's work has also attracted philosophical and psychological analysis, unsurprisingly, since no other Russian writer, with the exception of Dostoevskii, has raised so many issues in these areas via their fiction and other writings. William James thought it worth including Tolstoi in his pioneering psychological work, *The Varieties of Religious Experience*. In James' view 'Tolstoy's trajectory' is 'an example of positive religious experience that led from doubt and melancholy to a fruitful resolution of "unity and level"'.[60] In fact there are two stages in conversion according to James. The first is 'anhedonia' in which the subject's surroundings and life in general lose all pleasure and meaning. This is then followed in the case of conversion (but not of melancholia) by the reverse process – 'a new heaven seems to shine upon a new earth'.[61]

James' conclusions may seem over-reductive by today's standards, though in yielding to the temptation to schematize Tolstoi he is not alone. In an attempt to redress the widespread contemporary view (1875) that Tolstoi was a better artist than he was a thinker, the populist writer N.K. Mikhailovskii formulated the notion of a left-handed and a right-handed Tolstoi, not in the literal sense

---

57 Raymond Williams, 'Lawrence and Tolstoy', *Critical Quarterly*, II, 1, 1960, pp. 33–9 in Gifford, ed., pp. 304–11 (305).
58 F.R. Leavis, 'Anna Karenina: Thought and Significance in a Great Creative Work' (extract) from Anna Karenina *and Other Essays* (1967) in Gifford, ed., pp. 372–5, (374).
59 'Shestov on Tolstoy's Lack of Compassion' (1900) in Knowles, ed., pp. 387–94 (393–4).
60 Moulin (a), p. 586.
61 See William James, *The Varieties of Religious Experience*, Longmans. Green and Co., New York, London, 1917, p. 148.

of ambidexterity but to figuratively represent the creative side (left) and the rationalizing side (right) of Tolstoi, both of which are of equal importance.[62] Perhaps the most striking feature of this dichotomy is its anticipation of brain lateralization. A better known and more ingenious dichotomy is Isaiah Berlin's 'hedgehog and fox', whereby thinkers and artists are deemed to be either hedgehogs or foxes, according to whether, in the former case, they know how to do one thing very well, or, like the fox, excel in knowing how to do many things. Less simplistically, those in the former category 'relate everything to [...] a single, universal, organizing principle in terms of which all that they are and say has significance [...]' while those on the latter 'pursue many ends, often unrelated and even contradictory [...]' and 'entertain ideas that are centrifugal rather than centripetal'.[63] According to Berlin, while it is fairly clear that Pushkin was a fox and Dostoevskii was a hedgehog, 'Tolstoy was by nature a fox, but believed in being a hedgehog; [...] his gifts and achievement are one thing, and his beliefs, and consequently his interpretation of his own achievement, another [...]'.[64] The implication of this is that the late Tolstoi, far from withdrawing as an artist, as André Gide maintained, because he 'felt his literary career was finished', was yielding to his hedgehog impulse, at the expense of his earlier creative fox.[65]

Philosophers with existentialist tendencies have sometimes been attracted to Tolstoi, as they have to Dostoevskii, and the attention paid to this aspect of their writings has contributed to the sense that their works have a philosophical profundity. Berdiaev voices the idea neatly encapsulated in the title of Steiner's study: *Tolstoy or Dostoevsky*, inasmuch as '[p]eople may be divided into two types: those who are drawn to Tolstoy's mind and those who are drawn to Dostoevsky's'; they are separated, he says, by mutual misunderstanding. Dostoevskii's entertainment in his novels, of extreme anti-Christian ideas, albeit juxtaposed with Christian ones, seems anti-Christian to the Tolstoians, who prefer Tolstoi's unequivocal interpretation of the Gospel, although it was Dostoevskii who was the fervent Orthodox believer while Tolstoi 'lacked any personal feeling for our Lord' and found 'the idea of the Redemption [...] quite foreign'.[66] As Hugh Maclean notes, Tolstoi would invert Dostoevskii's famous apothegm expressed in his letter to Natalia Vonvizina (1854): 'If anyone could

---

62   See 'Mikhailovsky on Tolstoi's Left Hand' in Knowles, ed., pp. 274–81 (274).
63   Isaiah Berlin, *The Hedgehog and the Fox: An Essay on Tolstoy's View of History*, Weidenfeld and Nicolson, London, 1953, p. 1.
64   Ibid., p. 4.
65   André Gide, extract from his *Journals* in Gifford, ed., pp. 197–8 (197).
66   Nicolas Berdyaev, extract from *Dostoievsky* (1936), in Gifford, ed., p. 215.

prove to me that Christ is outside the truth, and if the truth really did exclude Christ, I should prefer to stay with Christ and not the truth'.[67]

Heidegger also bears mention here, for footnoting *The Death of Ivan Ilich* in his *Being and Time*: 'In his narrative [...] *The Death of Ivan Il'ich* [...] L. N. Tolstoy has presented [...] the phenomenon of the shattering and breakdown of (that) "one dies / people die" [...].[68] As Natalie Repin notes, 'in spite of its brevity, [it] is rather significant, since it amounts to Heidegger's unequivocal recognition of Tolstoy's successful comprehension of the question of death, a recognition that has proved not easy to gain'.[69] The similarity between Heidegger's and Tolstoi's views of death in *The Death of Ivan Ilich* lies in their shared notions of an authentic and inauthentic attitude to death, the latter being to regard death as something that happens to others and the former being death as it happens to me. The structure of Tolstoi's story ensures that these two perspectives on death (how I view other people's death and how I view my own) are explored in detail.

Another philosopher, Wittgenstein, also drew upon Tolstoi when considering the nature of life and death. According to Tolstoi's translator Aylmer Maude, Tolstoi's *Confession* and *Gospel in Brief* 'altered the outlook on life of many men of many lands, and caused some to alter not their ideas merely but the settled habits and customs of their lives'.[70] Wittgestein was one such: in correspondence he attested to its influence on him: 'This book in its time has almost kept me alive. Would you buy yourself this book and read it? If you are not acquainted with it, then you cannot imagine how it can work on people'. Before reading the work he had, in his own words, been 'dogmatically antichristian'. He was transformed by what he referred to as 'the redeeming word' of Tolstoi's gospel.[71] This impact is also evident, according to David Woodruff, in Wittgenstein's *Tractatus*: he speaks with a 'Tolstoyan accent' when dealing with matters of life and death.[72] This may seem to be the case when one considers such a passage in the *Tractatus* as 'Death is not an event of life. Death is not lived through. If by eternity is understood not endless temporal duration

---

67 Hugh Mclean, *In Quest of Tolstoy*, Academic Studies Press, Boston, 2017, p. 118.
68 This translation is taken from Natalie Repin, 'Being-toward-Death in Tolstoy's the Death of Ivan Il'ich: Tolstoy and Heidegger', *Canadian-American Slavic Studies*, XXXVI, 1–2, 2002, pp. 101–32 (101). German has been omitted (ellipses).
69 Loc. cit.
70 Aylmer Maude, *The Life of Tolstoy*, I, p. 443. Quoted by T. David Joseph Woodruff 'Tolstoy and Wittgenstein: The Life Outside of Time', *The Southern Journal of Philosophy*, LX, 2002, 421–35 (428).
71 Ibid., p. 429.
72 Ibid., p. 430.

but timelessness, then he lives eternally who lives in the present',[73] which, for instance, evokes the protagonist's epiphany at the end of *The Death of Ivan Ilich*. On the other hand, it could be argued that such existential conclusions are not new and pre-date both Wittgenstein and Tolstoi himself.

The final issue I wish to discuss in this section may at first sight appear to be more literary than philosophical – it probably lies between both, in the area of rhetoric. It is *ostranenie*, variously translated as 'making strange', 'estrangement' or 'defamiliarization'. The term was invented by Viktor Shklovskii in his *Art as Device* (1917) to describe the manner in which art is capable of transforming perception so that things shed the formal contexts in which they are traditionally perceived and reveal themselves as they are in reality. Tolstoi is particularly noteworthy for his very explicit use of the device: in his story *Kholstomer*, for example, which, being narrated from a horse's point of view, makes many apparently normal human behaviours seem strange or unnecessary. Another example is the description of an opera in *What Is Art?* (chapter 13) intended to ridicule the pretensions of the performance, by emphasizing the reality behind the illusion: the false beards, tight-clad legs, a singer opening his mouth 'in a strange way'.[74] The technique was not new and a form of it was advocated by Stoic philosophers as a way of dismantling the attractions of a tempting object by methodically reducing them to their (less superficially attractive) component parts. Thus, although it can occur as a device within a literary text it can be used effectively to deconstruct established values in any context. One of these is literary criticism, particularly in the form which retells a plot in such a way as to undermine its coherence or credibility. Tolstoi's essay on Shakespeare falls into this category, his aim being 'to show why I believe that Shakespeare cannot be recognized either as a great genius, or even as an average author'.[75] This he does by turning his attention to *King Lear* 'one of Shakespeare's most extolled dramas'.[76] In his narration of *Lear*'s plot, in considerable detail, Tolstoi notes the points which, in his view, challenge plausibility: Lear's failure to recognize the disguised Kent is repeatedly

---

[73] Ludwig Wittgenstein, *Tractatus Logico-Philosophicus*, C.K. Ogden, trans., Kegan Paul Trench Trubner and Co., London, 1922, 6.4311, p. 88. Reproduced by Project Gutenberg: http://www.gutenberg.org/ebooks/5740 (accessed 15. 11. 2020).

[74] Leo Tolstoy, *What is Art?*, Richard Pevear and Larissa Volokhonsky, trans., Penguin, London, 1995, pp. 104–5.

[75] Leo Tolstoy, 'Tolstoy on Shakespeare: A Critical Essay on Shakespeare', V. Tchertkoff and I.F.M., trans., Funk and Wagnalls, New York and London, 1906, p. 6. Project Gutenberg, https://www.gutenberg.org/files/27726/27726-h/27726-h.htm (accessed 15. 11. 2020).

[76] Loc. cit.

emphasized; words are put in characters' mouths not because they are relevant to the action, but because the author thought them witty – though they are not even that. Tolstoi concludes by observing that '[h]owever absurd it may appear in my rendering (which I have endeavoured to make as impartial as possible), I may confidently say that in the original it is yet more absurd'.[77]

Tolstoi's treatment of the play excited the ire of George Orwell.[78] Orwell was, anyway, no fan of Tolstoi: he saw a dystopian potential in the prescriptive and restrictive ideas which the latter espoused.[79] He also attributes the ferocity of Tolstoi's attack on *Lear* specifically to the similarity between the predicaments of the two old men: particularly their renunciation of the world and social ties. The content of Orwell's riposte is significant, but the manner in which he makes it even more so. If Tolstoi's treatment of *Lear* is an exercise in defamiliarization, then Orwell's must exemplify refamiliarization. His strategy is to parry the force of Tolstoi's attack by exposing the nature of the *ostranenie*:

> To begin with, his examination of *King Lear* is not 'impartial', as he twice claims. On the contrary, it is a prolonged exercise in misrepresentation. It is obvious that when you are summarizing *King Lear* for the benefit of someone who has not read it, you are not really being impartial if you introduce an important speech (Lear's speech when Cordelia is dead in his arms) in this manner: 'again begin Lear's awful ravings, at which one feels ashamed, as at unsuccessful jokes'. And in a long series of instances Tolstoi slightly alters or colours the passages he is criticizing, always in such a way as to make the plot appear a little more complicated and improbable, or the language a little more exaggerated.[80]

One problem, then, with *ostranenie* is that the deconstruction it effects is reversible. Its target can be re-assembled by identifying its *modus operandi* and re-asserting the values that the *ostranenie* seeks to deny. At the same time *ostranenie* is profoundly monologic: it is offered as the true perspective, not one that is open to polemic. It is not unfeasible to see it, though it is an identifiable stylistic feature throughout Tolstoi's work, as an intellectual principle, too: what is generally valued is not really of value; what is thought to be like *this* is really like *that*.

---

77   Ibid., p. 46.
78   George Orwell, 'Lear, Tolstoy and the Fool' in Gifford, ed., pp. 238–55. Reprinted from *Collected Essays*, 1947.
79   On this see Robert Pearce, 'Orwell, Tolstoy and Animal Farm', *The Review of English Studies*, 1998, XLIX, pp. 64–9.
80   Orwell, p. 242.

5   Tolstoi in Post-revolutionary Russia

The fate of Tolstoi's legacy in post-revolutionary Russia is contradictory. Tolstoi was Lenin's favourite author, and his favourite novel *War and Peace*.[81] While opposed to the quietistic and Christian elements in Tolstoi's teaching he saw his chief value as a 'spokesman of the ideas and sentiments' of 'the millions of Russian peasants at the time the bourgeois revolution was approaching in Russia'.[82] Although his teachings were congenial to Marxists, there were differences in timing. The Tolstoians, with their emphasis on individual conversion, wanted change now, unencumbered by a teleology of the sort adhered to by the Marxists. In his article on Tolstoi and Gorkii Hugh Mclean argues that, like Gorkii, Tolstoi was a utopian. However, whereas Gorkii tended towards the more common view that the urban proletariat should be the dominant revolutionary force, Tolstoi's ideas for social transformation revolved around the peasant. Not only that, but Gorkii, and others of like mind, disagreed with Tolstoi on the matter of non-violent resistance, believing that 'Russians [...] had been passive long enough'.[83] The doctrine of non-resistance would have seemed to many of his contemporaries to rule Tolstoi out as a serious revolutionary, because it had never been tried, but history would prove this view to be false with the practical demonstration provided by Gandhi. Moreover, it is not easy to find the right pigeonhole for the kind of anti-establishmentarianism that Tolstoi represents. Berdiaev thought Tolstoi was an anarchist advocating 'a most thorough-going and radical form of anarchism, that is to say [...] a rejection of the principle of authority and force', unlike that of Bakunin.[84] Lavrin points to the paradox that Tolstoi became an 'indirect revolutionary force, even though his ideas and ideals had nothing to do' with the 'character' or 'consequences' of the revolution. 'His doctrine of non-resistance was anti-revolutionary in its very essence'.[85] In correspondence Tolstoi quoted a passage from Lao-Tse which was certainly not adhered to in Russia in the decades following the Revolution: 'When great sages have power over the people, the people do not notice them …' Such leaders follow

---

81   David Sloane, 'Rehabilitating Bakhtin's Tolstoy: The Politics of the Utterance', *TSJ*, XIII, 2001, pp. 59–77 (65). Hereafter Sloane (b).
82   V.I. Lenin, 'Leo Tolstoy as Mirror of the Russian Revolution' (1908) in Gifford, ed., pp. 135–6 (136).
83   Hugh McLean, 'A Clash of Utopias: Tolstoy and Gorky', *TSJ*, XIV, 2002, pp. 25–34 (26).
84   Nicolas Berdyaev, extract from *The Russian Idea* (1947) in Gifford, ed., pp. 236–8 (236).
85   Janko Lavrin, *Tolstoy: An Approach*, Methuen and Co., London, 1944, pp. 144–5.

the natural course of events, as Michael Denner notes, like Kutuzov.[86] From this idealization of governmental passivity it is but a short step to anarchy in its literal sense. However, for Tolstoi, it was a means of challenging authority by peaceful means, and thus refusing to acknowledge a government's power. As Denner puts it, with a hint of Tolstoian *ostranenie*, 'Tolstoy's plan' was 'to bring about the end of government by doing nothing'.[87]

According to Aylmer Maude, that great popularizer of Tolstoi and his works in the English-speaking world, Tolstoi himself did not approve of Tolstoianism, at least in its manifestation as communes formed to carry out his teachings, a view with which Maude came to concur: 'Tolstoyan principles when treated as axioms become unreasonable'.[88] As for practical implementations of Tolstoi's theories within Russia, these persisted for some time after the Revolution. Surprisingly, the last Tolstoian commune, near Kuznetsk, survived until 1939. The recollections of a surviving member illuminate the contrasting views of communists and Tolstoians at this time:

> Often in frank discussions we would hear such statements as this from Communists – highly placed figures, ordinary members, and investigators, as well as simple working people: 'It's all well and good, what you Tolstoyans say. That will all come about – a stateless society without violence and without frontiers, sober and industrious, and without private property. But this is not the right time for it – right now it is even harmful'. But we did not understand that. The 'Kingdom of God' that lived within us kept nudging us toward carrying out our ideals immediately, without delay. Putting off the fulfillment of our ideals until some indefinite time in the future seemed to us amazingly similar to the teachings of the church people, who urged us to be patient and endure our poverty and deprivation so that we would acquire the blessings we longed for in some future life beyond the grave.[89]

If the legacy of Tolstoi the moralist and teacher was being eradicated in Russia his stature as a literary figure was growing. Indeed, to the Soviet cultural

---

[86] Quoted by Michael Denner, 'Tolstoyan Non-Action: the Advantage of Doing Nothing', *TSJ*, XIII, 2001, pp. 8–22 (18).
[87] Loc. cit.
[88] See Daniel Moulin, *Tolstoy*, Bloomsbury, London and New York, 2014, pp. 142–3.
[89] Quoted by William Edgerton, ed. and trans., *Memoirs of Peasant Tolstoyans in Soviet Russia*, Indiana University Press, Bloomington, 1993, p. 97.

ideologues who were seeking to come to terms with the heritage of pre-revolutionary literature, Tolstoi was in many ways congenial, certainly much more so than Dostoevskii. As Sloane puts it, the centenary of Tolstoi's birth in 1928 supplied the pretext for the 'state-sponsored enshrinement of Lev Tolstoy'.[90] A few years later in 1934 'Emulation of Tolstoy' was an important ingredient in the creation of Socialist Realism at the first Congress of Soviet Writers.[91] The Congress sought to reset the norms of Soviet literature to accord with the aesthetics of nineteenth-century realism, abandoning the modernist techniques of the years immediately preceding and following the revolution. Those were represented by Tolstoi not Dostoevskii.[92] In doing this they were not only advocating the imitation of Tolstoi's style, characterization, and so on, but, according to Slonim, his aesthetics, particularly as articulated in *What Is Art?*.[93] Thus his advocacy of a moral message in literature was transformed into an official socio-political one in Socialist Realism, his rejection of elitist or bourgeois literature became an important element of communist censorship, his call for universal accessibility was answered by the use of literature for mass education. Indeed, the buzz words of the 'new' art – *dostupnost* (accessibility), *narodnost* (of the people), (*partiinost* [party loyalty] excepted) – are also consistent with Tolstoi's aesthetics.

Among prominent twentieth-century Russian writers whose works, it has been argued, show the influence of Tolstoi are Sholokhov (*Quiet Flows the Don*), Pasternak (*Doctor Zhivago*) and Solzhenitsyn (*First Circle*; *Cancer Ward*).[94] *Quiet Flows the Don* 'is full of stylistic and structural echoes of *War and Peace*' and has been 'referred to as the Soviet *War and Peace*', although there is an important difference: the authorial voice in Sholokhov's novel is more that of the classical epic author who describes the vicissitudes of the characters without, as in Tolstoi's case, using them to express his own ideas and moral struggles.[95] Pasternak's novel exhibits a hero, reminiscent of one of Tolstoi's truth-seekers, caught up in the great military struggles of the twentieth century. The distinction, however, is that he is himself a writer, and his own verse functions as a postscript to the main narrative. In this respect its

---

90   Sloane (b), p. 64.
91   Ibid., p. 65.
92   Loc. cit.
93   Marc Slonim, *Soviet Russian Literature: Writers and Problems, 1917–1967*, Oxford University Press, Oxford, 1967, pp. 177–8. Quoted by Sloane (b), 'Rehabilitating Bakhtin's Tolstoy', p. 65.
94   See Ernest J. Simmonds, *Tolstoy*, Routledge and Kegan Paul, London, p. 230.
95   See Helen Muchnic, 'Sholokhov and Tolstoy', *Russian Review*, XVI, 2, 1957, pp. 25–34 (25, 27, 30–1).

more plausible literary antecedent is Lermontov's *A Hero of Our Time*. One of the results of Tolstoi's legitimization in Soviet letters is that he exerted a considerable influence on the themes, content and style of writers who came to creative maturity in subsequent years. Solzhenitsyn is the prime example: his use of parallel plots and ideologically charged characters, such as Rubin *in First Circle*, is reminiscent of those used by Tolstoi in *Anna Karenina* and *Resurrection*. *Ostranenie* of a particular kind is evident in the protagonist's perspective in *One Day in the Life of Ivan Denisovich*. Solzhenitsyn's historical works also bear the imprint of *War and Peace*.

Simmons argued that, over time, 'the distinction between literary artist and religious and social reformer' has been accentuated.[96] It is probably true that in Tolstoi's heyday as, simultaneously a great European novelist and a controversial moralist and religious teacher, the two functions were inseparable, the one augmenting the popularity of the other. If time has overtaken the popularity of Tolstoi's views in the form in which he expressed them, they have not disappeared altogether. Moulin sees Tolstoi as part of a continuum of alternative thinkers about consciousness and spirituality:

> [Tolstoi] was part of a chain of intellectuals who followed their own paths, who then enabled further generations to strike their paths across wider horizons of possibilities. One possible such construction, for example, runs from Kant (1724–1804), to Schleiermacher (1768–1834), to Tolstoy (1828–1910), Younghusband (1863–1942) and then Watts (1915–73). In the space of four generations from Kant we can therefore see how popular and influential cultural movements such as New Age, western Buddhism, or the Beat Generation are possible.[97]

Thus Tolstoi's ideas have been subsumed into the ongoing tradition of secular spirituality with its emphasis today on such concepts as mindfulness and cognitive behaviour, alongside those like pacifism and vegetarianism which Tolstoi himself recognized.

6 Tolstoi Today

As for his fictional works they are as popular as ever, both in text form and on stage and screen. As the chapters in this collection show, Tolstoi's works

---

96   Simmonds, p. 234.
97   Moulin (a), p. 586.

have invited transposition to the stage and film and not merely his drama (*The Power of Darkness*). There is a particular challenge in the adaptation of substantial works such as *Resurrection* and *War and Peace*, but the ingenuity and persistence required to do this are propelled by the belief that these works still possess relevance and a message that can be formulated anew in a fresh medium. It is also the case that the availability in English of modern translations of Tolstoi has enhanced their attraction for new generations of readership. Continued popularity of literary works depends considerably on 'reader brand' – a reader's 'own conception of which books should be owned and which borrowed, which displayed and which merely consumed'.[98] Moreover, a book rebranded to appeal to an audience that had not hitherto imagined itself reading it, effectively 'becomes a new book'.[99] A modern example of this, mentioned by Blume, was Oprah Winfrey's choice of *Anna Karenina* for her Book Club list in 2004:

> Many of Oprah's largely female audience reported that they had feared the novel as too difficult, but they identified with their favorite talk-show host and so were convinced to buy her choice. This example thus hints at the democratizing work of the reader brand: Oprah's familiarity prompted a flood of new subjects to recognize themselves as readers of a previously unfamiliar and unknown text.[100]

As Blume points out, the publicity surrounding the launch of the 2000 award-winning translation by Pevear and Volokhonsky, had already helped to raise the novel's profile, but, it is claimed, in the wake of the Oprah announcement, Penguin decided to increase 'its press run by 800,000'.[101]

As for *War and Peace*, Covid-19 has, according to some reports, made it popular reading during lockdown, when many have had the time to embark upon it, but for other reasons too: 'readers are finding new urgency in [Tolstoi's] work at a time when the racial and economic inequities revealed by Covid-19 and police killings have inspired unprecedented numbers of people to question some of this country's [America's] foundational myths'.[102] A particularly interesting project is Yiyun Li's Tolstoy Together book club on the website

---

[98] Blume, p. 320.
[99] Ibid., p. 333.
[100] Loc. cit.
[101] Edward Wyatt, 'Tolstoy's Translators Experience Oprah's Effect', *The New York Times*, June 7, 2004.
[102] Jennifer Wilson, 'Leo Tolstoy vs. the Police', ibid., June 25, 2020.

'A public space'. Over 85 days from 18 March 2020 she proposed reading 12–15 pages of the novel per day, recording her thoughts in a blog, and inviting others to read in tandem with her, sharing their own reactions on Twitter and Instagram. The aim, which was achieved, was to finish the process by summer. Laura Waddell, one of the many participants, recorded her impressions in *The Scotsman* a short time into it: while 'engaging with others' on the project is entirely optional, it is its own private comfort to do something pleasurable in step with others'.[103] This kind of participative, open-ended response to a novel of which, as Waddell suggests, many people may have had 'a dusty copy on the bottom of [their] bookshelves' is something entirely of the internet age and gives the lie to the 'death of the novel' theory, and the exaggeration of that rumour as it pertains to Lev Tolstoi.

7   The Chapters

The first of the chapters in this collection, 'Does the Translation Matter?' by Carol Apollonio addresses one of the media, perhaps the most significant, by which the continuing popularity of Tolstoi has been sustained. Apollonio notes that, until recently, translators were given little credit for their role in making literary works available to a wider readership. She detects 'something feminine' in the traditional invisibility of translators and, indeed, when it comes to Tolstoi, some of the more significant translators of them *were* women. This situation has thankfully changed and Apollonio notes that recent successful translations of the Russian classics have 'restored the translator to the conversation about world literature'. This is one way in which translation matters, but another is the very real scope that the translation process uniquely offers to interpret, indeed to perform, the source text in an original way. Apollonio demonstrates this by comparing extracts from up to ten translations of *War and Peace* that particularly exemplify characteristic Tolstoian techniques such as the physical description of characters, philosophical exposition and defamiliarization (*ostranenie*). Apollonio also compares and contrasts the apparatus and presentation of the translations. Her conclusion is that the 'ideal physical embodiment of *War and Peace* is a composite' of all of them.

Tolstoi's creative history is remarkable for its sharp turn towards didactic literature in the last thirty years of his life. He offers the key to this in *What Is Art?*,

---

[103]   Laura Waddell, 'Coronavirus Limbo Is Perfect Time to Finally Read *War and Peace*', *Scotsman*, 1 April, 2020.

a treatise which not only provides an idiosyncratic assessment of the literary canon but also explains the moralistic aesthetics by which he will henceforth abide. Richard Peace's chapter ('Feeling and Contradiction in Tolstoi's *What Is Art?*') highlights a fact often overlooked in the general assumption of the uniqueness of Tolstoi's ideas on art, namely that they have much in common with those enunciated in the 1850s and 1860s by Chernyshevskii, Dobroliubov and Pisarev, progressive radicals whom Tolstoi ignored at that time and does not reference in *What Is Art?* In other ways, though, Peace argues, one can see more contemporary affinities in the work, such as Tolstoi's aspiration to create art for the people, which anticipates the work of the Proletkult movement in the early years of the Revolution. The anarchic nature of Tolstoi's prescriptions about art is also stressed by Peace – that it was better to have no art than bad art. In sum Peace argues that Tolstoi's aesthetics, as articulated in *What Is Art?*, forms 'a bridge between the radicals of the 1860s and the theoreticians of the early Soviet Union'; however Tolstoi refuses to succumb to the rationalism espoused by these thinkers, preferring to retain a sentimentalist subjectivism, even at the risk of contradiction.

Is the Tolstoi who held such controversial views about art, so forthrightly, even provocatively expressed, the Tolstoi we have in mind when we read his best-known classics: *War and Peace* and *Anna Karenina*? It is simplest to say 'no', on the grounds that these views only emerged fully after those works were written. But the question of how, if at all, an author is 'present' in his or her works is peculiarly complex in the case of Tolstoi, as Willem Westeijn points out in his chapter 'Tolstoi in the Work of Tolstoi'. While we may know little about the lives of Homer or Shakespeare, we have a large amount of information about Tolstoi: his diaries and confessional works, the diaries and memoirs of his relatives and friends, photographs and even voice recordings and film footage. All these are in addition to his works of fiction, which form of writing, as Westseijn explores in detail, is notoriously problematic as a source of information about its author. By contrast, in Tolstoi's non-fiction there is no doubt about the status and role of the author. From all of this Weststeijn can conclude that 'Tolstoi *has* a biography and *does* exist in the reader's, almost any reader's, consciousness'. This, however, is quite different from the 'image' of Tolstoi that a given reader may have, for the latter depends on the social, cultural and historical location of the reader and the degree to which he or she is familiar with Tolstoi's biography. Weststeijn's conclusion is partly a formalist one: we can enjoy a literary work on its merits alone, without knowing anything of its author; on the other hand the very reading will inevitably excite our curiosity to discover the author's biography. This, though, comes with a caveat to avoid 'the pitfalls narrative theory is warning us against': in particular, confusion of the real author with the implied author.

Among the more intriguing influences on Tolstoi's creative and spiritual life was the Orthodox tradition of the 'elder' (*starets*), a theme explored by Nel Grillaert in 'Dostoevskii's Zosima and Tolstoi's Father Sergius: Literary Representations of Starchestvo'. The tradition of the Elder, it is claimed, goes back to the early days of Russian Orthodoxy but, having fallen out of favour was revived again only in the eighteenth century. Elders, attached to certain monasteries, were renowned for their piety and often attracted large numbers of pilgrims and petitioners. Both Tolstoi and Dostoevskii admired and visited the most famous elder of their time, Amvrosii, at the monastery of Optina Pustyn. As Grillaert points out, both writers were attracted to the religious basis of elderhood, for its exemplification of a direct relationship with God, and its emphasis on reaching out to the common people. Both produce a fictional representation of an elder, Dostoevskii in *The Brothers Karamazov* (Zosima) and Tolstoi in the eponymous *Father Sergius*. However, in Grillaert's view, the two writers differ in their aims and portrayals. Dostoevskii embeds his description of Zosima in the hagiographical tradition; he aims at creating a 'credible saint', as Grillaert puts it, 'as a counterweight' against Ivan Karamazov's atheistic arguments in the novel'. By contrast, Tolstoi's Father Sergius is shown throughout his story as someone struggling to adapt himself to the religious life and unable to slough off the failings and temptations that had driven him to become a monk in the first place, particularly ambition and lust. Predictably, perhaps, given Tolstoi's antipathy to the Orthodox Church, his hero only finds peace by leaving the monastery to live a life of humble anonymity. As Grillaert concludes, '[f]or Tolstoi, real spiritual elderhood can only be effective in a context that cuts off all ties with the established church'.

While moral and spiritual values are never far from the surface in Tolstoi's works, their settings and topoi often owe much to pre-existing literary templates, as this introduction has already discussed. One of these is the 'society tale' which centres on the lives and loves of genteel characters in a given social setting. A favoured setting is the spa, an early example of which is found in Lermontov's *Princess Mary*. Susan Layton ('Tolstoi and Lidiia Veselitskaia's *Mimi at the Spa*: The *Fin de Siècle* Tourist Adulteress') explores the contrasts between Tolstoi's treatment of this theme (in, for instance, *Family Happiness* and *Anna Karenina*) and his younger contemporary's presentation of it in *Mimi at the Spa* (1891). Tolstoi admired the work which, in Layton's words, bore witness to creative dialogue with his own 'treatments of femininity, marriage, adultery, and the disorienting potential of travel'. However, he viewed vacations taken for pleasure in a negative light – Anna and Vronskii's time in Italy being an example – whereas Veselitskaia avoids moralizing. She also modernizes the travel story to depict the destination's potential for broadening an individual's horizons, and developing the character, rather than for flirtation and seduction. In this, concludes Layton, she anticipates (via the character Vava) Soviet notions of the wholesome effects of vacation, whereas the protagonist, Mimi, 'represents the comfort-loving bourgeois type Soviet tourist officials sought to root out'.

Tolstoi's 'extreme' views on sex are well known. But he was far from alone in Russia at the end of the nineteenth century in examining issues of sexuality, particularly in relation to marriage. As Henrietta Mondry shows ('Legitimate and Illegitimate Children: Rozanov's "Indecent Proposal" to Tolstoi'), Vasilii Rozanov was equally active in publishing his views on the subject. He was particularly exercised by what he saw as the 'disintegration of the contempoarary Russian family' and, after the publication of *The Kreutzer Sonata* in 1890, became convinced that Tolstoi was an ideal interlocutor in his discussion of the institution. Rozanov blamed Russian literature for undermining, or at least failing to uphold traditional family values, even *Eugene Onegin* suffering censure for consigning its heroine to the role of 'a childless wife without hope of motherhood'. Tolstoi, by contrast, does offer wholesome portraits of family life. Realizing the advantages of Tolstoi's authoritative support, Rozanov approached Tolstoi in the wake of a new law of 1902 concerning the status of illegitimate children which allowed them to be legitimized on birth certificates, or retrospectively if their parents later married. Rozanov wished to go further, promoting a form of common-law marriage which would abolish the difference between officially sanctioned marriage and cohabitation. It was for this proposal that he sought Tolstoi's support. Rozanov discusses the issue with Tolstoi but is non-committal about Tolstoi's response, which suggests something less than full-throated support. Above all, this incident illustrates the extraordinary status that Tolstoi had acquired in his final years; as Rozanov acknowledges: 'I thought that it could be done only by a person with international authority whom nobody will dare to accuse of immorality'.

As noted earlier in this introduction, after the Revolution Tolstoi's particular brand of critical realism was adopted and adapted by Soviet aestheticians as a template for Socialist Realism. In her chapter on the staging of an adaptation of Tolstoi's novel *Resurrection* by the Moscow Art Theatre ('Tolstoi's *Resurrection* on the Russian Stage') in 1930, Olga Sobolev emphasizes that its performance was not the most obvious one to undertake, since it not only required abridgement from its substantial novel form, but considerable adjustment of its thematics in order to make it acceptable to a Soviet audience. Nevertheless, since it is a work highly critical of the Tsarist status quo, it contains elements that could be ideologically foregrounded as well as others that could be conveniently excised. Accordingly, the role of the central character of the novel, Nekhliudov, a landowner anxious to atone for his social privilege and his behaviour as a young man, is 'practically reduced to that of a melodramatic seducer'; while Maslova, the heroine, becomes 'an optimistic embodiment of the socialist realist scheme'. Moreover, these modifications in characterization are mutually dependent: Maslova, seduced in her youth by Nekhliudov and ashamed of having fallen into prostitution, is in danger of assuming a victimhood incompatible with a positive Soviet heroine, whereas '[b]y presenting Nekhliudov as an utterly unsympathetic and even repulsive character, the sense of guilt [is] completely effaced from [her] image'. By the mid-1930s, as Sobolev notes, the Socialist Realist canon was already well established, making it easier for writers and directors to navigate official expectations. The Moscow Art Theatre production of *Resurrection* in 1930 was in this sense a pioneering work of its kind.

Tolstoi's teachings, as well as producing numbers of individual 'Tolstoians', also inspired some of them to found colonies in which the teacher's principles could be put into practice. The attempts of one such adherent, Nicholas Illin (1852–1922), to carry out such projects, is the subject of Elena Govor and Kevin Windle's chapter 'The Dreamer and the Destroyer: Two Unconventional Tolstoians and their Impact in Australia', the second Tolstoian being Alexander Zuzenko (1884–1938), whose affiliation to Tolstoi's teachings was less wholehearted.

Illin's enthusiasm for Tolstoi was initially intense, but in the 1890s he denounced him as a hypocrite, while, paradoxically, not abandoning the basic principles of Tolstoianism. He attempted to found Tolstoian colonies in Patagonia, Australia (Queensland) and Honduras (where he died). Despite his repudiation of Tolstoi, while in Australia he himself came to be regarded 'by some in the Russian community as a kind of spiritual leader, although he never aspired to exert any practical direction'. Zuzenko, who spent over seven years in Australia as a political agitator and trades unionist, seems initially to have thought of him in this light, but fell out with Illin over his public condemnation of the execution of the Russian royal family in 1918. Having taken the well-trodden path from Tolstoian to anarchist to confirmed Bolshevik, Zuzenko returned to Russia to work as a sea captain, but was charged with espionage and executed during Stalin's purges. The biographies of these two men exemplify the potent influence, for good or ill, that Tolstoi's ideas had on the lives of many Russians.

Alexandra Smith's examination of Fomenko's stage adaptation of *War and Peace* ('Reconfiguring the Empire through Performance: Petr Fomenko's 2001

Production of Tolstoi's *War and Peace*') provides an interesting contrast with Olga Sobolev's chapter on staging *Resurrection* in 1930. Whereas the earlier performance was navigating the pitfalls of an emergent and not fully defined Socialist aesthetic, Fomenko was seeking to break out of the creative fetters of the past and produce a version of *War and Peace* which spoke to the post-Soviet condition. Smith sees a connection between Tolstoi's search for a cohesive vision of the Russian empire, via his novel, in the 1860s and Fomenko's search, via its adaptation, 'for a cohesive narrative of continuity at the beginning of the twenty-first century'. Because of the canonical status of the novel the theatre audience is invited to engage in a dialogue between the innovative performance and their established ideas of Russian history, based on the novel. In Fomenko's view, therefore, theatre has the power to transform established beliefs. In the case of adaptations he seeks to bridge the gap between source and performed texts, and indeed to lay this process bare: thus, actors periodically read from a copy of *War and Peace* placed on a table on stage. What is not lost in the transposition, according to Smith, is the optimistic tone on which the novel ends: 'Fomenko's production celebrates the notion of youthful optimism, the vision of family happiness and the resilience of Russians to survive any corruptive influences from the west'.

As Cynthia Marsh points out in her chapter, 'Bridging Cultures? John McGahern's *The Power of Darkness*', stage adaptations of Tolstoi's novels considerably outnumber performances of his drama in the UK. However, his best known play, *The Power of Darkness*, received a particularly interesting reception when it was performed at the Abbey Theatre in Dublin in 1991. John McGahern had initially adapted it as a play for Radio 3 as long ago as 1972, significantly using Irish English (at the BBC's request) as a way of distancing itself from the language of the English target audience and, more controversially, relying upon certain assumptions about the nature of rural Irish culture. Marsh also notes the erasure of Tolstoi's authorship in credits for the stage adaptation of the play in favour of the adapter, an interesting inversion of a phenomenon identified in her chapter by Carol Apollonio: the anonymization of the translator. Indeed, so hibernicized was the play and its performance, that heated critical discussion followed about the legitimacy of such a harsh representation of Irish life and morals. As Marsh notes, the critical furore engendered by the Irish version of the play in many way replicated the outrage provoked by the Russian original.

The final chapter, by Katherine Jane Briggs ('A Tale of Two Centenaries: Elizabeth Gaskell and Lev Tolstoi') reviews and compares the creative paths of two great European writers in the wake of, in Gaskell's case, the bicentenary of her birth in 1810 and, in Tolstoi's, the centenary of his death in 1910. Gaskell was first introduced to a Russian readership by the serialization of *Mary Barton* in *Vremia* in 1861; Dostoevskii used his preface to its publication to favourably compare Russia's treatment of the poor with England's. A strong sense of social justice is a feature common to both Tolstoi's and Gaskell's works, as is an interest in moral and religious questions. Although overtly clerical themes are not as prominent in Russian literature as they are in English, Briggs' comment about Trollope's novels, that they explore 'the conflict between Christian poverty, humility and service, on the one hand, and the craving for power, preferment and authority [...] on the other' is certainly applicable to Tolstoi's *Father Sergius*. Briggs discusses the similarities between *Anna Karenina* and *North and South*, particularly in the characterization of John Thornton and Levin; she also discusses the degree to which both writers portray themselves in their novels (Gaskell as Margaret Hale and Tolstoi as Levin).

The chapters which comprise the present volume are largely based on papers delivered at an international conference – 'Tolstoi 100 Years On' – held under the auspices of the Neo-Formalist Circle at Mansfield College, Oxford from 13–15 September 2010. The editors warmly thank the participants in that conference for their contributions and for their co-operation in preparing this work for publication. The volume has been updated to take account of new work that has emerged since the original papers were given. The chapters have been arranged in thematic order. Titles of well-known Russian works have been given in established English translation only; for lesser known works the Cyrillic original has also been supplied at first mention. Quotations from Tolstoi and other writers are given in English translation except where reference to the original was considered essential. Citation of Russian titles in the notes is via transliteration, the system used being that of the Library of Congress without diacritics. The spelling of 'Tolstoi' used in this volume conforms to this system. This is the second of two volumes arising from papers delivered at the 'Tolstoi 100 Years On' conference. The first, entitled *Tolstoi and the Evolution of His Artistic World*, was published by Brill in 2021.

Bibliography

Adams, Maurice, 'The Ethics of Tolstoy and Nietzsche', *International Journal of Ethics*, XI, 1, 1900, pp. 82–105.

Allen, Elizabeth Cheresh, ed., *Before They Were Titans: Essays on the Early Works of Dostoevsky and Tolstoy*, Academic Studies Press, Boston, 2019.

Barran, Thomas, 'Rousseau's Political Vision and Tolstoy's *What Is Art?*', *Tolstoy Studies Journal*, V, 1992, pp. 1–13.

Bartlett, Rosamund, *Tolstoy: A Russian Life*, Houghton Mifflin Harcourt, Boston and New York, 2011.

Berlin, Isaiah, *The Hedgehog and the Fox: An Essay on Tolstoy's View of History*, Weidenfeld and Nicolson, London, 1953.

Bloom, Harold, ed., *Leo Tolstoy*, Chelsea House Publishers, Broomhall, 2003.

Blume, Gwendolyn, J., 'The Reader-Brand: Tolstoy in England at the Turn of the Century', *Texas Studies in Literature and Language*, LIII, 3, 2011, pp. 320–37.

Børtnes, Jostein, 'Religion' in *The Cambridge Companion to the Classic Russian Novel*, Jones, Malcolm and Feuer Miller, Robin, eds, Cambridge University Press, Cambridge, 1998, pp. 104–29.

Briggs, A.D.P., *Alexander Pushkin: A Critical Study*, Croom Helm, London, 1983.

Bunin, Ivan Alekseevich, *The Liberation of Tolstoy: A Tale of Two Writers*, Marullo, Thomas Gaiton and Khmelkov, Vladimir T., eds and trans., Northwestern University Press, Evanston, ILL, 2001 (first published as *Osvobozhdenie Tolstogo*, 1937).

Coetze, J.M., 'Confession and Double Thoughts: Tolstoy, Rousseau, Dostoevsky', *Comparative Literature*, III, 37, 1985, pp. 193–232.

Decker, Clarence, 'Victorian Comment on Russian Realism', *PMLA*, LII, 1937, pp. 542–9.

Denner, Michael, 'Tolstoyan Non-Action: the Advantage of Doing Nothing', *Tolstoy Studies Journal*, XIII, 2001, pp. 8–22.

Diment, Galya, 'Tolstoy and Bloomsbury', *Tolstoy Studies Journal*, V, 1992, pp. 39–53.

Edgerton, William, ed. and trans., *Memoirs of Peasant Tolstoyans in Soviet Russia*, Indiana UP, Bloomington, 1993.

Fennell, John, ed. and trans., *Pushkin*, Penguin, Harmondsworth, 1964.

Freeborn, Richard, *Russian Literary Attitudes from Pushkin to Solzhenitsyn*, Macmillan, London, 1976.

Gifford, Henry, ed., *Leo Tolstoy*, Penguin, Harmondsworth, 1971.

Hickey, Steve, *Second Tolstoy: The Sermon on the Mount as Theo-tactics*, Wipf and Stock Publishers, Eugene, Oregon.

James, William, *The Varieties of Religious Experience*, Longmans. Green and Co., New York, London, 1917.

Knapp, Liza, 'Language and Death in Tolstoy's *Childhood* and *Boyhood*: Rousseau and the Holy Fool', *Tolstoy Studies Journal*, X, 1998, pp. 50–62.

Knowles, A.V., ed., *Leo Tolstoy: The Critical Heritage*, Routledge, London and New York, 1997 (first published 1978).

Lavrin, Janko, *Tolstoy: An Approach*, Methuen and Co., London, 1944.

Lermontov, Mikhail, *A Hero of Our Time* and *Princess Ligovskaya*, Martin Parker and Neil Cornwell, trans., Oneworld Classics Ltd., 2009.

Maertz, Gregory, 'Elective Affinities: Tolstoy and Schopenhauer', *Wiener Slavistisches Jahrbuch*, XL, 1994, pp. 53–62.

McKeogh, Colm, *Tolstoy's Pacifism*, Cambria Press, Amherst, New York, 2009.

McLean, Hugh, 'A Clash of Utopias: Tolstoy and Gorky', *Tolstoy Studies Journal*, XIV, 2002, pp. 25–34.

McLean, Hugh, *In Quest of Tolstoy*, Academic Studies Press, Boston, 2017.

Medzhibovskaya, Inessa, *Tolstoy and the Religious Culture of His Time: A Biography of a Long Conversion, 1845–1885*, Lexington Books, Washington, 2009.

Mirsky, D.S., *A History of Russian Literature from Its Beginnings to 1900*, Francis J. Whitfield, ed., Northwestern University Press, Evanston, 1999 (first published 1926).

Moulin, Daniel, *Tolstoy*, Bloomsbury, London and New York, 2014.

Moulin, Daniel 'Tolstoy, Universalism and the World Religions', *Journal of Ecclesiastical History*, LXVIII, 3, 2017, pp, 570–87.

Muchnic, Helen, 'Sholokhov and Tolstoy', *Russian Review*, XVI, 2, 1957, pp. 25–34.

Pearce, Robert, 'Orwell, Tolstoy and Animal Farm', *The Review of English Studies*, 1998, XLIX, pp. 64–9.

Pickford, Henry H., 'Of Rules and Rails: On a Motif in Tolstoy and Wittgenstein', *Tolstoy Studies Journal*, XXII, 2010, pp. 40–53.

Repin, Natalie, 'Being-toward-Death in Tolstoy's *The Death of Ivan Il'ich*: Tolstoy and Heidegger', *Canadian-American Slavic Studies*, XXXVI, 1–2, 2002, pp. 101–32.

Scanlan, James P., 'Tolstoy among the Philosophers: His Book on Life and Its Critical Reception', *Tolstoy Studies Journal*, XVIII, 2006, pp. 52–69.

Scanlan, James, 'From William James to Karl Marx: David Kvitko's Studies of Tolstoy the Thinker', *Tolstoy Studies Journal*, XV, pp. 67–78.

Simmonds, Ernest J., *Tolstoy*, Routledge and Kegan Paul, London, 1946.

Sloane, David, A., 'Pushkin's Legacy in Anna Karenina', *Tolstoy Studies Journal*, IV, 1991, pp. 1–23.

Sloane, David, 'Rehabilitating Bakhtin's Tolstoy: The Politics of the Utterance', *Tolstoy Studies Journal*, XIII, 2001, pp. 59–77.

Slonim, Marc, 'Four Western Writers on Tolstoy', *Russian Review*, XIX, 2, 1960, pp. 187–204.

Slonim, Marc, *Soviet Russian Literature: Writers and Problems, 1917–1967*, Oxford University Press, Oxford, 1967.

Steiner, George, *Tolstoy or Dostoevsky*, Penguin, Harmondsworth, 1967.

Toland, Kristina, 'Path of Life: Lev Tolstoy's Prescriptive Spiritual Diaries', *Tolstoy Studies Journal*, XXIV, 2012, pp. 15–25.

Tolstoy, Leo, 'Tolstoy on Shakespeare: A Critical Essay on Shakespeare', V. Tchertkoff and I.F.M., trans., Funk and Wagnalls, New York and London, 1906. Project Gutenberg, https://www.gutenberg.org/files/27726/27726-h/27726-h.htm (accessed 15. 11. 2020).

Tolstoy, Leo, *What is Art?*, Pevear, Richard and Volokhonsky, Larissa, trans., Penguin, London, 1995.

Troyat, Henri, *Tolstoy*, Amphoux, Nancy, trans., Doubleday and Co., New York, 1968.

Waddell, Laura, 'Coronavirus Limbo Is Perfect Time to Finally Read *War and Peace*', *Scotsman*, 1 April, 2020.

Williams, Raymond, 'Lawrence and Tolstoy', *Critical Quarterly*, II, 1, 1960, pp. 33–9.

Wilson, Jennifer, 'Leo Tolstoy vs. the Police', *The New York Times*, June 25, 2020.

Wittgenstein, Ludwig, *Tractatus Logico-Philosophicus*, C.K. Ogden, trans., Kegan Paul Trench Trubner and Co., London, 1922. Reproduced by Project Gutenberg: http://www.gutenberg.org/ebooks/5740 (accessed 15. 11. 2020).

Woodruff, T. David Joseph, 'Tolstoy and Wittgenstein: The Life Outside of Time', *The Southern Journal of Philosophy*, LX, 2002, 421–35.

Wyatt, Edward, 'Tolstoy's Translators Experience Oprah's Effect', *The New York Times*, June 7, 2004.

CHAPTER 1

Does the Translation Matter?

Carol Apollonio

Abstract

This chapter addresses one of the media, perhaps the most significant, by which the continuing popularity of Tolstoi has been sustained. Until recently, translators were given little credit for their role in making literary works available to a wider readership. There is something feminine in the traditional invisibility of translators and, indeed, when it comes to Tolstoi, some of the more significant among them were women. The situation has thankfully changed, and recent successful translations have restored the translator to the conversation about world literature. This is one way in which translation matters, but another is the very real scope, that the translation process uniquely offers, to interpret, indeed to perform, the source text in an original way. Extracts from up to ten translations of *War and Peace* are compared, with particular emphasis on characteristic Tolstoian techniques such as the physical description of characters, philosophical exposition and defamiliarization (*ostranenie*). The chapter also compares and contrasts the apparatus and presentation of the translations.

Keywords

Tolstoi in translation – translators of Tolstoi – Tolstoi's novels

∴

> [...] many heroes and men of genius are described to us in accounts of this period of the campaign, but of Dohturov nothing is said, or but few words of dubious praise. This silence in regard to Dohturov is the plainest testimony to his merits.[1]

∴

---

1   Leo Tolstoy, *War and Peace*, Constance Garnett, trans., in four volumes, Konemann, Hungary, 1999 (1904) (hereafter CG), p. 1616.

In this excerpt from book four, part two, chapter 15 of *War and Peace*, Tolstoi praises the valour of the 'modest, unpretentious little general Dohturov,' the 'small cog-wheel, which turns inaudibly' and is 'one of the essential parts of the machine'.[2] Replace 'Dohturov' with 'the Translator' and you'll realize that the virtues that Tolstoi values most are those most often praised in translators: modesty, silence, invisibility, and service to the greater cause. There's something feminine about these attributes:

> [Pierre] experienced that rare pleasure which is granted by women when they listen to a man – not intelligent women, who, when they listen, try either to memorize what they are told in order to enrich their minds and on occasion retell the same thing, or else to adjust what is being told to themselves and quickly say something intelligent of their own, worked out in their small intellectual domain; but the pleasure granted by real women, endowed with the ability to select and absorb all the best of what a man has to show. Natasha, not knowing it herself, was all attention: she did not miss a word of Pierre's, not a waver in his voice, not a glance, not the twitch of a facial muscle, not a gesture. She caught the not-yet-spoken word in flight and brought it straight into her open heart, guessing the secret meaning of all Pierre's inner work.[3]

Pierre's feminine ideal listener manifests the values that the monolingual reader generally seeks in the translator. Pierre is the author (Tolstoi), and Natasha is the translator – catching everything, adding nothing of her own. This listening is the first half of the translator's work, the understanding part. The second half, though, that active part where the listener has to convey that essential Pierre into a foreign language, to speak in his place, is where the trouble begins. There's no place for that person. Readers prefer the translator to remain silent, in that state that Lawrence Venuti calls 'invisibility',[4] maintaining the illusion that the master himself, in this case, Tolstoi, is speaking directly to them with no intermediary. This assumption is pervasive. The cover of my edition of Ann Dunnigan's 1968 translation of *War and Peace* reads, in its entirety:

---

2 Leo Tolstoy, *War and Peace*, Leo Wiener, trans., *The Complete Works of Count Tolstoy*, V–VIII, Dana Estes & Company, Boston, 1904 (hereafter LW), VIII, pp. 151–2.
3 Leo Tolstoy, *War and Peace*, Richard Pevear and Larissa Volokhonsky, trans., Alfred A. Knopf, New York, 2007 (hereafter PV), p. 1117.
4 Lawrence Venuti, *The Translator's Invisibility: A History of Translation*, Routledge, London, 1995, p. 1.

> LEO TOLSTOY
> WAR AND PEACE
> With a New Introduction by PAT CONROY[5]

Open the cover, and there on the first page are two blurby bios: one, longer and on top, is Count Leo Tolstoy's. Below follows a shorter one telling who Pat Conroy is. That is all. Only after you turn another page do you see that someone named Ann Dunnigan has written every word in the novel you hold in your hands. There is something feminine about the fact that translators are so often not credited, though throughout the twentieth century, classic Russian literature spoke to English readers in the voice of a woman (the astonishingly productive, though famously modest, Constance Garnett). Until recently, two of Tolstoi's female translators – Dunnigan and Edmonds – appeared at the top of a Google search in the form of obituaries. In the twenty-first century, the field of Translation Studies has brought much-needed attention to translators, including these pioneering women. And our analysis reveals an unusual case where a female translator (Kropotkin) receives too much credit for her work. But, mainstream readers persist in associating translation with feminine virtues such as docility, selflessness, and devotion to their master, the author.

The title of this chapter, 'Does the Translation Matter?', comes in response to Edith Grossman's much praised 2010 book on translation, entitled *Why Translation Matters*. Arguing the importance of translation in making great literature accessible to readers around the world, Grossman lists many writers she read first in translation:

> I never have forgotten my adolescent self discovering nineteenth-century Russian and French novelists [...]. [W]riters like Stendhal and Balzac, Gogol and Tolstoy, created entire galaxies in their writing. It is unthinkable, almost unbearable to contemplate the possibility of being deprived of those universes because one does not know French and Russian well enough to read their books.[6]

Grossman follows up these great names with those of Homer, Sophocles, Sappho, Catullus, Virgil, Dante, Petrarch, Leopardi, Cervantes, Lope, Quevedo,

---

5 Leo Tolstoy, *War and Peace*, Ann Dunnigan (hereafter AD), trans., Signet Classics, New York, 1968.
6 Edith Grossman, *Why Translation Matters*, Yale University Press, New Haven, 2010, p. 25.

Ronsard, Rabelais, Verlaine, Tolstoi (again), Chekhov, Goethe, and Heine, and many others, including Akhmatova, Brecht, Montale, Garcia Lorca, Valéry, Kazantzakis, Ibsen, Strindberg, Saramago, and Singer. The point is that without translation our lives would be impoverished. Grossman notes, with some fervour: 'the fact is that many readers tend to take translation so much for granted that it is no wonder translators are so frequently ignored'.[7] Oddly enough, though, in these early chapters, arguing that 'translation matters', Grossman herself neglects to mention the name of a single translator. That comes at the end of the book, where she offers a list of translated books, 'not necessarily the best or most recent translations', but books that 'made a deep and long-lasting impression and certainly influenced the way I write and translate'. Even as she acknowledges their influence, she notes that if they were not still on her shelves, she could never 'reconstruct the titles and their translators from memory'.[8] Edith Grossman's answer to my question, sadly, would be that translation matters, but not 'the' translation.

Given that this admission comes to us from one of the most famous living translators (if that is not an oxymoron) of literature – Cervantes – into English, we must deduce that the translator's invisibility is a pernicious thing indeed. Why is it so hard for even translators themselves to credit other translators? The very informative front page of the John C. Winston Company's 1949 edition of *War and Peace*, tells the reader that the novel has been illustrated by J. Franklin Whitman, revised by Somerset Maugham, and that 'a translation' has been 'revised by' Princess Alexandra Kropotkin, but does not inform the reader who did that translation.[9] (There will be more on this specific case later.) This sort of information can be difficult to track down. What is the precise relationship between Leo Wiener's translation of the novel in his edition of Tolstoi's *Collected Works* and Nathan Haskell Dole's 1898–9 version? Translation matters, of course. It is one of the achievements of Richard Pevear's and Larissa Volokhonsky's translations of Russian literature that they and their publishers have restored the translator to the conversation about world literature. In doing so, they have brought the Russian classics a readership that, without this conversation, would never have come into being. At the same time, as Gary Saul Morson argues, the conversation may very well be as much

---

7 Ibid., p. 27.
8 Ibid., pp. 121–4.
9 Leo Tolstoy, *War and Peace*, translation revised by Princess Alexandra Kropotkin, W. Somerset Maugham, ed., The John C. Winston Company, Philadelphia and Toronto, 1949 (hereafter AK), title page.

about the vagaries of marketing and publishing as it is about translation.[10] How important are the distinctions we make among translations of a great classic like Tolstoi's *War and Peace*, and how important are other factors, such as the novel's editorial packaging? With these questions in mind, I offer here a necessarily cursory comparison of ten translations of the novel. These are, in chronological order: Nathan Haskell Dole (1898–9); Constance Garnett (1904); Leo Wiener (1904); Aylmer and Louise Maude (1922–3); Alexandra Kropotkin (1949); Rosemary Edmonds (1957; 1978); Ann Dunnigan (1968); Anthony Briggs (2005); Andrew Bromfield (2007); and Richard Pevear and Larissa Volokhonsky (2007). Kropotkin's version is abridged and, at least based on the excerpts analyzed here, seems actually to be unabashedly Dole. Bromfield's is based on a different edition of the novel from all the others, so his figures here only incidentally.

In the first Epilogue, Tolstoi (or is it his translator?) writes: 'As the sun and every atom of ether is a sphere perfect in itself, and at the same time only an atom in the mighty All inaccessible to man, so each individual has within himself his own objects, and at the same time serves the common object inaccessible to man'.[11] In the second Epilogue, they write:

> Only the expression of the will of the Deity, not dependent on time, can relate to a whole series of events occurring over a period of years or centuries, and only the Deity, independent of everything, can by His sole will determine the direction of humanity's movement; but man acts in time and himself takes part in what occurs.[12]

The relationship between the sun and the atom of ether, or between the individual human act and the will of the Deity, is similar to the relationship between the great novel as a whole, whose value is 'not dependent on time', and a whole range of lesser, but essential elements such as, say, the individual words. On the one hand the sick beehive of abandoned Moscow, the anthill, the great forces of history, the infinite sky; on the other hand the sick bees, the ants, the soldier, the wounded man gazing up. Even as readers stand in awe before the majesty of the novel, we also realize that its power – like that of

---

10   Gary Saul Morson, 'The Pevearsion of Russian Literature', *Commentary*, July / August 2010, pp. 92–8 (92).
11   Lyof N. Tolstoi, *War and Peace*, Nathan Haskell Dole, trans., Thomas Y. Crowell Co, New York, 1926–7 (1898–9), III, part 14, (hereafter NHD), p. 166.
12   Leo Tolstoy, *War and Peace*, Aylmer and Louise Maude, trans., Amy Mandelker, ed., Oxford University Press, Oxford, 2010, p. 1287.

human history that is its subject – derives from the accumulation of its smallest component parts. We all have our favourites: 'A doctor in a bloodstained apron came out of the tent, holding a cigar between the thumb and little finger of one of his bloodstained hands to keep the blood off it'.[13]

At the large end, Tolstoi's landscape sweeps across the screen, beginning underfoot and encompassing everything in sight:

> Every day fleecy clouds floated across the sky, occasionally shutting out the sun, but towards evening the sky would clear again and the sun set in a sombre red haze. Only the heavy night-dews refreshed the earth. The wheat left in the fields was burnt up and dropping out of the ear. The marshes dried up. The cattle lowed from hunger, finding nothing to graze on in the sun-baked meadows. Only at night and in the forests while the dew lasted was it ever cool. But on the road, the high road along which the troops marched, there was no coolness even at night or where the road passed through the forest: the dew made no impression on the sandy dust inches deep. As soon as it was daylight the soldiers began to move. The artillery and baggage-wagons ploughed along noiselessly, buried almost to their axles, and the infantry sank ankle-deep in the soft, choking burning dust that never cooled even at night. Sandy dust clung to their legs and to the wheels, rose and hung like a cloud overhead, and got into eyes, ears, hair and nostrils, and worst of all, settled in the lungs of the men and beasts that moved along the road.[14]

Like Natasha when Pierre is talking, at those moments when we readers give ourselves fully to the novel, it seems petty to quibble over something so microscopic as the wording (those tiny distances that Tolstoi's Achilles, in book three, part three, chapter one, must cover as he tries to overtake the tortoise on their way to the majestic panoramic whole of the novel, and of history). It's a matter of perspective. Are we allowing ourselves to enter Tolstoi's epic world in its full majestic sweep, to empathize with the characters, to see the landscapes, to experience the battle? At such moments the translations can seem almost interchangeable. *The translation does not matter.* But when we squint up close to get a good look, say, at the individual bees, to feel the language in its full tangibility – its sounds and rhythms, we realize that the translations

---

13 Leo Tolstoy, *War and Peace*, Anthony Briggs, trans., Viking Penguin, New York, 2006 (hereafter AB), p. 902.
14 Leo Tolstoy, *War and Peace*, Rosemary Edmonds, trans., in two volumes, Penguin, Middlesex, England, 1957 (hereafter RE), pp. 832–3.

are in fact quite different. *The translation matters.* It is not so much a question of which is the best, but rather, what is unique and different about each translation. Which translator would you invite into your room at night to read Tolstoi's novel to you?

Did the translation matter in the excerpts from the novel cited above? For each quote, I chose the particular translations completely at random; my only concern was to give each translator a voice in the conversation, and to cite each translation only once. Would a different translation have conveyed each point more effectively? How important was the identity or style of the translator to the argument I was developing? My point is twofold: that we look at translation in different ways depending on our goals great and small, and that these different ways of looking at translation can be presented in terms of Tolstoi's world view and novelistic vision. The argument can be made *regardless of who translated the excerpts*. But now we turn our attention to the text of the novel, quoting and juxtaposing translations of key passages. Tolstoi's, and his translators', language is now our focus, rather than serving as a mere vehicle for demonstrating my points about translation. From this up-close perspective, we can come to a better sense of just how, where, and why 'the' translation matters.

The passages presented below exemplify features that are generally recognized as distinctively Tolstoian. The categories are as follows:

1. Physical Description (Pierre)
2. Descriptive Detail (the bloodstained finger)
3. Non-standard Speech (the huntsman; Denisov's lisp)
4. Tolstoi's Epic Landscape (the dusty march)
5. Philosophical Exposition (the life of nations)
6. *Ostranenie (Defamiliarization)* (Natasha at the opera)
7. Metaphor; the French language (the watch mechanism)
8. Emotional Climax (Prince Andrei's death)

Each set of excerpts is accompanied by some preliminary comments, along with speculative generalizations. An exhaustive analysis is of course impossible here, but the material should give my readers the opportunity to compare and evaluate the translations according to their own taste. The translators are listed in the same order for each quote, chronological based on the translation's publication date. For reasons given above there is not a Bromfield or Kropotkin passage for every example. In each case, the translations are preceded by the Russian original.

1 Physical Description: Pierre (I: ii: 5)

The first excerpt has to do with Tolstoi's physical description of characters. As we know, in Tolstoi's works a character's moral identity and character pervades his physical being, and at the same time he is fully and completely 'real'.

Пьер был неуклюж. Толстый, выше обыкновенного роста, широкий, с огромными красными руками, он, как говорится, не умел войти в салон и еще менее умел из него выйти, то есть перед выходом сказать что-нибудь особенно приятное. Кроме того, он был рассеян. Вставая, он вместо своей шляпы захвлатил треугольную шляпу с генеральским плюмажем и держал ее, дергая султан, до тех пор, пока генерал не попросил возвратить ее.[15]

a. Pierre, as we have already said, was awkward. Stout, of more than the average height, broad-shouldered, with huge red hands, he had no idea of the proper way to enter a drawing-room, and still less the proper way of making his exit; in other words he did not know how to make some especially agreeable remark to his hostess before taking his leave. Moreover, he was absent-minded. He got up, and instead of taking his own hat he seized the plumed three-cornered hat of some general, and held it, pulling at the feathers until the general came and asked him to surrender it. (NHD I: i: 27).

b. Pierre was clumsy, stout and uncommonly tall, with huge red hands; he did not, as they say, know how to come into a drawing-room and still less how to get out of one, that is, how to say something particularly agreeable on going away. Moreover, he was dreamy. He stood up, and picking up a three-cornered hat with the plume of a general in it instead of his own, he kept hold of it, pulling the feathers till the general asked him to restore it (CG 34).

c. Pierre was clumsy. He was fat, taller than the average, broad, and had immense red hands; he, as they say, did not know how to enter a parlour, and still less did he know how to come out of it, that is, he did not know how to say something very pleasant before taking his leave. He was, in addition, absent-minded. Upon getting up, he picked up a three-cornered

---

[15] L.N. Tolstoi, *Voina i mir* in *Polnoe sobranie sochinenii*, V.G. Chertkov, ed., Gosudarstvennoe izdatel'stvo khuzhestvennoi literatury Moscow-Leningrad, IX–XII, 1930–3, 1, p. 27 (hereafter quotations in the text refer to this edition).

d. Pierre was ungainly. Stout, above the average height, broad, with huge red hands, he did not know, as the saying is, how to enter a drawing room and still less how to leave one; that is, how to say something particularly agreeable before going away. Besides this he was absent-minded. When he rose to go, he took up instead of his own, the general's three-cornered hat, and held it, pulling at the plume, till the general asked him to restore it (MM 23–4).

e. Pierre, as we have already said, was awkward. Stout, of more than average height, broad-shouldered, with huge red hands, he had no idea of the proper way to enter a drawing-room, and still less the proper way of making his exit; in other words, he did not know how to make some especially agreeable remark to his hostess before taking his leave. Moreover, he was absent-minded. He got up, and instead of taking his own hat he seized the plumed three-cornered hat of some general and held it, pulling at the feathers until the general came and asked him to surrender it (AK 13).

f. Pierre was ungainly, stout and uncommonly tall, with exceptionally large red hands; as the saying is, he had no idea how to enter a drawing-room and still less of how to get out of one. In other words, he did not know how to make some especially agreeable remark to his hostess before leaving. Moreover, he was absent-minded. He got up and, instead of his own, seized the plumed three-cornered hat of a general and stood holding it, pulling at the plume, until the general claimed it from him (RE 24).

g. Pierre was awkward; above average height, broad and stout, with huge red hands, he did not know how to enter a drawing room, as they say, and still less how to leave one, that is, how to say something particularly agreeable before going. Moreover he was absent-minded. Now when he got up to go he picked up a general's three-cornered hat instead of his own and stood there plucking at the plume till the general asked him to return it (AD 49–50).

h. Pierre was ungainly, stout, quite tall and possessed of huge red hands. It was said of him that he had no idea how to enter a drawing room and was worse still at withdrawing from one, or saying something nice as he left. He was also absent-minded. He stood up now, picked up a general's nicely plumed three-cornered hat instead of his own, and held on to it, pulling at the feathers, until the general asked for it back (AB 24).

i. Pierre was clumsy. Fat, unusually tall, broad, with enormous red hands, he did not, as they say, know how to enter a salon, and still less did he know how to leave one, that is, by saying something especially pleasant at the door. Besides that, he was absentminded. Getting up, he took a three-cornered hat with a general's plumage instead of his own and held on to it, plucking at the feathers, until the general asked him to give it back (PV 22).

j. Pierre was ungainly. Fat and broad, with huge hands that seemed to have been made for swinging one-*pood* weights, he had no idea, as they say, of how to enter a salon and even less idea of how to leave it, that is, of how to make his farewells and say something particularly agreeable before his exit. In addition, he was absent-minded. As he stood up, instead of taking his own hat he grabbed hold of a three-cornered hat with a general's panache and held it, tugging at the plume, until the general finally requested him with some animosity, or so it seemed to Pierre, to hand it back. (Bromfield 34 – here and always, Bromfield translated a different version of the novel)

Dole's 'surrender' represents what is usually a good impulse – using one verb instead of a verb-preposition alternative – in translating Russian. In this regard, 'surrender' is in solidarity with the 'restore' and in opposition to the 'give it back' that we find in later versions. Edmonds makes some additions ('to his hostess'; 'stood holding'). Garnett's entry in the originality category is 'dreamy', which seems excessive but may be an anachronism that served well in her time. 'Restore', too, may fit into that category. Wiener's 'panache' dates the translation. His choice of the literal 'fat' for толстый will lie dormant until the twenty-first century. Elsewhere Wiener tends to offer extremely literal versions, though that is not necessarily the case in this excerpt. The Maudes use 'restore' as well. 'Broad' may have sounded more natural in the early twentieth century than it does now. The careful reader of Kropotkin's translation soon realizes, with a sense of indignation that spills into outrage, that it is identical to Dole's. Dunnigan adds an adjective: broad *and* stout. Dunnigan generally will adhere fairly closely to the rhythm of Tolstoi's text and, when all is said and done, will show a tendency to simplify the original, both in grammar and in vocabulary. Like some of her freer renderings, the additions are presumably motivated by the aim of achieving good English style, and at least to this reader, they serve the spirit of Tolstoi's text and are justified. Edmonds' 'the general claimed it' is a deft transposition. Briggs offers a series of weak verbs ('was'); prepositions also abound. He, Dunnigan, and Garnett repeat 'up' in verb-preposition phrases. On the positive side Briggs' 'possessed of' is a nice touch. Pevear and Volokhonsky's decision to add 'at the door' may be the equivalent of Edmonds' addition of the hostess, and here too, it is amply justified. One of Pevear and Volokhonsky's most pronounced tendencies, at least in comparison with the others, is to adhere to *grammatical and syntactical literalism*. So the verbal adverb 'вставая' comes across as 'getting up' – an accurate but by no means the only correct rendition. As for Bromfield, like Pevear and Volokhonsky and their distant predecessor Wiener, he chose to translate 'толстый' as 'fat', an iron-clad literalism which to some may be a controversial choice – though the reader of the original will note an almost terrifying tendency for Pierre to grow even fatter (yes, Tolstoi repeats and repeats this word) with every new stage in his life throughout the novel. Bromfield, like Briggs, will always go for the most modern colloquial variant – in this example, 'grabbed hold of' – and makes no pretence at matching words to their historical time. In this excerpt that jars with 'something particularly agreeable', which would probably not be said by a person who could say 'grabbed hold of'. Similarly, the phrase conflicts with what Pevear and Volokhonsky elsewhere might call the 'grabbed object', the 'three-cornered hat with a general's panache'. I wonder if Bromfield's ideal reader would know what a 'panache' is. Pevear and Volokhonsky, by contrast, and true to their emphasis on *vocabulary* in translation, make a point of not using words that were not in the Oxford dictionary during the time the novel was written.[16]

2   Descriptive Detail: The Bloodstained Finger (III: ii: 37)

Tolstoi is the master of the tiny detail, the drop of water in which the entire world is reflected. These gems can present a serious challenge to the ablest translator; just as in the original, every word, and every word's placement, is important.

Один из докторов в окровавленном фартуке и с окровавленными небольшими руками, в одной из которых он между мизинцем и большим пальцем (чтобы не запачкать ее) держал сигару, вышел из палатки (XI: 253).

a. One of the surgeons, with a blood-soaked apron and with his small hands covered with gore, holding a cigar between thumb and little finger so as not to besmear it, came out of the tent (NHD II: ix: 329).
b. One of the doctors came out of the tent with a blood-stained apron, and small, blood-stained hands, in one of which he had a cigar, carefully held

---

16   Jeffrey Trachtenberg, 'Translating Tolstoy', telephone and email interview with Richard Pevear and Larissa Volokhonsky, 'Books and Ideas', *The Wall Street Journal*, 17 November 2009.

between his thumb and little finger, that it might not be stained too (CG 1283).
c. One of the doctors in a blood-stained apron and with small, blood-stained hands, in one of which, between his little finger and thumb (in order not to soil it), he was holding a cigar, came out of the tent (LW VII: 363).
d. One of the doctors came out of the tent in a bloodstained apron, holding a cigar between the thumb and little finger of one of his small blood-stained hands, so as not to smear it (MM 872).
e. One of the surgeons, with a blood-soaked apron and with his small hands covered with gore, holding a cigar between thumb and little finger so as not to besmear it, came out of the tent (AK 508).
f. One of the doctors came out of the tent in a blood-soaked apron, holding a cigar between the thumb and little finger of one of his blood-stained hands, so as not to besmear it (RE 965).
g. One of the doctors came out of the tent in a bloodstained apron with a cigar held between the thumb and little finger of his small, bloody hand, to avoid smearing it (AD 976).
h. A doctor in a bloodstained apron came out of the tent, holding a cigar between the thumb and little finger of one of his bloodstained hands to keep the blood off it (AB 902).
i. One of the doctors came out of the tent in a bloody apron and with small, bloody hands, in one of which, between the thumb and the little finger (so as not to stain it), he was holding a cigar (PV 812).

Dole's (and the larcenous Kropotkin's) 'gore' for the second reference to blood may be gratuitous. His and Edmonds' 'besmear' is a strange word. Syntax becomes important in conveying these precise, unforgettable images. Briggs is ever colloquial ('to keep the blood off it'). Pevear and Volokhonsky's word order, with the cigar at the end, introduces some awkwardness and, though their parentheses (and Wiener's) duplicate Tolstoi's text, the phrase falls flat. The other translators recognize the importance of the phrase and place it in the power position at the end of the sentence. In Garnett's version, the apron and hands are in the same semantic field; lingering on the implications may cause some queasiness in the reader. That could use some tweaking. But her elegant, pitch-perfect 'that it might not be stained too' redeems the sentence. Here, as so often is the case, Garnett deserves far more credit than she gets. Remember, she was a pioneer.

3 Non-standard Speech

Rendering the speech of non-literate speakers in a work of literature is a problem whether the text is an original or a translation. Two examples are presented here: (A) peasant speech and (B) Denisov's lisp. In judging these it is recommended to keep a sense of measure, and even indulgence. No matter how these utterances are translated, they will not be fully 'authentic'; rather they are stylized, literate approximations of how peasants speak. That said, it is here that translators show the most variety. One senses that those who go the extra mile tend to draw on the substandard speech of the substandard speakers closest to them. This will satisfy no-one. The versions cited here range from the tasteful and reticent to the downright weird.

A. Peasant Speech: the huntsman (II: iv: 4)

– Картину писать! Как намеднись из Заварзинских бурьянов помкнули лису. Они перескакаивать стали, от уймища, страсть – лошадь тысяча рублей, а седоку цены нет! Да, уж такого молодца поискать! (X: 249)

a. 'Like a picture! How he run that fox t'other day out of the steppe at Zavarzino! How he did gallop out of the woods, t'was a caution! Horse worth a thousand but the rider beyond price! 'T would be a hard job to find such another young fellow' (NHD II: vi: 127).
b. 'A perfect picture he is! How he drove the fox out of the Zavarzinsky thicket the other day. He galloped down from the ravine, it was a sight – the horse worth a thousand roubles, and the rider beyond all price. Yes, you would have to look a long while to find his match!' (CG 785).
c. 'Like a picture! The other day he chased a fox in the Zavarzin steppe. He took some terrible leaps, – his horse is worth a thousand roubles, but there is no price to the rider himself. Yes, it would be hard to find such a fine fellow!' (LW VI: 356)
d. 'A perfect picture! How he chased a fox out of the rank grass by the Zavarzinsky thicket the other day! Leapt a fearful place; what a sight when they rushed from the covert … the horse worth a thousand rubles and the rider beyond all price! Yes, one would have to search far to find another as smart' (MM 532).
e. (not present in AK)
f. 'A reg'lar picture! How he run that there fox out of the steppe Zavarzino way t'other day! Come flying out of them woods, 'twas a caution! Horse

worth thousand roubles but nobody could set no price to the rider. Aye, a man'd need to go a long way to find the likes of him!' (RE 586).

g. 'A picture, he is! He made short work of running that fox out of the Zavarzinsky high grass the other day. Came galloping out like a fury – the horse worth a thousand rubles and the rider beyond price! Yes, one would have to search far and wide to find the likes of him!' (AD 602).

h. 'Perfect picture! The other day he run this fox out of yon patch at Zavarzino. Flew down that ravine, he did, sight for sore eyes – horse worth a thousand roubles, no price on the rider. Aye, you'd go a long way to find another like him!' (AB 544).

i. 'A real picture! Like the other day when we chased a fox from the Zavarzinsky thicket. The master went hurtling to cut it off from the forest, something fearsome – a thousand-rouble horse, but the rider's priceless! Yes, a fine fellow like that is hard to find!' (PV 498).

j. 'A real picture. The way as he drove that fox out of the Zavarzins' thickets the other day – what a sight: the horse is worth a thousand, but the rider's priceless. Where would you find a fellow to match him' (Bromfield 590).

Dole, Briggs and Edmonds take the most risk, in Briggs' case in particular, maybe too much risk. The Maudes' 'leaped a fearful place' is striking, though its meaning is elusive; here even more than in the other versions one feels the full struggle between the elemental distinctiveness of the man's way of talking and the upward tug of English style. Ultimately, they, like Dunnigan, Garnett, Pevear and Volokhonsky, and Bromfield show restraint, opting for more standard, and safe, literary language.

A related category is pronunciation (German, French accents, peculiarities of speech).

A. Denisov's lisp (IV: iii: 4)

This particular example raises some questions of a textual nature. Denisov has an unusual, manly, guttural lisp; he pronounces 'r' like 'g' (– Г'остов! Петя! [...] – Ну, я г'ад тебя видеть [XII: 127–8]). Here, though, Denisov is *not speaking, but thinking*, and the original (or at least the Jubilee edition) lacks the lisp:

«Едва ли выйдет другой такой случай, как нынче, напасть на транспорт. Одному нападать слишком рискованно, а отложить до другого дня, – из-под носа захватит добычу кто-нибудь из больших партизанов», – думал Денисов [...] (XII: 127).

a. 'We shan't be likely to find another chance like to-day's to stwike the twansport twain. To attack them alone is too much of a wisk; and to wait till another day – some of those big bands of partizans will be sure to snatch it away from under our vewy noses,' said Denisov [...] (NHD III: vi, 13).
b. 'We shall never have such another chance to fall on the transport as today. To attack them alone would be risky and to put it off to another day – some of the bigger leaders will carry the booty off from under our noses', thought Denisov [...] (CG 1645).
c. 'There will hardly present itself another such an opportunity as to-day to attack the transport. It is too risky for me to attack it alone, and if I put it off to another day, some one of the greater partisans will snap it up under my nose', thought Denisov [...] (LW VIII: 183).
d. 'There'll hardly be another such chance to fall on a transport as today. It's too risky to attack them by oneself, and if we put it off till another day one of the big guerrilla detachments will snatch the prey from under our noses', thought Denisov [...] (MM 1117).
e. 'We won't be likely to find another chance like today's to stwike the twansport twain. To attack them alone is too much of a wisk; and to wait till another day – some of those big bands of pa'tisans will be sure to snatch it away from under our vewy noses', said Denisof [...] (AK 646).
f. 'We aren't likely to get another chance to fall on a twansport twain like today. To attack them alone is too much of a wisk, and if we put it off till another day one of the big guewwilla detachments will snatch the pwey from under our vewy noses', thought Denisov [...] (RE 1229).
g. 'We're not likely to have another chance like this to fall on a twansport twain. To attack them alone is too wisky but if we put it off to another day, one of the big guewwilla detachments will snatch the pwey fwom under our noses', thought Denisov [...] (AD 1240).
h. 'There'll never be a chance like this to attack that wagon-twain. It's too wisky to attack on our own, but if we put it off some of the big boys will gwab the spoils wight under our noses', said Denisov to himself [...] (AB 1154–5).
i. 'There could hardly be another such occasion as today for attacking the transport. To attack alone is too risky, but put it off to another day and some bigger party will snatch the booty right from under our noses', thought Denisov [...] (PV 1038).

When dealing with Denisov's lisp, some translators render it with 'w' replacing the intended 'r' sound; only PV, further down and throughout, cling to Tolstoi's guttural 'r' ('Ghrostov! Petya!') when it is present in the original (1039).

Oddly enough, some translators convey the lisp, absent in the original here (if they, as I presume, were using the Jubilee edition). The effect – baby talk reproduced in Denisov's unspoken thoughts – is hilarious, but wildly unjustified. This is particularly noticeable with 'guewwilla detachments' and 'snatch the pwey'. Garnett, Wiener, the Maudes, and Pevear / Volokhonsky show good taste. As for the others, one senses that later translators – not just the thief Kropotkin – were using their predecessors as well as or even instead of the original. The Maudes came up with the deft phrases 'guerrilla detachments' and 'snatch the prey from under our noses'; Edmonds restored the lisp, Dunnigan quoted them both, and Briggs added his usual colloquial variant ('gwab the spoils'). Kropotkin, true to form, and not bothering to check the original, repeated Dole's 'said' for Tolstoi's 'thought' (думал), compounding the colossal weirdness of the passage. Briggs at least corrects this by adding 'to himself' to 'said', though his choice to keep the lisp is still baffling.

4 Tolstoi's Epic Landscape: The Dusty March (III: ii: 5)

It is in his panoramic landscapes and mass scenes that Tolstoi's genius is most distinctive and inimitable. Given that translation is a form of imitation, these passages either present translators a chance to shine, or present an insurmountable challenge, depending on the point of view:

Каждый день по небу ходили курчавые облака, изредка заслоняя солнце; но к вечеру опять расчищало, и солнце садилось в буровато-красную мглу. Только сильная роса ночью освежала землю. Оставшиеся на корню хлеба сгорали и высыпались. Болота пересохли. Скотина ревела от голода, не находя корма по сожженным солнцем лугам. Только по ночам и в лесах, пока еще держалась роса, была прохлада. Но по дороге, по большой дороге, по которой шли войска, даже и ночью, даже и по лесам, не было этой прохлады. Роса не заметна была на песочной пыли дороги, встолченной больше чем на четверть аршина. Как только рассветало, начиналось движение. Обозы, артиллерия беззвучно шли по ступицу, а пехота по щиколку в мягкой, душной, не остывшей за ночь, жаркой пыли. Одна часть этой песочной пыли месилась ногами и колесами, другая поднималась и стояла облаком над войском, влипая в глаза, в волоса, в уши, в ноздри и главное в легкие людям и животным, двигавшимся по этой дороге (XI: 120).

a. Each day cirrus clouds moved across the sky and occasionally veiled the sun; but by evening the heavens were clear again, and the sun set in brownish purple haze. The only refreshing that the earth got was from the heavy dew at night. The standing crops of wheat were parched, and wasted their seed. The marshes dried up. The cattle bellowed from hunger, finding no pasturage along the ponds, which had shrunk to nothing in the sun. Only at night and in the depths of the forest, before the dew evaporated, was there any freshness.

But on the roads, on the highroad where the troops were marching, even at night, even in the shelter of the forests, this coolness was not to be found. The dew was imperceptible on the sandy dust, which was more than a quarter of an arshin deep.

At the first ray of dawn the troops were set in motion. The baggage train and the field-pieces plowed along noiselessly, sinking almost up to the hubs of the wheels, and the infantry struggled through the soft, stifling, heated dust which settled not even at night. One part of this sandy dust impeded feet and wheels; the other arose in the air and hovered like a cloud over the troops, filling eyes, hair, ears, and nostrils, and above all the lungs, of men and beasts alike as they moved slowly along this highway (NHD II: X, 155–6).

b. Every day curly clouds passed over the sky, rarely covering the sun; but towards evening the sky cleared again and the sun set in a glowing, red mist. But a heavy dew refreshed the earth at night. The wheat left in the fields was burnt up and dropping out of the ear. The marshes were dry. The cattle lowed from hunger, finding nothing to graze on in the sun-baked meadows. Only at night and in the woods, as long as the dew lasted, it was cool. But on the road, on the high-road along which the troops marched, there was no coolness even at night, and even where the road passed through the woods. The dew was imperceptible on the sandy dust of the road, more than a foot deep. As soon as it was daylight, the soldiers began to move. The transports and artillery moved noiselessly, buried up to their axles, and the infantry sank to their ankles in the soft, stifling, burning dust, that never got cool even at night. The sandy dust clung to their legs and to the wheels, rose in a cloud over their heads, and got into the eyes and hair and nostrils and lungs of the men and beasts that moved along the road (CG 1113).

c. Fleecy clouds had been scudding every day across the sky, occasionally shrouding the sun; but toward evening it cleared up again, and the sun went down in a brownish red mist. Nothing refreshed the earth but a heavy dew each night. The grain on the stalk was burnt and fell out.

DOES THE TRANSLATION MATTER? 51

      The swamps were dried up. The cattle bellowed from hunger, being unable to find food on the sunburnt meadows. Only at night and in the forests was there any freshness, and then only as long as there was any dew. But on the road, on the highway, over which the troops marched, there was no coolness even at night, and even in the forests. The dew could not be noticed on the sandy dust of the road, which was turned up to the depth of more than half a foot. The moment day broke, the troops began to move. The baggage-train and the artillery proceeded noiselessly up to the hub, and the infantry up to the ankle, in the soft, strangling, hot dust, which had not cooled off through the night. One part of this sand dust was kneaded by the feet and wheels, while another rose in the air and stood in a cloud above the army, getting into the eyes, the hair, the ears, the nostrils, and, above all, into the lungs of the men and the animals that were moving along this road (LW VII: 170–1).

d.   (not in AK)

e.   Each day fleecy clouds floated across the sky and occasionally veiled the sun, but towards evening the sky cleared again and the sun set in reddish-brown mist. Heavy night dews alone refreshed the earth. The unreaped corn was scorched and shed its grain. The marshes dried up. The cattle lowed from hunger, finding no food on the sun-parched meadows. Only at night and in the forests while the dew lasted was there any freshness. But on the road, the highroad along which the troops marched, there was no such freshness even at night or when the road passed through the forest; the dew was imperceptible on the sandy dust churned up more than six inches deep. As soon as day dawned the march began. The artillery and baggage-wagons moved noiselessly through the deep dust that rose to the very hubs of the wheels, and the infantry sank ankle deep in that soft, choking, hot dust that never cooled even at night. Some of this dust was kneaded by the feet and wheels, while the rest rose and hung like a cloud over the troops, settling in eyes, ears, hair, and nostrils, and worst of all in the lungs of the men and beasts as they moved along that road (MM 752).

f.   Every day fleecy clouds floated across the sky, occasionally shutting out the sun, but towards evening the sky would clear again and the sun set in a sombre red haze. Only the heavy night-dews refreshed the earth. The wheat left in the fields was burnt up and dropping out of the ear. The marshes dried up. The cattle lowed from hunger, finding nothing to graze on in the sun-baked meadows. Only at night and in the forests while the dew lasted was it ever cool. But on the road, the high road along which the troops marched, there was no coolness even at night or where the road passed through the forest: the dew made no impression on the sandy dust inches deep. As soon as it was daylight the soldiers began to move. The artillery and baggage-wagons ploughed along noiselessly, buried almost to their axles, and the infantry sank ankle-deep in the soft, choking burning dust that never cooled even at night. Sandy dust clung to their legs and to the wheels, rose and hung like a cloud overhead, and got into eyes, ears, hair and nostrils, and worst of all, settled in the lungs of the men and beasts that moved along the road. (RE 832–3).

g. Every day fleecy clouds floated across the sky, occasionally hiding the sun, but toward evening the sky would clear again and the sun set in a russet haze. Only the heavy night dews refreshed the earth. The standing wheat was scorched and shed its grain. The marshes dried up. The cattle lowed from hunger, finding nothing to graze on in the sun-baked meadows. Only at night and in the forests while the dew lasted was it cool. But on the roads and the highway along which the troops marched there was no such freshness even at night or when the road passed through the forest. The dew made no impression on the sandy dust which was churned up more than six inches deep. As soon as it was daylight, the soldiers began to move. The artillery and transport wagons advanced noiselessly, buried up to their hubs, and the infantry sank ankle deep in the soft, hot, stifling dust that never cooled, even at night. This sandy dust, kneaded by wheels and marching feet, rose in a cloud over the troops, settling in eyes, ears, hair, nostrils, and, worst of all, in the lungs of the men and beasts as they marched along the road (AD 844).

h. Every day fleecy clouds floated across the heavens, now and then hiding the sun, but the sky always cleared in the late afternoon and the sun went down in a deep red haze. The earth got its only refreshment from a heavy dew at night. Any wheat left in the fields was scorched and scattered. The marshes had dried up. The cattle bellowed from hunger, finding nothing to graze on in the sun-baked meadows. Only at night and in the woods was there any cool air, and then only while the dew lasted. Out on the road, the high road where the troops were marching, there was never any cool air, not even at night, not even when the road went through a wood. No dew touched the six inches of churned-up sandy dust. They were on the road at first light. Axle-deep, the wagons and big guns trundled on without a sound, while the infantry marched up to their ankles in soft, choking, burning dust that never cooled off overnight. Sandy dust stuck to feet and wheels, and rose in a cloud over the marching men, getting into eyes and hair and nostrils and, worst of all, down into the lungs of man and beast moving down the road (AB 777).

i. Every day fleecy clouds crossed the sky, occasionally covering the sun; but towards evening it cleared up again, and the sun set in a reddish brown murk. Only the heavy dews at night refreshed the earth. The standing wheat was scorched and spilled its grains. The swamps dried up. The cattle lowed from hunger, finding no food in the sun-parched meadows. It was cool only at night and in the woods, while the dew lasted. But on the road, on the high road along which the troops were marching, there was not that coolness even at night and in the woods. There was no dew to be seen on the sandy dust of the road, churned up more than half a foot deep. As soon as dawn broke, movement began. Baggage trains and artillery went noiselessly, sunk to the hubs, and infantry sunk to the ankles in the soft, suffocating, hot dust that did not cool down overnight. Part of this dust was kneaded by feet and wheels, the rest rose and hung in a cloud over the troops, filling the eyes, hair, ears, nostrils, and, above all, the lungs of the men and animals moving along this road (PV 700).

One could discuss the difference between legs and feet, whether cattle can 'bellow' (Dole, Briggs), and other trivialities. The translators here adhere to their own distinctive strategies; Briggs likes his prepositions ('out on the road'; 'marched up to their ankles'); and there's some bumpiness: 'no dew touched the six inches of churned-up sandy dust'. The same can be said for the ever-cautious Dunnigan. Caution, literalism, and awkwardness go hand in hand. Garnett misses the mark here and there in the purely lexical sense ('rarely' instead of 'occasionally' for изредка; 'were dry' possibly should be 'had dried up'; 'a foot deep', etc.). But she was the pioneer, and the English is astonishing. The Maudes provide many improvements (Garnett's 'curly' clouds become 'fleecy' from the Maudes on). With her bold transpositions and her awareness of the greater text beyond the words, Edmonds is a gift to the reader. But it is Tolstoi who awes me the most.

5 Philosophical Exposition: The Life of Nations (Epilogue II: 5)

Tolstoi's philosophical and historical passages in *War and Peace* are integral to the novel's design.

Жизнь народов не вмещается в жизнь нескольких людей; ибо связь между этими несколькими людьми и народами не найдена. Теория о том, что связь эта основана на перенесении совокупности воль на исторические лица, есть гипотеза, не подтверждаемая опытом истории (XII: 313).

a. The life of the nations cannot be summarized in the lives of a few men, for the bond connecting these few persons with the nations has not been discovered. The theory that this bond of union is based on the will of the masses transferred to historical personages is an hypothesis not confirmed by the experience of history (NHD III: Epilogue ii, 254).

b. The life of nations is not contained in the life of a few men, since the connection between those few men and the nations has not been found. The theory that this connection is based on the delegation of the combined will of a people to its historical leaders is an hypothesis, not supported by the testimony of history (CG 1891).

c. The life of the nations is not embraced by the lives of a few men; for the connection between these few people and the nations has not been found. The theory that this connection is based on the transference of the sum of the wills to the historical persons is a hypothesis which is not confirmed by historical experience (LW VIII: 453).

d. AK unsurprisingly dispenses with the epilogues.

e. The life of the nations is not contained in the lives of a few men, for the connection between those men and the nations has not been found. The theory that this connection is based on the transference of the collective will of a people to certain historical personages is a hypothesis unconfirmed by the experience of history (MM 1284).

f. The life of nations cannot be summarized in the lives of a few men, for the connexion between those men and the nations has not been discovered. The theory that this connexion is based on the transference of the collective will of a people to certain historical personages is a hypothesis not supported by the experience of history (RE 1416).

g. The life of nations is not contained in the lives of a few men, for the connection between these few men and the nations has not been found. The theory that this connection is based on the transference of the collective will of a people to certain historical personages is a hypothesis not confirmed by the testimony of history (AD 1428).

h. The lives of nations cannot be contained within the lives of a few men, since the connection between those few men and the nations has never been discovered. The theory that this connection is based on

a transfer of collective popular will from a people to its historical leaders is a hypothesis not borne out by historical experience (AB 1333).
i. The life of peoples cannot be contained in the lives of several men, for the connection between these several men and the peoples has not been found. The theory that this connection is based on the transfer of the sum total of wills to historical figures is a hypothesis not confirmed by the experience of history (PV 1192).

Tastes differ. No doubt that historians could get very excited about the translation differences in this example. Truly, though, the problem of whether 'nations' or 'peoples' is a better translation for народов, like the other issues of language in this excerpt and in Tolstoi's historical musings generally has more to do with history than literature. In that sense reading and comparing the translations holds about the same interest as reading the original text.

6   *Ostranenie*: Natasha at the Opera (II: v: 9)

At key moments of moral and emotional stress, Tolstoi's syntax gets very simple. This feature of his style is key to understanding the workings of *ostranenie*. The best example, of course, is Natasha's visit to the opera in Volume two, Part five. Fresh from the country, surrounded by dangerous, corrupt influences, cruelly separated from Prince Andrei, she is about to fall victim to Anatole's wiles. She sees but does not understand:

На сцене были ровные доски по середине, с боков стояли крашеные картины, изображавшие деревья, позади было протянуто полотно на досках. В середине сцены сидели девицы в красных корсажах и белых юбках. Одна, очень толстая, в шелковом белом платье, сидела особо, на низкой скамеечке, к которой был приклеен сзади зеленый картон. Все они пели что-то. Когда они кончили свою песню, девица в белом подошла к будочке суфлера, и к ней подошел мужчина в шелковых, в обтяжку, панталонах на толстых ногах, с пером и кинжалом и стал петь и разводить руками (X: 324).

a. Smooth boards formed the center of the stage, on the sides stood painted canvases representing trees, in the background a cloth was stretched out on boards, in the foreground girls in red bodices and white petticoats were sitting around. One, who was exceedingly stout, wore a white silk dress. She sat by herself on a low footstool, to the back of which was glued green cardboard. They were all singing something. After they had finished their chorus the girl in white advanced toward the prompter's box, and a man in silk tights on his stout legs, and with a feather and a dagger, joined her, and began to sing and wave his arms (NHD. II: vi, 231)

b. The stage consisted of a boarded floor in the middle, with painted cardboard representing trees at the sides, and linen stretched over boards at the back. In the middle of the stage there were sitting maidens in red bodices and white skirts. An excessively stout woman in a white silk dress was sitting apart on a low bench with green cardboard fixed on the back of it. They were all singing something. When they had finished their song, the woman in white moved towards the prompter's box, and a man, with his stout legs encased in silk tights, with a plume and a dagger, went up to her and began singing and waving his arms (CG 888).

c. On the stage there were smooth planks in the middle; at the sides stood painted pictures, representing trees; in the background a canvas was drawn over boards. In the middle of the stage sat maidens in red corsages and white skirts. One of them, who was very stout and dressed in a white silk dress, was sitting apart on a low stool, to the back of which was pasted up a green pasteboard. They were singing something. When they had all finished their song, the maiden in white walked over to the prompter's box, and was accosted by a man in closely fitting silk trousers over stout legs, with feather and poniard, and he began to sing and wave his arms (LW VI: 466).

d. The floor of the stage consisted of smooth boards, at the sides was some painted cardboard representing trees, and at the back was a cloth stretched over boards. In the center of the stage sat some girls in red bodices and white skirts. One very fat girl in a white silk dress sat apart on a low bench, to the back of which a piece of green cardboard was glued. They all sang something. When they had finished their song the girl in white went up to the prompter's box and a man with tight silk trousers over his stout legs, and holding a plume and a dagger, went up to her and began singing, waving his arms about (MM 601).

e. Astoundingly, AK omits this famous passage.

f. Smooth boards formed the centre of the stage, at the sides stood painted canvases representing trees, and in the background was a cloth stretched over boards. In the middle of the stage sat some girls in red bodices and white petticoats. One extremely fat girl in a white silk dress was sitting apart on a low bench, to the back of which a piece of green cardboard was glued. They were all singing something. When they had finished their chorus the girl in white advanced towards the prompter's box, and a man with stout legs encased in silk tights, a plume in his cap and a dagger at his waist, went up to her and began to sing and wave his arms about (RE 663).

g. The stage consisted of smooth planks in the center, with some painted cardboard representing trees at the sides, and a canvas stretched over boards in the back. Girls in red bodices and white petticoats sat in the middle of the stage. One extremely fat girl in a white silk dress was sitting apart on a low bench, to the back of which was glued a piece of green cardboard. They were all singing. When they had finished their song the girl in white advanced to the prompter's box, and a man with stout legs encased in silk tights, with a plume and a dagger, began singing and waving his arms about (AD 678).

h. The stage consisted of flat boards down the middle with painted cardboard representing trees at both sides and cloth-covered boards at the back. Several young girls in red tops and white skirts were sitting in the middle of the stage. One very fat girl in a white silk dress sat to one side on a low bench with green cardboard glued on the back of it. They were all singing something. When they had finished their song the woman in white came forward to the prompter's box, and a man with fat legs squeezed into silk tights, with a feather in his hat and a dagger in his belt, came up to her and burst into song with much waving of his arms (AB 617).

i. The stage consisted of flat boards in the middle, with painted pieces of cardboard on the sides representing trees, and canvas stretched over boards at the back. In the middle of the stage sat girls in red bodices and white skirts. One, very fat, in a white silk dress, sat apart on a low stool with a piece of green cardboard glued to the back of it. They were all singing something. When they finished their song, the girl in white went up to the prompter's box, and a man with tight silk breeches on his fat legs, and with a feather and a dagger, came up to her and began singing and spreading his arms (PV 560).

j. There were level boards in the centre of the stage and sheets of cardboard at the side, painted green, supposedly to represent trees. Men in frock coats and a few girls were sticking their heads out from behind the sheets of cardboard, and at the back there was a very poorly painted town – the kind you always see in the theatre, but which doesn't exist in reality. Sheets of canvas were stretched over the top of everything. There were young ladies in red bodices and little white skirts sitting on the boards and one in a white silk dress who was sitting apart from the rest, all of them dressed in a way that people never are in reality, but always are in the theater. And they were all singing something. Then the maiden in white walked over to a little hut, and a young man in skin-tight silk breeches (he had fat legs), with a feather in his hat and a dagger at his side, walked up to her and began trying to persuade her of something, clutching at her bare arm, running his fingers along the arm and singing (Bromfield).

The fact that this excerpt does not offer much of interest either may say as much about the features of Tolstoi's *ostranenie* as it does about translation. *Ostranenie* is a deliberate simplification to highlight the character's detachment, emotional vulnerability, and naïveté. By necessity, then, such texts must be simple in their language, and that simplicity will transfer without too much resistance into English.

7   **Tolstoi's Metaphors: The Watch Mechanism (III: ii: 29).**

As the original text is in French, this passage gives the opportunity to mention the problem of French in *War and Peace* overall. Pevear and Volokhonsky and Amy Mandelker's Maudes give us the French in the text, translated in bottom-of-page footnotes. In the text overall, the others offer a range of options. Dunnigan, Edmonds, and Garnett insert minimal French to set the tone. Bromfield gives practically no French, and Briggs doesn't bother; his goal is readability to a contemporary audience. As for the translation of this passage, the similarities are striking, which might suggest that the translators are in dialogue, and occasionally borrow one another's wording. In addressing this question, which is beyond the scope of this chapter, it is instructive to be aware of chronology: NHD-CG/LW-MM-AK-RE-AD-and the other three in a close cluster, these latter presumably operating independently from one another.

Notre corps est comme une montre parfaite qui doit aller un certain temps; l'horloger n'a pas la faculté de l'ouvrir, il ne peut la manier qu'à tâtons et les yeux bandés. Notre corps est une machine à vivre, voilà tout (XI: 223).

a.   'Our body is like a perfect watch which is meant to go a certain time; the watchmaker cannot open it; he can only regulate it by his sense of feeling and with his eyes shut. Our body is a living-machine, that is all it is' (NHD II: x, 290).

b. 'Our body is a perfect watch, meant to go for a certain time; the watchmaker has not the power of opening it, he can only handle it in fumbling fashion, blindfold. Our body is a machine for living, that's all' (CG 1244).
c. *LW provides only the French text* (VII: 318).
d. 'Our body is like a perfect watch that should go for a certain time; the watchmaker cannot open it, he can only adjust it by fumbling, and that blindfold ... Yes, our body is a machine for living, that is all' (MM 844).
e. *AK does not include this part. Generally the French in this edition is minimal – as in her puppetmaster, Dole; when present it appears with no translation.*
f. 'Our body is like a perfect watch meant to go for a certain time; the watchmaker cannot open it – he can only adjust if by fumbling his way blindfold. Yes, our body is a machine for living, that is all' (RE 935).
g. 'Our body is like a perfect watch, meant to go for a certain time; the watchmaker can't open it, he can only fumble with it blindfold. Our body is a machine for living, that's all' (AD 946).
h. 'Our body is like a perfect watch with only a fixed time to run. The watchmaker has no power to get inside it, he can only fumble with it blindfold. Our body is a machine for living, and that's all there is to it' (AB 874).
i. *PV quote the French in the text and provide the following translation in a footnote*: 'Our body is like a perfect watch that must run for a certain time; the watchmaker is not able to open it, he can only handle it by feel and blindfolded. Our body is a machine for living, that's all' (PV 787).

8   Emotional Climax: Prince Andrei's Death (IV: i: 16)

It is at such cathartic moments that we feel the full emotional power of Tolstoi's novel:

Наташа и княжна Марья теперь тоже плакали, но они плакали не от своего личного горя; они плакали от благоговейного умиления, охватившего их души перед сознанием простого и торжественного таинства смерти, совершившегося перед ними (XII: 65).

a. Natasha and the princess also wept now, but they wept not because of their own personal sorrow; they wept from a reverent emotion which took possession of their souls in presence of the simple and solemn mystery of death, which had been accomplished before their eyes (NHD III: xi, 252–3).

b. Natasha and Princess Marya wept too now. But they did not weep for their personal sorrow; they wept from the emotion and awe that filled their souls before the simple and solemn mystery of death that had been accomplished before their eyes (CG 1557).

c. Natasha and Princess Marya also wept, but they did not weep from their personal grief; they wept from that sensation of reverent awe which held possession of their souls before the consciousness of that simple and solemn mystery of death, which had taken place before them (LW VIII: 90).

d. Natasha and Princess Mary also wept now, but not because of their own personal grief; they wept with a reverent and softening emotion which had taken possession of their souls at the consciousness of the simple and solemn mystery of death that had been accomplished in their presence (MM 1060–61).

e. Natasha and the princess also wept now, but they wept not because of their own personal sorrow; they wept from a reverent emotion which took possession of their souls in presence of the simple and solemn mystery of death, which had been accomplished before their eyes (AK 621).

f. Natasha and Princess Maria wept too now, but they wept not because of their own personal grief: they wept from the emotion and awe which took possession of their souls before the simple and solemn mystery of death that had been accomplished before their eyes (RE 1167).

g. Natasha and Princess Marya also wept now, but not because of their own personal grief; they wept out of a reverent emotion that filled their souls before the solemn mystery of a death that had been consummated in their presence (AD 1177).

h. Natasha and Princess Marya now also gave way to tears, but not from personal sorrow. They wept with a melting sensation of reverence gripping their souls as they contemplated the simple and solemn mystery of death that had been accomplished before their eyes (AB 1095).

i. Natasha and Princess Marya also wept now, but they did not weep from their own personal grief; they wept from a reverent emotion that came over their souls before the awareness of the simple and solemn mystery of death that had been accomplished before them (PV 986). Wording like 'softening emotion' and 'melting sensation of reverence' will distract some readers, including this one. Lexical chains such as 'wept out of a reverent emotion' and 'before the awareness of the simple and solemn' may reflect Tolstoi's precise wording but Edmonds' decision to cut and trim reflects what is, in her translation generally, almost perfect pitch. Here, as with *ostranenie*, simplicity is of the essence. The power of these moments in the novel derives, among other things, from the length of time we have awaited them. A principle here might be advanced: the longer the text, the more important the plot and the passage of time, the less important minor differences in wording; the obvious comparison is with lyric poetry. Whatever the differences here, it is likely that any translation will bring tears to the reader's eyes.

9   General Impressions

Translation matters more in some cases than in others. When discussing the rules of history, Tolstoi's language flattens out; his message is well conveyed by all the translators. Interestingly enough, where he is most distinctive – at key moments of emotional catharsis – Tolstoi writes very simply; here, too, all of the translators convey the essence of the text. Garnett comments on this when she says: 'Tolstoy's simple style goes straight into English without any trouble. There's no difficulty'.[17] It's always rash to say something like this when you're translating, particularly when bilingual specialists might be micro-analyzing your work a hundred years later. But Garnett conveys a basic truth. Tolstoi's literary style, when moral stakes are high, is simple. Those passages conveying distinctive features of Russian speech present the greatest challenge to translators; my sense is that adherence to literary language can be more effective than attempting to find equivalent dialect features in English. It is when dealing with Tolstoi's magisterial descriptive passages that a translator can demonstrate real mastery of the English language. Some issues that come up repeatedly have to do with the basic structural differences between the languages. Russian lacks articles and in many cases can do without prepositions, covering the gap with inflection. The Russian verbal adjective packs

---

17   Constance Garnett, 'The Art of Translation', conversation recorded in *The Listener*, 30 January 1947, *Translation: Theory and Practice: A Historical Reader*, Daniel Weissbort and Ástráður Eysteinsson, eds, Oxford University Press, Oxford, 2006, p. 292.

precise, dense meaning into a single word, impossible to mirror in English. Tense depends less on 'helping verbs' than in English and is built into the verb itself, through conjugation patterns. Aspect, too, is built in. In translating a single Russian word, then, English often offers a string of short ones (an article, a helping verb, a preposition). The unique richness of English is our vocabulary. The best translators take the extra step to provide a richer word than might spring to mind at first glance.

In sum:
- Dole deserves considerable credit for producing the first English version of Tolstoi's novel, one that is reliable, with a quirky charm.
- Garnett's pioneering version features elegant English with occasional awkwardness and here and there a minor error in comprehension. In spite of her pride in her Tolstoi, I do not think this is her best work; she had not yet hit her stride. Or perhaps it was the haste and stress. Her grandson and biographer Richard Garnett gives the slightest glimpse: 'Fortunately she had managed to complete *War and Peace* before her eyes broke down'.[18]
- Wiener's is the most earnestly literal translation, with attendant infelicities of style. That said, some wording is quaint and endearing – possibly as a result.
- The Maudes should be at the top of the list for serious readers. Amy Mandelker's meticulously produced Oxford edition updates and corrects infelicities in earlier versions.
- Dunnigan's vocabulary tends to the basic and she often simplifies.
- Edmonds always goes the extra mile, converting Tolstoi's Russian into eloquent English by converting syntax in almost every sentence. Here and throughout she demonstrates the most creative approach to Tolstoi's text, working well beyond his wording to recreate the situation he is describing at any given moment. This means that she adds elements when it seems warranted – I think, mainly, for purposes of creating a literary text worthy of the author. In a majority of cases, I prefer her solutions, although more literal-minded readers will find a great deal to cavil at. Of all the translations, she commits the fewest literalisms. Interestingly, her edition is the least impressive physically (see below).

---

18   Richard Garnett, *Constance Garnett: A Heroic Life*, London, Sinclair-Stevenson, 1991, p. 204.

- Bromfield's and Briggs' translations tend to be the most colloquial; they both occasionally use wording that is jarringly modern. Bromfield's translation clunks frequently: 'She stood up, wearing that same constant smile of a perfectly beautiful woman with which she had entered the drawing room' (17); '[h]er tone was peevish now, her short little lip was raised, lending her face an expression that was not joyful, but feral, squirrel-like. She stopped speaking, as if she found it improper to talk of her future delivery in front of Pierre, while this was in fact the very essence of the matter' (41). In Briggs, the best example may be that famous passage where Kutuzov stirs the troops by using some obscenity to refer to the French: 'Поделом им, м... и.. в г....' (II: 489). CG: 'It serves them right, the b – b' (1727). LW: 'Serves them right, those ...' (VIII: 273); MM: 'Serves them right, the bloody bastards!' (963). RE: 'It serves them right, the b – b...s!'(1290); AD, always reticent: 'Serves them right, the ... !' (1302); PV: 'It's their own doing, f...th...in the f...' (1089). Briggs just lets fly: 'They asked for it, the fucking bastards!' (1213). Just idly, I wonder if there exists the sort of reader who would tackle *War and Peace* to begin with and find this jazzy and unfluent approach to Tolstoi's language appealing. But that may be a sign of my own obsolescence.
- PV are conscientious, adhering closest to the Russian syntax. They make the least effort in converting grammar. Their habits include adverb strings and literalisms: 'He was not thinking about anything, but looked around cheerfully and meaninglessly' (419); 'Goodbye, Count,' she said to him aloud. 'I'll be waiting very much for you' (PV 1122). Root-literal adjectives are common: strengthlessness (987); countlessness (987), as are verbal adjectives appearing as adjectives preceding their noun: 'these enamoured girls' (45); 'the not-yet-spoken word' (1117).

Comparing the language of translation demonstrates marked differences among all nine versions of the novel. Given a page or so of text, a careful reader might be able to identify the translation based on its stylistic peculiarities. Here, clearly, the translation matters. But the edition matters too. Kropotkin is to be immediately discarded. Bromfield's book falls out of the running at this point; Bromfield is for anyone who wants to read one of Tolstoi's versions of *War and Peace*, but the absence of decent scholarly notes renders this a frustrating experience. One of the joys of reading is to talk about the book with other readers; Bromfield's readers will be alone.

At this point, then, questions of the 'packaging' take on importance, first and foremost, what the scholarly editor contributes: introductions, annotations, maps. Here, PV, the Maudes, and Briggs are the clear winners, especially

P/V. To this we can add the issue of the French. All, none, or some? Most serious readers will prefer in-text French, with footnotes.

Physically, *War and Peace* is huge and ungainly, like Pierre. This may seem a trivial point, but it may very well be the most important factor for the majority of book purchasers who are interested in reading some Tolstoi. For these readers, and to stimulate reflection on our own tastes, a brief physical description of the books is presented in the appendix. Since the focus here is the edition rather than the translation, the publisher and editor should be getting the credit, but as a sign of respect for translators generally, I identify the editions by their names – in a feeble attempt to rectify past wrongs and slights.

Appendix

Description of the Editions used in this analysis (with no reference to translation features)

1. Dole (Crowell). I have fallen in love with my 1926–7 edition of these three books. They are compact and portable (though too precious to carry around), with tasteful frontispieces in each with that crinkly translucent filmy cover.
2. Constance Garnett (Konemann). The edition I used is a beautifully produced Hungarian boxed set, in four volumes; you can take the one you're reading on the subway and leave the others at home. The proofreading is abysmal, though. May I recommend the publisher hire a native speaker of English to proof-read. No French except for '*soirée*' and '*grippe*' and suchlike. There are some useful notes (at the end of each volume), very subtly cued in with a faint icon in the margins, but otherwise it's just the book in its pure state. Physically, this edition is my ideal.
3. Wiener (Dana Estes & Co.). Four volumes with excellent, if sparse, illustrations. Rough page edges.
4. Maudes a. (Norton). A large floppy paperback that stays open and can be carried around. Very thin pages. Excellent maps, supporting materials, and actual footnotes. Some French, mercifully with translations, though in annoying parenthetical phrases that break up the flow of the text. The chapter divisions are idiosyncratic and do not match Tolstoi's. A crippling flaw is the presence of subtitles that occasionally give away important plot details. Someone please edit these out. As always in the Norton Critical Editions, there are a number of abridged

critical materials at the end. But how many of us teach Lenin and Pisarev in our Tolstoi class?

5. Maudes b. (Oxford): In this superb edition Amy Mandelker corrects all the flaws of the Norton edition listed above. The pages are extremely thin. Affordable, portable, this is the best edition for classes.

6. Edmonds (Penguin). There is a gentle introduction, a short Tolstoi chronology and a useful character list, without stresses. The French is there in the form of tasteful introductory words and clues. No footnotes, though there are four quaint but valuable notes after the introduction giving basic information about such matters as Russian names and Tolstoi's French. This is a two-volume edition, so you can take one and leave the other at home. But, like Dunnigan, it won't stay open when you lay it down on the table. The covers, with their photographs of actors from a BBC TV production of the novel, are the worst of the lot, and lack the austere dignity of the covers of all of the other editions' covers. Sadly, any copy that you are likely to find will be dilapidated, with fragile, yellowed and foxed pages.

7. Dunnigan (Signet). There is an introduction and a helpful character list, with accent marks. No footnotes. Pat Conroy is, oddly, your guide. Too small and thick to be of any real use. Won't stay open, keeps flopping closed on you. Cheap, rough paper, very little white space; don't even try to make marginal notes. That said, it's the cheapest. For the desperate, budget reader it will do.

8. Briggs (Viking). Also a nicely produced hardback. No French. Good supplementary material at the end, including a very useful chapter-by-chapter plot summary, a description of three key battles, annotations, character list (with stresses), maps, a short afterword (really an introduction to the novel) and, at last, the vaunted though cursory afterword by Orlando Figes. This serves, we presume, the same function as Pat Conroy's introduction to the Dunnigan edition, and has about as much value. This edition is a B+ where PV is an A+.

9. Pevear / Volokhonsky (Knopf). This hardback is by far the most physically impressive version. With its elegant font, high paper quality, dignified cover, useful maps, notes at the end, historical index and chapter-by-chapter plot summary, its French translations at the bottom of the page, its Appendix by Count Leo Tolstoy, the entire thing, from detail to the whole, rises to the challenge of conveying Tolstoi's majestic masterpiece to the English-language reader.

10. Electronic versions:

    a. An online Maudes is available with one click from the excellent Project Guttenburg series: https://www.gutenberg.org/files/2600/2600-h/2600-h.htm (accessed 29 October 2020). Other online versions appear to also be the Maudes, but the translators are not credited. Any such version is to be avoided.

    b. You can choose from several editions on your Kindle, including a Maudes that is absolutely free and one that will cost you $4.74, and a cheap uncredited translation for $1.99 (reduced from a baffling $19.99). Like other bottom-of-the-barrel editions, these cut right to the chase, like my Garnett – obtained for free on Kindle ten years ago – starting abruptly with book one, chapter one and ending equally abruptly with the last words of the epilogue. $14.99 will get you a Kindle P/V. And there are other options listed, if you have the patience to scroll through them.

11. Bromfield (Ecco), though it's a different Tolstoi original, deserves to be recognized. This is the only one of these English editions that has illustrations (beyond maps), and they are marvellous – mostly contemporary drawings by M.S. Bashilov, plus some engravings, lithographs, and a couple of images of manuscripts. Instead of the standard character list this edition begins with a conversion table of Russian weights and measures. This edition has its quirky aspects. The Conroy-Figes stand-in here is a Nikolai Tolstoi, who introduces the text and offers, we presume, a living link to the master. A Note on the Translation is signed by Bromfield and his editor Jenefer Coates. The paper is rougher than in the other two new hardbacks.

My ideal physical embodiment of *War and Peace* is a composite of all of these books: the tasteful physical virtues of Garnett's four-volume set; Wiener's and Dole's feel for their time; the Maudes' apparatus and ease of handling; Dunnigan's thrifty qualities; Bromfield's illustrations; Briggs' chapter summaries, battle outlines and maps; Pevear and Volokhonsky's French, supplemental matter, and production quality; the Kindle Maudes' price and portability. The version that is least appealing physically, is Rosemary Edmonds' Penguin. But as happens so often in life, an unprepossessing exterior conceals riches within.

Bibliography

Garnett, Constance, 'The Art of Translation,' conversation recorded in *The Listener*, 30 January 1947, *Translation: Theory and Practice: A Historical Reader*, Weissbort, Daniel and Eysteinsson, Ástráður, eds, Oxford University Press, Oxford, 2006, p. 292.

Garnett, Richard, *Constance Garnett: A Heroic Life*, London, Sinclair-Stevenson, 1991.

Grossman, Edith, *Why Translation Matters*, Yale University Press, New Haven, 2010.

Morson, Gary Saul, 'The Pevearsion of Russian Literature', *Commentary*, July/August, 2010, pp. 92–8.

Tolstoi, L.N., *Voina i mir* in *Polnoe sobranie sochinenii*, Chertkov, V.G., ed., Gosudarstvennoe izdatel'stvo khuzhestvennoi literatury, Moscow-Leningrad, IX–XII, 1930–3.

Tolstoy, Leo, *War and Peace*, Briggs, Anthony, trans., Viking Penguin, New York, 2006.

Tolstoy, Leo, *War and Peace*, Bromfield, Andrew (Original Version), trans., HarperCollins, New York, 2007.

Tolstoy, Leo, *War and Peace*, Dole, Nathan Haskell, trans., Thomas Y. Crowell Co, New York, 1926–77 (1898–9), 3 vols.

Tolstoy, Leo, *War and Peace*, Dunnigan, Ann, trans., Signet Classics, New York, 1968.

Tolstoy, Leo, *War and Peace*, Edmonds, Rosemary, in two volumes, trans., Penguin, Middlesex, 1957.

Tolstoy, Leo, *War and Peace*, Garnett, Constance, in four volumes, trans., Konemann, Hungary, 1999 (1904).

Tolstoy, Leo, *War and Peace*, translation revised by Kropotkin, Princess Alexandra, Maugham, W. Somerset, ed., The John C. Winston Company, Philadelphia and Toronto, 1949.

Tolstoy, Leo, *War and Peace*, Maude, Aylmer and Louise, trans., Norton Classics, New York, 1966 (1920/1930s).

Tolstoy, Leo, *War and Peace*, Maude, Aylmer and Louise, trans., Mandelker, Amy, ed., Oxford World's Classics, Oxford, 2010.

Tolstoy, Leo, *War and Peace*, Pevear, Richard and Volokhonsky, Larissa, trans., Alfred A. Knopf, New York, 2007.

Tolstoy, Leo, *War and Peace*, *The Complete Works of Count Tolstoy*, 5–8, Wiener, Leo, trans., Dana Estes & Company, Boston, 1904.

Trachtenberg, Jeffrey, 'Translating Tolstoy', telephone and email interview with Richard Pevear and Larissa Volokhonsky, 'Books and Ideas', *The Wall Street Journal*, 17 November, 2009.

Venuti, Lawrence, *The Translator's Invisibility: A History of Translation*, Routledge, London, 1995.

CHAPTER 2

Feeling and Contradiction in Tolstoi's *What Is Art?*

Richard Peace

Abstract

Tolstoi's creative history is remarkable for its turn towards didactic literature in the last thirty years of his life. He offers the key to this in *What Is Art?*, a treatise which not only provides an idiosyncratic assessment of the literary canon but also explains the moralistic aesthetics by which he now abides. This chapter highlights a fact often overlooked in the general assumption of the uniqueness of Tolstoi's ideas on art, namely that they have much in common with those enunciated in the 1850s and 1860s by Chernyshevskii, Dobroliubov and Pisarev, progressive radicals whom Tolstoi ignored at that time and does not reference in *What Is Art?* In other ways, though, one can see more contemporary affinities in the work, such as Tolstoi's aspiration to create art for the people, which anticipates the work of the Proletkult movement in the early years of the Revolution. The anarchic nature of Tolstoi's prescriptions about art is also stressed – that it was better to have no art than bad art. In sum, the chapter concludes that Tolstoi's aesthetics, as articulated in *What Is Art?*, forms a bridge between the radicals of the 1860s and the theoreticians of the early Soviet Union.

Keywords

Tolstoi's *What Is Art?* – Tolstoi's views on art – influences on Tolstoi's aesthetics

Tolstoi's title poses a question to which he attempts an answer. It is, he claims in his conclusion, a problem which has occupied him for 15 years, and he has already made attempts to address the issue, most notably in the essay *About Art* (*Об искусстве*, 1889).

Tolstoi's views on art are extreme, iconoclastic and seem, at first sight, to be at variance with his own practice. His own novels are regarded as a major contribution to the realistic tradition, yet in *What Is Art?* he dismisses realism as something which it is more true to call 'provincialism in art',[1] and in a footnote renounces all his writing as bad, with the exception of *The Prisoner of the Caucasus* (*Кавказский пленник*) and the later pamphlet-like story *God Sees the Truth* (*Бог правду видит* [16: 163 n. 219]). He further claims that '[a]lmost all that is considered art, as both good and entirely art in our society, not only is not real and good art, and is not entirely art, but even is not art at all, but its imitation' (14: 140).

Tolstoi has indeed done research, particularly in the area of aesthetic theory, but strangely there is one group of home-grown theoreticians whom he does not mention: the young radicals of the 1860s (Chernyshevskii, Dobroliubov and Pisarev) – the dominant intellectual force during the period that Tolstoi himself entered the literary scene. Yet the iconoclasm of the later Tolstoi has much in common with the radical thinkers he ignored in his youth. In his magisterial thesis 'The Aesthetic Relations of Art to Reality' ('эстетические отношения искусства к действительности' [1855]), Chernyshevskii saw the aesthetic principle not in abstract theories but in life itself, and advanced the formula 'beauty is life' ('прекрасное есть жизнь'),[2] whilst at the same time arguing that art must also have an instructive purpose, that it must be 'a textbook of life' ('учебник жизни').[3] Like the later Tolstoi, Chernyshevskii condemned any purely aesthetic concept of art, and argued for a more didactic purpose. Significantly, Chernyshevskii appreciated aspects of Tolstoi's early works: *Childhood, Boyhood* and the war stories which he reviewed for *The Contemporary* in 1856. In these he found accurate descriptions of 'the psychic process itself, its forms, its laws, [...] the dialectic of the soul'. As Gustafson notes, the dialectic of the soul is essentially the same concept as 'the empiricist notion of the association of ideas'. Gustafson concludes that Chernyshevskii 'was able to perceive and describe the internal monologue because he shared with Tolstoy the general assumptions and even the language of associationist psychology'.[4]

---

1 *Chto takoe iskusstvo?* in L.N. Tolstoi, *Polnoe sobranie sochinenii*, xxx: *Proizvedeniia 1882–1898*, V.S. Mishin and N.V. Gorbachev, eds, Gosudarstvennoe izdatel'stvo khudozhestvennoi literatury, Moscow, 1951, pp. 27–195, chapter 15, p. 410. ⟨http://tolstoy.ru/online/90/30/⟩ (Hereafter quoted in the text by chapter and page number.) Translations are the author's own.
2 N.G. Chernyshevskii, 'Esteticheskie otnosheniia iskusstva k deistvitel'nosti' in N.G. Chernyshevskii, *Polnoe sobranie sochinenii v 15 tomakh*, V.Ia. Kirpotin et al., eds, Goslitizdat, Moscow, II, 1949, pp. 5–92 (10).
3 Ibid., p. 90.
4 Richard F. Gustafson, *Leo Tolstoy: Resident and Stranger. A Study in Fiction and Theology*, Princeton University Press, Princeton, New Jersey, 2014, p. 293.

In *What Is Art?* Tolstoi rejects the aesthetic values of the upper classes: 'the art of the upper classes in the course of time ceased to be art and began to change into an imitation of art' (11: 111). Chernyshevskii's colleague, Dobroliubov, in an article seemingly pre-empting that of Tolstoi, 'What is Oblomovism?' ('Что такое обломовщина?' [1859]) and in reviews of Turgenev's novels, had already attacked upper-class culture, though more in moral terms. In 'A Ray of Light in a Kingdom of Darkness' ('Луч света в царстве тьмы' [1860]) Dobroliubov developed his own theory of criticism, which strongly rejected the influence of aesthetic authority – a position echoed by Tolstoi, when he writes: 'nothing to such a degree has aided, and aids the distortion (извращение) of art than the authorities established by criticism' (12: 123).

But it is the most extreme iconoclast of the 1860s, D.I. Pisarev, who seems closest to Tolstoi. He too was a renegade nobleman with a strong social conscience. Pisarev was contemptuously dismissive of Pushkin and his ilk. Tolstoi in *What Is Art?* attempts to see Russia's national poet through the eyes of a literate member of the lower classes, to whom he explains the immorality of the life lived by Pushkin, and 'that all the service he provided was that he wrote verses about love, and often very indecent ones' (17: 170).

Pisarev's anti-aestheticism is proclaimed in his most notorious essay with the provocative title 'The Destruction of Aesthetics' ('Разрушение эстетики' [1865]). He deplored the waste of resources and labour involved in the production of objects of beauty – a constant theme in Tolstoi's essay.[5] When, however, Tolstoi writes: 'Our refined art can only come about through the slavery of the popular masses' and that writers and other artists can achieve perfection 'only on condition of the intensive labour of the workers' (8: 82), it is well to bear in mind Tolstoi's own exploitation of his wife and daughters in the drudgery of copying and re-copying his own works.

When he proclaims: 'Free the slaves of capital and it will be impossible to produce such refined art' (8: 82), we appear to hear a more twentieth-century note. Marxism was indeed fashionable in Russia at the time of writing, but Tolstoi appears to condemn it out of hand. He writes: 'Such is now the much disseminated theory of Marx on the inevitability of economic progress, consisting of the swallowing up of all private products by capitalism' (7: 77). Yet what he is condemning is merely the second stage of Marx's triadic view of

---

5 Even so, argues Tatyana Gershkovich, Tolstoi was 'no destroyer of aesthetics'. What he denies is the role of artistic craftsmanship, so that he can aver that 'peasant tales are […] preferable to the works of Shakespeare'. Tatyana Gershkovich, 'Infecting, Simulating, Judging: Tolstoy's Search for an Aesthetic Standard', *Journal of the History of Ideas*, LXXIV, 1, 2013, pp. 115–37 (136).

progress – a stage he considered still applicable to backward Russia.[6] In Tolstoi's view the art produced for capitalism is as wasteful as that produced for an aristocracy. Industry with its modern resources, such as water power, squanders them on trivial and harmful things: 'But the trouble is that this power of the waterfall we force to work not for the advantage of the people, but for the enrichment of capitalists, producing objects of luxury or weapons of human destruction' (20: 189).

Tolstoi's views on art are close to those that ruled at the beginning of the Revolution, in the movement known as *Proletkult*. He, like the members of this movement, is looking for examples of a new type of art which will come from 'all the artists of genius, now hidden in the people' (19: 181), and he looks forward to a time when 'the most gifted from all the people will be the participants in art, and there will be more of these examples' (loc. cit.). Yet, whereas these early Soviet theoreticians wanted to bring out this talent through helpful instruction, Tolstoi appears to view it as a self-generating process.

Nevertheless, the yardstick of the 'people' also has authoritarian implications, as we see from Tolstoi's condemnation of contemporary music:

> Worthless, exclusive melodies have piled on them harmonic, rhythmic and orchestral complications, in order to make them attractive, and therefore become even more exclusive and not only not universal but even not of the people, i.e. accessible only to certain people and not to the whole of the people (16: 163).

Here are views which find an echo in the later persecution of Soviet composers – notably Shostakovich. Indeed, the anti-authoritarian Tolstoi can reveal a proto-Stalinesque side of his nature when it comes to art of which he disapproves. He suggests that everything that fails to meet his double criteria of Christian art 'must be acknowledged as bad art, which not only must not be encouraged, but must be driven out, denied and despised as art which does not unite people but separates them' (16: 164).

At the end of chapter 17 Tolstoi posits an attitude to 'bad art' even more severe than his own, suggesting that 'every rational and moral person' would have solved the question, as did Plato in his *Republic*, and as it was decided by all Church Christians and Muslim teachers – that it was better to abolish

---

6 On Lenin's partial approbation of Tolstoi's social views see Roland Boer, 'Lenin on Tolstoy: Between Imaginary Resolution and Revolutionary Christian Communism', *Science & Society*, LXXVIII, 1, pp. 41–60.

art than to let it continue in its corrupted form. Tolstoi's own attitude is much milder: 'It is to understand the error, in which we find ourselves, and not to persist in it, but find a way out of it' (17: 175).

The degree of Tolstoi's iconoclasm can be seen in his assertion that beauty has little to do with art. It is, he maintains, a vague muddled concept, and he likens its interpreters to the superstitious theologians he so much despises. He argues that a certain confusion has arisen over the word for 'beauty' (красота) in Russian: 'In the word "*krasota*" in Russian we understand only what pleases our eyes. Although, lately they have even begun to say "an ugly act", "beautiful music", but this is not Russian' (2: 38). This new usage derives from the influence of foreign languages, and its adoption must be blamed on the Russian upper classes. It would not be understood by a representative of the simple Russian people.

At the same time Tolstoi concedes that there is an ambiguity in the Russian word for good – *khoroshii* – 'which contains within itself the concept of the "beautiful", but not the other way round: the concept of the "beautiful" does not cover the concept of the "good"'. These are the meanings ascribed to these words 'in the Russian popular sense' (loc. cit.).

Tolstoi also argues that the ancient Greeks saw a similar confusion of the 'beautiful' and the 'good', but that modern philosophers did not understand the Greek idea of beauty, and the Greek idea of the 'good' was on a lower moral scale when compared to Christianity (2: 41). He scornfully dismisses the ancient Greeks themselves as: 'a half-wild, slave-owning little nation, very good at depicting the nakedness of the human body and constructing buildings pleasant to the eye' (7: 78). Tolstoi himself is clear on this aesthetic / ethical confusion: 'The concept of beauty not only does not coincide with the good, but rather is opposed to it, since the good for the most part coincides with the conquering of addictions (пристрастия), whereas beauty is the basis of all our addictions' (7: 79).

If beauty has nothing to do with art, what then could be the essence of art? Tolstoi's answer is, in the purest sense, that of a sentimentalist – feelings: '… art is a human activity, consisting of one person consciously and by certain outward signs transmitting the feelings he experiences to others, and other people are infected (заражаются) by these feelings and experience them' (5: 65).

The vocabulary here is worth noting: feelings are transmitted '*by certain outward signs*', suggesting the device of gesture employed throughout Tolstoi's novels, and ultimately traceable back to Sterne's concept of 'translations'.[7] These feelings must be those of the artist himself, indeed in this respect the artist must be entirely self-centred, as Tolstoi later makes clear: 'As soon as the viewer, the listener the reader feels that the artist himself is infected by his work, and is writing, singing, playing for himself, and not just to have an effect on others, this inner state of the artist infects the recipient' (15: 150).[8]

Such self-centredness may help to explain the autobiographical element prominent in Tolstoi's writing. The choice of the verb 'to infect' is also illustrative. It leaves open the possibility of using feelings, either for commercial purposes, as in advertising, for propaganda, as in Soviet art, or, as in Tolstoi's own case, the didacticism of strongly held convictions.[9]

Tolstoi appears to have adopted an absolutist sentimentalist approach to art. In chapter five he asserts that the most diverse of feelings, be they strong or weak, significant or worthless, bad or good, all comprise the matter of art as long as they 'infect' the recipient, and in chapter 15 he italicizes his belief that '[t]*he stronger the infection, the better the art, as art, not to speak of its content, that is independent of the merit of those feelings it transmits*' (15: 149).

It is, however, not only the subject which is irrelevant to art. Tolstoi ends this chapter with a further definition. The merit of art, as art, is defined 'independently of its content, that is independently of whether it conveys, or not, good or bad feelings' (15: 151). Given such a fundamentalist approach to the centrality of 'feeling' in art, it is scarcely surprising that Tolstoi denigrates the importance of the formalized and unspontaneous – the role of technique. In chapter 12 he refuses to admit that dancers, singers, violinists, painters and poets can be taught their art; it is only discovered through feeling. Schools may teach something similar to art, but not real art (12: 126); they may even get in the way because 'for the most part concerns about technique and beauty replace feeling' (16: 161) Nevertheless, such absolutism in regard to the integrity of *all* forms of feeling cannot hold out long against Tolstoi's own prejudices:

---

7 Laurence Sterne, *A Sentimental Journey through France and Italy*, John Bumpus, London, 1824, pp. 74–7.

8 This raises the question whether a *treatise* on art conforms to the same principle. See Douglas Robinson, *Estrangement and the Somatics of Literature: Tolstoy, Shklovsky, Brecht*, part one: 'Zarazhenie: Tolstoy's Infection Theory', The Johns Hopkins University Press, Baltimore, 2008, pp. 1–76 (4).

9 For a proposal that 'infectiousness' is a ubiquitous metaphorical presence in Tolstoi's work more generally, see Jacob Emery, 'Art Is Inoculation: The Infectious Imagination of Leo Tolstoy', *The Russian Review*, LXX, 4, 2011, pp. 627–45 (644–5).

> In reality almost all the feelings of the people of our circle come down to three, quite worthless and uncomplicated feelings: to the feeling of pride, of sexual lust, and of boredom with life. And these three feelings and their offshoots almost exclusively comprise the content of the art of the rich classes (9: 87).

Although this passage strongly implies criticism, it is not fully stated, because, as we have seen, Tolstoi believes that it is the strength of the 'infection' which determines the quality of art, irrespective of content and '... independent of the merit of those feelings it transmits' (15: 149). As though in response to the three worthless and uncomplicated feelings of the upper classes, Tolstoi gives his own three criteria for 'infection':

> Art becomes more or less infectious as a result of three conditions: 1) as a result of the greater or lesser particularity of the feeling transmitted; 2) as a result of the greater or lesser clarity of the transmission of this feeling and 3) as a result of the genuine nature of the artist, that is the greater or lesser strength, with which the artist himself experiences the feeling, he transmits (loc. cit.).

Yet, in this reasoned categorization itself we have something at work, which is opposed to the primacy of feeling – rational analysis, even though the demotion of the rational forms part of Tolstoi's theory, as we can see from the following statement: 'Art is the organ of human life translating people's rational consciousness into feeling' (20: 194).

If we examine Tolstoi's great novels (admittedly, now rejected by him) in the light of this formula, we see that the movement in *War and Peace* is the opposite of what he now maintains – it ends in an epilogue attempting a rational summation of what the novel itself has tried to demonstrate artistically. Tolstoi's assertion may hold some truth for *Anna Karenina*, beginning, as it does, with a *sententia*, which the novel then explores, but not only through feeling; there are many rational interventions on the part of the author. The central figure of Levin is caught up in this ambivalence, and it is only through abandoning the search for truth through rationality that he feels he is on the right track. Yet the novel itself does not fully confirm Levin's final position.

Resurrection gives us an example of Tolstoi using art to eliminate feeling in his description of the Orthodox Mass. He describes the ritual in a dry rationalistic way, in which the elimination of associated emotion and religious feeling reduces the ritual to the absurd. Moreover, it is a *technique* – that of *reductio ad absurdum* – which Tolstoi employs elsewhere and which, significantly, also figures in *What Is Art?* itself, when Tolstoi seeks to debunk the music of Richard Wagner (13: 133–7).[10] There is throughout Tolstoi's writing this creative tension between the emotional and the rational, and although in *What Is Art?* he seeks to dethrone rationality in favour of feeling, the very form of his essay, with its reasoned arguments, negates the attempt.

In spite of this, academics and critics who attempt to bring intellectual analysis to bear on works of art are dismissed with contempt. Tolstoi quotes the witticism of a friend: 'critics are the stupid making judgements on the intelligent' (12: 122). His definition of art is impervious to rational interpretation: 'An artist, if he is a real artist, has in his work transmitted to other people the feeling which he has experienced. What then is there to explain here?' (12: 123) and he goes on to aver: 'all interpretations are superfluous' (loc. cit.). This is not just the usual artists' distrust of critics; it may well reflect the need for a defence mechanism against probing rationality at a deeper level; for Tolstoi's arguments are shot through with inconsistencies.

If the fundamental nature of his sentimentalism seems at first sight to fail in distinguishing between the good and the bad (both morally and aesthetically), the final paragraph of the final chapter (before the 'Conclusion') makes clear that his demotion of rationality has a religious dimension. He looks forward to a time when people will be brought together 'by the mechanism of transferring Christian religious consciousness from the domain of reason and rationality to the domain of feeling' (19: 185).

In chapter 10 he had stated:

> They talk of incomprehensibility. But if art is the transmission of feelings, flowing from people's religious consciousness, then how can a feeling based on religion, that is – on the relationship of God to man, be incomprehensible? Such an art must be, and really always has been, comprehensible to all, because every person's relation to God is one and the same (10: 109–10).

This latter statement may well represent Tolstoi's own *feeling*, but reason would surely argue otherwise: the various discrepancies surrounding this posited immutable relationship have had disastrous consequences world-wide.

---

10   Douglas Robinson argues that this technique, identified by Shklovskii as *ostranenie*, is compatible with Tolstoi's aesthetics as enunciated in *What Is Art?* because it enables a true vision of things to replace the false one portrayed by false art: 'Tolstoy's Infection Theory and the Aesthetics of De- and Repersonalization', *TSJ*, XIX, 2007, pp. 33–53 (49).

In promoting his insistence on the primacy of feelings in art Tolstoi appears initially to have overstated his case – all feelings, whether bad or good, are the real matter of art. Yet Tolstoi, the moralist, cannot hold such an absolute view for long; another factor is involved:

> The evaluation of the merit of art, that is of the feelings which it transmits, depends on people's understanding of life's sense, on what they see as the good, and what they see as the bad, in life. The good and the evil in life are defined by what we call religions (6: 68).

It is religions (not just religion), Tolstoi says, that act as arbiters: 'and therefore it is only religions that serve and always have served as the basis of the evaluation of people's feelings' (loc. cit.). He adds that '[t]here has always been at all times, in all societies, a religious consciousness of what is good and bad, and it is this religious consciousness that defines the worth of the feelings transmitted through art' (6: 69).

In conformity to this religious consciousness, good feelings were approved, bad ones rejected. Yet not all art has a strictly religious dimension: 'All the remaining, huge area of art, through which people associated with one another, was not evaluated at all and was only rejected when it was contrary to the religious consciousness of its time' (loc. cit.). The rich diapason of feelings at first outlined by Tolstoi, is not only at the mercy of religions, but is further constrained by Tolstoi's own rational drive to categorization:

> All people are united by only two types of feeling: the feelings which flow from the consciousness of being God's children and human brotherhood, and the most simple of feelings, everyday ones, accessible to everyone without exception, such as the feelings of jollity, tenderness, cheerfulness, calm, etc. Only these two types of feeling comprise the matter of art of our time which is good as regards its content. (15: 158).

These two types of feeling find corresponding expression in Christian art 'of our time': the first is religious; the second universal art: 'Only these two types of art can be considered good art of our time' (15: 159).

Earlier Tolstoi had introduced another qualification to his view of the central role of feeling in art: 'A work of art is only a work of art, when it introduces a new feeling (however insignificant it might be) into the everyday round of human life' (9: 85). But not only art and religion are seen through the prism of feelings; the nineteenth-century concern with progress is interpreted by Tolstoi, less in terms of ideas than of feelings: 'At every step forward taken by humanity – and these steps are brought about by greater and greater elucidation of religious consciousness – people experience all the time new and new feelings' (9: 86).

Tolstoi draws his imagery for art from the moral sphere, reflecting the values of the family:

> Real art, like the wife of a loving husband, has no need for embellishment. Imitation art, like a prostitute, must always be highly decorated.
> The cause of true art is an internal need to express the build-up of feeling, just as for a mother the cause of sexual conception is love. The cause for imitation art is monetary gain, exactly like prostitution (18: 178).

For Tolstoi the bringing of a new feeling into daily life is thus like the birth of a new human being (loc. cit.).

Tolstoi's sexual preoccupations are another underlying, but often undisclosed, layer in his arguments on art. He recalls the way he was affected by the singing of peasant women, and on the same evening heard an accomplished violinist play Beethoven's Sonata No. 101: '... the song of the peasant women was real art, transmitting definite and strong feeling. The hundred and first sonata of Beethoven, though, was merely an unsuccessful attempt at art, containing no definite feeling, and therefore in no way infecting one' (14: 145). The statement is striking, and, on the face of it, could appear merely to be an ideological commonplace *à la* Rousseau – the apposition of the art of the simple, unspoilt people to the sophisticated art of the salons. Yet what Tolstoi does not mention is that the violinist was Taneev, whom Tolstoi suspected of having a relationship with his wife and, indeed, in this case feeling did inspire art. Tolstoi's wild jealousy resulted in a tale bearing the title of another of Beethoven's works: *The Kreutzer Sonata*, whose protagonist rejects all sexual activity as bad. Nor is Tolstoi's enjoyment of the peasant choir without its personal element; the women were singing in praise of his newly-wed daughter, and celebrating her arrival on the family estate.

The Kreutzer Sonata gives us an example of a bad feeling inspiring art, but Tolstoi's real tastes, as he exemplifies them in *What is Art?*, are really more 'goody, goody' – not only sentimentalist but embarrassingly sentimental. The chief elements he appears to admire could even be called, albeit anachronistically, 'Disneyesque': children and animals. He is impressed by a story by an author of peasant origin, F.F. Tishchenko, whom he claims not to know: 'I could not tear myself away from a tale by an unknown author about children and chickens, because I immediately became infected with the feeling which the author had obviously felt, experienced and transmitted' (14: 145). He likes a tale about the theatre of a primitive people, the Voguls, which involves children and a mother deer and Bambi-like offspring pursued by huntsmen (14: 147). In painting he likes a picture by Vasnetsov (illustrating a story of Turgenev), which depicts a sleeping child apparently disturbed by the image of a quail shot by his father (14: 146). Another painting by the minor English artist Langley also appeals to him. It shows a hungry beggar boy being fed by a rich lady and observed by a young upper-class woman (loc. cit.).

Such motifs may take him back to his sentimentalist roots and to his first published work *Childhood*. Yet this was an account without the debased sentimentality that appears to have affected the tastes of the later Tolstoi, who is now capable not only of condemning Beethoven's Sonata No. 101, and the Ninth Symphony (16: 165), but also of rejecting the bulk of European literature (including his own works) in favour of cloying sentimental pieces by minor artists. It may be the result of Tolstoi's attempt to transmit rational consciousness into feeling but it smacks of ideology.

The influence of Rousseau's teaching on the 'noble savage', and the corrupting effect of civilization can certainly be felt in Tolstoi's arguments, but there is also a religious dimension:[11]

> Since the time that the upper classes of Christian peoples lost their faith in church Christianity, the art of the upper classes separated from the art of the whole people, and two forms of art came into being: the art of the people and the art of the masters (7: 74).

Because of this separation, Tolstoi argues, art became impoverished in content and vitiated in form, growing less and less capable of being understood: 'The art of the upper classes in the course of time even ceased to be art, and began to be substituted by imitation of art' (11: 112). Nevertheless, in this argument cause and effect soon become muddled. At the end of chapter 11, he argues that it is this very imitation of art which is the chief reason for this separation (rather than its effect [11: 121]).

In his championship of 'the people' as the only true arbiters of art, Tolstoi looks forward to the future (and, one may say, with prescience): his aesthetic yardstick would not be dissimilar from that later adopted by Soviet criticism:

> And the judge of art, in general, will not be a separate class of rich people, as happens today, but the whole people. So that in order for a work to be

---

11 For discussion of this see Thomas Barran, 'Rousseau's Political Vision and Tolstoy's *What Is Art?*', *TSJ*, 1992, V, pp. 1–13 (8).

recognized as good, be approved and disseminated, it must satisfy the demands, not of people in similar and often unnatural conditions, but the demands of all the people, the great masses of people in natural, working conditions (19: 180).

There is, however, an ominous note in the discernment which Tolstoi ascribes to the 'people': 'In people not perverted by the false theories of our society, in working people, in children, there exists a definite concept of what it is that people are esteemed for and praised' (17: 170). This quality, admired by the common man, is physical strength. The common man cannot understand the veneration accorded to Pushkin, but a Stalin-figure might well be understood (to take once more an anachronistic example):

> That Russian knights and Alexander of Macedon, Genghis-Khan or Napoleon he understands were great, because any one of them could squash him and a thousand like him; that Buddha, Socrates and Christ are great, he also understands, because he knows and feels that he and all people should be like that; but why a person should be great, because he wrote verses about the love of women, that he cannot understand (17: 171).

Nevertheless, only a couple of pages later the argument has changed; it is now the upper classes who see the tyrannical figures as great. Of the ideas of the French critic de Vogüé, and the German philosopher Nietzsche, Tolstoi says:

> In essence these propositions are included in the ideal of art serving beauty. The art of our upper classes has fostered in people this ideal of the superman [which is] in essence the old ideal of Nero, Stenka Razin, Genghis Khan, Robert Macaire, Napoleon and all those of like mind, their hangers-on, and flatterers and it is wholly directed towards sustaining this ideal among the people (17: 173).

The rejection of the idea that aesthetic criteria could replace ethical criteria is an argument that looks back to the 'nihilists' of the 1860s, and in its embodiment in the figure of Napoleon it is also explored by Dostoevskii in *Crime and Punishment*. Significantly, in *War and Peace* Tolstoi was more concerned with pitting the decisive influence of Napoleon against that of mass movements, and here again the real arbiter was seen as the people.

The aesthetic theories of Tolstoi appear, then, as a bridge between the radicals of the 1860s and the theoreticians of the early Soviet Union; yet, for all the apparent similarities, there is one important difference: both nineteenth-century radical thought and Soviet aesthetic theory promoted rationalism – Tolstoi, in attempting to suppress the rationalism of his own nature, would only acknowledge feeling as the true yardstick for art and, as we have seen, it was an extreme sentimentalist position which led him into many contradictions.

Bibliography

Barran, Thomas, 'Rousseau's Political Vision and Tolstoy's *What Is Art?*', *TSJ*, V, 1992, pp. 1–13.

Boer, Roland, 'Lenin on Tolstoy: Between Imaginary Resolution and Revolutionary Christian Communism', *Science & Society*, LXXVIII, 1, pp. 41–60.

Chernyshevskii, N.G., 'Esteticheskie otnosheniia iskusstva k deistvitel'nosti' in id., *Polnoe sobranie sochinenii v 15 tomakh*, II, Kirpotin, V.Ia. et al., ed, Goslitizdat, Moscow, 1949, pp. 5–92.

Emery, Jacob, 'Art Is Inoculation: The Infectious Imagination of Leo Tolstoy', *The Russian Review*, LXX, 4, 2011, pp. 627–45.

Gershkovich, Tatyana, 'Infecting, Simulating, Judging: Tolstoy's Search for an Aesthetic Standard', *Journal of the History of Ideas*, LXXIV, 1, 2013, pp. 115–37.

Gustafson, Richard F., *Leo Tolstoy: Resident and Stranger. A Study in Fiction and Theology*, Princeton University Press, Princeton, New Jersey, 2014.

Robinson, Douglas, 'Tolstoy's Infection Theory and the Aesthetics of De- and Repersonalization', *Tolstoy Studies Journal*, XIX, 2007, pp. 33–53.

Robinson, Douglas, *Estrangement and the Somatics of Literature: Tolstoy, Shklovsky, Brecht*, The Johns Hopkins University Press, Baltimore, 2008.

Sterne, Laurence, *A Sentimental Journey through France and Italy*, John Bumpus, London, 1824.

Tolstoi, L.N., *Chto takoe iskusstvo?* in id., *Polnoe sobranie sochinenii, Proizvedeniia 1882–1898*, XXX, Mishin, V.S. and Gorbachev, N.V., eds, Gosudarstvennoe izdatel'stvo khudozhestvennoi literatury, Moscow, 1951, pp. 27–195. ⟨http://tolstoy.ru/online/90/30/⟩.

CHAPTER 3

Tolstoi in the Work of Tolstoi

Willem G. Weststeijn

Abstract

The question of how, if at all, an author is 'present' in his or her works is peculiarly complex in the case of Tolstoi. While we may know little about the lives of Homer or Shakespeare, we have a large amount of information about Tolstoi: his diaries and confessional works, the memoirs of relatives and friends, photographs and voice recordings, all these are in addition to his fiction, which form of writing is notoriously problematic as a source of authorial information. By contrast, in Tolstoi's non-fiction there is no doubt about the status and role of the author. From all of this we can conclude that Tolstoi has a biography and does exist in the reader's consciousness. This, however, is quite different from the 'image' of Tolstoi that a given reader may have, for the latter depends on the social, cultural and historical location of the reader and the degree to which he or she is familiar with Tolstoi's biography. The conclusion is partly a formalist one: we can enjoy a literary work on its merits alone, without knowing anything of its author; on the other hand, the very reading will inevitably excite our curiosity to discover the author's biography.

Keywords

Tolstoi's biography – Tolstoi's diaries and confessional works – the reader's 'image' of a writer

From the title of this chapter it will be clear that I want to find out whether – and, if so, in what way and where – we can find Tolstoi, the real Tolstoi, the writer who lived, loved and quarrelled, worked, thought, and expressed his opinions more than one hundred years ago, in his own work. More generally the question would be: what is the exact relation between the writer and his or her work? The question is not new, of course, and has been dealt with in various ways. One of the oldest and best-established traditions in literary criticism is to assume that there is a one-to-one relationship between the work and the writer, that is to say that everything in the work directly concerns the writer herself or himself. In other words, one may establish who and what the writer is on the basis of his / her works; there is a causal relation between the writer and his work: every statement in a play, a novel or a poem can and should be taken as literal biographical truth. This 'biographical method' in literary criticism was particularly popular in pre-Formalist times and has been aptly described and, subsequently, rejected as inadequate and even mistaken by Wellek and Warren in their *Theory of Literature*:

> One cannot, from fictional statements, especially those made in plays, draw any valid inference as to the biography of a writer. One may gravely doubt even the usual view that Shakespeare passed through a period of depression, in which he wrote his tragedies and his bitter comedies, to achieve some serenity of resolution in *The Tempest*. It is not self-evident that a writer needs to be in a tragic mood to write tragedies or that he writes comedies when he feels pleased with life [...] authors cannot be assigned the ideas, feelings, views, virtues, and vices of their heroes. And this is true not only of dramatic characters or characters in a novel but also of the *I* of the lyrical poem. The relation between the private life and the work is not a simple relation of cause and effect.[1]

A work of art, Wellek and Warren maintain, is quite different from a personal statement of an autobiographical nature as, for instance, a letter or a diary:[2]

> Even when a work of art contains elements which can be surely identified as biographical, these elements will be so rearranged and transformed in a work that they lose all their specifically personal meaning and become simply concrete human material, integral elements of a work [...] The whole view that art is self-expression pure and simple, the transcript of personal feelings and experiences, is demonstrably false. Even when there is a close relationship between the work of art and the

---

1 René Wellek and Austen Warren, *Theory of Literature*. Jonathan Cape, London, 1954, p. 70 (first published 1948). The authors are adherents of the idea of the 'autonomy' of the literary work, one of the central notions of New Criticism. See also T.S. Eliot, who speaks of 'a continual extinction of personality' in art. The poet does not have a 'personality to express, but a particular medium' (T.S. Eliot, 'Tradition and the Individual Talent' [first published 1917] *Selected Essays*, Faber and Faber, London, 1934, pp. 13–22; p. 17; 20).
2 Although even letters and diaries need not contain autobiographical 'truth'.

life of an author, this must never be construed as meaning that the work of art is a mere copy of life.[3]

A work of art has an entirely different relation to reality than a personal document or statement, but it often happens, it perhaps generally happens, that readers and often even critics relate or try to relate the literary work directly to its writer. When Charlotte Brontë published her novel *Jane Eyre* under the pseudonym Currer Bell, there were some early reviewers who, in this case rightly, claimed that the book must have been written by a woman. George Eliot's case was different. When her pseudonym was lifted shortly after her first novel, *Scenes of Clerical Life*, had been published, some readers were angry: the writer of this Christian, moralistic book, was not a clergyman, but a female freethinker, moreover, living 'in sin' with another woman's husband.

George Eliot's case shows how difficult it can be to draw the right conclusions about the 'real', 'empirical' writer – I will call him henceforth the historical author – on the basis of the text he / she has written.[4] That holds true, at least, for fictional texts. When we read a newspaper report or a scientific essay the question simply does not arise as to whether there is a difference between the historical author and the intratextual instance that expresses the text – the narrator. We assume that in these cases the historical author and the narrator coincide and that the ideas, feelings and opinions expressed in these texts can be ascribed to the author him / herself.

---

3   Wellek and Warren, pp. 71–2. Before Wellek and Warren the question whether we need or do not need a writer's autobiography in order to understand his work had been posed more cautiously by Boris Tomashevskii in his article 'Literatura i biografiia', *Kniga i revoliutsiia*, IV, 1923, pp. 6–9 (translated as 'Literature and Biography' in *Readings in Russian Poetics. Formalist and Structuralist Views*, Ladislav Matejka and Krystyna Pomorska, eds, The University of Michigan, Ann Arbor, 1978, pp. 47–55). Tomashevskii is perfectly aware of the fact that there are writers with and writers without a biography and that in the former case one has to consider how a writer's biography operates in the reader's consciousness.

4   An interesting and rather characteristic case is that of a Dutch feminist critic (Maaike Meijer) who in her analysis of a collection of poetry by a female poet (Neeltje Maria Min) concluded that this poet must have been the victim of incest. She had no problem conflating the lyric I or lyric subject, the speaker in the poem, with the historical author. Fortunately, the poet was still alive when the critic published her article, so she could protest and deny, because the incest existed only in the imagination of the critic. See Rudi Wester, 'Neeltje Maria Min slaat terug' ('Neeltje Maria Min hits back') in *Opzij*, XVIII, 4, 1990, pp. 82–4. Dead authors, however, cannot defend themselves. There is still much criticism in which authors are 'explained' on the basis of their works and are sometimes burdened with traumas, depressions and aberrations of which they did not have the faintest notion themselves. For a lucid discussion of the role of psychoanalysis in literary criticism, see Peter Lamarque, *Fictional Points of View*. Cornell University Press, Ithaca and London, 1996, pp. 181–98.

In fiction the situation is entirely different. In the first place we are confronted with a fictional world, which may resemble the real world but, in principle, does not coincide with it, and is peopled by characters that do not really exist, but exclusively belong to the fictional world created by the text. When a writer decides to introduce a historical figure into this fictional world, this figure becomes part of the fictional world, which means that the writer, at least to a certain extent, can do with him / her what he wants. An example is Napoleon in *War and Peace*. In the fictional world of the novel, which closely resembles the real world, Napoleon is the French emperor, as he was in reality, and Tolstoi could not possibly introduce him as a mere soldier in the French army or, still less veridical, as a woman (which might be possible in a postmodernist novel). However, Tolstoi had the freedom to present Napoleon, or any other historical figure, such as Kutuzov, in a certain way, sympathetic or unsympathetic, magnanimous or self-satisfied and attribute words and thoughts to them, which in reality they never uttered and never thought. In this way the reader may be confronted with historical figures whose images do not agree with the images the reader has created for himself on the basis of, for instance, history-books.

What holds true for historical figures concerns any character, even if it is based on someone the author (and also the reader) knows quite well, and even if the author introduces himself into his work. In the latter case he easily can and often will put on a mask behind which he hides himself and deliberately change himself into a character who is considerably different from the person he is in real life. A second feature which makes fiction different from other texts is its complex narrative situation. In contrast to letters, essays, scientific articles *et cetera*, in which the spokesman or narrator coincides with the historical author, in fiction there is often a narrator who cannot be identified as the writer outside the text. Think for instance of a character in the fictional world who tells a story about himself or about one or more other characters in this world.[5] Such a narrator may resemble the historical author, but can also be an entirely different person. Take for example Dostoevskii's underground man, who as the narrator of his own story is a purely fictional character and certainly not Dostoevskii himself. Despite these evident differences between the character-narrator and the historical author there are many critics who discuss the underground man's ideas as the ideas of Dostoevskii himself.

---

5 Norman Friedman's seminal article 'Point of View in Fiction: The Development of a Critical Concept', PMLA, LXX, 1955, pp. 1160–84 classified the '"I" as Protagonist'. An early, not often quoted, but interesting study on first-person narrative is Bertil Romberg, *Studies in the Narrative Technique of the First-Person Novel*, Almqvist & Wiksell, Stockholm, 1962.

There is a vast amount of structuralist theory on the narrator in fiction and on the possible forms in which he can appear. One of the best known classifications of narrators is that of Gérard Genette, the French father of structuralist narratology, who apart from the important notions of 'focalization' and 'voice' introduced four perhaps rather awkward, but theoretically appropriate terms to define the four fundamental types of narrators.[6] I will concentrate on one type of narrator, in Genette's terms the extradiegetic-heterodiegetic one, by other theorists called the impersonal, authorial or omniscient narrator. We find such a narrator in many nineteenth-century novels, including *Anna Karenina* and *War and Peace*. The narrator in these novels does not belong to the fictional world that he creates by telling his story and reigns supreme over this world; he is invisibly present everywhere, knows what will happen, what the characters are saying to each other and even what they are feeling and thinking. Accordingly, we sometimes get to know fictional characters much better than we will ever know people in the real world, whose thoughts are not accessible to us.

One of the terms used for the narrator in *Anna Karenina, War and Peace* and other novels is 'authorial narrator' and, indeed, such a narrator is, at least formally, not distinguishable from the historical author. But do authorial narrator and historical author really coincide? Writers themselves have given entirely different answers to this question. In his prefaces to his novels Henry James contends that he himself, as the historical author, is the narrator and he claims the full authority for the meaning and intention behind his works. For Proust, on the other hand, a book written by him is the product of a self that is different from the self manifested in his social life. It may happen that the authorial narrator, consciously or subconsciously, expresses opinions contrary to what the historical author professed or professes in real life. A fictional text may escape the author's control, so that, as Paul Valéry has said, when you try to

---

6 The four terms concern the narrator's narrative level: extradiegetic or intradiegetic and the narrator's relation to the story: heterodiegetic or homodiegetic. Genette's four types of narrators are therefore: 1) extradiegetic-heterodiegetic (a narrator on the first level, the level above the primary story, who does not take part in the story he tells – Homer; 2) extradiegetic-homodiegetic (a narrator on the first level who tells his own story – Dostoevskii's underground man); 3) intradiegetic-heterodiegetic (a narrator on the second level, i.e. inside the story, who tells a story in which he does not take part – Sheherazade); 4) intradiegetic-homodiegetic (a narrator on the second level who tells his own story – Pozdnyshev in Tolstoi's *The Kreutzer Sonata*). See Gérard Genette, 'Discours du récit', *Figures III*, Éditions du Seuil, Paris, 1972, pp. 255–7.

reconstitute the historical author on the basis of his work you necessarily construct an imaginary character.[7]

In order to catch this imaginary character, the author's second self, the term 'implied author' has been introduced, initially by Wayne Booth in his *The Rhetoric of Fiction* (1961). Like many other narratological notions this is a rather elusive one and has been used and understood in various ways. For some theorists, including Booth himself, the implied author is a distinct agent between the narrator and the historical author, the real author's 'second self', as it comes to the fore in the style of the work and the 'particular ordering of values'.[8] Seymour Chatman does not consider the implied author as an agent, but as the textual principle of 'unified invention and intent'.[9] He also uses words as 'text implication' and 'text design'. The implied author is 'nothing other than the text itself in its inventional aspect'.[10] Another way to look at the implied author is to see him or her in the sense of Valéry's imaginary character: the implied author as the image of the author that the reader infers from the work. As such, the implied author is a construct inferred from the text and, accordingly, dependent on the interpretation by the reader. Such a construct is, generally, not a mental picture of a person (although it was for George Eliot's disappointed readers) but, rather, a set of ideas, opinions and implicit norms and meanings.[11]

In describing and establishing the implied author of a work the reader has to be very careful. In his book *Frameworks* William Nelles mentions the interesting case of a critic who commented on an expression in Herman Melville's *White-Jacket*. The expression was 'soiled fish of the sea', which the critic praised in the following words:

---

7   'C'est pourquoi celui qui veut reconstituer un auteur à partir de son œuvre se construit nécessairement un personnage imaginaire.' Paul Valéry, Œuvres, II, Gallimard, Paris, 1960, p. 569.
8   Wayne C. Booth, *The Rhetoric of Fiction*, The University of Chicago Press, Chicago and London, 1961, pp. 71–4.
9   Seymour Chatman, *Coming to Terms. The Rhetoric of Narrative in Fiction and Film*, Cornell University Press, Ithaca and London, 1990, p. 82.
10   Ibid., p. 86. In an earlier study Chatman wrote: 'Unlike the narrator, the implied author can *tell* us nothing. He, or better, *it* has no voice, no direct means of communicating. It instructs us silently, through the design of the whole, with all the voices, by all the means it has chosen to let us learn': *Story and Discourse*, Cornell University Press, Ithaca, New York, 1978, p. 148.
11   See also Shlomith Rimmon-Kenan, *Narrative Fiction: Contemporary Poetics*, Methuen, London and New York, 1983, pp. 86–8.

Hardly anyone but Melville could have created the shudder that results from calling this frightening vagueness some '*soiled* fish of the sea'. The *discordia concors*, the unexpected linking of the medium of cleanliness with filth, could only have sprung from an imagination that had apprehended the terrors of the deep, of the immaterial deep as well as the physical.

Poor critic: in reality Melville had written 'coiled fish of the sea', soiled being just a misprint in the edition the critic was using. In this way an accidental error can become part of the implied author's meaning.[12]

The terms connected with the production of the narrative – historical author, implied author, narrator – are mirrored by terms connected with the reception of the text. Accordingly we have the reader in the text who is directly addressed by the narrator; next, the implied reader, also called the ideal or perfect reader; the super-reader who would understand and discern all the subtleties and ambiguities of a text; and, on a par with the historical author, the historical reader who exists, of course, always outside the text. The 'good' historical reader will, when reading a narrative text, set aside the personal prejudices and idiosyncrasies, that characterize him or her in real life and strive to become someone like the implied reader of the text.

Is all this theory really helpful for answering the question that I stated at the beginning of this chapter: where and how to find Tolstoi in Tolstoi's works? The theory, of course, cannot answer this particular question, but, I think, makes us at any rate aware of how problematic the issue is. We do not know much about Shakespeare's life, nothing at all about, for instance, Homer's life, but, fortunately or unfortunately, there is quite a lot of information about the historical author Tolstoi. We have his own extensive diaries, the diaries of his wife, the memoirs of at least eight of his 12 or 13 children, some of them siding with their father, some with their mother. We have the notes and diaries of his secretaries, the countless reports of visitors, particularly during the last years of his life, when he was world-famous, a great number of biographies and photographs, an entire library of criticism. It is almost impossible to disregard this information or at least part of it. Tolstoi *has* a biography and *does* exist in the reader's, almost any reader's, consciousness. So what does it mean when we say: Tolstoi in the work of Tolstoi? The historical author Tolstoi is dead; what remains is an image of this historical author, a construction made by the

---

12   William Nelles, *Frameworks. Narrative Levels and Embedded Narrative*, Peter Lang, New York, 1997, p. 72.

historical reader based on the information the reader has. Accordingly, 'the' image of Tolstoi does not exist. The Tolstoi expert will have a different image, and I venture to say a better image, of the historical author than a reader who hardly knows anything about Tolstoi's life and is only aware of and conforms to the public myth of the author. Such a public myth can be very different from the historical author – think, for instance, of the lofty public myth of Aleksandr Blok as the wonderful poet who praised his Beautiful Lady, while in reality he was a habitué of St Petersburg's brothels.

'The' image of Tolstoi does not exist, not only because it varies from reader to reader, but also because it is not a fixed image for one and the same historical reader. Tolstoi lived quite a long time and the image the reader has of him as a young man, writing his early autobiographical stories and taking part in the Crimean war is not necessarily the same as the reader's image of Tolstoi after the writer's so-called confession: the bearded preacher of sexual abstinence and pacifism in his Russian peasant shirt.

Back to Tolstoi's works, which are, after all the main, I would say the only reason why the historical author interests us. When we look for Tolstoi in his work we are trying to establish the implied author of a work. Every single work has its implied author, the author inferred by the reader. In Tolstoi's case this inferred author is not only a construct based on the work itself, but, I would say, almost inevitably also based on what we know of his biography and on the biographical legend he has himself created.[13] When we read *Anna*

---

13   Tolstoi introduced important elements of this biographical legend in his *Confession* (1882), which contains merciless self-examination and a solemn vow to search for a new way of life and moral perfection. Although Tolstoi wrote about himself in this text, inviting the reader to identify the 'I' in the text with the historical author, one may doubt (perhaps) not the author's serious intent, but the 'truth' of his self-accusations, which seem to be rather exaggerated.: 'I cannot think of those years without horror, loathing and heartache. I killed men in war and challenged men to duels in order to kill them. I lost at cards, consumed the labour of the peasants, sentenced them to punishments, lived loosely, and deceived people. Lying, robbery, adultery of all kinds, drunkenness, violence, murder – there was no crime I did not commit, and in spite of that people praised my conduct and my contemporaries considered and consider me to be a comparatively moral man.
So I lived for ten years.
During that time I began to write from vanity, covetousness, and pride. In my writings I did the same as in my life. To get fame and money, for the sake of which I wrote, it was necessary to hide the good and to display the evil. and I did so. How often in my writings I contrived to hide under the guise of indifference, or even of banter, those strivings of mine towards goodness which gave meaning to my life! And I succeeded in this and was praised' (L.N. Tolstoy, *The Confession*, Louise and Aylmer Maude, trans. at http://www.classicallibrary.org/tolstoy/confession/index.htm).

Karenina and *War and Peace* this biographical legend does, perhaps, play a less important role than in Tolstoi's later works, particularly those written after his 'confession'. For that reason there is, perhaps, more resemblance between the implied authors constructed by various historical readers of *War and Peace* than between those of, for instance, *The Kreutzer Sonata*. In *War and Peace* there is authorial narration, which means that the narrator of the novel and its creator, the historical author, to a certain extent coincide. Nobody would doubt, I think, that the negative image of Napoleon, which is evoked by the narrator's description, is the same as Tolstoi's own image of Napoleon, or that the narrator's conception of history, extensively elaborated at the end of the novel, is Tolstoi's own conception. In this case aspects of the implied author can be connected, I would say objectively, with the historical author. In *The Kreutzer Sonata* there is an I-narrator, who in his story introduces a character, Pozdnyshev, who as embedded narrator tells the primary narrator about his life. This narrative construction makes it much more difficult to relate the two narrators to the historical author, but knowing the facts of Tolstoi's biography many readers are inclined to do so, considering Pozdnyshev Tolstoi's mouthpiece and reading the story as an autobiographical account. Now, it is true that Pozdnyshev's story contains some autobiographical allusions, such as the presenting of his diary, containing a record of his various liaisons with women, to his future wife, and the later quarrels with her over sex and the education of their children, but Tolstoi did not murder his wife as Pozdnyshev did and, of course, deliberately wrote a story in which he presented a fictional character under a different name from his own. Pozdnyshev is not Tolstoi, but you might say that on a more general level Pozdnyshev's dilemma and his moral struggle against his former ideas and the conventions of society is Tolstoi's own struggle. The great impact the story has is, undoubtedly, a result of Tolstoi's own engagement with Pozdnyshev's story. The implied author that we infer from *The Kreutzer Sonata* is a Tolstoi who with artistic brilliance writes a narrative in which elements from his own biography are fused with moral and psychological problems that are close to his heart.

Is it relevant to try to find Tolstoi, the real Tolstoi in so far as we can reconstitute him, in his work? It is not relevant, of course, when you are only interested in the work of art itself and do not care about whether the image of the implied author you inferred from the text conforms to the historical author. Even if we do not know anything of the historical author we can consider a work of literature great literature, and enjoy it aesthetically. Knowledge of the historical author does not, or rather should not, affect our appraisal of the work, but it inevitably affects our construction of the implied author. It seems to be the case that a hectic life and suicide is a better guarantee of immortality than an uneventful existence as a civil servant. Poets, in particular, do better to die young. And men and women are inquisitive. When we are dealing with a great work of literature we do want to know something about its creator and when we know something about the creator we will invariably make a connection between the creator and the work. Let us keep doing it, professionally, without prejudices and avoiding the pitfalls narrative theory is warning us against.

Bibliography

Bartlett, Rosamund, *Tolstoy: A Russian Life*, Profile, London, 2010.

Booth, Wayne C., *The Rhetoric of Fiction*, The University of Chicago Press, Chicago and London, 1961.

Chatman, Seymour, *Story and Discourse*, Cornell University Press, Ithaca, New York, 1978. Chatman, Seymour, *Coming to Terms. The Rhetoric of Narrative in Fiction and Film*, Cornell University Press, Ithaca and London, 1990.

Eliot, T.S., 'Tradition and the Individual Talent' in id., *Selected Essays* (first published 1917), Faber and Faber, London, 1934, pp. 13–22.

Emer, Jacob, 'Art Is Inoculation: The Infectious Imagination of Leo Tolstoy', *The Russian Review*, LXX, 4, 2011, 627–45.

Friedman, Norman, 'Point of View in Fiction: The Development of a Critical Concept', *PMLA*, LXX, 1955, pp. 1160–84.

Genette, Gérard, 'Discours du récit', *Figures III*, Éditions du Seuil, Paris, 1972.

Ginzburg, Lidiia, *O psikhologicheskoi proze*, Sovetskii pisatel', Leningradskoe otdelenie, Leningrad, 1971.

Knapp, Liza, Anna Karenina *and Others: Tolstoy's Labyrinth of Plots*, The University of Wisconsin Press, Madison, Wisconsin, 2016.

Lamarque, Peter, *Fictional Points of View*, Cornell University Press, Ithaca and London, 1996.

McLean, Hugh, *In Quest of Tolstoy*, Academic Studies Press, Boston, 2017.

Medzhibovskaya, Inessa, ed., *Tolstoy and His Problems: Views from the Twenty-First Century*, Northwestern University Press, Evanston, Illinois, 2019.

Nelles, William, *Frameworks. Narrative Levels and Embedded Narrative*, Peter Lang, New York, 1997.

Orwin, Donna Tussing, *Consequences of Consciousness: Turgenev, Dostoevsky and Tolstoy*, Stanford University Press, Stanford, 2007.

Paperno, Irina, *'Who, what am I?': Tolstoy Struggles to Narrate the Self*, Cornell University Press, Ithaca, New York, 2014.

Rancour-Laferriere, Daniel, *Tolstoy on the Couch: Misogyny, Masochism and the Absent Mother*, Macmillan, London and New York University Press, New York, 1998.

Rimmon-Kenan, Shlomith, *Narrative Fiction: Contemporary Poetics*, Methuen, London and New York, 1983.

Romberg, Bertil, *Studies in the Narrative Technique of the First-Person Novel*, Almqvist & Wiksell, Stockholm, 1962.

Tapp, Alyson, '"Как быть писателем?": Boris Eikhenbaum's Response to the Crisis of the Novel in the 1920s', *Slavonica*, XV, 1, 2009, pp. 32–47.

Tolstoy, L.N., *The Confession*, trans. Louise and Aylmer Maude, at http://www.classicallibrary.org/tolstoy/confession/index.htm.

Tomashevskii, Boris, 'Literatura i biografiia'in *Kniga i revoliutsiia*, IV, 1923, pp. 6–9 (translated as 'Literature and Biography' in Matejka, Ladislav and Pomorska, Krystyna, eds., *Readings in Russian Poetics. Formalist and Structuralist Views*, The University of Michigan, Ann Arbor, 1978, pp. 47–55).

Valéry, Paul, *Œuvres*, II, Gallimard, Paris, 1960.

Weir, Justin, *Leo Tolstoy and the Alibi of Narrative*, Yale University Press, New Haven and London, 2011.

Wellek, René and Warren, Austen, *Theory of Literature*, Jonathan Cape, London, 1954 (first published 1948).

Wester, Rudi, 'Neeltje Maria Min slaat terug' ('Neeltje Maria Min hits back') in *Opzij*, 18, 4, 1990, pp. 82–4.

CHAPTER 4

Dostoevskii's Zosima and Tolstoi's Father Sergius: Literary Representations of *Starchestvo*

Nel Grillaert

Abstract

Among the more intriguing influences on Tolstoi's creative and spiritual life was the Orthodox tradition of the 'elder' (*starets*). This tradition, it is claimed, goes back to the early days of Russian Orthodoxy and, having fallen out of favour, was revived again only in the eighteenth century. Both Tolstoi and Dostoevskii admired and visited the most famous elder of their time, Amvrosii, at the monastery of Optina Pustyn. Both produce a fictional representation of an elder, Dostoevskii in *The Brothers Karamazov* (Zosima) and Tolstoi in the eponymous *Father Sergius*. Dostoevskii embeds his description of Zosima in the hagiographical tradition; he aims at creating a credible saint as a counterweight against Ivan Karamazov's atheistic arguments in the novel. By contrast, Tolstoi's Father Sergius struggles to adapt himself to the religious life and is unable to fend off the temptations that have driven him to become a monk in the first place, particularly ambition and lust. Predictably, perhaps, given Tolstoi's antipathy to the Orthodox Church, his hero only finds peace by leaving the monastery to live a life of humble anonymity. For Tolstoi, real spiritual elderhood can only be effective in a context that cuts off all ties with the established church.

Keywords

Tolstoi's Father Sergius – Dostoevskii's *The Brothers Karamazov* – the Russian Orthodox elder (*starets*)

In the nineteenth century, a substantial number of Russian intellectuals made a pilgrimage to Optina Pustyn, a monastery in the Kaluga province near the town of Kozelsk, around 200 kilometers south of Moscow.[1] The Optina mon-

---

1 See, for example, I.M. Kontsevich, *Optina Pustyn' i ee vremia*, Holy Trinity Monastery, Jordanville, New York, 1970; Sergius Chetverikov, *Optina Pustyn'*, YMCA Press, Paris, 1926.

astery occupies a special place in Russian religious consciousness because it was an important centre of the revival of *starchestvo* or elderhood, which is a special monastic discipline that revolves around spiritual guidance in the mystical prayer practice of *hesychasm*. The tradition dates back to the Desert Fathers, saw a revival on Mount Athos in the fourteenth century and was introduced to Russia by Nil Sorskii in the fifteenth century. Nil founded a hermitage in the Volga forest lands (at the Sora river) and inspired a whole movement of 'Transvolgan elders'. In spite of their popularity in monastic and lay circles, the elders were soon suppressed, because of their independent status within the hierarchy of the Russian church, as well as conflict with the movement of the Josephite 'possessors'.[2] At the end of the eighteenth century, elderhood was revived by Paisii Velichkovskii and his disciples and adopted by some monastic communities. It was the monastery of Optina Pustyn that became especially renowned for the renaissance of elderhood and made the nineteenth century the Golden Age of Russian *starchestvo*. Optina acquired great fame because of its three *startsy*: Leonid (1821–1841), a direct disciple of Paisii Velichkovskii, Makarii (1841–1860) and Amvrosii (1860–1891). Their spiritual and ascetic charisma spread far outside the monastery walls and attracted hordes of lay pilgrims, who had broken away from the secularized church and were in search of a more spiritual faith. The hermitage had a special appeal for religious intellectuals who were aware of the poor moral state of the majority of the Russian clergy and longed to find a sufficient religious counterweight against the atheist theories now becoming prevalent in Russia. Nikolai Gogol and Ivan Kireevskii were, amongst others, frequent visitors to the hermitage. The most famous visitors, though, were undoubtedly Fedor Dostoevskii and Lev Tolstoi: each from his own ideological background was impressed by the elders' aura and decided, each for his own purposes, to immortalize elderhood in a piece of fiction. This was a daring project: within the restrictive atmosphere of the Russian state church, the Optina elders represented a current of freedom. They revived a social engagement with the common people and the typical Orthodox mystical spirituality that had been gradually pushed to the margins of the established church. Their growing popularity among lay believers was a thorn in the side of the church authorities, who made severe, but fruitless, attempts to discredit them and stop the hordes of pilgrims.[3]

---

2 For Nil Sorskii's theology and his place in the history of Russian Christianity, see George A. Maloney, *Russian Hesychasm: The Spirituality of Nil Sorskij*, Mouton, The Hague, 1973.
3 In his biography of the elder Leonid, Kliment Zedergol'm devoted a whole chapter to the opposition to elderhood. He describes, for instance, how at some point visitors were no

Together with the young philosopher Vladimir Solovev, Fedor Dostoevskii made a pilgrimage to Optina in the summer of 1878, in the hope of finding some spiritual comfort there after the sudden death of his son Alesha.[4] Dostoevskii and Solovev arrived in Kozelsk at the beginning of July after a rather adventurous journey. They stayed in the monastery only a couple of days, but in this short period of time Dostoevskii met with the celebrated *starets* Amvrosii three times: he had two long private conversations with him and met him a third time with a group of other visitors. He related his impressions to his wife, who wrote them down in her memoirs:

> Fedor Mikhailovich returned from Optina Pustyn seemingly at peace and much calmer, and he told me a great deal about the customs of Pustyn, where he spent two days. Fedor Mikhailovich met three times with the renowned 'starets' Amvrosii, once in a crowd of people, and twice alone, and from these conversations he brought a profound and lasting impression [...] From his stories it was clear, what a profound knower of the heart and seer this honoured 'starets' was.[5]

The writer was so impressed by the spiritual atmosphere of the monastery and the charisma of *starets* Amvrosii, that he decided to portray the specific monastic customs and the institution of *starchestvo* in his novel *The Brothers Karamazov*, on which he was working at the time. In addition to the monastic setting, he created – obviously inspired by Amvrosii – the fictional *starets* Zosima, whom he gave a central place in the narrative and envisioned as the

---

longer allowed in Leonid's cell. See *Elder Leonid of Optina*, St Herman of Alaska Brotherhood (Optina Elders Series), Platina, CA, 1990.

4 Dostoevskii's wife Anna Grigor'evna had asked Solov'ev, who was in those days a personal friend of the family, to accompany her grieving husband on this pilgrimage. In her memoirs, she wrote: 'Fedor Mikhailovich was terribly crushed by this death [...] In order to comfort him a little and distract him from his sad thoughts, I begged Vl.S. Solov'ev, who often visited us in these days of our mourning, to persuade Fedor Mikhailovich to accompany him to Optina Pustyn', where Solov'ev was planning to go this summer. A visit to Optina Pustyn' had long been a dream of Fedor Mikhailovich' (See Anna Grigor'evna Dostoevskaia, *Vospominaniia*, Khudozhestvennaia literatura, Moscow, 1971, pp. 321–2).

5 Dostoevskaia, *Vospominaniia*, p. 323.The feelings of warmth and sympathy Dostoevskii felt for the elder seem to have been reciprocal: there is evidence that Amvrosii liked the writer a great deal. See John B. Dunlop, *Staretz Amvrosy: Model for Dostoevsky's Staretz Zossima*, Nordland Publishing Company, Belmont, Mass., 1972, p. 59.

'culminating point' of the novel.[6] He devoted a whole book in the novel (book six), 'A Russian Monk' ('Русский инок') exclusively to his elder; this book functions as a hagiography of Zosima and serves as the spiritual and moral counterweight against the atheism voiced by Ivan in book five, 'Pro et Contra'. When writing the book on Zosima, Dostoevskii was well aware of the controversial status of *starchestvo* and even anticipated criticism of his 'Russian monk': in his notes to *The Brothers Karamazov* he wrote: 'I have entitled this sixth book: "a Russian Monk", a bold and provocative title, because all the critics who do not like us will scream: "is that what a Russian monk is like, how can you dare to put him on such a pedestal?"' (PSS XXX, 1, 102).

Lev Tolstoi visited the Optina monastery four or five times.[7] He made his first trip to Optina – together with the critic Nikolai Strakhov – in the summer of 1877, in other words, during a period in his life when he had just finished *Anna Karenina* and was already struggling with the religious and existential questions that would finally lead to his 'crisis'.[8] He had high expectations of the visit: he wanted to discuss with the Optina elder his growing inability to believe and hoped that the elder would be able to calm his troubled mind and refute his reasons for questioning religion. In sum, his plan was 'to explain to the monks all the reasons why I cannot believe'.[9] Tolstoi returned to Optina four years later, in June 1881, that is, right after his so-called conversion. He travelled with his valet Arbuzov and dressed as a *muzhik* to arrive incognito, but the monks and other pilgrims soon discovered his true identity, which evidently caused a great commotion. At that time, Tolstoi was still experiencing

---

6 F.M. Dostoevskii, *Polnoe sobranie sochinenii v tridtsati tomakh*, Nauka, Leningrad, 1972–1990, XXX, 1, p. 75. Further references to Dostoevskii's works will be given in the text, citing the standard abbreviation PSS, volume and page numbers. For translations of *The Brothers Karamazov*, I used Fyodor Dostoyevsky, *The Brothers Karamazov*, translated with an introduction and notes by David McDuff, Penguin Books, 2003. I made some minor changes in the translations where I found them appropriate for reasons of style and clarity. Other translations are mine.

7 For a detailed account of Tolstoi's numerous visits to Optina, see Leonard Stanton, *The Optina Pustyn Monastery in the Russian Literary Imagination: Iconic Vision in Works by Dostoevsky, Gogol, Tolstoy, and Others*, Peter Lang, New York, Middlebury Studies in Russian Language and Literature, 1995, pp. 203–28, and Pål Kolstø, 'The Elder at Iasnaia Poliana: Lev Tolstoi and the Orthodox *Starets* Tradition', *Kritika: Explorations in Russian and Eurasian History*, IX, 3, Summer 2008, pp. 533–54. See also Vladimir Kotel'nikov, *Pravoslavnye podvizhniki i russkaia literatura: na puti k Optinoi*, Progress-Pleiada, Moscow, 2002, pp. 321–32.

8 As the last words of *Anna Karenina* were sent to the publisher of *The Russian Herald* in April 1877, Tolstoi wrote to Strakhov: 'let's go as soon as possible to the Optina monastery' (*Pis'ma 1842–1881*, in L.N. Tolstoi, *Sobranie sochinenii v dvadtsati dvukh tomakh*, Khudozhestvennaia literatura, Moscow, 1978–1985, XVIII, p. 802.

9 Quoted in Stanton, p. 204.

great inner moral and religious struggle, and he spoke with the *starets* about his growing aversion to the church, as well as the authority of the Gospel. He went back to Optina nine years later, in February 1890, with his wife and three of his children. On his first three visits, he spoke several times with the elder Amvrosii, who died in 1891; the subsequent *startsy*, Anatolii and Iosif, did not have the same spiritual charisma as their predecessors, and, as a result, the number of visitors to the monastery gradually dropped. Some sources claim that Tolstoi travelled again to Optina in 1896, but the evidence is conflicting.[10] His last visit to Optina is the most dramatic one, and is one that fires the imagination. In the autumn of 1910, tired of the endless quarrels with his wife, Tolstoi fled from Iasnaia Poliana to Optina, where he stayed at the monastery inn. He did not meet up with the *starets* Iosif, but wandered around the monastery and spoke with several Optina monks. He also visited his sister Mariia who lived as a nun in Shamordino; Tolstoi discussed with her his plans to rent a small cottage near the convent to lead a simple life, close by Optina. But, in the end, he decided to flee once more. The rest is history: his next stop was the train station Astapovo, where he fell ill and died.[11]

The scenario of Tolstoi's visits to Optina was always basically the same: he travelled there in moments of spiritual and existential distress and hoped to find some guidance or answers there. There is, however, much disagreement as regards his impressions of Optina and its elders. According to his wife Sofiia, Tolstoi, upon his return from his first visit in 1877, was 'greatly satisfied with the wisdom, education and way of life of the monastic elders' and 'acknowledged the wisdom and spiritual strength of father Amvrosii'.[12] According to Henri Troyat, however, Tolstoi was disappointed by his meeting with the elder, and both Amvrosii and Tolstoi were worn out after their conversation and 'parted in mutual dissatisfaction'.[13] According to one report, Amvrosii was displeased because Tolstoi had kissed him on the cheek, a gesture of respect in secular contexts, but quite out of place when directed to a man so close to God.[14] Strakhov however gives another picture of the elder's reaction to Tolstoi; he writes to Tolstoi that 'the fathers [at Optina] praise you highly and find in

---

10   There is no doubt that in 1896, Tolstoi visited the Shamordino Convent not far from Optina – which was founded by Amvrosii – where Tolstoi's sister Mariia lived as a nun. There is, however, no definitive evidence that he also made a side visit to Optina.
11   See Stanton, pp. 209–13.
12   Quoted in N.N. Gusev, *Lev Nikolaevich Tolstoi: materialy k biografii s 1870 po 1881 god*, Akademiia nauk, Moscow, 1963, p. 441.
13   Henri Troyat, *Tolstoy*, translated from the French by Nancy Amphoux, Harmondsworth, Penguin Books, 1980, pp. 528–9.
14   Kolstø, pp. 541–2.

you a wonderful soul'. Tolstoi replied that he had joyful memories of Optina.[15] After his second visit to the hermitage in 1881, Tolstoi stated – according to Amvrosii's biographer – that 'Father Amvrosii is absolutely a holy man. I talked with him, and my soul felt light and joyful. When you speak to such a man, you sense the nearness of God'.[16] In a letter to Ivan Turgenev, Tolstoi spoke highly of his visit: 'My pilgrimage was a wonderful success. I would take five years from my life in return for these ten days'.[17] His daughter Aleksandra, by contrast, claims that his second visit alienated him further from Orthodoxy.[18]

To sum up, on the basis of these conflicting sources, there is no unequivocal answer to the question of how Tolstoi related to Optina and its elders. Even so, his recurring visits to Optina testify that Tolstoi was to a great extent attracted to the hermitage and could not get its elders out of his mind. In the authoritative life of elder Amvrosii, we read that 'Leo Tolstoy visited the elder several times, and it must be said that he always related respectfully to the Optina monastery and to monasticism in general'.[19] There can be no doubt that, in the light of his growing resistance to, and final rejection of, official Orthodoxy, Tolstoi was attracted to the Optina *startsy* because of their independent status in the hierarchy of the Russian church.

In spite of his ambiguous responses to the Optina elders, Tolstoi, like Dostoevskii, wrote down his impressions of *starchestvo* in a fictional work, namely the short story *Father Sergius* (*Отец Сергий*). Whereas Dostoevskii began working on Zosima soon after his trip to Optina, that is, in 1878, Tolstoi started working on *Father Sergius* only in 1890, in other words, only after his third

---

15 Gusev, pp. 441–2.
16 Sergius Chetverikov, *Elder Ambrose of Optina*, translated from the Russian edition, *Opisanie zhizni blazhennoi pamiati Optinskago startsa Amvrosia*, St Herman of Alaska Brotherhood, Platina, CA, 1997 (first published 1912), p. 290.
17 See Tolstoi, *Pis'ma 1842–1881*, p. 896.
18 Kolstø, p. 543. In his essay 'Optina Pustyn', Vasilii Rozanov gives a vivid insight into Tolstoi's third visit to Optina, written down on the basis of an eye-witness report given to him by Konstantin Leont'ev, who spent the last years of his life as a monk in Optina: 'After his meeting with Father Amvrosii, L.N. dropped in on K.N. Leont'ev, as if he were visiting an old acquaintance [...] the conversation touched on the elder, Father Amvrosii. "There is a good man! I've been to see him, and I'm thinking of going again tomorrow. He teaches the Gospel, only not quite the pure thing, and here is my Gospel", at which point he took a book from his pocket and gave it to Leont'ev [...] Leont'ev could contain himself no longer. He flared up and said: "How is it possible to be here in the hermitage, where there is such an elder as Father Amvrosii, and talk about one's own Gospel?"' See Vasilii Rozanov, 'Optina Pustyn', in V.V. Rozanov, *Religiia, Filosofiia, Kul'tura*, A.N. Nikoliukin, ed., Respublika, Moscow, 1992, pp. 273–4; see also Stanton, pp. 205–6.
19 Chetverikov, p. 214.

visit to Optina, and more than a decade after his 'conversion'. Perhaps Tolstoi was even inspired by Dostoevskii's Zosima to write down his own version of elderhood: in 1886, he had the ambition to publish Dostoevskii's 'A Russian Monk' in a separate book under the title *The Story of Starets Zosima*, but these plans were hindered by the censor because he foresaw 'obvious harm in the distribution of Zosima's mystical and social teaching, which shows only a visible resemblance to Christ's teaching, but is in essence completely opposite to the doctrine of orthodox faith'.[20] Work on *Father Sergius* proceeded in fits and starts: Tolstoi often laid the story aside to engage in other projects, but in 1898 he wanted to finish it as part of his plan to finance the collective move of the persecuted Dukhobors to Canada; however, he still wasn't pleased with it, and decided not to publish it (instead, it was the profits of his novel *Resurrection* that were used to support the Dukhobors). Eventually, the story was posthumously published – without thorough editing – in 1911.[21]

The aim of this chapter is to compare both Dostoevskii's and Tolstoi's fictional representations of the Optina tradition of *starchestvo*; through an analysis of both Zosima and Sergius, I will illustrate the similarities and differences in Dostoevskii's and Tolstoi's views of the Optina *startsy*.

Let us first take a look at the explicit references to the Optina tradition in both narratives. In book one of *The Brothers Karamazov*, a separate chapter, with the eponymous title 'Startsy', is devoted to elderhood. In this chapter, the narrator begins by sketching the origins of *starchestvo* in Sinai and on Mount Athos and describes the evolution of it in Russian monasticism:

> In the first place, then, those competent in the specialism assert that the elders and elderhood have been with us in our Russian monasteries only since very recent times, even less than a century, while in the rest of the Orthodox East, in Sinai and on Mount Athos in particular, they have already existed for well over a thousand years. It is claimed that elderhood also existed among us in Russia in the most ancient times, or

---

[20] V.K. Lebedev, 'Otryvok iz romana *Brat'ia Karamazovy* pered sudom tsenzury', *Russkaia literatura*, 1970, 2, pp. 123–5.

[21] For the genesis of the story, see the editors' note, in Lev Nikolaevich Tolstoi, *Sobranie sochinenii v dvenadtsati tomakh*, Khudozhestvennaia literatura, Moscow, 1975, X, p. 428. References to *Father Sergius* are also from volume X in this edition, and in the rest of this chapter will be given in the text, citing the standard abbreviation ss, volume and page numbers. I have based my translation of *Father Sergius* on the translation by Louise and Aylmer Maude, published on *Project Gutenberg* (http://www.gutenberg.org/ebooks/985). I have made minor changes where I found them appropriate for reasons of style and clarity.

that it certainly must have existed, but that in consequence of Russia's tribulations – the Tatar invasions, the mass upheavals, the break in our former relations with the East after the subjugation of Constantinople – this institution became forgotten among us and the elders died out (PSS XIV, 26).

Still, as the narrator relates, elderhood was revived in Russia at the end of the last century by 'one of the great ascetics (as they call him), Paisii Velichkovskii and his disciples' (PSS XIV, 26), who instigated the recovery of hesychastic practice and the tradition of elderhood by his Slavonic translation of the *Philokalia* (*Dobrotoliubie* [*Love of Virtue*]). The narrator, then, does not refrain from mentioning that elderhood only exists in a few monasteries and 'has even on occasion been subjected to what almost amounts to persecution as an unprecedented novelty in Russia', and continues that elderhood has 'thrived in particular among us here in the land of Rus at a certain renowned hermitage, the Kozelsk Optina [since the monastery was so closely located to the village of Kozelsk, it was also called "Kozelskaia Optina", NG]', thus indicating the special role of the Optina hermitage in the renaissance of hesychasm and the related institution of elderhood (PSS XIV, 26). Reference is then made to the three renowned elders of Optina: 'there have been three elders in succession, and Zosima was the last of them': Zosima is thus explicitly placed within the tradition of the Optina elders and is from the start surrounded with their charisma (PSS XIV, 26). The narrator then overtly talks about the popularity of the elders and their historical status of seemingly posing a threat to the established church, thereby also mentioning the church's suspicious and even hostile reaction to them:

> It [the monastery, NG] throve and became renowned all over Russia because of its elders, to whom pilgrims thronged in their multitudes for thousands of versts from all across the land [...] That is why in a large number of our Russian monasteries elderhood was initially met with what almost amounted to persecution. At the same time the elders immediately began to acquire a high degree of respect among the common people. To the elders of our monastery, for example, there thronged both simple people and the most learned, with the purpose of submitting to them, of confessing before them their doubts, their sins, their sufferings, and ask them for counsel and teaching (PSS XIV, 27).

Tolstoi also places Father Sergius – though much more briefly than Dostoevskii – explicitly in the tradition of the Optina elders. When Sergius – whose secular name is Kasatskii – enters monastic life, the abbot of his first monastery is a 'starets', 'who was a disciple of the famous starets Amvrosii, who was a disciple of Makarii, who was a disciple of starets Leonid, who was a disciple of Paisii Velichkovskii' (SS X, 346).[22]

The *zhitiia* of Sergius and Zosima can be compared on both a stylistic and thematic level. Let us first start with the stylistic embedding of both fictional elders. Both Zosima and Sergius are placed in a narrative setting that hints at and is demarcated by the rich medieval tradition of hagiographical literature; in the second half of the nineteenth century, there was in Russian secular circles a renewed interest in medieval religious literature, which emerged in part from a growing frustration with the secularized and westernized church. To compensate for the loss of spirituality in the official church and to create a counterweight against the ever more popular atheist and nihilist theories, many intellectuals looked back at medieval Russia and attempted to restore this heritage in Russian culture. The genre of Russian hagiography became a new source of inspiration for writers, philosophers and painters alike, who took an original and creative approach to this genre. Some, like Nikolai Leskov, adapted a series of medieval hagiographies (from the so-called *Prologue*) to the nineteenth-century context, and chose to depict in particular those saints that challenged church authorities; others, like Alexander Herzen, played with hagiographical themes in a new narratological context.[23]

Both Dostoevskii and Tolstoi were inspired in the creation of their elders by the medieval tradition of hagiographical literature. Both diverge markedly, however, in their approach to and handling of the hagiographical genre. To start with, there is a conspicuous difference between the composition of Zosima's and Sergius' life. Zosima's *zhitie* is – consistent with the typical composition of a *vita* – split up in two parts: 1) his biography, entitled *From the Life of the Departed in God the Hieroschemonach the Elder Zosima, collated from his own words by Aleksei Fedorovich Karamazov*; and 2) his teachings, *From the Discourses and Teachings of the Elder Zosima*. His biography – again according to traditional hagiographies – consists of three conversion stories. The first one relates the spiritual transformation of Zosima's brother Markel, a consumptive freethinker who regains his belief in face of his impending death. The second conversion story is that of Zosima himself: Zosima – his secular

---

22 Since Sergius lived in the time of Nicholas I, this is chronologically impossible: Amvrosii was the elder of Optina between 1860 and 1891. See Kolstø, p. 550.

23 For a discussion of the reworking of the hagiographical genre by nineteenth-century writers, see Margaret Ziolkowski, *Hagiography and Modern Russian Literature*, Princeton University Press, Princeton, 1988.

name is Zinovii – was an army officer who prided himself on 'drunkenness, debauchery and devilry' (PSS XIV, 268). He provokes a romantic rival into a duel, but, the day before the duel is to take place, he undergoes a spiritual transformation: after violently lashing out at his servant Afanasii in uncontrolled anger, Zosima suddenly remembers Markel's message of active love and moral responsibility for each other. He shows repentance for all his former acts of misbehaviour and inflicting suffering upon others, resigns from military service and enters monastic life. The third conversion story is that of the mysterious visitor, who confesses a murder to Zosima. These conversion stories are typical *hagiographical topoi*: they serve to show the reader that each sinner – even a murderer – can come to repentance and turn towards the good. As such, these stories illustrate Zosima's moral sermons in the second part of the *zhitie*, and, on a broader level, function to epitomize the underlying message of the whole novel, that each human being has the potential for spiritual rebirth.

The *zhitie* of Sergius, by contrast, lacks the typical hagiographical composition: it reads more like a *Bildungsroman*, in which attention is drawn to the psychological transitions he undergoes in his development towards a *starets*, rather than to the content of his teachings. Put briefly, *Father Sergius* is the story of a very ambitious young man, Prince Stepan Kasatskii, who abandons a promising military career to become a monk, after he discovers that his fiancée has been the mistress of Nicholas I. But, as it turns out, monastic life is marked by numerous worldly temptations. His monastic career begins as a simple monk in a cenobitic monastery, but, after a conflict with his abbot, his elder commands him to adopt the solitary life-style of a hermit. After some time, he is declared an elder and becomes famous for his gift of healing and miracle-working powers. His fame spreads and attracts hordes of pilgrims, who come from afar to receive his advice or blessing. But throughout his whole career as *starets*, he is in a constant struggle between his worldly ambitions and the spiritual expectations that are connected to his position as a *starets*. On two occasions, his chastity is put to the test. The first time, he is tempted by the widow Makovkina; he only is able to resist the temptation by chopping off his finger. The second temptation comes from a simple and feeble-minded merchant's daughter, Maria; overcome by lust, he gives in this time. The next day, he puts on peasant's clothes, cuts his hair and leaves the monastery in shame. Only then, by withdrawing from monastic life and living like a *strannik* or wanderer in Christ, he finds true spiritual fulfillment. The story of Sergius breaks off here, there is no supplement that describes his teachings, as in Zosima's *zhitie*. The detailed psychological analysis of Sergius' sufferings, torments and motivation stands in sharp contrast to the shroud of mystery surrounding Zosima's spiritual development. A diary entry from June

1890 shows that Tolstoi envisioned the story first and foremost as a vehicle to analyze Sergius' psychology: 'My entire interest is in the psychological stages that Father Sergius passes through'.[24]

Dostoevskii's intentions were clearly different: he wanted to create a credible saint, or, in his words 'a pure, ideal Christian', because this image would be the only sufficient counterweight against Ivan's atheism in book five:

> This [book six, NG] is not a sermon, but more like a story, a tale about actual life. If it succeeds, I shall have done something good: I will make people realize that the pure, ideal Christian is not an abstract matter, but is figuratively real and possible, and stands before our very eyes, and that Christianity is for the Russian Land the only shelter for all her ills (PSS XXX, 1, 68).

Dostoevskii deliberately embedded his fictional elder in the hagiographical tradition to underscore the seriousness of his teachings. In one of his letters to the editor of *The Russian Herald*, in which *The Brothers Karamazov* was published in serial form, he stated that 'I have taken his character and figure [Zosima's, NG] from Old Russian monks and saints' (PSS XXX, 102). Bakhtin explicitly labels Dostoevskii's portrayal and description of Zosima as 'hagiographical discourse' (*житийное слово*): it was his purpose to create within the polyphony of the novel a setting in which Zosima would be able to convey an authoritative word without being interrupted by the words of the other characters.[25] The authoritative status of Zosima's word is further established by its special embedding in the narrative: book six is cast in the form of a *zhitie* as written down by his disciple Alesha on the basis of previous conversations with the elder. Through this procedure, Zosima's sayings, which were initially part of a dialogue, are now expressed in the form of a monologue, which reinforces his message, since it is no longer disturbed by the comments or objections of others. In addition, in order to emphasize the credibility of his fictional saint, Dostoevskii copied the naive and sentimental style of hagiographical literature and adopted various rhetorical strategies that are typical of this genre. For instance, Zosima frequently addresses the readers, a procedure that makes his *zhitie* look like an oral narrative, thus embedding it in the medieval tradition of transmitting saint's lives orally. He speaks in a somewhat

---

24   *Dnevniki 1847–1894*, in L. N. Tolstoi, 1978–1985, XXI, p. 429.
25   Mikhail Bakhtin, *Problems of Dostoevsky's Poetics*, edited and translated by Caryl Emerson, introduction by Wayne C. Booth, Manchester University Press, Manchester, 1984, p. 248.

archaic Russian that is full of Church Slavonic words; a lot of sentences start with 'and', and he uses a lot of imperatives, all formulas that are characteristic of hagiographical discourse.

The sincere hagiographical style of Zosima's *zhitie* is in sharp contrast to the style of Sergius' life, which drips with irony most emphatically. Whereas Dostoevskii intentionally copied hagiographical style and *topoi* to underline the saintliness of his *starets*, Tolstoi chose to overturn typical hagiographical *topoi* in order to undermine the saintly status of Sergius. In medieval hagiographical literature, *topoi* were used as types of universal markers that, first, imply the hero's saintliness, and, second, are guidelines for moral conduct. Tolstoi inserts many of these *topoi* in the life of Sergius, but instigates a break with their traditional underlying meaning by revealing to the reader how in Sergius' life there is a gap between *topos* or outward behaviour, and inward motivation. The *topoi* in Sergius' life are no more than fixed forms of hagiographical outward behaviour and are in sharp contrast to his inner psychology.[26] Tolstoi subtly lays bare the fact that, in spite of his outward appearance as a saint, Sergius is in reality – just as he was in his secular life – driven by feelings of ambition and the desire to be applauded by others. Already from the start of Sergius' *zhitie*, the reader is directed to be aware that outward behaviour and inward motivation do not correspond. As in traditional hagiographies, Sergius / Kasatskii already in his youth and childhood is portrayed as excelling in personality and high moral character: 'the boy distinguished himself by his brilliant capacities [...] he did not drink, did not lead a dissolute life, and was remarkably truthful' (SS X, 340). He is portrayed as generous and faithful to his beliefs. However, this image is immediately undercut by revealing his true motive for his outstanding conduct: 'essentially, he had but one striving, this was to attain perfection and success in all matters that he took up, and evoke praise and admiration from the people [...] this striving to distinguish himself [...] filled his whole life' (SS X, 342). Also, the young Kasatskii has a furious temper that often gets him into trouble. His extreme self-love does not disappear once he sets out on the religious path. His motivation for entering monastic life is far from pious: deeply offended by the betrayal of his fiancée, he becomes a monk to show those who mock him that he is morally above them. His sister senses his real motivation for becoming a monk: 'she

---

26 Margaret Ziolkowski's article 'Hagiographical Motifs in Tolstoy's *Father Sergius*' was a great source of inspiration for this topic. For a more detailed analysis of Tolstoi's use of hagiographical *topoi*, see this article, in *South Atlantic Review*, XLVII, 2, May 1982, pp. 63–80.

understood that he had become a monk in order to be above those who considered themselves his superior' (ss x, 346). It soon becomes clear that the pride and competitive nature that were his main drives in the world have not been extinguished by his becoming a monk. As in his secular life, he is mainly driven by the ambition to outsmart his fellow monks: 'Here in the monastery, besides the feeling of ascendancy over others that such a life gave him, he felt much as he had done in the world: he found satisfaction in attaining the greatest possible perfection outwardly as well as inwardly' (ss x, 346). His vanity inevitably crops up when reflecting on his career as a *starets*: 'He was often amazed that this had happened, that he, Stepan Kasatskii, had come to be such an extraordinary saint and even a worker of miracles […] people come to me from a thousand versts, they write about it in the papers, the Emperor knows me, and they even know me in Europe, where they do not believe' (ss x, 369–70). In Sergius' *zhitie*, Tolstoi uses hagiographical *topoi*, not – like the traditional hagiographer – to underline the saintliness of his hero, but, on the contrary, to break intentionally with the hagiographical pattern of expectations and unmask Sergius' profane motivation.

In addition to the significantly different use of hagiographical devices, Dostoevskii and Tolstoi also diverge in their thematic portrayal of *starchestvo*, and its framing in the ecclesiastical context.

In Zosima's *zhitie* the institution of the church is notably absent: it has already been noted by other scholars that the traditional practices of the church, its liturgy, rituals and sacraments play only a minor, as it were insignificant, role in Zosima's biography and teachings.[27] His first and later steps in monastic life are recounted without any reference to priests or church practices. He even takes a daring critical position towards the contemporary clergy for their complaints about their small income and unwillingness to perform their duties (PSS XIV, 265). In sum, Dostoevskii's Zosima functions already from the start of his life as an elder largely outside of the strictly clerical realm, and conveys a monastic ideal that is separate from the official church; he is rather the spokesman of a very personalistic interpretation of Russian orthodoxy.[28] Instead of placing God in the church, Zosima finds Him in the whole of

---

27   See, amongst others, Sergei Hackel, 'The Religious Dimension: Vision or Evasion? Zosima's Discourse in *The Brothers Karamazov*', in Malcolm V. Jones and Garth M. Terry, eds, *New Essays on Dostoyevsky*, Cambridge University Press, Cambridge, 1983, pp. 139–68.
28   For my interpretation of Zosima's religious views, see, my 'Dostoevskij's Portrait of a "Pure, Ideal Christian": Echoes of Nil Sorskij in the Elder Zosima', *Russian Literature*, LXVII, 2, 2010, pp. 185–216.

nature and all living creatures. His teachings are infused with a strong dimension of nature mysticism: 'Brothers, love the whole of creation, both the whole and each grain of sand. Each leaf, each sunbeam of God, love it. Love the animals, love the plants, love everything in nature. If you love everything in nature, you will perceive the mystery of God' (PSS XIV, 289).

The mystical pantheism in Zosima's sermons is unorthodox for a 'Russian monk' and provoked – right from the publication of book six – much controversy in clerical circles.[29] Furthermore, at the core of Zosima's teachings is a message of mutual moral responsibility and an appeal for active love (*деятельная любовь*: PSS XIV, 292), which seems to compensate for the loss of social engagement in the Russian secularized church. The controversial status of Zosima's function is further highlighted in book seven, which describes the atmosphere in the monastery after Zosima's death: contrary to the anticipation that Zosima's body will be miraculously immune against the natural laws of decomposition and that this will prove his saintly status, a putrid smell emerges from the body. The rotting of Zosima's body is received with mocking glee by the opponents of the *starets*. A real scandal breaks out at the coffin of the deceased, which reveals the 'old ingrained hostility' towards the institution of *starchestvo*, a hostility still deeply rooted in the minds of many brethren in the monastery:

> For although the departed elder had drawn many to his side, and not so much by miracles as by love, and had erected around him almost an entire world of those who loved him, he had nevertheless and, even perhaps because of this, brought into being those who envied him, and, in the time that followed also bitter enemies, both open and concealed, and not among the monastics only, but even among the secular (PSS XIV, 299).[30]

---

29 Sergius displays a very different attitude to nature, Immediately before he succumbs to the second temptation, a sparrow hops towards him, but suddenly, 'frightened of something', flies away. Just minutes later, he crushes a beetle that crept up the back of his neck (SS X, 369–70). Both incidents not only represent the opposite of Zosima's pantheism, but also, in a broader context, are a reversal of a common hagiographical *topos* which stresses the close connection between saint and nature. Sergius' namesake, Sergius of Radonezh, for example, lived in harmony with the wild animals in the forests in which he had settled. The fictional Sergius' relationship with animals is not incidental: it reveals the falseness and artificiality of his saintliness and unmasks his petty, all too human nature.

30 Dostoevskii copied this scene and the controversy surrounding elderhood from the *zhitie* of *starets* Leonid, written by Kliment Zedergol'm: *Elder Leonid of Optina*, St Herman of Alaska Brotherhood (Optina Elders Series), Platina, CA, 1990.

Tolstoi's fictional *starets*, on the other hand, is portrayed as having a relationship with the clerical establishment, and this will be an important cause for his moral decay and final break with traditional *starchestvo*. His life as an elder is juxtaposed with his life in the world: there is a similar rule of conduct that allows him to be driven by the same desire for recognition of others and pride, that were also his main motivations in his life in the world. Tolstoi gives us a profane and disturbing picture of monastic life: at the beginning of his career – the process of becoming a *starets* is indeed described as a career – Sergius is soon irritated by the crowds of visitors that overrun the monastery, by the monotony of the numerous church services, and by the moral flaws of his fellow monks. He is only able to bear these annoyances by submitting himself to the monastic rule of obedience:

> If many of the demands of life in the monastery [...] did not please him and were temptations to him, they were all nullified by obedience: 'it is not my duty to reason, it is my task to carry out the obedience set for me, be that standing beside the relics, singing in the choir or doing the accounts in the monastery guest-house [...] I don't know why it is necessary to hear the same prayers several times a day, but I know, that it is necessary' (SS X, 347).

After some years, he is mentally worn out by the daily routine of the church and prayer services, to the point that he starts regretting his decision to become a monk. Sergius is then sent to a new monastery, whose abbot is a very worldly figure, driven by sensual and opportunist desires. The abbot makes no secret of his ambition to turn the monastery into some kind of fashionable attraction; this monastery is popular with women, who shamelessly flirt with the monks. Sergius has great difficulty in controlling himself from giving in to these temptations. Much later in his career, after he achieved much fame as a *starets*, he realizes that he has become a bait to attract financial contributors to the monastery: a church and hostelry is built close to his cell to accommodate rich visitors and 'the monastic authorities arranged matters in such a way as to make as much use of him as possible' (SS X, 363). His inner life is wasted away and absorbed by outward rituals and meetings with visitors: he feels that 'the source of living water had dried up in him, and that what he did, he did more and more for the people, and not for God' (SS X, 364). Although they attempt to cloak their true motives in the guise of Christian charity, the monastic authorities are only driven by mere greed. In this description of monastic life Tolstoi's hostility towards the ecclesiastical establishment emerges very clearly. Tolstoi's fictional *starets* only discovers true Christian feelings after his escape from the monastery. After he has yielded to the seduction of the merchant's simple daughter Maria, he leaves the monastery and takes up an entirely new religious path, that of a *strannik* or a wanderer in Christ. Only in this calling, at the end of his life, does Sergius – who has resumed his secular name Kasatskii – finally find peace of mind and spiritual fulfillment. The true Christian path is shown to him by a woman whom he knows from his childhood, Pashenka, who appears to him in a dream at a moment of existential despair (when he contemplates suicide). He decides to visit her, and finds an aged woman who has had a hard and unfortunate life: she was married to a violent man, her son died, her daughter is married to an alcoholic and they are in a very poor financial state. Yet, this simple and unfortunate woman instigates Sergius' salvation. Pashenka, a lay woman who even excuses herself for hardly ever attending church services, embodies the Christian spirit that has been lacking in Sergius' role as a *starets*: 'Pashenka is exactly what I should have been, and what I was not. I lived for the people, on the pretext of living for God, while she lives for God, imagining that she lives for the people' (SS X, 379).

Pashenka's moral touchstone is an instinctive feeling of goodness, humility and complete self-sacrifice for the well-being of others. Sergius, by contrast, has been driven by the narcissistic ambition to gain recognition and praise from others. Pashenka's self-effacement and humility become Sergius' new religious ideal. He now understands that seeking admiration corrupts one's moral character: 'yes, there is no God for the man who lives, as I did, for human praise'. He becomes, in his own words, 'a servant of God' ('*раб божий*': SS X, 379–80). After this 'epiphany', Sergius chooses to disappear into anonymity: he is arrested for not having a passport, refuses to reveal his identity and is sent to Siberia, where he teaches children and cares for the sick on the estate of a rich peasant. The break with his former life – both in his secular and monastic career – in which he was driven by his pride and desire for recognition, is complete: he has no name, no particular professional or social status, and devotes himself entirely to others.

The story of Father Sergius should obviously be read against the background of Tolstoi's views on religion after his conversion. True Christianity, he now believed, can only be attained when one strives for moral self-perfection on the basis of Christ's law of love, as set out in the Sermon on the Mount. It is not to be found in the church, which has corrupted Christ's authentic words, but in the common Russian people, epitomized in the image of the Russian *muzhik*. Both Zosima and Sergius eventually concur in the fact that for them true Christian feelings are separate from the established church.

Before concluding, it is interesting to note that, in Tolstoi's mind, Optina was always in some way linked to Dostoevskii's portrayal of it. Not long before his final and fateful flight to the hermitage in October 1910, Tolstoi started reading *The Brothers Karamazov*. He mentions Zosima in a diary entry of 19 October, just nine days before he was at Optina.[31] In spite of the undeniable attraction Dostoevskii's fictional elder held for him, he depicted *starchestvo* in a very different way, clearly motivated by his own religious and ideological agenda.

Although quite different in their Christian positions, Dostoevskii and Tolstoi were fascinated by the Optina elders for similar reasons: the elders represented for both of them a counterweight against the rigid and formalized church. Whereas Dostoevskii held elderhood in high esteem, Tolstoi's impressions of it were more ambivalent. This is reflected in their fictional representation of it. Dostoevskii deliberately embedded Zosima in the form of a hagiography to give extra spiritual weight to his teachings; the naïve and elevated style of Zosima's *zhitie* is in sharp contrast to the realistic and profane style of the story of Sergius. Whereas Dostoevskii used hagiographical *topoi* to underscore his portrayal of his 'pure, ideal Christian', Tolstoi used these *topoi* only to reveal the inconsistencies between Sergius' outward behaviour and his inner psychology. Dostoevskii thus gives an idealized picture of *starchestvo*, whereas Tolstoi's depiction of it is almost naturalistic. Zosima, from the very beginning, is portrayed as being separate from, and taking a critical position towards, the ecclesiastical authorities. In Dostoevskii's interpretation and description, *starchestvo* is thus an institution that thrives largely outside of the official church: it represents a brand of spirituality and a concern with the common folk that he missed in the secularized church. Although Tolstoi also values *starchestvo* for its independent status within the church, he finds that – evidently in the light of his growing conflict with the ecclesiastical authorities – it is still too closely connected to it. The irony of Sergius' life is that, in his official position as a *starets*, he is hindered, both by his ambitious nature and the monastic environment, from reaching the spiritual and moral state of mind that is traditionally expected from an Optina elder; Sergius only becomes a true Christian – in Tolstoian terms – after he breaks with the ecclesiastical establishment. Tolstoi's depiction of elderhood reflects the ambivalence in his viewpoint of it: on the one hand, he does portray elderhood as an institution that can guide people in their spiritual development; on the other hand, by

---

31   *Dnevniki 1895–1910*, in L. N. Tolstoi, 1978–1985, XXII, p. 409. Two days before his departure, Tolstoi noted in his diary that he had a dream in which Grushenka had a romance with Nikolai Strakhov. See Stanton, p. 210. Stanton wonders whether Tolstoi's plan to go to Optina prompted him to take up Dostoevskii's final novel, or *vice versa*, whether his reading of *The Brothers Karamazov* gave him the idea to go to Optina.

unmasking the psychological torments and moral pitfalls of it, he reduces its spiritual splendour. For Tolstoi, real spiritual elderhood can only be effective in a context that cuts off all ties with the established church. Is it not then remarkable – or, we might even say, ironic – that, at the end of his life and even more so after his death, Tolstoi himself was frequently called a *starets*? In his obituary article, 'In front of Tolstoi's coffin' ('Перед гробом Толстого'), Rozanov called Tolstoi 'a great elder' ('великий старец').[32] Tolstoi's biographer Troyat even entitles him 'the lay equivalent of starets Ambrose'.[33] As such, Tolstoi, although unintentionally, fulfilled his own ideal of *starchestvo*.

Bibliography

Bakhtin, Mikhail, *Problems of Dostoevsky's Poetics*, ed. and trans. Emerson, Caryl, Manchester University Press, Manchester, 1984.

Chetverikov, Sergius, *Elder Ambrose of Optina*, translated from the Russian edition, *Opisanie zhizni blazhennoi pamiati Optinskago startsa Amvrosia* (1912), St Herman of Alaska Brotherhood, Platina, CA, 1997 (first published 1912), p. 290.

Chetverikov, Sergius, *Optina Pustyn'*, YMCA Press, Paris, 1926.

Dostoevskaia, Anna Grigor'evna, *Vospominaniia*, Khudozhestvennaia literature, Moscow, 1971.

Dostoevskii, F.M., *Polnoe sobranie sochinenii v tridtsati tomakh*, Nauka, Leningrad, 1972–1990, XXX.

Dostoyevsky, Fyodor, *The Brothers Karamazov*, translated with an introduction and notes by McDuff, David, Penguin Books, 2003.

Dunlop, John B., *Staretz Amvrosy: Model for Dostoevsky's Staretz Zossima*, Nordland Publishing Company, Belmont, Mass., 1972, p. 59.

Grillaert, Nel, 'Dostoevskij's Portrait of a "Pure, Ideal Christian": Echoes of Nil Sorskij in the Elder Zosima', *Russian Literature*, LXVII, 2, 2010, pp. 185–216.

Gusev, N.N., *Lev Nikolaevich Tolstoi: materialy k biografii s 1870 po 1881 god*, Akademiia nauk, Moscow, 1963.

Hackel, Sergei 'The Religious Dimension: Vision or Evasion? Zosima's Discourse in *The Brothers Karamazov*', in Jones, Malcolm V. and Terry, Garth M,. eds, *New Essays on Dostoyevsky*, Cambridge University Press, Cambridge, 1983, pp. 139–68.

---

32 Quoted in Henrietta Mondry, *Vasily Rozanov and The Body of Russian Literature*, Slavica Publishers, Bloomington, Indiana, 2010, p. 125.

33 See Troyat, p. 652. Two years after Tolstoi's death, Iakov Protazanov – who was the first director to adapt *Father Sergius* for the screen in 1917 – directed a short film about Tolstoi's last days, and gave it the title *The Departure of the Great Elder* (*Уход Великого Старца*).

Kolstø, Pål, 'The Elder at Iasnaia Poliana: Lev Tolstoi and the Orthodox *Starets* Tradition', *Kritika: Explorations in Russian and Eurasian History*, IX, 3, Summer 2008, pp. 533–54.

Kontsevich, I.M., *Optina Pustyn' i ee vremia*, Holy Trinity Monastery, Jordanville, New York, 1970.

Kotel'nikov, Vladimir, *Pravoslavnye podvizhniki i russkaia literatura: na puti k Optinoi*, Progress-Pleiada, Moscow, 2002, pp. 321–32.

Lebedev, V.K., 'Otryvok iz romana *Brat'ia Karamazovy* pered sudom tsenzury,' *Russkaia literatura*, 2, 1970, pp. 123–5.

Maloney, George A., *Russian Hesychasm: The Spirituality of Nil Sorskij*, Mouton, The Hague, 1973.

Mondry, Henrietta *Vasily Rozanov and The Body of Russian Literature*, Slavica Publishers, Bloomington, Indiana, 2010.

Rozanov, V.V., *Religiia, Filosofiia, Kul'tura*, Nikoliukin, A.N., ed., Respublika, Moscow, 1992.

Stanton, Leonard, *The Optina Pustyn Monastery in the Russian Literary Imagination: Iconic Vision in Works by Dostoevsky, Gogol, Tolstoy and Others*, Peter Lang, Middlebury Studies in Russian Language and Literature, New York, 1995, pp. 203–28.

Tolstoi, Lev Nikolaevich, *Sobranie sochinenii v dvenadtsati tomakh*, X, Khudozhestvennaia literatura, Moscow, 1975.

Tolstoi, L.N., *Sobranie sochinenii v dvadtsati dvukh tomakh*, M.B. Khrapchenko et al., eds, Khudozhestvennaia literatura, Moscow, 1978–85.

Tolstoy, Graf Leo, *Father Sergius*, trans. Maude, Louise and Maude, Aylmer, Project Gutenberg, http://www.gutenberg.org/ebooks/985.

Troyat, Henri, *Tolstoy*, Amphoux Nancy, trans., Penguin Books, Harmondsworth, 1980.

Zedergol'm, Kliment, *Elder Leonid of Optina*, St Herman of Alaska Brotherhood (Optina Elders Series), Platina, CA, 1990.

Ziolkowski, Margaret, 'Hagiographical Motifs in Tolstoy's *Father Sergius*', *South Atlantic Review*, LXVII, 2, May 1982, pp. 63–80.

Ziolkowski, Margaret, *Hagiography and Modern Russian Literature*, Princeton University Press, Princeton, 1988.

CHAPTER 5

Tolstoi and Lidiia Veselitskaia's *Mimi at the Spa*: The *Fin de Siècle* Tourist Adulteress

Susan Layton

Abstract

While moral and spiritual values are never far from the surface in Tolstoi's works, their settings and topoi often owe much to pre-existing literary templates. One of these is the 'society tale' which centres on the lives of genteel characters in a given social setting. A favoured setting is the spa, an early example of which is found in Lermontov's *Princess Mary*. This chapter explores the contrasts between Tolstoi's treatment of this theme (in, for instance, *Family Happiness* and *Anna Karenina*) and Veselitskaia's presentation of it in *Mimi at the Spa* (1891). Tolstoi admired this work which creatively engaged with his own treatments of such themes as femininity, marriage, adultery, and the disorienting potential of travel. However, he viewed vacations taken for pleasure in a negative light – Anna and Vronskii's time in Italy being an example – whereas Veselitskaia avoids moralizing. She also modernizes the travel story to depict the destination's potential for broadening an individual's horizons, and developing the character, rather than for flirtation and seduction. In this, she anticipates (via the character Vava) Soviet notions of the wholesome effects of vacation, whereas the protagonist, Mimi, represents the comfort-loving bourgeois type Soviet tourist officials sought to root out.

Keywords

Lidiia Veselitskaia – *Mimi at the Spa* – the 'vacation' as a literary theme in Tolstoi's work

Tolstoi was among the many late nineteenth-century admirers of Lidiia Veselitskaia's *Mimi at the Spa* (Мимочка на водах, 1891), the vacation adultery story that brought the author literary celebrity.[1] Born into a noble military

---

[1] A portion of this chapter appears in the author's *Contested Russian Tourism: Cosmopolitanism, Nation, and Empire in the Nineteenth Century*, Academic Studies Press, Boston, MA, 2021.

family in 1857 in Riazan province, Veselitskaia took teacher-training courses in Pavlovsk and St Petersburg.[2] Soon after graduating in 1874, she married a Russian army officer. The marriage ended in divorce, as had her own parents' union, and those experiences of marital strife would find reflection in her fiction. Published in 1877, Veselitskaia's first literary efforts were short tales for young readers. Then in 1883, her story *Mimi the Bride* (*Мимочка – невеста*) appeared in the prestigious *Herald of Europe* (*Вестник Европы*) under the pseudonym V. Mikulich. Following the international success of *Mimi at the Spa*, Veselitskaia-Mikulich produced the sequel, *Mimi Has Taken Poison* (*Мимочка отравилась*, 1893), to comprise the *Mimi* trilogy.[3] Tolstoi found the spa story so impressive that he initiated a correspondence with Veselitskaia in 1892 after obtaining her address from Aleksei Suvorin. Tolstoi established a mentor relationship to her. From the first, he found her a 'very intelligent and serious woman', a 'sensitive woman', and he enlisted her as a translator for his Intermediary press.[4] Between 1893 and 1905, Veselitskaia visited the Tolstois several times at Iasnaia Poliana or at their home in Moscow, and she became friendly with Tolstoi's wife and daughters Tatiana and Maria. In 1913 Veselitskaia would reverently recall how Tolstoi had offered her advice about writing and conversed with her about literature, the arts, and religion.[5] Tolstoi's views strongly influenced her collections of stories of 1911, 1914 and 1915. While dealing primarily with the suffering of the Russian proletariat, those included tales of adultery on the Grand Tour circuit ('In Venice', 'In Florence'). Veselitskaia subsequently published translations of French literature and memoirs of meetings with Dostoevskii and other Russian writers. She died alone in poverty in 1936 in Tsarskoe selo (now Pushkin).

The entire *Mimi* trilogy creatively interacts with Tolstoi's treatments of femininity, marriage, adultery, and the disorienting potential of travel. *Mimi the*

---

2   For the biographical details, see Olga Demidova and Mary Zirin, 'Lidiia Ivanovna Veselitskaia', in *Dictionary of Russian Women Writers*, Marina Ledkovsky, Charlotte Rosenthal, and Mary Zirin, eds, Greenwood Press, Westport, Conn., 1994, p. 705.

3   *Mimochka – nevesta. Ocherk*, in *Vestnik Evropy*, September 1883, pp. 5–30; *Mimochka na vodakh. Ocherk*, ibid., February 1891, pp. 526–68 and March 1891, pp. 30–60; and *Mimochka otravilas'. Ocherk*, ibid., September 1893, pp. 112–40 and October 1893, pp. 417–54.

4   L.N. Tolstoi, *Polnoe sobranie sochinenii*, 90 vols, Khudozhestvennaia literatura, Moscow 1928–58, letters to E.I. Popov, 13 May 1893; and to L.L. and M.L. Tolstaia, 15 May 1893, 66, pp. 316, 323.

5   V. Mikulich, 'Ten' proshlogo', *Istoricheskii vestnik*, CXXXI, February 1913, pp. 362–83; March 1913, pp. 778–813; and 132, April 1913, pp. 41–81. On such mentor relationships in the Silver Age, see Charlotte Rosenthal, 'Carving out a Career: Women Prose Writers, 1885–1917', in *Gender and Russian Literature. New Perspectives*, Rosalind Marsh, ed., Cambridge University Press, Cambridge, 1996, pp. 133–5.

Bride traces the heroine's life from childhood up to the age of twenty when a financial disaster in her Petersburg high-society family forces her to marry Spiridon Ivanovich, a well-to-do but oafish, fat, balding general 'no longer young'.[6] *Mimi at the Spa* finds the heroine weary of marriage and motherhood.[7] She follows her doctor's advice to go to the Caucasus for a cure, a journey she makes by train. At the spa she has an affair with Valerian Nikolaevich, a rich married man of thirty-five. In the short run, the affair causes Mimi no suffering. However, in *Mimi Has Taken Poison* she has become a confirmed adulteress and attempts suicide when her children's French tutor breaks off their affair to marry another Russian woman. Unlike Emma Bovary, Mimi survives, apparently doomed to a dreary life with her husband.[8] This third tale lacks the sly irony, the thematic coherence, and the structural elegance of the round-trip spa vacation story. Nonetheless, thanks primarily to the first two narratives, the *Mimi* trilogy succeeds in painting what Mirsky called 'a witty picture of the average *jeune fille* of Petersburg bureaucratic society – the incarnation of placid futility'.[9]

The present study of *Mimi at the Spa* centres on the Tolstoian depiction of adultery as a danger for the unsupervised woman traveller. How did Veselitskaia update Tolstoian travel concerns in the 1890s when a commercialized 'idea of a vacation' had become pervasive among the Russian bourgeoisie?[10] The exploration of this problem brings to light Veselitskaia's engagement with

---

6   *Mimochka – nevesta*, p. 5.
7   *Mimi at the Spa* was reprinted with *Mimi the Bride* prior to Veseltskaia's writing the third story: see commentary in V. Mikulich [Lidiia Veselitskaia], *Mimochka*, Eksmo, Moscow, 2003, p. 283. On the contemporary readership's avid interest in sex, see Peter Ulf Møller, Postlude to The Kreutzer Sonata. *Tolstoj and the Debate on Sexual Morality in Russian Literature in the 1890s*, John Kenda, trans., Brill, Leiden, 1988, pp. xi-xviii, 92–162; and Laura Engelstein, *The Keys to Happiness: Sex and the Search for Modernity in Fin de Siècle Russia*, Cornell University Press, Ithaca, 1992, pp. 218–32.
8   On suicide as Madame Bovary's ultimate escape, consult Susan J. Rosowski, 'The Novel of Awakening', in *The Voyage In. Fictions of Female Development*, Elizabeth Abel, Marianne Hirsch and Elizabeth Langland, eds, University Press of New England for Dartmouth College, Hanover and London, 1983, p. 52.
9   D. S. Mirsky, *A History of Russian Literature from Its Beginnings to 1900*, Vintage, New York, 1958, p. 352.
10 Quotation from Louise McReynolds, 'The Prerevolutionary Russian Tourist: Commercialization in the Nineteenth Century', in *Turizm. The Russian and East European Tourist under Capitalism and Socialism*, Anne E. Gorsuch and Diane P. Koenker, eds, Cornell University Press, Ithaca, 2006, pp. 17–42 (39). On the emergence of a Russian 'consumer market' for tourism in the 1880s, see also Christopher Ely, 'The Origins of Russian Scenery: Volga River Tourism and Russian Landscape Aesthetics', *Slavic Review*, LXII, 4, 2003, pp. 666–82 (675).

Anna Karenina, Tolstoi's novel of adultery associated with the railroad. The dialogue with *Anna Karenina* offers a rather obvious yet productive line of analysis that previous commentators have neglected. Peter Ulf Møller mentioned *Mimi at the Spa* as one of many marital problem stories of the time related to *The Kreutzer Sonata*. As Møller put it, Veselitskaia assessed upper-class Russian 'sexual morality from a basically Tolstoian position', while refraining from moralizing.[11] My chapter concurs with that view, yet reveals the more pervasive resonance of *Anna Karenina* rather than *The Kreutzer Sonata* not only in *Mimi at the Spa* but in Veselitskaia's whole trilogy.

Along with the Tolstoi connections, *Mimi at the Spa* also engages with the *Princess Mary* episode of *A Hero of Our Time*. As Olga Demidova and Mary Zirin remarked, Valerian's seduction of Mimi parodies the Pechorin-Princess Mary relationship.[12] More generally, we should add, Veselitskaia stands in continuity with Lermontov's elaboration of the 'chronotope of the spa'. A staple of the society tale genre prominent in the Romantic era, the chronotope of the spa models a place and time away from home. The cure site emerges as a more or less exotic 'parade ground' (or 'amphitheatre,' in Lermontov's term) where the *dramatis personae* recreate the social hierarchy of their quotidian realms.[13] Clothing carries semiotic weight, psychological power games unfold, and love affairs abound. In the relaxed, vacation atmosphere, naive young women elude the watchful gaze of their mothers, and worldly women change their lovers with each season, as Lermontov put it. *Mimi at the Spa* sustains those conventions.[14] However, Veselitskaia enfolds Mimi's sojourn in the Caucasus into a larger structure, the narrative of a train trip with many allusions to *Anna Karenina*.

My investigation of *Mimi at the Spa* as a *fin de siècle* vacation story that parodies *Anna Karenina* takes methodological inspiration mainly from the

---

11 See Møller, pp. 191, 227. Veselitskaia attended a public reading of *The Kreutzer Sonata* just prior to the summer of 1891, as noted in ibid. p. 97.
12 Demidova and Zirin, p. 706.
13 See Joe Andrew, 'Another Time, Another Place: Gender and the Chronotope in the Society Tale', in *The Society Tale in Russian Literature from Odoevskii to Tolstoi*, Neil Cornwell, ed., Rodopi, Amsterdam and Atlanta, 1998, pp. 127–32. In the same collection, see also Robert Reid, '*Princess Ligovskaia* and *Princess Mary*: The Society Tale Goes to the Caucasus'. pp. 49–56; and W. Gareth Jones, 'Tolstoi's Alternative Society Tales', pp. 110–12. For further discussion of the spa chronotope, consult Joe Andrew, *Narrative, Space and Gender in Russian Literature, 1846–1903*, Rodopi, Amsterdam and New York, 2007, pp. 94–6, 100–1.
14 Veselitskaia may have presumably known other examples of the genre, including Mariia Zhukova, *Self-Sacrifice (Samopozhertvovanie)*. For a translation, see Joe Andrew, ed. and trans., *Russian Women's Shorter Fiction. An Anthology, 1835–1860*, Clarendon Press, Oxford, 1996, pp. 220–71.

interdisciplinary literature on tourism. Most stimulating for this project was Shelley Baranowski's and Ellen Furlough's discussion of the modern concept of a vacation as 'getting away from it all'. In their formulation, the vacation is a round trip to a specific destination for purposes of 'recuperation and liberation from the stresses of daily life'. Liberated from work, modern vacationers often feel they are finding 'their "true" selves', now free to spend time as they like. Such travellers experience the vacation not only as a spatial displacement but as a 'time apart' conducive to experimenting with their social identity and behaving in ways they might not at home.[15] This modern concept of the vacation originated in Britain in the Romantic era, as epitomized by the often-quoted travel programme of William Hazlitt. 'We go a journey', he wrote, 'chiefly to be free of all impediments and of all inconveniences; to leave ourselves behind, much more to get rid of others ... We are not the same, but another, and perhaps more enviable individual, all the time we are out of our own country. We are lost to ourselves, as well as our friends'.[16] If not specifically reacting to Hazlitt, Tolstoi always stigmatized the escapist pursuit of leisure travel as an evasion of responsibilities and a falsification of the self, as in *Family Happiness* (Masha at Baden) and *Anna Karenina* (Kitty at the German spa, Anna and Vronskii in Italy). In a playful rather than moralistic manner, *Mimi at the Spa* extends Tolstoi in imagining the vacation as a chance to slip the domestic leash, to find 'time apart' and liberate potentials of the self frustrated at home.

In modelling Mimi as a commodity-conscious bourgeois consumer, Veselitskaia assumes a Tolstoian stance on many particulars. Those include woman as fashion plate and Romantic poetry as an incitement to lust (a salient motif

---

15 See Shelley Baranowski and Ellen Furlough, 'Introduction'. in *Being Elsewhere. Tourism, Consumer Culture, and Identity in Modern Europe and North America*, Baranowski and Furlough, eds, University of Michigan Press, Ann Arbor, 2001, pp. 4–7, 19. On tourism in relation to consumption, consult also Dean MacCannell, *The Tourist. A New Theory of the Leisure Class*, Schocken Books, New York, 1976, reprinted 1989, pp. 11, 22–3; John Urry, *Consuming Places*, Routledge, London and New York, 1995, reprinted 1997, p. 130; and Hartmut Berghoff, 'From Privilege to Commodity? Modern Tourism and the Rise of the Consumer Society', in id., Barbara Korte, Ralf Schneider and Christopher Harvie, eds, *The Making of Modern Tourism: The Cultural History of the British Experience, 1600–2000*, Palgrave, New York, 2002, pp. 164–8.

16 William Hazlitt, 'On Going a Journey' (1822), in his *Table Talk; or, Original Essays on Men and Manners*, Bell and Daldy, rev. eds, London, 1869, p. 261. On Hazlitt, see James Buzard, *The Beaten Track. European Tourism, Literature, and the Ways to 'Culture'. 1800–1918*, Oxford University Press, New York, 1993; rprt. 2001, pp. 103–4, 117; and George G. Dekker, *The Fictions of Romantic Tourism. Radcliffe, Scott, and Mary Shelley*, Stanford University Press, Stanford, 2005, pp. 26, 46, 101.

of *The Kreutzer Sonata*). Yet Veselitskaia also goes beyond Tolstoi to anticipate two modern-day cultural phenomena. First, *Mimi at the Spa* foreshadows official Soviet discourse on tourism as of the 1920s. Socialist tourism was supposed to be a politically purposeful, wholesome and often physically taxing project of self-improvement, as opposed to the 'decadent' mode of capitalist leisure travel.[17] Secondly and more up to the minute, Mimi and her fashion-hound partner in adultery in the Caucasus resemble the glamour-seeking 'new Russians' of our time. Veselitskaia situates her *fin de siècle* heroine in a 'commodified milieu' where the self is defined through consumption.[18] This dimension of the *Mimi* trilogy no doubt facilitated its entry into the post-Soviet literary marketplace in 2003 when it was reprinted in the series 'Bestsellers of Ladies' Reading.[19] *Mimi* thus stands as a fascinating case of a literary work that enjoyed great success in its time, fell into obscurity, but struck a receptive chord in Russian readers of the twenty-first century.

Each *Mimi* narrative is subtitled 'An Essay', a designation proclaiming the author's aspiration to illuminate Russian society and culture through a realistic literary lens. Such an orientation emulates Tolstoi and centres on the Tolstoian issue of feminine self-realization. Functioning as a vital prelude to the spa story, *Mimi the Bride* parodies Kitty Shcherbatskaia, to pose serious questions about a young woman's upbringing. Mimi's education is similar to Kitty's, consisting mainly of French and music lessons.[20] Both *jeunes filles* love balls; pink and white are their signature colours, and Mimi's chosen fiancé resembles Vronskii. He is a handsome guardsman with gleaming teeth, excellent French, and impeccable command of the waltz. But Mimi's carefree life

---

[17] Consult Anne E. Gorsuch and Diane P. Koenker, 'Introduction', in *Turizm*, pp. 6–8. See also Diane P. Koenker, 'Travel to Work, Travel to Play: On Russian Tourism, Travel and Leisure', *Slavic Review*, LXII, 4, 2003, pp. 657–63.

[18] Quotation from Olga Mesropova, '"The Discreet Charm of the Russian Bourgeoisie": OKsana Robski and Glamour in Russian Popular Culture', *Russian Review*, LXVIII, 1, 2009, p. 97. See also Mark Lipovetsky, 'New Russians as Culture Myth', *Russian Review*, LXII, 1, 2003, pp. 54–71. On 'emotional responses to life as commodities', see also Alexandra Smith, 'The Effacement of History, Theatricality and Postmodern Urban Fantasies in the Prose of Petruševskaja and Pelevin', *Die Welt des Slaven*, LIV, 2009, p. 54.

[19] *Mimochka* (2003). This edition lacks some material contained in the *Herald of Europe* texts. The post-Soviet editors have translated Veselitskaia's French in footnotes. In the text, however, misprints occur in French including *ge* for *je*.

[20] Veselitskaia stresses the corrupting influence of light French literature. On antecedents of that motif and the general preoccupation with woman's education, see Carolyn Jursa Ayers, '*L'éducation sentimental* or the School of Hard Knocks? The Heroine's Education in the Society Tale', pp. 162–4; and Neil Cornwell, 'Vladimir Odoevsky and the Society Tale in the 1820s and 1830s', pp. 9–20, both in *Society Tale*.

falls apart when her father dies under the shadow of financial scandal. Mimi's *maman* is left saddled with debts, Mimi has no dowry, and her fiancé abandons her. Time passes. No other suitors come forth, and Mimi begins wasting away.

In seeking a solution to Mimi's predicament, mama makes plain her role in producing a consumer daughter. What is abandoned Mimi to do? Marriage to a rich man is the only future she, her mother, and aunts can conceive. After all, Mimi has acquired a taste for *chocolat mignon* (chocolate dainties), expensive clothes and accessories purchased at the finest stores. As she and her female relatives see it, she *needs* those things. Moreover, in mama's view, Mimi is perfectly qualified for wifehood because she knows 'how to spend money, how to dress, and how to behave in society'.[21] Mimi's consumer skills turn her into a commodity. Through mama's eyes, Veselitskaia models Mimi as a trophy on the marriage market where 'rich old bachelors' shop for young wives, to 'buy' them as 'property'.[22] In such terms, the bourgeois wife emerges as a 'ceremonial consumer of goods' that provide evidence of her husband's 'wealth and dominance in a social hierarchy of invidious distinction'.[23] This vision of woman as a chattel-consumer anticipates *The Kreutzer Sonata*, while insinuating the question of what might have happened to Kitty Shcherbatskaia had she lost her father and been left alone with a mother as materialist as Mimi's.

In introducing Mimi as a consumer who is simultaneously a commodity, Veselitskaia broaches the issue of women's work. Mama, Mimi, and Mimi's aunts consider paid labour vulgar, even dangerous for an attractive young woman. There might be Jews, for example, among Mimi's co-workers in an office. And while walking to meet a pupil, an unescorted woman tutor is liable to be taken for a prostitute. Again, the older women of Mimi's family push her into the marriage market. Since no Konstantin Levin waits in the wings to rescue Mimi, her plot now veers toward Anna Karenina's. As in the case of young Anna, one of Mimi's aunts (Julie) steps in to arrange her marriage to a wealthy older man with no erotic magnetism.

An image of Mimi before a mirror on her wedding day brilliantly forecasts the yearning she will display for a vacation as a time apart from the marriage about to imprison her. Up to the actual ceremony, the day unfolds as

---

21 *Mimi the Bride*, p. 16.
22 Ibid. p. 22. This passage is missing in *Mimochka* (2003), p. 33.
23 For this extension of Thorstein Veblen's *Theory of the Leisure Class* (1899), see Mary Louise Roberts, 'Gender, Consumption, and Commodity Culture', *American Historical Review*, CIII, 3, 1998, p. 819.

consumer bliss, with more ironic reminiscences of Kitty Shcherbatskaia. Both brides wear Parisian gowns and have a French hairdresser to do their wedding coiffeurs. Veselitskaia describes Mimi's sumptuous dress at length, conveying the pleasure it gives the bride. This wedding day is much more about her regalia rather than a husband and their future together. The future, in fact, is what Mimi would like to block out. In representing Mimi alone in her boudoir gazing at herself in the mirror in her wedding attire, Veselitskaia captures the bride's narcissistic desire to freeze that moment into 'fashion time', Roland Barthes' term for fashion's festive illusion of a 'utopian "elsewhere"' beyond the flux of real time.[24] Veselitskaia draws out the fashion moment through an authorial apostrophe to Mimi. Do you really want to go through with this marriage, Mimi? Such is the gist of the apostrophe, which commands the reader's attention, while leaving the heroine in temporal suspension, transfixed by her reflection in the mirror. As though in the fitting room of a store, Mimi has achieved her own little consumer-paradise time apart in her boudoir.

When fashion time ends, however, real time sweeps Mimi to the church and into a climactic intertextual confrontation with the 'great author of *Anna Karenina*'.[25] Veselitskaia gives Tolstoi the last word, ending her story with a re-accentuated quotation from his novel. As Mimi arrives at the church, bystanders speak of her just as a corresponding 'crowd of women spectators' had spoken of Kitty: 'What a sweetie the bride is, done up like a ewe-lamb! Say what you like, one feels pity for a sister'.[26] For Kitty, the strangers' commiseration is misplaced. For Mimi, though, the lamb-to-the-slaughter scenario seems apt in light of the groom. The dialogism gives the authorial perspective a compassionate edge. No Kitty or Anna, Mimi has a skin-deep identity, manifested primarily in what she buys and wears. She rarely speaks and will never grow. But for all her vapidity and materialism, she retains something of the little lost lamb in the trilogy's first two stories. She is an object of lively authorial mockery rather than moral indignation.

Mimi at the Spa opens with a flashback that highlights how readily the heroine (now in her sixth year of marriage) has assumed her role as a ceremonial consumer. Her peak consumption experience occurred in Paris during the three-month honeymoon she and Spiridon Ivanovich spent primarily taking the waters in Vichy. Not attracted to scenery, Mimi enjoyed the spa as

---

24 Roland Barthes, *The Fashion System*, trans. Matthew Ward and Richard Howard, Jonathan Cape, London, 1983, pp. 250–1. See also Mesropova, p. 99.
25 *Mimi the Bride*, p. 30.
26 Leo Tolstoy, *Anna Karenina*, trans. Richard Pevear and Larissa Volokhonsky, Penguin, London, 2000, reprinted 2003, p. 457.

a fashion opportunity 'to see and be seen'.²⁷ She had eyes only for elegant *toilettes*, her own and those of others. But the 'real honeymoon' started afterwards in Paris where Mimi 'was in heaven, buying right and left whatever she liked'. Mimicking the heroine's choppy, rudimentary speech style, the authorial voice twice interjects into the flashback, 'What a honeymoon she had!' ('О, ее медовый месяц!'). After sightseeing with her husband every morning, Mimi would 'go shopping, buying and buying'.²⁸ While his ceremonial shopper spent his money, Spiridon Ivanovich napped in their luxury hotel, limiting his own material consumption to food. *Anna Karenina* and *The Kreutzer Sonata* (the Paris honeymoon) relate gourmet cuisine to carnal appetite.²⁹ *Mimi at the Spa* implies instead that honeymoon gluttony compensated for the couple's tepid physical relations. In joining her husband for brunch each day, Mimi, having finally arisen and gussied herself up, would extend her hand for him to kiss and give him a peck on his bald pate. Then they would attack the food – the likes of 'cutlets *en papillote*, lobster, and hors d'oeuvres'.³⁰

With the honeymoon long behind her, Mimi in present time experiences marriage as entrapment. She feels like a 'fly in a spider's web'.³¹ Veselitskaia lets this metaphor do the spatial work of evoking Mimi's Petersburg home. Neither the building nor its interiors are described. Veselitskaia relies instead on the metonymic evocation of stagnant time. Mimi's days are all the same, and her pleasures are paling (shopping, social calls, and carriage rides). Routine has its purely revolting side as well. At dinner, mama and Spiridon Ivanovich bore Mimi with their conversations about politics. Food, too, signifies monotony. Over and over, mama prepares cutlets that please Spiridon Ivanovich but get on Mimi's nerves. Nor has their son brought Mimi joy. Mimi leaves to mama the care of the child, whose name is never mentioned. The boy is simply known as 'bebi' (бэби) (or the diminutive 'bebichka' [бэбичка]), a phonetic rendering of 'baby' that objectifies the child, as though he were but an accessory in Mimi's wardrobe. The son's strange-looking Cyrillic appellations underline motherhood's foreignness to Mimi, while also mocking the contem-

---

27 The quoted topos dates back at least to Thomas Nugent, *The Grand Tour, or A Journey through the Netherlands, Germany, Italy, and France*, 4 vols, London, 1749; 3rd ed., 1778, IV, p. 109.
28 *Mimi at the Spa*, February 1891, p. 528.
29 Helena Goscilo-Kostin, 'Tolstoian Fare: Credo à la Carte,' *The Slavonic and East European Review*, LXII, 4, 1984, pp. 481–95; and Ronald LeBlanc, 'Unpalatable Pleasures: Tolstoi, Food, and Sex,' *Tolstoi Studies Journal*, VI, 1993, pp. 1–3, 9–20.
30 *Mimi at the Spa*, February 1891, pp. 528–9.
31 Ibid. p. 531.

porary Russian bourgeois fad for things English.³² Needless to say, baby will be left behind (with Aunt Julie) when Mimi, her maid Katia, mama, and Julie's tomboy daughter Vava go to the Caucasus. 'Vava for baby, baby for Vava' ('Вава за бэби, бэби за Вава'), quips the author on this exchange.³³

In sending Mimi to the Caucasus for a reinvigorating vacation, Veselitskaia establishes ironic interplay with the up-market Vichy honeymoon. As we will see shortly, Mimi recaptures the Vichy fashion-parade experience in the Caucasus. With respect to travellers' amenities, however, Veselitskaia conveys the Caucasus' actual reputation as a place for roughing it. In hopes of keeping rubles at home, Russian tourism promoters touted the Crimean seacoast and the Caucasian spas as alternatives to resorts in Western Europe.³⁴ Throughout the imperial age, however, Western Europe remained the preferred destination for Russians with sufficient means.³⁵ Furthermore, only on the eve of World War I did tourist development of the Caucasus begin catching up with the Crimea.³⁶ The fourth edition (1888) of John Murray's guide to Russia had duly warned would-be travellers. For scenery, mountain climbing, hunting, and the quality of the mineral waters, Murray gave the Caucasus high marks. But the guide found no spa hotels worth describing, warned of dirt and bugs in sleeping quarters at posting stations, and advised tourists going to the Caucasus to 'provide themselves with everything requisite in a country where modern appliances of civilized life are often wanting'. Recommended items included a 'small cork bed' or a bag to stuff with hay to serve as a mattress, a portable bath, a store of tea, brandy, candles, preserved meats, and a 'good supply of Keating's insect-powder'.³⁷

Mimi at the Spa corroborates Murray in many respects. In view of Mimi's low spirits and recent hysterics, both her husband and mama feel she needs a cure. When their doctor recommends the Caucasus, Mimi is secretly glad since a friend of hers was sexually 'emancipated' during a recent summer

---

32   On Russian Anglomania at this time, see Stephen Lovell, *Summerfolk: A History of the Dacha, 1710–2000*, Cornell University Press, Ithaca, 2003, p. 80.
33   *Mimi at the Spa*, February 1891, p. 539.
34   See McReynolds, pp. 40–2.
35   G.P. Dolzhenko, *Istoriia turizma v dorevoliutsionnoi Rossii i SSSR*, Rostovskii universitet, Rostov-on-Don, 1988, p. 19, and Christopher Ely, *This Meager Nature: Landscape and National Identity in Imperial Russia*, Northern Illinois University Press, DeKalb, 2002, p. 4.
36   See Dolzhenko, pp. 22–5; and Andrei Mal'gin, *Russkaia Riv'era. Kurorty, turizm i otdykh v Krymu v epokhu Imperii. Konets XVIII-nachalo XX v.*, SONAT, Simferopol', 2004, p. 326–7.
37   *Handbook for Travellers in Russia, Poland, and Finland, Including the Crimea, Caucasus, Siberia, and Central Asia*, 4th ed., John Murray, London, 1888, p. 404.

vacation in Kislovodsk.[38] Mama, however, had assumed the doctor would propose a spa abroad, and the prospect of the Caucasus horrifies her. Many people have told her, says mama, that everything in the Caucasus is 'so primitive, so undeveloped. There are no apartments, no doctors. Just awful quacks, I hear. And there's nothing to eat'.[39] Even as the travellers prepare to start the train trip to the Caucasus, Mimi's Aunt Sophie tells them they should be going to Karlsbad instead. Aunt Mary, too, considers Russia's resort periphery a wasteland: 'I know perfectly well what the Crimea means, what the Caucasus means: hunger, boredom, and dirt. It's a waste of money'.[40] Mama's worries about 'quacks' prove well grounded: at the spa Mimi's doctor turns out to be a venal philanderer with erotic designs on her.[41] With respect to tourist comforts, though, the situation proves better than expected. Mimi's hotel room in Kislovodsk has a poor bed and a crooked mirror. But she and the rest of her party adore the shashlik, they learn about hiring a laundress, they find a cook, and rent a decent apartment in Zheleznovodsk.

With many parodic echoes of *Anna Karenina*, Veselitskaia's depiction of the journey treats the railroad as a facilitator of adultery. Mimi and her companions travel in style, in a ladies sleeping car with a tea service, velvet sofa-seats, mirrors, blue window-shutters, and lilac shades on the night-lights. At the outset of the trip, Mimi settles into the compartment, takes off her new travel hat, and passes the time playing with her lapdog Monique.[42] In her berth the first night, Mimi finds the train's motion and noise lulling as it speeds through the night, away from Petersburg and the marital bed she associates with insomnia, crushing silence, sheer 'torture'. Mimi is now alone with her thoughts. But unlike Tolstoi's Anna, who tries to read a novel on the train but slips into reflecting on her life instead, Veselitskaia's consumer heroine anticipates fashion time at the spa. Mimi has brought so many clothes that her outfits require planning. Which of her five hats, for example, will go with the mousseline dress? Three days into the journey, reality disrupts the fashion reverie when the travellers have to change trains in Rostov. They enter the train station to eat their pre-paid meal, a realistic detail bespeaking commercialized travel. What a revolting spectacle meets Mimi's eyes in the smoke-filled, dusty café: a mob of visibly sick people bound for Caucasian spas. Mimi and mama also recoil

---

38   *Mimi at the Spa*, February 1891, p. 535.
39   Ibid. p. 534.
40   Ibid. pp. 540–1.
41   A French doctor in Vichy also ogles Mimi: ibid. p. 527.
42   Mimi's lapdog is the first of several intriguing anticipations of Chekhov's Crimean vacation adultery story *The Lady with the Little Dog* (*Dama s sobachkoi*, 1899).

from the multitude of 'provincial Russian women' in the crowd, an indication of the varied social composition of domestic vacationers at this time.[43]

But standing out from the crowd is the Byronic figure who will become Mimi's lover. She spots him at once when he enters the cafe: an 'elegantly dressed man of thirty-five' with a porter carrying his stylish suitcase and an English-type travel blanket (плед).[44] To complete the impression of the Anglomanic Russian dandy, the stranger is travelling with his Newfoundland dog Rex, a name introduced in Latin script in the text. The man takes a seat at our ladies' table. Vava begins feeding Rex her chicken, a spontaneous adolescent gesture that sparks conversation among the adults.[45] Huge Rex scares Monique, but this too helps break the ice between travelling strangers.[46]

A parodic Tolstoian motif of the language of the eyes begins in the café, where the dandy frequently meets Mimi's gaze. More thrilling looks pass between them after they get on the train. Mimi gazes out her window in his direction, only to find he is looking her way. At every rest stop, the man (yet to reveal his name) strolls on the platform in front of Mimi's car, trying to catch her eye. She, though, pretends to be looking at the sky or the station, yet mentally registers his excellent wardrobe. He too has brought more than one hat and has stylish boots Mimi takes to be French. Such details link Rex's owner to *The Kreutzer Sonata* violinist Trukhachevskii who wears fashionable, elegant clothing attractive to women. On the last night of Mimi's journey Veselitskaia imitates the classic Anna-Vronskii railroad platform moment during the snowstorm. While everybody else is sleeping, Mimi glances out at a rest-stop station just before going to bed. Lo and behold, the dandy is there on the platform, staring right into her window. Mimi returns his penetrating gaze, an act that makes her feel 'a little to blame' the next morning, another reminiscence of Anna.[47]

Upon arrival at the resort station, Mimi, in 'ghastly' shape, heads for the ladies toilet, another mundane detail typifying Veselitskaia's assault on Romanticism. In passing through the station Mimi pretends not to notice the dandy drinking tea but sees he has changed his clothes. He continues to stand out from the crowd and soon acquires in Mimi's mind the appellation *l'homme*

---

43   *Mimi at the Spa*, February 1891, pp. 542–3, 546, 548.
44   Ibid. 547.
45   In *The Lady with the Little Dog* Gurov strikes up his acquaintance with the heroine Anna by asking her permission to give her dog a bone in the Yalta hotel restaurant.
46   Veselitskaia's use of dogs as erotic surrogates parallels Gogol's *The Diary of a Madman*. Note in this light the comic assonance of Mimochka and her *sobachka* Monichka.
47   *Mimi at the Spa*, February 1891, p. 550. Cf. *Anna Karenina*, p. 98.

au chien – the man with the dog.⁴⁸ Passengers have poured from the train in a hectic rush to find porters and hire carriages. Having obtained the best carriage, the dandy speeds past all the other vacationers, to take the road to Piatigorsk. Mimi manages to observe, however, that he is now wearing a third hat.

In tracking the trip to the south, Veselitskaia starts projecting sixteen-year-old Vava's vacation agenda as a foil to Mimi's. Vava prefigures the model *komsomolka* type of Soviet times. Athletic, idealistic, and socially concerned, she is in revolt against her mother's plan to transform her into a high-society belle like her older sister. The journey from Petersburg is barely underway when Vava embarks on her quest to commune with untamed nature, a theme engaging with both Lermontov and Tolstoi. Standing in the train car's corridor, she looks up at the sky and recites Lermontov's Caucasian exile lyric 'Celestial clouds, eternal wanderers …' ('Тучки небесные, вечные странники').⁴⁹ At the resort, Vava goes hiking on her own or with other wholesome vacationers. She returns home every day with scratches on her face, brambles in her hair, and pleasant memories of exploring the mountain terrain and listening to the 'choir of grasshoppers' she prefers to the music in town (a reminiscence perhaps of Olenin in the lap of nature in the Caucasus in Tolstoi's *The Cossacks*).⁵⁰ In addition to active leisure and revelling in nature, Vava socializes with thoughtful tourists at the spa. They discuss the 'immortality of the soul, the woman question, the views and opinions of Leo Tolstoi', a cultural hero for Vava who has long desired to write him a letter.⁵¹ Vava also makes friends with representatives of the working class – the nannies and *bonnes* of vacationing families. Finally, Vava maps out humanitarian work for the future, planning to stay single and use her dowry to establish a home for abandoned children. In her commitment to Tolstoian ideals, Vava comes across as an absurdly zealous teenager, yet one with her heart in the right place. Vacation for her is a salutary time apart, strengthening her resolve to resist the high-society norms of her mother and sister.

Mimi by contrast seizes the vacation as a chance to reassume her Vichy tourist persona, using clothes to proclaim her husband's wealth and dominance in the imperial Russian hierarchy of socio-regional distinction. Erotic promiscuity reigns at the spa, but Mimi remains aloof, following her cure

---

48   *Mimi at the Spa*, p. 551.
49   Ibid. p. 541.
50   Ibid. p. 555.
51   Ibid. p. 545; and *Mimi at the Spa*, March 1891, p. 38.

and dressing to impress. She parades many outfits, each signifying an activity or time as dictated by the vestimentary coding of a modern-day fashion magazine (white for summer, casual for weekend, and so forth).[52] When Mimi lends a hand at a charity bazaar in Zheleznovodsk, for instance, she wears an 'exquisite peached-coloured dress' ('нежнейшное платье цвета pêche').[53] Clothes make this woman and even convey her assumption that Russians of Petersburg crown the imperial power structure. At the spa Mimi's mama learns that *l'homme au chien* is Valerian Nikolaevich, a lawyer from Kiev married to the rich daughter of a factory owner.[54] In his campaign to seduce Mimi, Valerian strategically flirts with a woman of easy virtue named Lenskaia, the sister of an actress in the Kiev vaudeville troupe in the Caucasus for the summer season. Veselitskaia casts Mimi's jealousy in terms of the status-conscious semiotics of clothing. With her wardrobe befitting the wife of a Petersburg general, Mimi believes she is the best dressed woman at the spas. She therefore feels superior in every way to the less elegantly clothed demimondaines from Kiev.

On the Pechorin-Princess Mary model, Valerian's courtship grows more aggressive but manipulates Mimi's distinct obsession with clothes. The two fashion plates often go riding together, allowing Mimi to sport the sexy equestrian outfit whose price Spiridon Ivanovich found outrageous. Valerian, too, takes riding as a fashion opportunity. As usual, he has brought from home his vacation outfit of Circassian clothing.[55] During their encounters he quotes Pechorin and recites or alludes to wonderful poetry (Fet, de Musset, Byron) – all for the purpose of persuading Mimi that love is exalted even if adulterous. Valerian's ultimate ploy is to praise Lenskaia as a passionate woman as opposed to high-society 'dressmakers, mannequins for Parisian toilettes'.[56] The remark greatly upsets Mimi, who had come to trust Valerian's advice about how to dress.

At last Mimi adds sex to her vacation regime but in a manner that continues to demonstrate her mannequin character. The decisive erotic encounter collapses into a wardrobe crisis, a comic deflation of the *Anna Karenina* metaphor

---

52   See Barthes, pp. 15, 47, 249–53. Mimi follows what sounds like a newspaper fashion page, 'le chronique de l'élégance', in *Mimi the Bride*, p. 23.
53   *Mimi at the Spa*, March 1891, p. 30.
54   The dandy's name ironically proclaims him the man to cure what ails Mimi, a habitual user of valerian drops.
55   On the Russian fad of dressing up as Caucasian mountaineers, see Susan Layton, 'Colonial Mimicry and Disenchantment in Alexander Druzhinin's "A Russian Circassian" and Other Stories', *Russian Review*, LX, 1, 2001, pp. 57–8.
56   *Mimi at the Spa*, March 1891, p. 40.

of sex as murder. Mimi's parodic fall occurs on a moonlit night when she and Valerian go riding with the mountaineer guide Osman to see a rock formation, the Castle of Treachery and Love. In the canyon-like enclosure of the rocks, the tourists sit on a Caucasian felt cloak and gaze at the site. '*C'est féerique*', ('it's magical') murmurs Mimi. They embrace and then disappear from the reader's view. The curtain rises again with Mimi's mental question: 'How had it happened?'[57] The moonlight scene had seemed so romantic; she had even begun to understand why people make a fuss about scenery. And now adultery! Yet, soon after 'it' is over; Mimi on the ride back home realizes she has lost her new riding crop, a smart accessory to her equestrian outfit. Valerian and Osman set about searching and find the crop.[58] In Mimi's consciousness, the near loss of a stylish commodity takes precedence over the loss of virtue. At home in her room that night, she assesses the experience of 'sin'. It was not at all the horror people pretend it to be. In fact, she feels 'happy and calm'.[59]

Subsequent episodes displace emotional intimacy with Mimi's expanded, commodity-conscious knowledge of Valerian's wardrobe. The day after the Castle rocks excursion, the vacationers confess they fell in love at first sight in the Rostov station cafe. However, the comic substitute for authentic-sounding feeling is Mimi's new access to Valerian's closet.[60] They now begin to meet regularly in his rented apartment where Mimi discovers the forty neckties and matching socks he has brought on vacation. She sorts through the ties and picks out her favourites. She is also impressed by the abundance of 'watch fobs, pins, and rings' lying about.[61] There too are photographs of Valerian's wife and children, but those images of humans are made secondary to Mimi's preoccupation with his material possessions.

At this stage of the affair Valerian reveals his essential make-up as bourgeois materialist. Unlike Pechorin, Valerian has no profound, intensely private

---

57 Ibid. pp. 50–1.
58 The equestrian theme links *Mimi at the Spa* to *Madame Bovary* as well as *Anna Karenina*. Of particular note, as Helena Goscilo remarked at the 2010 conference, is Flaubert's motif of the riding crop. Wearing a new *amazone*, Emma waves her riding crop in answer to the kiss her little daughter blows to her as she rides off with Rodolphe into the woodlands where they first have sex. Emma subsequently gives him an expensive crop as a gift. For an overview of the novel's 'equine theme,' see Vladimir Nabokov, 'Gustave Flaubert: *Madame Bovary*,' in his *Lectures on Literature*, Fredson Bowers, ed., with an Introduction by John Updike, Picador, London, 1980, reprinted 1983, pp. 175–6.
59 *Mimi at the Spa*, March 1891, p. 52.
60 On the topos of 'male inner space', including Evgenii Onegin's study, see Andrew, 1998, p. 143.
61 *Mimi at the Spa*, March 1891, p. 53.

aesthetic appreciation of nature. Veselitskaia's debased version of the Byronic hero has simply exploited the Castle rocks for the purpose of sexual conquest. In one of their last rendezvous, Mimi histrionically tests his sentiments. Now calling him Val, she cries, '*Je suis une femme perdue*' ('I'm a fallen woman'), 'you must despise me.' Val speaks words to the contrary, and they swap stories about marital misery. Val now maligns his wife as a 'callous pedant' and 'mere female [самка], *une femelle*' devoted to raising their children instead of trying to please her husband.[62] 'Самка' ironically alludes to Anna Karenina, whose pursuit of erotic fulfilment at the expense of maternal duty ends in suicide.[63] But while pretending to glorify passion, Val is already trying to disengage. When Mimi reveals the history of her unhappy marriage, he tells her she was prudent to marry a rich man because 'money is the key to happiness'.[64] Mimi must simply take charge of her life, adds Val. Vowing their love will last forever, he promises to come to Petersburg, to take her to concerts and the theatre. In fact, though, Mimi and *l'homme au chien* will never see each other again.[65]

Mimi's vacation comes to an end, but the 'magical' time apart endures in photographs the two materialists exchange upon parting. Although feeling weepy, Mimi sits for a portrait in her equestrian outfit on the horse she rode to the Castle rocks. In turn, she receives from Val a photograph of him in Circassian garb. Like the *Mimi the Bride* image of the heroine gazing at herself in the mirror on her wedding day, the souvenir photographs freeze the adulterers in the 'elsewhere' of fashion time. Those costumes mean vacation experienced as escape from home. Mimi and Val also exchange turquoise rings, a commonplace souvenir on sale at the spa.[66]

With a final allusion to *Anna Karenina*, Veselitskaia reasserts the dreariness of the quotidian world awaiting Mimi in Petersburg. The author skips describing the return trip except for the last stretch into the capital:

---

62 Ibid. p. 55.
63 Just before introducing Levin to Anna, her brother Stiva describes her as a 'remarkable' woman, no 'mere female' (самка): *Anna Karenina*, p. 695.
64 *Mimi at the Spa*, March 1891, pp. 54–5.
65 *The Lady with the Little Dog* reverses this situation: vacation adultery evolves into genuine love, as Gurov and Anna affirm when he goes to her home town and finds her at the theatre.
66 Piatigorsk shops for souvenir-hunting are featured in *Hero of Our Time* and Alexander Druzhinin's 'A Russian Circassian'. See my 'Russian Military Tourism' in *Turizm*, pp. 49–50.

Rain, rain, rain ... the morose grey sky ... rows and rows of Petersburg dachas in pine groves. Flashing by were dirty, muddy little roads bordered by ditches full of thick fern bushes. Moss, marsh, fog ...

And now the familiar cabbage gardens, the barracks, and the platform of the Petersburg station.[67]

There on the platform, like Aleksei Karenin, stands Mimi's defamiliarized husband. As the train pulls in, she spots him and sees him anew: 'How old he is, how alien, alien! She wished the train would not stop, she wanted it to go on and on, to speed past with her in it.'[68] Being elsewhere has become Mimi's permanent desire. The train has enabled her temporary liberation and now stirs her longing for motion ever onward toward a time and place, any time and place apart from her marriage.

At the end of the story Mimi appears guilt-free – a very un-Tolstoian finale. Back home, Mimi and Vava relive the vacation through commercialized pictures they share with relatives. This affords ironic contrast to the private photos Mimi and Val exchanged. While in the Caucasus, Vava compiled a scrapbook of her vacation, a practice publicly discussed in Russia by the late 1830s.[69] But in addition to this personal creative project, Vava bought a set of stereoscope pictures. The vicarious tourism thrills Aunt Mary. 'How beautiful! What's that?' she exclaims, passing the stereoscope to Mimi. That, explains Mimi, is the Castle of Treachery and Love. 'Is it really so beautiful? Were you there?' asks Mary. Mimi answers: 'Yes, I took a horse ride there. It's very beautiful. Especially in moonlight...c'est féerique'.[70] Those are the final words of the story – the phrase Mimi uttered to Valerian at the place where they first had sex. The purchased souvenir thus does double duty for Mimi. It augments her cultural capital as tourist who has seen such wonders with her own eyes. But it also serves as a secret memento of her affair with Val whose photograph she must hide at home.

The spa story's great success apparently prompted Veselitskaia to write the melodramatic sequel *Mimi Has Taken Poison*. Set in Petersburg, the tale begins just after the heroine's suicide attempt. Mimi is distraught because the French

---

67 *Mimi at the Spa*, March 1891, p. 57.
68 Ibid. p. 58.
69 Ivan Golovin, 'Puteshestvennik nashego vremeni,' *Syn otechestva*, v, 1838, part 1, p. 75. Golovin (1816–1883), who emigrated to the West in 1845, featured as a repellent, 'insolent and quarrelsome man' in Herzen's *My Past and Thoughts* (*Byloe i dumy*), *Sobranie sochinenii*, 30 vols, Izdatel'stvo Akademii nauk SSSR, Moscow, 1954–65, XI, pp. 404, 406.
70 *Mimi at the Spa*, March 1891, p. 60.

tutor Jules left her to go and live with his fiancée Olga, the gorgeous, brainy daughter of a rich Russian businessman. Mimi confesses all to mama who goes to Jules and recovers the potentially compromising letters Mimi wrote to him. Veselitskaia pads out this slender plot with flashbacks concerning mama's past, Olga's past, Spiridon Ivanovich's past, and Mimi's past with Jules and a previous lover, her husband's nephew.[71]

Now nearing thirty, Mimi has become a coarse adulteress enmeshed in a rotten society. After the vacation, Mimi soon ceased to cherish the memory and the photograph of Val. She came to perceive adultery as a high-society norm that people simply hide behind proprieties. Even Spiridon Ivanovich turns out to have a second family – a mistress of long standing and an illegitimate daughter. This revelation exhausts whatever moral capital Mimi's husband ever had as a Karenin surrogate. The closing episode stresses Spiridon Ivanovich's grossness. After Mimi's convalescence, they join the fashionable crowd at a club on an island in the Neva where Spiridon Ivanovich ogles the show girls through opera glasses. The closing image shows Mimi riding back home with her husband. In the carriage Mimi sinks into a bitter, self-pitying reverie about a love that might have been, a reminiscence of Anna Karenina's final stream of consciousness. Mimi's future appears bleak, but she has become so pathetic it is hard for the reader to care. Digressions also try the reader's patience. Wandering from the problem of adultery, Veselitskaia paints a broader canvas of upper-class corruption. Religious hypocrisy receives much attention in two depictions of the principal *dramatis personae* mingling with other rich people in church to parade their clothes or pray for material bounties. A political subplot develops as well, exposing mama's reactionary views of the Russian peasantry and the urban poor. Such material makes clear the author's Tolstoian values. Yet, interestingly enough Tolstoi did not much care for *Mimi Has Taken Poison*. He considered it exaggerated and repetitive.[72]

The deficiencies of the poisoning story make all the more plain the artistic achievement of *Mimi at the Spa*, the literary gem of the trilogy. In privileging the prism of vacation as a time apart, my study has sought to demonstrate how Veselitskaia modernized Tolstoian travel concerns at the *fin de siècle*

---

71 The affair with Jules begins when he, Mimi, her children, and mama summer in the country while Spiridon Ivanovich works in the city: *Mimi Has Taken Poison*, October 1893, p. 429. On public discourse concerning such risks for the 'dacha husband', see Lovell, pp. 106–7.

72 See Tolstoi (1928–58), letter to S. A. Tolstaia, 26 or 27 October 1893, 84, p. 200.

when a consumer market for tourism and active leisure had emerged in Russia. Veselitskaia's anti-Romantic narrative exploited the traditional society-tale construction of the spa as a parade ground where naive and worldly quests for grand passion are played out. But *Mimi at the Spa* also projected a new, late-nineteenth-century image of the Caucasus as a hiking arena for asexual, Tolstoi-worshipping young people such as Vava. More pervasively, Veselitskaia pursued the anti-Romantic strategy of saturating her literary 'essay' with travel trivia, to insist on the prosaic, material dimensions of Mimi's trip: the well-appointed train car for ladies; the pre-paid meal; the train station café, refreshment bar, and toilet; practical problems of hiring porters, carriages, a laundress, and cook; the quality of accommodations and food; hotel prices and doctors' fees; the charity bazaar; the vaudeville troupe; souvenirs on sale; photography services at the spa; the scrapbook; and the purchased pictures to exhibit as tourist capital at home. In essence, Veselitskaia's anti-Romantic posture accords with Tolstoi's treatments of Russian leisure travel as an overly consumerist, hedonistic practice especially pernicious for 'unsupervised' women. *Mimi at the Spa* nonetheless declines to judge the heroine. The tale has a typically modern open end, shying away from a conclusive moral reckoning.

Veselitskaia's modernity resides as well in her anticipation of Soviet and post-Soviet cultural phenomena. The clash between Vava's and Mimi's vacation regimes prefigures the official Soviet position on tourism as of the 1920s. Vava anticipates the ideal socialist *turistka* actively harnessing her vacation to self-improvement. Day after day, she pushes herself as a hiker. The Caucasus sojourn also fosters her political growth. She mingles at the spa with domestic servants and intellectual people and vows to devote her life to needy children. Mimi, on the other hand, represents the comfort-loving bourgeois type Soviet tourist officials sought to root out. She hates politics and thinks only of her own pleasure. In linking tourism and consumption, Veselitskaia's spa story speaks as well to the cult of glamour among today's 'new Russians'. The product of a commodity culture from girlhood onward, Veselitskaia's Mimi has virtually no self outside consumption. The light-handed irony the author brings to bear on this predicament gives *Mimi at the Spa* its continuing appeal as a critical but amusing literary representation of the vacation construed as a consumer good.

Bibliography

Andrew, Joe, 'Another Time, Another Place: Gender and the Chronotope in the Society Tale' in Cornwell, Neil, ed., *The Society Tale in Russian Literature from Odoevskii to Tolstoi*, Rodopi, Amsterdam and Atlanta, 1998, pp. 127–32.

Andrew, Joe, *Narrative, Space and Gender in Russian Literature, 1846–1903*, Rodopi, Amsterdam and New York, 2007.

Ayers, Carolyn Jursa, '*L'éducation sentimental* or the School of Hard Knocks? The Heroine's Education in the Society Tale', in Cornwell, Neil, ed., *The Society Tale in Russian Literature from Odoevskii to Tolstoi*, Rodopi, Amsterdam and Atlanta, 1998, pp. 153–68.

Baranowski, Shelley and Furlough, Ellen, eds, *Being Elsewhere. Tourism, Consumer Culture, and Identity in Modern Europe and North America*, University of Michigan Press, Ann Arbor, 2001.

Barthes, Roland, *The Fashion System*, Ward, Matthew and Howard, Richard, trans., Jonathan Cape, London, 1983.

Berghoff, Hartmut, 'From Privilege to Commodity? Modern Tourism and the Rise of the Consumer Society', in id., Korte, Barbara, Schneider, Ralf and Harvie, Christopher, eds, *The Making of Modern Tourism: The Cultural History of the British Experience, 1600–2000*, Palgrave, New York, 2002, pp. 164–8.

Buzard, James, *The Beaten Track. European Tourism, Literature, and the Ways to 'Culture', 1800–1918*, Oxford University Press, New York, 1993 (reprinted 2001).

Cornwell, Neil, 'Vladimir Odoevsky and the Society Tale in the 1820s and 1830s', in id., ed., *The Society Tale in Russian Literature from Odoevskii to Tolstoi*, Rodopi, Amsterdam and Atlanta, 1998, pp. 9–20.

Dekker, George G., *The Fictions of Romantic Tourism. Radcliffe, Scott, and Mary Shelley*, Stanford University Press, Stanford, 2005.

Demidova, Olga and Zirin, Mary, 'Lidiia Ivanovna Veselitskaia', in Ledkovsky, Marina, Rosenthal, Charlotte and Zirin, Mary, eds, *Dictionary of Russian Women Writers* Greenwood Press, Westport, Conn., 1994, pp. 705-6.

Dolzhenko, G.P., *Istoriia turizma v dorevoliutsionnoi Rossii i SSSR*, Rostovskii universitet, Rostov-on-Don, 1988.

Ely, Christopher, *This Meager Nature: Landscape and National Identity in Imperial Russia*, Northern Illinois University Press, DeKalb, 2002.

Ely, Christopher, 'The Origins of Russian Scenery: Volga River Tourism and Russian Landscape Aesthetics', *Slavic Review*, LXII, 4, 2003, pp. 666–82.

Engelstein, Laura, *The Keys to Happiness: Sex and the Search for Modernity in Fin de Siècle Russia*, Cornell University Press, Ithaca, 1992.

Golovin, Ivan, 'Puteshestvennik nashego vremeni', *Syn otechestva*, v, 1838, part 1, pp. 67–83.

Goscilo-Kostin, Helena,'Tolstoyan Fare: Credo à la Carte', *The Slavonic and East European Review*, LXII, 4, 1984, pp. 481–95.

Hazlitt, William, *Table Talk; or, Original Essays on Men and Manners*, Bell and Daldy, London, 1869.

Herzen, A. S., *Sobranie sochinenii*, 30 vols, Izdatel'stvo Akademii nauk SSSR, Moscow, 1954-65, XI.

Jones, W. Gareth, 'Tolstoi's Alternative Society Tales' in Cornwell, Neil, ed., *The Society Tale in Russian Literature from Odoevskii to Tolstoi*, Rodopi, Amsterdam and Atlanta, 1998, pp. 99–113.

Koenker, Diane P. 'Travel to Work, Travel to Play: On Russian Tourism, Travel and Leisure', *Slavic Review*, LXII, 4, 2003, pp. 657–65.

Layton, Susan, 'Colonial Mimicry and Disenchantment in Alexander Druzhinin's "A Russian Circassian" and Other Stories', *Russian Review*, LX, 1, 2001, pp. 56–71.

Layton, Susan, 'Russian Military Tourism: The Crisis of the Crimean War Period', in *Turizm. The Russian and East European Tourist under Capitalism and Socialism*, Gorsuch, Anne and Koenker, Diane P., eds, Cornell University Press, Ithaca, 2006, pp. 43–63.

LeBlanc, Ronald, 'Unpalatable Pleasures: Tolstoy, Food, and Sex', *Tolstoy Studies Journal*, VI, 1993, pp. 1–32.

Lipovetsky, Mark, 'New Russians as Culture Myth', *Russian Review*, LXII, 1, 2003, pp. 54–71.

Lovell, Stephen, *Summerfolk: A History of the Dacha, 1710–2000*, Cornell University Press, Ithaca, 2003.

MacCannell, Dean, *The Tourist. A New Theory of the Leisure Class*, Schocken Books, New York, 1976 (reprinted 1989).

Mal'gin, Andrei, *Russkaia Riv'era. Kurorty, turizm i otdykh v Krymu v epokhu Imperii. Konets XVIII-nachalo XX v.*, SONAT, Simferopol', 2004.

McReynolds, Louise, 'The Prerevolutionary Russian Tourist: Commercialization in the Nineteenth Century' in Gorsuch, Anne E., and Koenker, Diane P., eds, *Turizm. The Russian and East European Tourist under Capitalism and Socialism*, Cornell University Press, Ithaca, 2006, pp. 17–42.

Mesropova, Olga, '"The Discreet Charm of the Russian Bourgeoisie": OKsana Robski and Glamour in Russian Popular Culture', *Russian Review*, LXVIII, 1, 2009, pp. 89–101.

Mikulich, V. See Veselitskaia, Lidiia.

Mirsky, D. S., *A History of Russian Literature from Its Beginnings to 1900*, Vintage, New York, 1958.

Møller, Peter Ulf, *Postlude to* The Kreutzer Sonata. *Tolstoj and the Debate on Sexual Morality in Russian Literature in the 1890s*, Kenda, John, trans., Brill, Leiden, 1988.

Murray, John, *Handbook for Travellers in Russia, Poland, and Finland, including the Crimea, Caucasus, Siberia, and Central Asia*, fourth edition, John Murray, London, 1888.

Nabokov, Vladimir, *Lectures on Literature*, Bowers, Fredson, ed., Picador, London, 1980.

Nugent, Thomas, *The Grand Tour, or A Journey through the Netherlands, Germany, Italy, and France*, 4 vols, London, 1749, third edition, 1778, IV.

Reid, Robert, '*Princess Ligovskaia* and *Princess Mary*: The Society Tale Goes to the Caucasus' in Cornwell, Neil, ed., *The Society Tale in Russian Literature from Odoevskii to Tolstoi* Rodopi, Amsterdam and Atlanta, 1998, pp. 49–56.

Roberts, Mary Louise, 'Gender, Consumption, and Commodity Culture', *American Historical Review,* CIII, 3, 1998, pp. 817–844.

Rosenthal, Charlotte, 'Carving out a Career: Women Prose Writers, 1885–1917' in *Gender and Russian Literature. New Perspectives*, Marsh, Rosalind, ed., Cambridge University Press, Cambridge, UK, 1996, pp. 133–5.

Rosowski, Susan J., 'The Novel of Awakening', in Abel, Elizabeth, Hirsch, Marianne, and Langland, Elizabeth, eds, *The Voyage in Fictions of Female Development*, University Press of New England for Dartmouth College, Hanover and London, 1983, pp. 49-68.

Smith, Alexandra, 'The Effacement of History, Theatricality and Postmodern Urban Fantasies in the Prose of Petruševskaja and Pelevin', *Die Welt des Slaven*, LVI, 2009, pp. 53–78.

Tolstoi, L.N., *Polnoe sobranie sochinenii*, 90 vols, Khudozhestvennaia literatura, Moscow 1928–58, letters to E. I. Popov, 13 May 1893; and to L. L. and M. L. Tolstaia, 15 May 1893, 66, pp. 316, 323.

Tolstoy, Leo, *Anna Karenina*, Pevear, Richard and Volokhonsky, Larissa, trans., Penguin, London, 2000 (reprinted 2003).

Urry, John, *Consuming Places*, Routledge, London and New York, 1995 (reprinted 1997).

Veselitskaia, Lidiia Ivanovna, *Mimochka*, Eksmo, Moscow, 2003; *Mimochka – nevesta. Ocherk*, in *Vestnik Evropy*, September 1883, pp. 5–30; *Mimochka na vodakh. Ocherk*, ibid., February 1891, pp. 526–68 and March 1891, pp. 30–60; and *Mimochka otravilas'. Ocherk*, ibid., September 1893, pp. 112–40 and October 1893, pp. 417–54; 'Ten' proshlogo', *Istoricheskii vestnik*, CXXXI, February 1913, pp. 362–83; March 1913, pp. 778–813; and CXXXII, April 1913, pp. 41–81.

Zhukova, Mariia, *Self-Sacrifice*, in Joe Andrew, ed. and trans., *Russian Women's Shorter Fiction. An Anthology, 1835–1860*, Clarendon Press, Oxford, 1996, pp. 220–71.

CHAPTER 6

Legitimate and Illegitimate Children: Rozanov's 'Indecent Proposal' to Tolstoi

Henrietta Mondry

Abstract

Tolstoi was far from alone in Russia at the end of the nineteenth century in examining issues of sexuality, particularly in relation to marriage. Vasilii Rozanov was equally active in publishing his views on the subject. He was particularly exercised by what he saw as the disintegration of the contemporary Russian family and became convinced that Tolstoi was an ideal interlocutor in his discussion of the issue. Rozanov blamed Russian literature for helping to undermine traditional family values, even *Evgenii Onegin* suffering censure for consigning its heroine to the role of a childless wife. Tolstoi, by contrast, offers wholesome portraits of family life. Realizing the advantages of Tolstoi's authoritative support, Rozanov approached him in the wake of a new law of 1902 concerning the status of illegitimate children which allowed them to be legitimized on birth certificates, or retrospectively if their parents later married. Rozanov wished to go further, promoting a form of common-law marriage which would abolish the difference between officially sanctioned marriage and cohabitation. Rozanov discussed the proposal with Tolstoi but appears to have received something less than full-throated support for it. Above all, this incident illustrates the extraordinary status that Tolstoi had acquired in his final years.

Keywords

Tolstoi and Rozanov – Russian views on sexual morality – Russian views on the family

∴

It is easy for the Jews: they have been given a commandment to 'multiply', and they multiply without having to worry about this life and the life beyond the grave because of the obvious

> guarantee in each of these lives. It is not like this in Christianity.
> VASILII ROZANOV[1]

∵

This chapter examines Vasilii Rozanov's dialogic relationship with Tolstoi's views on sexuality, procreation and Christianity. In the span of some twenty years around the turn of the twentieth century Rozanov devoted his work to understanding the riddles of human sexuality in the context of the history of religion, metaphysics and cosmology, and societal and cultural prejudices. As a self-appointed preacher of sex he set out to rehabilitate sexuality from the stigma imposed upon it by Christianity and the Church, not through an abstract *theorization* of the topic but through the depiction of the relevance of this project to Russian society.

Although one of the most original and erudite thinkers of the turn of the century, Rozanov was also passionately involved in all the mundane aspects of Russian society. As a journalist he initiated a discussion on the divorce laws in Russia in 1902, most of which was published as the book *The Family Question in Russia* (Семейный вопрос в России, 1903). He thus provided a forum for public debate on the role of Church laws, as well as on Christianity's attitudes to marriage in the context of what he believed to be the disintegration of the contemporary Russian family. The topics which he opened for discussion included such intimate themes as the role of sexual attraction in marriage, the metaphysical meaning of human procreation and the role of the family in Russian society. As a self-proclaimed preacher of sexuality Rozanov had to be, and was, in constant contextual polemics with another authority on matters of human sexuality, Lev Tolstoi. Tolstoi's *The Kreutzer Sonata* (1890) was the first major subversive text to break the taboos on aspects of human sexuality in the context of physiological and psychological unsustainability within the institution of marriage. It also placed these questions in relation to the teachings of the Church. When *The Kreutzer Sonata* was published, its effect on society was likened to that of the blast of a bomb.[2] Similarly, when Rozanov's book *In*

---

1   V.V. Rozanov, *Semeinyi vopros v Rossii*, Respublika, Moscow, 2004, p. 722.
2   On the debate see Peter Ulf Møller, *Postlude to the Kreutzer Sonata: Tolstoj and the Debate on Sexual Morality in Russia in the 1890s*, E. J. Brill, Leiden, 1988.

the World of the Unclear and Undecided (*В мире неясного и нерешенного*) was published in 1901, it was described as a bomb which exploded in the faces of his contemporaries, demanding as it did a complete revision of all perspectives on sexuality: metaphysical, religious, biological, and societal.[3] In the same way in which Tolstoi developed the themes of family and marriage in relation to sexual love and procreation, Rozanov enlisted the theme of the family as one of the major building blocks of his writings on sexuality. It was thus to be expected that Rozanov would develop a special long-lasting attitude towards Tolstoi's work and persona; indeed, in Rozanov's parataxical texts there are numerous references to Tolstoi: his personality, his views, and the role that he played within Russian society.[4] In an article written a year after Tolstoi's death Rozanov declared that, in spite of the enormous turbulence which *The Kreutzer Sonata* had caused in Russian society, this story only raised issues and posed questions – it did not resolve them.[5] This statement implies that it was Rozanov himself who had succeeded in finding answers to the mysteries of sexuality to which he had indeed devoted his 'sermon of sex' ('проповедь пола').[6] Being Tolstoi's contemporary Rozanov was able to meet the great elder. In 1903 he made a pilgrimage to the Iasnaia Poliana estate, a visit which he later described in his articles 'L.N. Tolstoi' and 'A Trip to Iasnaia Poliana' ('Поездка в Ясную поляну'), both published in 1908.

In this chapter I focus on the theme of wanted and unwanted, legitimate and illegitimate, children, as well as that of infanticide in the context of the Russian family, in Rozanov's writings. I also demonstrate the polemical and dialogic nature of Rozanov's resolution of these key themes in relation to Tolstoi.

Viktor Shklovskii was one of the first commentators on Rozanov to notice the link between the core themes of Rozanov's work and those of Tolstoi. In his 1922 essay 'Rozanov' he develops his idea of the non-linear development of literary schools, genres and traditions, maintaining that Rozanov developed the themes which Tolstoi had started.[7] These themes are those first de-tabooed by

---

[3] Andrei Belyi, 'Kommentarii' in V.V. Rozanov, *V mire neiasnogo i nereshennogo, Polnoe sobranie sochinenii*, A. Nikoliukin, ed., Respublika, Moscow, 1995, p. 427.

[4] For a discussion of this, see Henrietta Mondry, *Vasily Rozanov and the Body of Russian Literature*, Slavica, Bloomington, 2010, pp. 115–30.

[5] See V.V. Rozanov, 'Priroda i tserkov', in *Terror protiv russkogo natsionalizma, Polnoe sobranie sochinenii*, A. Nikoliukin, ed., Respublika, Moscow, 1995, pp. 204–7.

[6] See V.V. Rozanov, *Opavshie list'ia*, in *Izbrannoe*, Neimanis, Munich, 1970, pp. 81–426 (112).

[7] Viktor Shklovskii, 'Rozanov' in *V.V. Rozanov. Pro et Contra*, second edition, D. K. Burlaka, ed., Izdatel'stvo RKhGI, St Petersburg, 1922, pp. 321–42. (Subsequent quotation from this source is indicated by page numbers in the text.)

Tolstoi: family, intimacy between husbands and wives, and the subject of the nursery. He quotes those passages from Tolstoi's letter to his wife of 10 December 1864 in which Tolstoi expresses his physical longing for her – a longing which he intends to satisfy on the floor of the nursery on his return home.

According to Shklovskii, Rozanov introduced the new themes of the 'kitchen' (326), the 'every day' and 'the family' (328) into Russian literature. The novelty of his method, Shklovskii argues, was to write about family life, the 'kitchen smells' (326) and 'woollen blankets', without a satirical attitude. Although Shklovskii maintains that Tolstoi did not leave true disciples in literature, he nevertheless points out the thematic link between Rozanov's work and that of Tolstoi.

In previous work on Rozanov's views on Russian writers I have demonstrated that, after the Revolution, Rozanov blamed the destruction of the Russian state on Russian literature; in particular he attacked novelists such as Turgenev and Goncharov for teaching the Russian public 'the wrong kind of love', a Romantic love which takes place outside the confines of marriage, the love which led Liza Kalitina, in Turgenev's *Home of the Gentry* (1859), to the monastery; and which was not consummated between Oblomov and Olga in Goncharov's *Oblomov* (also 1859).[8] In *The Family Question in Russia*, and in the discussion article 'Foundations of Family Structure' ('Стропила семейного уклада', 1900) Rozanov targets Pushkin's 'ideal, Tatiana' as a devastatingly wrong role model for Russian society. He maintains that, in *Evgenii Onegin*, Pushkin turns the 'shameful plot' of the loveless marriage of a young woman to a wealthy but sexless husband into a literary masterpiece. Tatiana is a childless wife without hope of motherhood; she is a sufferer, а 'страстнотерпица' (352) who crucifies her own flesh. In typical Rozanovian argumentation, he juxtaposes the Christian Russian family to the family of the Old Testament, pointing out that in Russia there is no broad knowledge of the Old Testament. This general ignorance concerning the Old Testament, both by the broad public and the clergy in Russia, becomes one of his explanations for the dominance of the New Testament's views in attitudes towards human sexuality. In Rozanov's philosophy of sexuality, sex is inseparable from metaphysics and cosmology; it is not a matter of nature, but one of the deepest riddles of human existence.

---

8   See Henrietta Mondry, 'A Wrong Kind of Love – A Teacher of Sex on a Teacher of Love: Rozanov on Turgenev and Viardot', in *Turgenev: Art, Ideology, Legacy*, Robert Reid and Joe Andrew, eds, Rodopi, Amsterdam, 2010, pp. 237–51.

It is in the understanding of sexuality in relation to religion that he sees the unbridgeable gap between the two Testaments.[9]

It is in this approach, based on the search for answers to the riddles of human sexuality in religion and various philosophical systems, where the link between Rozanov and Tolstoi is to be found. And it is in the desire to apply this understanding to the social good of Russian society where another link between Rozanov's and Tolstoi's views on family is evident. In his article 'Foundations of Family Structure' Rozanov reveals the utilitarian aspect of his quest to rehabilitate sexuality and procreation within the family: 'Give me only a loving family, and from this unit I will construct for you an eternal social building' (354).

This sentence has clear polemical connotations in regard to the sociological language of positivists and the utopian visions of Nikolai Chernyshevskii's *What is to be Done?*. Rozanov's challenge to positivism is apparent in this text as he stresses the mystery of love on the basis of the unconquerable strength of this emotion. The manifestation of this love is found not only in the love between a man and a woman, but also in the love which parents have towards their children. Given Tolstoi's views on the nature of sexual love as the strongest but most destructive feature of human life it becomes clear that Rozanov had to be in a quasi-dialogic relationship with this writer. But where Tolstoi struggled against the flesh Rozanov found evidence of the inexplicable mysteries of human sexuality. It must be remembered that Rozanov believed that human sexual organs were not of earthly but of meteoritic or cosmic nature.

In the above article Rozanov claims that 'in Russia we do not have a family, what we have is a *"semeika"*' (352), 'semeika', a dysfunctional family being a word which, after Dostoevskii's use of it in *The Brothers Karamazov*, acquired definite negative connotations of degeneration and immorality. Concern over the Russian family as a building block of Russian society is overt in Rozanov: he believes that the only way to save Russia as a nation is through reforming the nation's attitude towards the family. This Russocentric feature of Rozanov's body politics is reflected in his perception and representation of Tolstoi as a Russian citizen, a Russian genius. Rozanov often stresses that Tolstoi is more

---

9   Dukhanova maintains that Rozanov viewed Tolstoi either as a prophet of the family, 'representing an amalgam of pagan and Christian views' or as 'a defeated man whose pessimism over the possibility of renewing the Christian family led him to embrace asceticism'. See Diana Dukhanova, 'A Prophet of the Family: Vasily Rozanov Reads Tolstoy', in *Tolstoy and Spirituality*, Predrag Cicovacki and Heidi N. Grek, eds, Academic Studies Press, Boston, 2018, pp. 128–48 (128).

than a writer; he is, he argues, a thinker, somebody who is above literature. He makes this claim in order to enlist Tolstoi as a collaborator in his own political mission – the quest to change Russian people's habits, their way of thinking and their attitude towards family life.

In *The Family Question in Russia* Rozanov uses the authority of Tolstoi in application to the theme of illegally born children and infanticide. He quotes a long passage from Tolstoi's *Resurrection* in which Nekhliudov inquires about the fate of his child borne by Katiusha Maslova. He notes that the woman who took the child made sure that she positioned all the children destined for the orphanage in such a way that they would not damage one another: with their heads pressing not against each other, but against their neighbour's feet. Rozanov maintains that Tolstoi wrote the scene knowing that it would have a special significance for readers of the journal *Niva*. Rozanov stresses that Tolstoi 'tortures' (40) his reader and that he raises an eternal question: that of the mystery of childbirth. In a move characteristic of Rozanov's logic, he places the problem of Katiusha's child into a discussion on the difference between the attitude of the Old Testament and that of the New Testament towards human sexuality and children. But he also exposes the absurdity of the notion of illegitimate children from the point of view of a metaphysical understanding of childbirth. Framing the discussion as a dialogue between an ascetic and a philosopher he shows the absurdity of the ascetic's claim that Katiusha should not have given birth to the child because it was not legitimate.

Rozanov includes in his book a sub-chapter under the title 'An Event from the Life of Count L. N. Tolstoi' ('Случай из жизни гр. Л. Н. Толстого'), in which he quotes a long passage from P.A. Sergeenko's book *How Count L. N. Tolstoi Lives and Works* (*Как живет и работает гр. Л. Н. Толстой*). The passage relates to a case of infanticide on Tolstoi's estate Iasnaia Poliana. The corpse of a drowned child was discovered in the pond on this estate in August 1896. The whole of the Tolstoi family was shattered by the event, but one of the daughters was particularly upset. She was convinced that the dead child belonged to one of the widows on the estate who had been concealing her pregnancy. The widow in question, however, refuted the allegations and suspicion started to fall on other members of the peasant community. One evening Tolstoi visited the widow and allegedly told her: 'If the murder is not your doing, it will not bring you suffering. But if it was your doing, then it must be very difficult for you now, so difficult that nothing else in your life compares to this suffering' (195). The widow burst into tears and said: 'Yes, it so hard for me as if somebody put a stone on my heart'. She confessed to Tolstoi in detail how she tortured the child to death and then threw him into the pond.

Rozanov left this passage from P.A. Sergeenko without comment, and in this form it functions in his text as a parable or religious sermon. As such it serves as a parallelism to the Old Testament story of how Solomon solved the problem of the ownership of a child claimed by two women. Rozanov elsewhere in his book refers to this story: Solomon the Wise knew that a mother would never allow the torture or murder of her child; he therefore suggested that the child be divided into two halves, one for each of the claimants. The real mother of the child refused to take part in this act. For Rozanov, this serves as an example of the special attitude towards children in Judaism. In his parataxis, which in itself is a mode borrowed from the structure of the Old Testament, the story of Tolstoi's wise resolution of the infanticide case stands as a parallelism between Tolstoi's wisdom and that of Solomon. (Indeed, in one of his articles on Tolstoi of 1908 Rozanov compares him with Solomon, as will be shown later.) Yet this story also functions as a sad juxtaposition between the acts of Hebrew and Russian mothers: in the Old Testament a woman saves her child while in Russia a woman kills her child by torture and then drowns the corpse. For Rozanov the fact that both women in the parable about Solomon were prostitutes, is significant, because it shows that the children of prostitutes were not stigmatized by the ancient Hebrews. Rozanov, we may recall, viewed the issue of illegal children as the source of two evils: infanticide and prostitution.

On the 27 June 1902 a new law concerning illegitimate children in Russia was issued. It was called 'Law on the Improvement of the Status of Illegitimate Children' ('Закон об улучшении положения незаконнорожденных детей'). Significantly, after the publication of this law, Rozanov closed down his debate on the family question in Russia. In one of his concluding articles, 'Последние фрагменты о браке' ('The Last Fragments on Marriage', 1902) he offers his own comments on the new law while also publishing letters from his correspondents. Most of these letters congratulate Rozanov on the new law, thus stressing the role played by Rozanov in influencing changes in legislation concerning illegitimate children. The law divided illegitimate children into two categories: those born from unrecognized marriages and those born outside of marriage. The children of the first category had the rights of legitimate children and those in the second category could become legitimate if their parents got married. The consequence of this new law was the eradication of the word 'illegitimate' on birth certificates. There was considerable confusion among clergy on the issue of the entry of the child's status on the birth certificate, but the expectation was that all children born after the date of the issue of the law, June 1902, would no 'longer have the word 'illegitimate" in their papers.

Rozanov had very personal reasons to be concerned with the status of illegitimate children. After the collapse of his marriage, his wife, Apollinariia Suslova, did not want to grant him a divorce. The result of this was that, in terms of the Church Laws, Rozanov was secretly and therefore illegally married to his second wife, Varvara Butiagina (in 1891), and his children from this relationship were thus illegitimately born. He unsuccessfully applied many times (from 1886) to annul his marriage to Suslova, but technically it was not possible to do so without her agreement. The sadistic former mistress of Fedor Dostoevskii, Suslova, forgetting the Chernyshevskian principles of free love which she practised in her youth, hypocritically argued that men could not destroy that which was sanctioned by God.[10] The situation caused grief not only to the observant Christian Butiagina, but also to their children who were stigmatized at school.

While praising the new law, Rozanov also expresses the view that the law in itself would not solve the problem of the stigma attached to children born out of marriage. He argues that, because the tradition of victimizing young women who gave birth outside of marriage would continue, there would result from this persecution ongoing infanticide and prostitution. He also publishes the letter of one of his correspondents which suggests that further reforms were needed which would allow unmarried couples to give birth to legitimate children, and that it is only if this happens that the whole notion of illegitimate birth would disappear from society. Rozanov also mentions that some journalists had expressed the opinion that the new law subverted the very institution of marriage, by erasing the boundaries between legitimate and illegitimate children. But what Rozanov is about to propose turns this opinion upside down, and suggests that indeed there should be no difference between illegitimate and illegitimate children because a new idea of marriage should be accepted by Russian society – common-law marriage, marriage where the people who lived together should give birth to children and take care of them. He chose to vent this idea in his conversations with Tolstoi during his visit to Iasnaia Poliana.

It is significant that Rozanov decided to visit Tolstoi at Iasnaia Poliana in March 1903, less then a year since the new law on the status of illegally born children was introduced. Rozanov regarded Tolstoi as the most influential person in Russia and believed that, if Tolstoi wished, he could start a revolutionary

---

10   See Zinaida Gippius, 'Zadumchivyi strannik' in *V.V. Rozanov: Pro et Contra*, I, D.K. Burlaka, ed., Izdatel'stvo Russkogo Khristianskogo gumanitarnogo instituta, St Petersburg, 1995, pp. 142–85.

new behavioral trend. At that moment in time such a trend, from Rozanov's perspective, was the emergence of a new type of marriage. In his article 'A Trip to Iasnaia Poliana', Rozanov immediately sets the scene for the focus of his visit to the Tolstoi estate. He notes that his initial impression of Iasnaia Poliana was disappointing in that it was very empty and quiet, like any residence where children do not live.[11] For Rozanov, such a house was not quite a family home. This impression changed with the entrance of Tolstoi's wife, Sofia Andreevna. Rozanov notes her strong physical presence, and the theme of children is yet again brought to the forefront as she speaks of herself as a mother who has given birth to some fourteen children:

> In came Sofia Andreevna, and I immediately characterized her as a 'storm'. Her dress makes a noise. Voice is strong and self-assured. Beautiful, in spite of her age. She told me to my surprise: 'I am 58 and have had about fourteen children' (including those who passed away). This is good and classical [...] Obviously she is clever, but has a somewhat practical mind. (319)

Rozanov confesses that, apart from his desire to see one of the great personalities of his time, he had a 'special motive' for seeing Tolstoi. He wanted to ask him about a subject that he was particularly 'devoted to': 'I thought that it could be done only by a person with international authority whom nobody will dare to accuse of immorality' (321). This subject related to the question of infanticide, and could be addressed by Tolstoi because he had raised this issue in *Resurrection*. Rozanov describes the proposal which he wanted to make to Tolstoi:

> And I wanted partly to ask him, partly to reproach him and partly to appeal to him in this matter: Why he, *the world's moral authority*, does not let his daughters get married 'just like that', without wedding; he could thus set an example for the whole of Europe, so that his authority would sanction this *absolutely private* and *absolutely personal* form of marriage, which could become acceptable for society, and could sanction births of children out of wedlock and as a consequence save children from murder. (321–2; italics in the original)

---

[11] See V.V. Rozanov, 'Poezdka v Iasnuiu polianu', in *O pisatel'stve i pisateliakh*, Polnoe sobranie sochinenii, A. Nikoliukin, ed., Respublika, Moscow, 1995, pp. 319–23. (Subsequent quotation from this source is indicated by page numbers in the text.)

Rozanov claims that, when they started talking 'about sexuality and sexual purity and impurity' (322), Tolstoi himself, without Rozanov asking him the intended question, gave him a definitive answer to the proposal. What that answer was, however, Rozanov does not say – it is possible that Rozanov did not want to pass on information about Tolstoi's daughters that was given in confidence.

The Russianness of Tolstoi was a factor in Rozanov's choice of him as a collaborator for his project. In all of his articles on Tolstoi he stresses that Tolstoi's physique was that of a Russian person: a Russian Ivan, a simple Russian man. In 'A Trip to Iasnaia Poliana' he claimed that Tolstoi was as Russian as Solomon was Jewish and The Buddha Indian. The relevance of the theme of Tolstoi's ethnic Russianness as applied to Rozanov's project is quite obvious: it is the Russian family which Rozanov tries to save from disintegration and Russian children from being victims of infanticide. In 'The Last Fragments on Marriage', an entry in his book *The Family Question in Russia*, Rozanov quotes the 1897 statistics on illegitimate children, placing special significance on data relating to ethnicity and religion. Thus, among the Jews of St Petersburg, 0.65% of children were illegitimate; among the Muslims – 0. 3%; among Catholics – 13%; among Protestants – 9%. Rozanov makes it clear that it is among the Russian population that the birth of so-called illegitimate children is high: between 1897 and 1907 for every 1,000 births in St Petersburg 437 are born out of wedlock.

Rozanov clearly viewed infanticide in ethnic terms; in his work it is presented as a Russian phenomenon. During his trip to Estonia he notes that Estonian peasants tolerated the birth of children out of wedlock, that there was a financial arrangement between the family of the child's father, and that in most cases parents of the child did marry each other in due course.[12] In Russia, he believed, it would take somebody like Tolstoi to influence society in teaching uneducated people of the sin of child-murder and stopping the practice of infanticide.

In his 1911 article 'L.N. Tolstoi and the Russian Church' ('Л.Н. Толстой и русская церковь') Rozanov notes that the Russian clergy was completely insensitive towards Tolstoi's writing and did not understand the educational role which his work had for the simple people, 'темный народ'.[13] Here he turns to Tolstoi's play *The Power of Darkness* (*Власть тьмы*), focusing on one

---

[12] See V.V. Rozanov, 'Estonskoe zatish'e' in *Inaia zemlia, inoe nebo*, Tanais, Moscow, 1994, pp. 54–67.

[13] V.V. Rozanov, 'L.N. Tolstoi i russkaia tserkov'', in *Terror protiv russkogo natsionalizma*, in *Polnoe sobranie sochinenii*, A. Nikoliukin, ed., Respublika, Moscow, 2005, pp. 247–55 (249).

detail related to the case of infanticide described in this play. He reminds the reader that the parents put a cross around the child's neck before killing him so that he dies as a Christian. They thus baptize him, so making him a member of the church. This raises the question of how a religious Russian Christian peasant family did not perceive child-murder as a sin. Rozanov here blames the Russian clergy for not educating people, stressing that Tolstoi understood this paradox in peasants' beliefs. According to Rozanov, Tolstoi knew that, while there were many believers in Russia, there were not many honest, hardworking people who understood the call of duty and obligation, and that it was the Church and the clergy that were to blame because they did not educate the people in these aspects of life. Rozanov admits that Tolstoi was right in his accusations against the church in these matters. But he also corrects himself, noting that this was not the whole truth since Tolstoi failed to *note* the phenomenon of the 'saintly figure' among the people. Rozanov explains that Tolstoi failed to appreciate that the various elders – the *startsy* who lived in monasteries, like Dostoevskii's Zosima – were the products of the Orthodox faith. Rozanov's choice of Zosima as an example is relevant to the context of the problems relating to children, since Zosima in *The Brothers Karamazov* exhorts love of children and all living creatures. Also relevant for this discussion is the fact that Zosima refers to the Old Testament as a source of his attitude to living creatures.

Although Zosima is a monastery elder, and a saintly figure, he is an exception rather than the rule. In most of his writings Rozanov blamed the Church and Christianity for the dire state of the Russian family in the same way in which he blamed Russian literature and writers for introducing the 'wrong kind' of ideals of love. While in his 1911 article he stresses that uneducated Russian clergy could not appreciate the delicacy of feelings of Tolstoi's literary heroes such as Levin and Anna Karenina, after the October Revolution in *The Apocalypse of our Times* (*Апокалипсис нашего времени*, 1918) he attacks Tolstoi amongst other novelists for leading the Russian public astray, for teaching them an erroneous example of love. At the same time he also attacks the Church, claiming that these two main Russian social institutions, literature and the church, were responsible for the collapse of the Russian state and what he perceived to be the end of the Russian nation. He notes that, while the literary protagonists only talk and love, since Peter the Great the people, *narod*, lived in a state of primitive darkness, '*первобытно*'. Most literary characters in Russian novels loved outside of marriage, as did Count Vronskii and Anna Karenina:

> Good God, but one must love inside the family; but inside the family we, so it seems, did not show much loving, and here yet again this damned church divorce law exacerbated the situation ('love according to your duty, and not in accordance with your feeling of love'). And the church is the first one to collapse, and so it deserves to in accordance with the law.[14]

When the tragic circumstances of Tolstoi's death following his escape from his home and his wife became known, Rozanov authored a number of articles in which he demonstrated that Tolstoi's family tragedy was a manifestation of the gap between the Old and the New Testament in their attitudes towards the family. Rozanov searches for a rational explanation for Tolstoi's decision to deprive his widow of the publication rights for his books and to deprive their children of significant and firm inheritance. In his 1911 article 'The Fatal in Tolstoi's "Legacy"' ('Роковое в "наследии" Толстого')[15] he stresses that, had Tolstoi left the rights of publication of his work to his family, it would have been done in accordance with the Old Testament spirit. He insists that the whole of Russia's sympathy lay with Tolstoi's widow, who had been his friend and secretary for forty years, and the wife and mother whose interests centered around raising the family and caring for the children's future. Rozanov describes as a tragedy the fact that only one of the children, the youngest daughter Alexandra, inherited the rights for publication. He expresses his hostility to Alexandra by mentioning in passing that she is a 'девица' (332), which signifies that she is an unmarried virgin. The fact that she rebelled against her mother is as fatal and tragic as the circumstances of Tolstoi's death. Rozanov characterizes the questions surrounding this situation as 'tormenting' for the whole of Russia, and suggests that the court should overrule Tolstoi's final will as something written in a state of hesitation before his death. The fact that Tolstoi did not leave his inheritance to his family, so that 'his children, and the children's children' (331) could use it, was a decision not in the spirit of the Old Testament. While Rozanov appreciated that Tolstoi did not want the money to have a demoralizing effect on his children, he nevertheless states that the estate could have been used for education and modest and honest occupation, and not to fund a life of idleness and leisure. Rozanov thus rebels against the jurisdiction and the laws of inheritance in this case, in the same

---

14   V.V. Rozanov. *Apokalipsis nashego* vremeni, A. Nikoliukin, ed., Respublika, 2000, p. 7.
15   V.V. Rozanov, 'Rokovoe v "nasledii" Tolstogo' in *Terror protiv russkogo natsionalizma, Polnoe sobranie sochinenii*, A. Nikoliukin, ed., Respublika, Moscow, 2005, pp. 331–4. (Subsequent quotation from this source is indicated by page numbers in the text.)

way in which he rebelled against the church and the state laws on marriage, divorce and illegal children. He insists that the rights of inheritance belonged to Tolstoi's wife, reminding the reader that Tolstoi himself challenged the legal system in his novel *Resurrection*. The ambivalence of the word *'nasledie'* in the title of the article, delineated by inverted commas, is an important signifier. It is *'nasledie'* as legacy rather than the legalistic *'nasledstvo'*, or inheritance, that is the real centre of Rozanov's attention. It is indeed Tolstoi's legacy to Russia, the wrong kind of example which he presents to the nation, which makes the issue of the inheritance to be fatal and tormenting.

When Shklovskii wrote the then groundbreaking article on Rozanov in 1922 he applied the term 'oxymoron' to Rozanov's style and structure. In 1922 he had to explain the meaning of the term since it was not as trivialized as it is in contemporary language. He explained the term as a device of putting together contradictory words, and thus applicable to Rozanov's paradoxes. Shklovskii wrote his programmatic Formalist essay without bothering to expand his observations to include Rozanov's political message. But the term oxymoron in application to Rozanov was remembered by other commentators, such as the émigré religious philosopher Vladimir Ilin who, in his 1964 article 'Stylization and Style' ('Стилизация и стиль'), made a point of applying this term to what he describes as Rozanov's original contribution to Christian anthropology. Ilin based his observation on Rozanov's claim that a writer had to suppress the writer in himself in order to make pronouncements: neither The Buddha nor Jesus Christ wrote, claims Ilin, they just uttered ('изрекают').[16] It is my contention that Rozanov perceived the relationship between the Old and the New Testaments as the greatest oxymoron – he often maintained the difference in spirit between Christ's message to the world and the spirit of the Old Testament. He supported his philosophy of sexuality by exposing this oxymoron, the nature of which was implicit in the difference between the attitude towards sex, family and procreation in the Old Testament and the negation of these phenomena in the New Testament. He structures his attitude toward Tolstoi around the same oxymoron: when Tolstoi acts as an Old Testament patriarch in the midst of his large family, he is acceptable to Rozanov. When he acts under the pressure of Christian hesitation towards the call of flesh, he is the target of Rozanov's polemics. In Rozanov's description of his visit to Iasnaia Poliana we are told that, before leaving, he kissed Tolstoi's hand – the hand which, he states, wrote *War and Peace* and *Anna Karenina*.

---

16   V. N. Il'in, 'Stilizatsiia i stil''. Remizov i Rozanov, in *V.V. Rozanov. Pro et Contra.* second edition, D. K. Burlaka, ed., Izdatel'stvo RkhGI, St Petersburg, 1922, pp. 406–30 (423).

But he also stresses that all of Tolstoi's creations are the products of nature, the kind of nature which is God-given, which passes from 'father and mother', and which comes from the earth's and history's deepest bowels. He claims that, from these deep strata, came Schopenhauer, The Buddha and Solomon – personalities which were important to Tolstoi during the time when he wrote his *Confession*. Notably, Rozanov states that only Jesus Christ did not come out of these inner depths. To further advance his monistic view of nature and procreation, Rozanov notes that Tolstoi is dearer to the Russian heart than 'the Jewish, Indian and German sages' (323) because he is Russian by blood ('кровный'). For Rozanov, the Old Testament was the 'Family Testament', 'Семейный завет'. However, by assigning Tolstoi a place among the national sages in the context of his daring proposal to Tolstoi let his daughters set an example of bearing children outside official marriage, Rozanov reveals that his project was above all concerned with the future of the Russian family.

Bibliography

Dukhanova, Diana, 'A Prophet of the Family: Vasily Rozanov Reads Tolstoy', in Cicovacki, Predrag and Grek, Heidi N., eds, *Tolstoy and Spirituality*, Academic Studies Press, Boston, 2018, pp. 128–48.

Gippius, Zinaida, 'Zadumchivyi strannik' in *V.V. Rozanov: Pro et Contra*, I, Burlaka, D.K, ed., Izdatel'stvo Russkogo Khristianskogo gumanitarnogo instituta, St Petersburg, 1995, pp. 142–85.

Il'in, V.N., 'Stilizatsiia i stil'. Remizov i Rozanov', in *V.V. Rozanov. Pro et Contra*. second edition, D.K. Burlaka, ed., Izdatel'stvo RkhGI, St Petersburg, 1922, pp. 406–30.

Møller, Peter Ulf, *Postlude to the Kreutzer Sonata: Tolstoj and the Debate on Sexual Morality in Russia in the 1890s*, E. J. Brill, Leiden, 1988.

Mondry, Henrietta, 'A Wrong Kind of Love – A Teacher of Sex on a Teacher of Love: Rozanov on Turgenev and Viardot', in Reid, Robert and Andrew, Joe, eds, *Turgenev: Art, Ideology, Legacy*, Rodopi, Amsterdam, 2010, pp. 237–51.

Mondry, Henrietta, *Vasily Rozanov and the Body of Russian Literature*, Slavica, Bloomington, 2010.

Rozanov, V.V., *Opavshie list'ia*, in *Izbrannoe*, Neimanis, Munich, 1970, pp. 81–426.

Rozanov V.V., 'Estonskoe zatish'e' in *Inaia zemlia, inoe nebo*, Tanais, Moscow, 1994, pp. 54–67.

Rozanov, V.V., 'Priroda i tserkov'' in Nikoliukin, A., ed., *Terror protiv russkogo natsionalizma, Polnoe sobranie sochinenii*, Respublika, Moscow, 1995, pp. 204–7.

Rozanov, V.V., *V mire neiasnogo i nereshennogo, Polnoe sobranie sochinenii*, Nikoliukin, A., ed., Respublika, Moscow, 1995.

Rozanov, V.V., 'Poezdka v Iasnuiu polianu', in Nikoliukin, A., ed., *O pisatel'stve i pisateliakh, Polnoe sobranie sochinenii*, Respublika, Moscow, 1995, pp. 319–23.

Rozanov, V.V, *Apokalipsis nashego vremeni*, Nikoliukin, A., ed., Respublika, Moscow, 2000.

Rozanov, V.V., *Semeinyi vopros v Rossii*, Respublika, Moscow, 2004.

Rozanov, V.V., 'Rokovoe v "nasledii" Tolstogo' in *Terror protiv russkogo natsionalizma, Polnoe sobranie sochinenii*, Nikoliukin, A., ed., Respublika, Moscow, 2005, pp. 331–4.

Rozanov, V.V., 'L.N. Tolstoi i russkaia tserkov'', in *Terror protiv russkogo natsionalizma, Polnoe sobranie sochinenii*, Nikoliukin, A., ed., Respublika, Moscow, 2005, pp. 247–55.

Shklovskii, Viktor, 'Rozanov' in *V.V. Rozanov. Pro et Contra*, second edition, Burlaka, D.K., ed., Izdatel'stvo RkhGI, St Petersburg, 1922, pp. 321–42.

CHAPTER 7

Tolstoi's *Resurrection* on the Russian Stage

Olga Sobolev

Abstract

After the Revolution Tolstoi's particular brand of critical realism was adopted by Soviet aestheticians as a template for Socialist Realism. Even so, a staging of Tolstoi's novel *Resurrection* by the Moscow Art Theatre in 1930 was not the most obvious one to undertake: it not only required abridgement from its substantial novel form, but adjustment of its thematics to make it acceptable to a Soviet audience. However, since it is a work highly critical of the Tsarist status quo, it contains elements that could be ideologically foregrounded and others that could be conveniently excised. Accordingly, the role of the central character of the novel, Nekhliudov, a landowner anxious to atone for his social privilege and his behaviour as a young man, is practically reduced to that of a melodramatic seducer; while Maslova, the heroine, becomes an optimistic embodiment of the Socialist Realist ideal. Moreover, these modifications in characterization are mutually dependent: Maslova, seduced in her youth by Nekhliudov and ashamed of having fallen into prostitution, is in danger of assuming a victimhood incompatible with a positive Soviet heroine, whereas by presenting Nekhliudov as an utterly unsympathetic and even repulsive character, the sense of guilt is completely effaced from her image.

Keywords

Tolstoi's *Resurrection* – staging Tolstoi's works – Socialist Realism

There was no writer in Russia who in his lifetime experienced such unprecedented glory and success as Lev Tolstoi. In 1898, Chekhov wrote to Suvorin: 'I shall not be at Tolstoi's on 28 August. First of all, it is too cold and damp to make the journey, and secondly what for? His life is a permanent celebration anyway, and there is absolutely no reason to single out any particular day'.[1]

---

1 *Perepiska A.P. Chekhova*, M.P. Gromov and A.M. Dolotova, eds, Khudozhestvennaia literatura, Moscow, 1984, I, p. 261. In his jubilee article (1908) dedicated to the eightieth birthday of

When in 1909 the journal *The Herald of Knowledge* (*Вестник знания*) carried out a readership survey, Tolstoi was named as the most popular author by an overwhelming majority of 295 votes; Darwin came second with 152; while Karl Marx languished in sixteenth position with 52.[2] The situation had not changed in the post-revolutionary twenties, and, despite the efforts of Narkompros (The People's Commissariat for Education) to promote new works dealing with issues of socialist construction, Tolstoi remained a firm favourite even among the ideologically skewed readers of the Red Army.[3] Soviet directors were, nevertheless, slow in producing dramatic adaptations of his works. The sober realism of Tolstoi's writings did not appeal to the artists of the revolutionary avant-garde, and the only attempt at staging Tolstoi in the immediate aftermath of the Revolution was a 1919 adaptation of *First Distiller* (*Первый винокур*) produced by Iurii Annenkov. Performed not any old where but in the Heraldic Hall of the Winter Palace – *First Distiller* used Tolstoi's antiliquor theme as the basis for a mélange of circus, vaudeville, and *balagan*. The production was well crafted and well received, but it lasted only four days, after which it was banned on the grounds of the 'unacceptable resuscitation of bourgeois classics'.[4]

It was not until 1930 that the name of Tolstoi first appeared in the repertoire of the Moscow Art Theatre (MKhAT). Curiously enough, the choice made was not of one of his didactic dramas that would have adequately served the socialist agenda of the day, but one of his later novels, *Resurrection*, which required a considerable amount of reworking of the source text. By placing this work in the cultural context of the time, this chapter will examine it as a controversial theatrical event shaped by its aesthetic proclivities and political objectives; and as a major precursor of the canon that was soon to lay claim to being the only legitimate theatre of the state.

---

the great writer, Semen Frank claimed: that his fame could be compared only with that of Voltaire, Goethe and Victor Hugo: see S.L. Frank, *Russkoe mirovozzrenie*, Nauka, St Petersburg, 1996, p. 440. (This and all ensuing translations from the Russian are by the present author unless otherwise stated.)

2 See Dmitrii Oleinikov, 'Kumiry chitaiushchei publiki nachala stoletiia', *Rodina*, III, 1998, p. 72.

3 See *Massovyi chitatel' i kniga*, N.A. Rybnikov, ed. Gosudarstvennoe voennoe izdatel'stvo, Moscow, 1925, p. 76. At the Literary Post, a theoretical journal of RAPP, also reported that Tolstoi was placed at the top of the list by Komsomol members, as well as by workers of the proletarian districts of the Russian provinces: see *Na literaturnom postu*, 1, 1926, pp. 35–6.

4 See Iurii Annenkov, *Dnevnik moikh vstrech*, Zakharov, Moscow, 2001, p. 299–301. Annenkov's experimental work was highly commended by Viktor Shklovskii, who described it as 'a real tour de force, striking in its composition': see 'Dopolnennyi Tolstoi', in Viktor Shklovskii, *Gamburgskii schet: stat'i, vospominaniia, esse 1914–1933*, Sovetskii pisatel', Moscow, 1990, pp. 103–5 (103).

By the mid-twenties the idea of a world-wide socialist revolution had already faded away; and in 1925 the Party Conference put forward a different task, that of building socialism 'in one country'.[5] This involved creating a new ethnic entity, a Soviet 'people'. The emphasis was on building the nation. This required a radical shift in ideological and cultural policies, which included a step back to 'conservative' values, a vindication of the past and a re-establishment of the classical legacy.[6] Stalin himself paid close attention to the appropriate revision of the tradition. After Lunacharskii's resignation in 1929, he took personal control of the formation of cultural policy in the country, and in his letter to Demian Bednyi expressed his concerns about the misinterpretation of history by certain members of artistic circles:

> Instead of comprehending this event, so significant to the course of the revolution, and lifting themselves to sing the praises of the advanced proletariat, they have retreated to the depths, and, having buried themselves under the dullest quotes from Karamzin on the one hand, and equally dull citations from *Domostroi* on the other, they have declared to the world that, in the past, Russia was a desolate cradle of filth ... that 'idleness' and a desire to 'sit on the stove' are quintessential national traits, inherent to all Russians in general, which, needless to say, includes Russian workers, who, having carried out the October Revolution, never stopped being Russian.[7]

In 1926, nineteenth-century classic works were reinstalled on the shelves of local libraries: previously they had been kept only in a certain number of district centres to be accessed strictly by those specializing in the history of literature. Young authors started being encouraged to engage with examples from the past. The position of the RAPP (Russian Association of Proletarian Writers) on the question of writing was distilled down to three main slogans, two of which referred directly to the tradition. The first – learning from the classics – designated general good practice in writing; the second – the living

---

5 The resolution was read by Kamenev, who claimed: 'By pursuing the right policy, namely reinforcing the socialist elements in our economics, we will show that, despite the reluctant tempo of the international revolution, socialism must be built, can be built together with the representatives of peasants in our country, and it will be built' (*XIV Konferentsiia RKP(B)*, Gosizdat, Moscow-Leningrad, 1925, p. 267).
6 See David Elliot, *New Worlds: Russian Art and Society 1900–1937*, Thames and Hudson Ltd., London, 1986, pp. 22–6.
7 Letter to Demian Bednyi 12 December 1930, in I.V. Stalin, *Collected Works*, R.I. Kosolapov, ed., Informatsionno-izdatel'skii tsentr 'Soiuz', Tver', 2006, XVIII, pp. 31–5 (33).

man – the anticipated result of implementing this practice in relation to the portrayal of the contemporary character; and the third – the 'Red Lev Tolstoi' – the yet-to-appear writer, whose work would represent the recapitulation of the highest achievement of nineteenth-century critical realism.

By 1930, historic and literary films began to dominate the repertoire of the Soviet screen. In this context it is worth mentioning Protazanov's *Ranks and People* (Чины и люди, 1929) – an adaptation of Chekhov's stories; *The Decembrists* (Декабристы, 1926) by Aleksandr Ivanovskii, or *The Poet and the Tsar* (Поэт и царь, 1927) by Vladimir Gardin, which was based on the life of Pushkin.[8] The aim of these films was a politically correct revision of the past, which in practice meant the replacement of real history by legend that was subsequently mythologized and ingrained in the consciousness of the mass viewer. It was precisely in this genre of legend that Soviet cinema was most successful in creating both canon and continuity, elaborating stereotypes and methods that could later be transplanted into any time and place.

The same role was forced on the theatre of the late twenties, which had important implications for the state-assisted 'academic' companies, including MKhAT.[9] This theatre was not in a strong position at the time. It expressed no interest in the experimentation and innovation of early Soviet avant-garde drama, nor would it bow to demands to put on new Soviet plays of inferior quality for the sake of propaganda. Moreover, with the NEP calling for market forces to control theatrical activity, the company was in danger of not being able to meet the economic targets set for the theatre. The running budget of the MKhAT was about 1.5 billion rubles and the box-office takings were just 600 thousand rubles.[10] The Theatre was being pressurized to 'pay back' for the state support, to increase its productivity and to put on more plays more quickly. Its repertoire was also far from satisfactory to the taste of RAPP critics. Despite the fact that by 1928 – the Theatre's thirtieth anniversary – it had produced a number of highly successful political plays (such as Trenev's *The*

---

8   Other examples included *The Collegiate Registrar* (*Kollezhskii registrator*, 1925) by Iurii Zheliabuzhskii – an adaptation of Pushkin's story *The Station Master*; *The House of Ice* (*Ledianoi dom*, 1928) and *The Lame Baron* (*Khromoi baron*, 1928) by Konstantin Eggert based on the eponymous novels of Lazhechnikov and Aleksei Tolstoi respectively, and *The Son of a Fisherman* (*Syn rybaka*, 1929) about the life of Lomonosov by Aleksandr Ivanovskii.

9   In 1920 all Russian theatres were reclassified: governmental financial support was given to a group of the so-called 'academic' theatres, while others were required to be self-supporting and were subjected to severe control by the Party. The favoured 'academic' theatres included the former Imperial Theatres, the Moscow Art Theatre, and Tairov's Chamber Theatre, none of which were strong supporters of the regime.

10 See Jean Benedetti, *Stanislavski: A Biography*, Methuen, London, 1988, p. 250.

Pugachev Rebellion [Пугачевщина, 1925] and Ivanov's Armoured Train 14–69 [Бронепоезд 14–69, 1927],[11]) it was largely dependent on pre-revolutionary productions of the classics and had been persistently criticized for 'its bourgeois aestheticism and middle-class complacency'.[12]

The authorities were beginning to tighten their control over the company,[13] but the new attitude in Soviet cultural policy cast a new light on its traditionalist orientation. For the theatre, it was an excellent opportunity to take the lead and establish itself as a new model in shaping the canon of staging the classics.

The idea of including Tolstoi in the Theatre's repertoire surfaced already in the mid-twenties, and was recorded in the minutes of the Repertoire Committee meeting on 15 November 1925:

> In connection with the upcoming jubilee to plan for the discussion of the revival of *The Living Corpse* (*Живой труп*) and the stage adaptation of *War and Peace*.
>
> Luzhskii – Why not *And the Light Shineth in the Darkness* (*И свет во тьме светит*), or if the worse comes to the worst *The Fruits of Enlightenment* (*Плоды Просвещения*)?
>
> Stanislavskii – Of course, *And the Light Shineth in the Darkness* is Tolstoi's best play. It would be a good idea to announce this production before someone else gets to it first; *The Living Corpse* is also needed.[14]

Tolstoi's dramas were the highlights of MKhAT's pre-revolutionary repertoire. In 1902 Stanislavskii mounted *The Power of Darkness* (*Власть тьмы*) and in 1911 *The Living Corpse*.[15] In his early career, Stanislavskii also staged *The Fruits of Enlightenment* when in 1891 he took over The Society of Literature and Arts.

---

11 Bulgakov's *The Days of the Turbins* (1926) presented a controversial case for the theatre. Approved initially by Glavrepertkom (The Central Repertoire Committee), it was banned from the stage in 1929, to be reinstated only in 1932 when it emerged that Stalin saw the play no fewer than fifteen times. Stalin's backing of this production was of great help to Stanislavskii when he fell out with the authorities and RAPP over closer control of the MKhAT in the late twenties.

12 Edward Braun, *Meyerhold: A Revolution in Theatre*, Methuen, London, 1995, p. 248.

13 In 1929 the directorate of the theatre was 'reinforced' by Heitz, a Communist official, who was supposed to mediate between the government and the company.

14 P.A. Markov, *V Khudozhestvennom teatre. Kniga zavlita*, Vserossiiskoe teatral'noe obshchestvo, Moscow, 1976, p. 527.

15 In accordance with Tolstoi's wishes, *The Living Corpse* was premiered only after the death of the author. Nemirovich-Danchenko visited Tolstoi back in 1900 and asked for permission to stage the play at MKhAT. 'Play it when I die…' replied the writer (*Studia*, 1, 1911, p. 5;

With its light-hearted humour and distinct social slant, *The Fruits of Enlightenment*, which satirizes the ignorance of the Russian landed aristocracy and favours the wit of their servants, would have made an excellent choice for Tolstoi's debut on the Soviet stage. The intention to revive this play was reiterated in meetings of MKhAT's Repertoire Committee in 1926–27,[16] but the project was never realized. Stanislavskii, who had a heart attack at a gala performance of *The Three Sisters* (29 October 1928), never returned to active stage-work again,[17] and the company was led by Nemirovich-Danchenko.

Why Nemirovich-Danchenko dropped the project remains unclear. He might not have been willing to deal with Stanislavskii's productions. He might have had a personal interest in adapting novels for the stage (after two successful adaptations of Dostoevskii's novels: *The Brothers Karamazov* in 1910 and *Nikolai Stavrogin* – a stage version of *The Devils* in 1913).[18] He might have had certain 'political' considerations. It is known that he was under considerable pressure to accept the script of *Resurrection* written by Feodor Raskolnikov. The latter was a Bolshevik writer and a Soviet diplomat, well connected in Party circles (his play *Robespierre* [1930] was staged by a number of Soviet theatres in the thirties). Raskolnikov's version of Tolstoi's novel was not particularly valued by the company, but in the words of Viacheslav Polonskii, the theatre was not in a position to reject it:

> Raskolnikov read 'his own' version of *Resurrection* at the Art Theatre. Shameful! The play is made up of just the dialogue – i.e. the conversations are cut out and stuck together; and he tries to impose it on

---

quoted in Iu.P. Rybkova, 'Kommentarii, L.N. Tolstoi Zhivoi trup', in L.N. Tolstoi, *Collected Works in 22 volumes*, M.B. Krapchenko, ed., Khudozhestvennaia literatura, Moscow, 1982, XI, p. 499).

16 'Regarding the classic plays, this coming season the following are planned for staging: a Shakespeare tragedy, most likely *Othello*, Ostrovskii's *Without a Dowry* (*Bez pridanogo*) and Tolstoi's *The Fruits of Enlightenment* (P.A. Markov, 'Teatr o sebe. Itogi, uroki, perspektivy', *Novyi zritel'*, 14, 1926, pp. 12–13); or 'To celebrate Tolstoi's birthday, *The Fruits of Enlightenment* is to be staged, as almost the entire cast can be involved' (From the minutes of the Repertoire Committee meeting, 5 October 1927, P.A. Markov, 1976, p. 560).

17 After *The Three Sisters*' incident, Stanislavskii rehearsed plays and operas in his apartment and spent much time at health spas in Germany and in Paris. For the years 1928 to 1930 the only major work he did for MKhAT was to write two-thirds of a production plan for *Othello*.

18 Stanislavskii, on the other hand, had very limited experience in staging plays adapted from prose fiction; his only major work, with Nemirovich-Danchenko as co-director, was Dostoevskii's, *The Village of Stepanchikovo* in 1917 – the last production of the pre-revolutionary MKhAT.

the company. And they (the management!) are embarrassed, they are afraid – it looks as if they'll take it. A. Ganetskii[19] strongly 'recommends' it – defends it. This is worse than Lunacharskii's lot.[20]

Finally Nemirovich might have thought, not without good reason, that an adaptation of a novel had greater scope for being expanded to fit the Soviet tenets of the time. Whatever his rationale was, in April 1929 the company began rehearsals and in September *Izvestia* announced that MKhAT was working on a production of *Resurrection*, which would be presented in the first half of the season: 'This season, MKhAT will be staging Raskolnikov's adaptation of Tolstoi's *Resurrection*. The aim of this show is to present a stage version of a "social novel". The production will be premiered in the first half of the season'.[21]

Given its explicit social content, of Tolstoi's three major novels, *Resurrection* was undoubtedly the most suitable for serving the new socialist agenda. According to Markov, the head of MKhAT's Literature Department at the time, the intention was to bring Tolstoi to a modern audience and to create a social drama that would be relevant for the issues of the day.[22] In an attempt to meet requirements of ideological acceptability, the importance of the love story between Katiusha and Nekhliudov was considerably diminished; and the emphasis was placed on the panorama of pre-revolutionary Russia; in the words of Markov: 'In *Resurrection*, Nemirovich-Danchenko saw a stern and expressive portrayal of Tsarist Russia. This was the line the play took'.[23]

The company had limited experience in staging novels. Their recent versions of Bulgakov's *The White Guard* [*The Days of the Turbins*] and Belyi's *Petersburg* were both based on the authorial scripts. The most significant benchmark in the domain of dramatic adaptation was still the 1910 production of *The Brothers Karamazov*, which Nemirovich-Danchenko used as a template for his re-working of Tolstoi's text. Following *The Karamazovs* pattern, the play was divided into four self-contained scenes – 'the court', 'the prison', 'the village' and 'St Petersburg' – each of which represented various layers of

---

19   A powerful Soviet functionary, a former diplomat, and from 1923 one of the leaders of the Soviet Ministry of Foreign Trade, Ganetskii met Raskolnikov when both were employed in the diplomatic corps.
20   V. Polonskii, 'Moia bor'ba na literaturnom fronte. Denvnik mai 1920 – ianvar' 1932, S.V. Shumikhin', ed., *Novyi Mir*, 11, 2008, pp. 133–52 (142).
21   'Khronika MKhATa', *Izvestiia*, 5 September, 1929, p. 4.
22   See P.A. Markov, 1976, p. 380.
23   Ibid. p. 380.

pre-revolutionary society and exposed social injustice in Tsarist Russia. For instance, in the opening scene of the trial, the setting and the *mise-en-scène* were rendered with a caricatured one-sidedness and depicted the court as the archetype of hypocrisy and betrayal. Nikolai Liubimov in his memoirs makes a special mention of the prosecutor (Mark Prudkin), who upon entering the scene was trying to ignore (rather unsuccessfully) an overtly friendly greeting from the madam of a brothel.[24] In the same vein, the sharp and almost grotesque manner of the officials, their mechanical gestures and squeaking voices contrasted with the monotonous speeches of the jury, which were full of abstractions and thus largely incomprehensible, engaged the audience in a collective experience of pity and dismay. From the very first minutes the scene announced one of the main themes of the performance – Katiusha Maslova needs neither vindication nor forgiveness from the dehumanized and rotten state-machine. In its powerful catharsis, it was seen as a swingeing diatribe against falsehood and bureaucracy, and evoked the trial of Ivan in the closing episode of the adaptation of *Brothers Karamazov*.

This allusion to Dostoevskii was a deliberate reprise. Bearing in mind that the staging of *The Karamazovs* had been highly successful, Nemirovich relied on the devices that came off effectively in the earlier work. As in *The Karamazovs*, the scenes in *Resurrection* were linked together through the figure of a 'raconteur' ('чтец'), whose initial task was to advance the action and to fill in the gaps between the episodes. In the course of rehearsals, however, this figure acquired a different dramatic function and became one of the pivotal parts of the performance. The raconteur – who was now referred to as 'the voice of the author' ('лицо от автора') was granted the ability to portray other characters and to provide the audience with the insights they needed. Performed by Vasilii Kachalov, one of MKhAT's leading actors, who also played the part of Ivan in the production of *Brothers Karamazov*, this role became the epitome of Stanislavskii's 'method', with its emphasis on authenticity of feelings and psychological transformation. It was through the eyes of Katiusha that Kachalov watched the train speeding away in the warm, windy autumn night; it was in her place that he turned abruptly at the scream of a little girl, who was trying to catch up with Katiusha on the platform: 'You've lost your shawl, Katerina Mikhailovna!'

The 'raconteur' was no longer perceived as an unintrusive narrator, but rather as the 'moral barometer' of the play – an active commentator, who directed the reaction of the audience; and, in other words, took upon himself

---

24   Nikolai Liubimov, *Neuviadaemyi tsvet*, Iazyki russkoi kul'tury, Moscow, 2000, III, p. 245.

the function of a Greek chorus. One could say that in some respects such a transformation was slightly ironic. A device that was initially introduced out of sheer necessity to bridge the gap between stage conventions and narrative prose was transformed into a quintessential component of classical drama. From the contextual perspective, its function also appeared to be somewhat peculiar – needless to say, the needle of this so-called 'moral barometer' was carefully guided by the dictates of ideological perspective. The audience's response was shaped in such a way that it excluded any ambiguity in the message, which undoubtedly is a cardinal concern of any form of propaganda.

Speaking of the early screen adaptations of Russian classics, Evgenii Dobrenko argued that the pattern was commonly based on giving 'a visual impact to a treatment that the critics have already developed and consolidated'.[25] MKhAT's reworking of *Resurrection* could not rely on any secure interpretation of the source, as the canon had not yet been developed; and the only 'politically correct' guidelines available to the dramatists were Lenin's account of Tolstoi's writings – his seminal article *Tolstoi as a Mirror of the Russian Revolution* (1908). As Raskolnikov wrote in his letter to Gorkii:

> Perhaps I am mistaken, but I do not consider my re-working of *Resurrection* as a mechanical one; it is creative, for I refracted it all through my own artistic prism and offered a new interpretation of this classic work. The reactionary philosophy of Tolstoi is not acceptable to me, but his 'social' aspect is dear and close to my heart. I based my re-working on Lenin's articles on Tolstoi. It is certainly not up to me to judge the success of this venture. In any case, I tried to efface all traces of 'tolstoianism', as I do not have the slightest intention of implanting the reactionary ideas of Tolstovian anarchism and 'non-resistance' into Soviet soil.[26]

In an attempt to make him conform with Lenin's reading, Tolstoi's negation of the existing order was seen as a severe criticism of capitalist exploitation. The ambiguous and unsettling aspects of his Christian philosophy were largely effaced, and the focus was on the author's striving towards spiritual and moral perfection. His notions of the common purpose in life and his altruistic service to others were successfully turned into the irreversible triumph of the collective.

---

25   Evgenii Dobrenko, 'The Russia We Acquired, Russian Classics, the Stalinist Cinema and the Past from Revolutionary Perspective', *Russian Studies in Literature*, XXXVII, 4, 2001, pp. 61–91 (66).
26   Quoted in *M. Gor'kii i sovetskaia pechat'. Arkhiv A.M. Gor'kogo*, R.P. Panteleeva, ed., Nauka, Moscow, 1965, X, book two, p. 84.

In this first 'introduction' to the world of the great writer, positive overtones were regarded as particularly important. The emphasis was placed on the idea of purity and light, which was accentuated in every detail of the production. Scenic design, for instance, strongly contributed to the desired perception. The entire *mise-en-scène*, created by Vasilii Dmitriev,[27] was elaborated in bright and airy tones: a soft-cream curtain that set the atmosphere of the performance was echoed in the elongated white birch-trees of the village, in the pristine white wall of the court room and in the radiant snowy road, meandering in the backdrop of the solemn finale of the closing scene.

Characterization was resolved along similar lines. The image of Nekhliudov (performed by Vladimir Ershov) was practically reduced to that of a melodramatic seducer; while Katiusha (played by Klavdiia Elanskaia) stood out as an optimistic embodiment of the socialist realist scheme. Although the latter was to be established and shaped only two years later in 1932, Nemirovich-Danchenko's interpretation of the heroine matched perfectly all the necessary criteria of the canon. A Socialist Realist work can be generally described as a *Bildungsroman*, concerned with the acquisition of ideologically charged consciousness: in the process of fulfilling a task, the hero or heroine, under the tutelage of a communist mentor, acquires an enhanced understanding of self, the surrounding world and the mission of building the bright future. The leitmotif of Katiusha acquiring this consciousness under the guidance of Shchetinina and Simonson – the exiled political prisoners who loved her with the brotherly love of a human being – became the focus of the performance. Having experienced the joy of pure truth, she could no longer abide the hypocrisy and lies of her rotten surroundings. It was a story of moral awakening, of a woman of great civic courage.

The implications of this moral stance tied in well with the political agenda of the time. Introduced in 1928, Stalin's Five Year Plan required mass mobilization of the workforce of the country. Women's participation in socially productive work was vital for its fulfilment; and a strong campaign to get them out of the pettiness of their domestic affairs was carried out under the leadership of the Women's Department of the Central Committee of the Russian Communist Party.[28] Founded in 1920, it was led by Alexandra Kollontai – the leading champion of liberal feminism, who in her numerous articles, pamph-

---

27 Vladimir Dmitriev became one of the leading artists of MKhAT and designed all its major production of the thirties, such as Gorkii's *Enemies* (*Vragi*, 1937), Tolstoi's *Anna Karenina* (1937) and Chekhov's *Three Sisters* (1940).
28 The organization was eventually dissolved in 1930.

lets and prose works, persistently fought for women's equality and promoted the new marriage and working laws set forth by the Revolution.

Kollontai's novel *Love of Worker Bees* (*Любовь пчел трудовых*, 1924) was a best-seller of its day. Reprinted several times in the late twenties, it set the framework for the image of a self-confident builder of the new system. In the text of the novel words like 'parents', 'marriage', 'God', 'children' – that are key to the Russian spiritual tradition – were all given in quotation marks, to mark them as profoundly alien to a socialist style of living. The novel focuses on the story of Dasha Chumakova, and traces her transformation from an idle, politically indifferent young woman into an ardent follower of the Bolshevik cause. Dasha was seen as the national ideal of a new woman, and it is not coincidental that Katiusha Maslova's image referred directly to the poetics of Kollontai's text. On the one hand, such reference was appealing to the younger audience, who were able to relate more easily to the recognizable stereotype. On the other hand, it created a certain sense of continuity – the past was seen through the prism of the present which was an essential feature in the emerging ideological scheme.

In this sense, the love story between Katiusha and Nekhliudov presented a certain amount of controversy for the director. Despite the forceful and persistent denial of the melodramatic motif in the production of *Resurrection*, the submissive sentimentality of the young heroine, as well as her guilt as a fallen woman, should have been resolved for the audience, for the shadow of Katiusha's past was not something that would easily find resonance in the heart of every *komsomolka*. A solution to this problem was found, however, by the manipulation of the moral hierarchy of the audience's emotions that is, as Peter Brooks put it, 'a public recognition of where virtue and evil reside'.[29] By presenting Nekhliudov as an utterly unsympathetic and even repulsive character, the sense of guilt was completely effaced from Katiusha's image. The weight of evil was transferred unreservedly onto society: she was seen as a 'ray of light in the kingdom of darkness',[30] and the redemptive mode of the original was entirely redressed.

Moreover, this little shift in the moral fabric of the production turned out to be rather effective in terms of projecting its political theme. Being able to relate to the most personal and intimate elements in the heroine's experience, the public became more receptive to its ideological connotations, and was

---

29　Peter Brooks, *The Melodramatic Imagination. Balzac, Henry James, Melodrama, and the Mode of Excess*, Yale University Press, New Haven and London, 1976, p. 32.

30　In this respect, it is slightly ironic that Elanskaia, who played Katiusha, also played Katerina in The Art Theatre's 1940 production of Ostrovskii's *The Thunder Storm*.

ready to appropriate the message alongside the implications of the heroine's story. Needless to say, after being inspired in this way, Nemirovich-Danchenko tended to repeat this practice in a number of his later adaptations, which were tinged with a somewhat uncalled-for melodramatic touch. This was the case in his libretto for *La Traviata* for the Bolshoi Theatre in 1935, where the heroine, haunted by society, committed suicide instead of dying of consumption;[31] or in MKhAT's version of *Anna Karenina* two years later, which became the real epitome of the 'social-realist' drama.

As far as *Resurrection* is concerned, it is worth bearing in mind that the need to negotiate the past with the socialist-realist canon, that was to become commonplace in the mid-thirties, was just emerging. Nemirovich had to proceed by trial and error, and one should certainly give him credit for his remarkable ingenuity in tracing the contour of a pattern that would not be fully apparent for another two years. It cannot be denied that he negotiated a path through the lines of the system. By reconfiguring and obscuring some of the main motifs of the novel, his version of *Resurrection* affirmed the role of the performing arts in the new political status quo. On the other hand, these compromises ensured that the play was not banned after the first night (in this respect, it is sufficient to recall the unfortunate fate of *First Distiller* or *The Days of the Turbins*) and paved the way for the numerous productions of Tolstoi on the Russian stage. Indeed, although it may seem far-fetched today, a performance of *Resurrection* even contributed to the international standing of the country in the period of the Cold War. As quoted in the *New York Times*, the incident is from the time when George Kennan was American Ambassador to Moscow (1952).

Watching a dramatization of Tolstoi's *Resurrection* at the Moscow Art Theatre, the American Ambassador [George Kennan] was electrified to hear the leading man, looking straight at him, say, 'There is an American by the name of George, and with him we are all in agreement'. Was this a daring political gesture? Back at the embassy, Kennan took down Tolstoi's novel and found that the line referred to Henry George, the champion of the single tax on unearned increase in land values and an American much admired by Tolstoi.[32]

Bibliography

Annenkov, Iurii, *Dnevnik moikh vstrech*, Zakharov, Moscow, 2001.

---

[31] See Vera Inber, *Za mnogo let*, Sovetskii pisatel', Moscow, 1964, p. 260–1.
[32] Arthur Schlesinger, 'By George!', *The New York Times*, 27 March, 1994, p. 27.

Benedetti, Jean, *Stanislavski: A Biography*, Methuen, London, 1988.
Braun, Edward, *Meyerhold: A Revolution in Theatre*, Methuen, London, 1995.
Brooks, Peter, *The Melodramatic Imagination. Balzac, Henry James, Melodrama, and the Mode of Excess*, Yale University Press, New Haven and London, 1976.
Dobrenko, Evgenii, 'The Russia We Acquired: Russian Classics, the Stalinist Cinema and the Past from Revolutionary Perspective', *Russian Studies in Literature*, XXXVII, 4, 2001, pp. 61–91.
Elliot, David, *New Worlds: Russian Art and Society 1900–1937*, Thames and Hudson Ltd., London, 1986.
Frank, S.L., *Russkoe mirovozzrenie*, Nauka, St Petersburg, 1996.
Gromov, M.P. and Dolotova, A.M., eds, *Perepiska A.P. Chekhova*, Khudozhestvennaia literatura, Moscow, I, 1984.
Inber, Vera, *Za mnogo let*, Sovetskii pisatel', Moscow, 1964.
'Khronika MKhATa', *Izvestiia*, 5 September, 1929, p. 4.
Liubimov, Nikolai, *Neuviadaemyi tsvet*, Iazyki russkoi kul'tury, Moscow, 2000.
Markov, P.A., 'Teatr o sebe. Itogi, uroki, perspektivy', *Novyi zritel'*, 14, 1926, pp. 12–13.
Markov P.A., *V Khudozhestvennom teatre. Kniga zavlita*, Vserossiiskoe teatral'noe obshchestvo, Moscow, 1976.
Na literaturnom postu, 1, 1926, pp. 35–6.
Oleinikov, Dmitrii, 'Kumiry chitaiushchei publiki nachala stoletiia', *Rodina*, III, 1998, p. 72.
Panteleeva, R.P., ed., *M. Gor'kii i sovetskaia pechat'. Arkhiv A.M. Gor'kogo*, Nauka, Moscow, 1965, X, book two.
Polonskii, V., 'Moia bor'ba na literaturnom fronte. Dnevnik mai 1920 – ianvar' 1932, in Shumikhin, S.V., *Novyi Mir*, II, 2008, pp. 133–52.
Rybkova, Iu.P., 'Kommentarii, L.N. Tolstoi Zhivoi trup', in Tolstoi, L.N., *Sobranie sochinenii v 22 tomakh*, Krapchenko, M.B., ed., Khudozhestvennaia literatura, Moscow, 1982, XI, p. 499.
Rybnikov, N.A., ed., *Massovyi chitatel' i kniga*, Gosudarstvennoe voennoe izdatel'stvo, Moscow, 1925.
Schlesinger, Arthur, 'By George!', *The New York Times*, 27 March, 1994, p. 27.
Shklovskii, Viktor 'Dopolnennyi Tolstoi', in *Gamburgskii schet: stat'i, vospominaniia, esse 1914–1933*, Sovetskii pisatel', Moscow, 1990, pp. 103–5.
Stalin, I.V., *Collected Works*, Kosolapov, R.I, ed., Informatsionno-izdatel'skii tsentr 'Soiuz', Tver', XVIII, 2006.
XIV Konferentsiia RKP(B), Gosizdat, Moscow-Leningrad, 1925, p. 267.

CHAPTER 8

The Dreamer and the Destroyer: Two Unconventional Tolstoians and Their Impact in Australia

Elena Govor and Kevin Windle

Abstract

Tolstoi's teachings, as well as producing numbers of individual 'Tolstoians', also inspired some of them to found colonies in which the teacher's principles could be put into practice. The attempts of one such adherent, Nicholas Illin (1852–1922), to carry out these projects, is the subject of this chapter, together with Alexander Zuzenko (1884–1938), whose affiliation to Tolstoi's teachings was less wholehearted. Illin's enthusiasm for Tolstoi was initially intense, but in the 1890s he denounced him as a hypocrite, while, paradoxically, not abandoning the basic principles of Tolstoianism. He attempted to found Tolstoian colonies in Patagonia, Australia and Honduras (where he died). Zuzenko, who spent over seven years in Australia as a political agitator and trades unionist, seems initially to have held Illin in high regard, but fell out with him over his public condemnation of the execution of the Russian royal family in 1918. Having taken the well-trodden path from Tolstoian to anarchist to confirmed Bolshevik, Zuzenko returned to Russia to work as a sea captain, but was charged with espionage and executed during Stalin's purges. The biographies of these two men exemplify the potent influence, for good or ill, that Tolstoi's ideas had on the lives of many Russians.

Keywords

Tolstoianism – Russians in Australia – evolution of Tolstoian ideas

The state of Queensland, in north-eastern Australia, has not, it is fair to say, ever been looked upon as a breeding ground for Tolstoian thought, or as a haven for the writer's followers.[1] In its short history it has, it is true, been noted for a brief period of determined activity by expatriate Bolsheviks, as we shall recount, and these were of much concern to the Australian government, but the fact that a small number of the leading agitators had at some stage fallen under the influence of Lev Tolstoi and regarded themselves as his followers – if only for a passing phase – is easily overlooked. This is understandable: by the time of the 'Bolshevik trouble' in Brisbane (1918–20), the protagonists saw themselves in a different light, and the police and military intelligence in their search for trouble-makers and revolutionaries did not associate these with the ideas of a Russian novelist.

Nevertheless, Tolstoian thought, that of his late period, which had such a powerful effect on so many of his fellow-countrymen, left its mark on the ideological development of some of those who made their way to Australia before World War I. Two who came to prominence in the Russian community in Queensland in the years 1910–1922 are of particular interest: Nicholas Illin (Nikolai Dmitrievich Il'in, 1852[2]–1922) and Alexander Zuzenko (Aleksandr Mikhailovich Zuzenko, 1884–1938).[3]

Nicholas Illin was born in the village of Ilinka, in the province of Saratov, into a family of provincial nobility which claimed an ancient lineage going back to the Riurik dynasty.

Nicholas, who lost his father early, received his education at a *gimnaziia* in Tambov and the St Petersburg Academy of Surgical Medicine, then a hotbed of student radicalism. In 1872, however, at the age of nineteen, he decamped to the United States without completing his degree (though later often referred to as a 'doctor'). This was the beginning of his rebellion against his family and its traditions: instead of pursuing a secure military career, he chose a more uncertain vocation as a seeker after truth and justice. A sense of guilt over his aristocratic origins would dog him until the October revolution of 1917. Disappointed with the form of society he found in America, he returned to Russia

---

1 An earlier version of this chapter was published in Russian in *Literaturnaia Amerika*, 2 in 2016: 'Dva neobychnykh tolstovtsa v Avstralii', pp. 375–95. The authors are grateful to the editors of *Literaturnaia Amerika*, for permission to make use of material published therein.

2 This date of birth seems the most reliable. It is based on Nicholas' statutory declaration for naturalization in Australia and his official service records, although he stated in his autobiography for the Russian biographical dictionary and in a book of poetry that he was born in 1849.

3 We have retained the forms of Russian names used by their owners in Australia, thus, for example, 'Illin', 'Yakunin' and 'Herman Bykoff'. This does not apply to Russian bibliographical references, in which, as elsewhere in this volume, standard Library of Congress transliteration is used: Il'in, German Bykov and Iakunin.

FIGURE 1   Nicholas Illin.
REPRODUCED BY KIND PERMISSION OF THE ILLIN FAMILY.

and Ilinka after six months, and toyed for a while with a *narodnik* approach, trying to lead his former serfs towards economic independence, but without success, and at the cost of his own financial security. In 1876 he left for newly conquered Central Asia as a junior civil servant, but his ten years in Turkestan ended when he clashed with the higher authorities of the region – an episode which provided the material for an exposé published as a novel, *In the New Land* (*В новом краю*).[4] By the time of its publication he had returned to St Petersburg to work as a lawyer, upholding the legal rights of the poor and growing increasingly critical of the Tsarist regime.

Such was Illin's frame of mind by the close of the 1880s that, at a time when the new Tolstoian philosophy was gaining ground, he was particularly receptive to it. He and his wife Alexandra read *The Kreutzer Sonata*, then banned but circulating widely, in May 1890, and immediately became converts. Nicholas records their first impressions:

---

4   N.D. Il'in, 'V novom kraiu: roman-khronika iz vremen zavoevaniia Turkestana', *Knizhki 'Nedeli'*, 1–11, St Petersburg, 1886.

> I am spending the third day at our *dacha* with my wife and two ladies, our close acquaintances. We have spent all this time reading *The Kreutzer Sonata*, which has recently become famous, and in endless debates and discussions about it. Our day-to-day life has been turned upside down; we forget to eat and drink; we stay awake at night. A strange thing this is: each of us, individually, knew everything depicted by Tolstoi and yet, reading this story, how can I say it – reading it opens up to you a new, unknown truth.... Yes, we have to ... scrape away the dirty layers of modern civilization's habits and customs; we have to reveal in ourselves the human being, which indeed was created in God's likeness. How lucky we are that our eyes have been opened while our children are young ... This rebirth will be a hard struggle for us but we will manage to guide our children along this pure and straight path.[5]

The Illins' obsession with Tolstoi's teachings was reinforced by their acquaintance with another Tolstoian, the painter Nikolai Ge (1831–94), a frequent visitor to Iasnaia Poliana, known for his portraits of Tolstoi, Nekrasov, Saltykov-Shchedrin and others.

Ge's painting of Pilate and Christ *What is Truth?* (*Что есть истина?* [1890]) had given deep offence to the Orthodox Church, and Konstantin Pobedonostsev exerted influence to have it banned from the *Peredvizhniki* exhibition for its inappropriate image of the figure of Christ, who resembled a vagabond and lacked any trace of the dignity usually accorded to him. So impressed was Illin with this painting that he spontaneously offered to take it abroad for exhibition in the West, to spread the artist's message, and, if possible, make a fortune for them both. However, the journey he proceeded to undertake with his eight-year old son Leandro, to Hamburg, Berlin, New York and Boston, did not bring the success he had confidently predicted; the venture proved an expensive failure. Nine months later he returned, bankrupt and bitter against his former idols Tolstoi and Ge. Financial wrangles and recriminations followed; he had simply made no provision for failure. Ge, who had supplied some funding, suspected – not implausibly – that Illin had gambled it away. Illin, whose devotion to Tolstoian ideals sometimes seemed to exceed that of Tolstoi himself, hastened to 'expose' the 'hypocrisy' of Tolstoi and Ge in his book *The Diary of a Tolstoian* (*Дневник толстовца*, 1892), which in fact was an anti-Tolstoian pseudo-diary with jumbled dates.[6] It provoked dismissive remarks from the Tolstoian camp. Ilia Repin called him a 'strange

---

5   N.D. Il'in, *Dnevnik tolstovtsa*, M. Iants, St Petersburg, 1892, pp. 14–15.
6   See ibid.

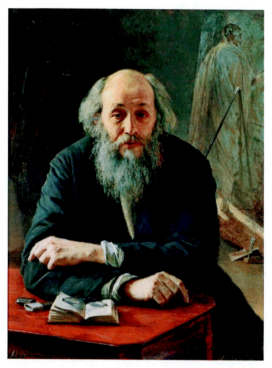

FIGURE 2   Nikolai Ge by Nikolai (Mykola) Iaroshenko. State Russian Museum.
PUBLIC DOMAIN.

dreamer', a 'cheat or psychopath' and a 'simple-minded thief';[7] an anonymous critic described him as a 'petty creature corroded with vanity and an aspiration for European fame' and 'a morally deformed personality',[8] while Nikolai Ge wrote, 'I think that he is ... simply mad, he is ill, there is no other explanation for such muddle-headedness in his enterprises'.[9] Lev Nikolaevich himself pronounced him 'insane', adding that 'in insanity, as in drunkenness, what was previously concealed becomes apparent'.[10] Maxim Gorkii would later refer to the *Diary* as 'a hysterically spiteful little book'.[11] Tolstoi's spiritual authority in

---

7   I.E. Repin, *Dalekoe blizkoe*, Iskusstvo, Moscow, 1964, p. 320; I.E. Repin, *Pis'ma k pisateliam i literaturnym deiateliam*, Iskusstvo, Moscow, 1950, p. 89.
8   See *Severnyi vestnik*, VI, 1892, pp. 75–9.
9   Quoted in V. Stasov, *Nikolai Nikolaevich Ge*, Posrednik, Moscow, 1904, p. 346.
10 L.N. Tolstoi, *Polnoe sobranie sochinenii*, Khudozhestvennaia literatura, Moscow, 1950, LXXXVIII, p. 200.
11 M. Gor'kii, 'O S.A. Tolstoi'. In: M. Gor'kii, *Vospominaniia. Rasskazy. Zametki*, Kniga, Berlin, 1925, p. 30.

FIGURE 3 Nikolai Ge's 'What is Truth?' Tretiakov Gallery, Moscow.
PUBLIC DOMAIN.

Russian society was such that Illin's bitter denunciation was soon forgotten, with its author, while Tolstoi's reputation remained untarnished. Illin himself disappeared from view, thought by many to have died soon after this episode.[12]

He was in fact alive and well, but had fled abroad, expecting prosecution for debt and embezzlement. His whereabouts and later life were known to very few, until a century later when Elena Govor investigated the family history of a large group of Australian Aborigines, named Illin, in Northern Queensland, who preserved memories of the forebear they called 'Deda', together with family relics and manuscripts in Russian, a language they had lost. It was Nicholas Illin's son, Leandro, who demonstrated that his father's idealism ran deeper than the rhetoric of a Chekhovian *intelligent*, when in 1915, in the face of strict racial segregation, he married an Aboriginal woman, and after her early death, brought up their six children in outback Queensland.

12   A Soviet edition of Tolstoi's complete works refers to Illin as having died in 1895. L.N. Tolstoi, *Polnoe sobranie sochinenii*, Khudozhestvennaia literatura, Moscow, 1952, LI, p. 225.

FIGURE 4   The Illin family (1929).
REPRODUCED BY KIND PERMISSION OF THE ILLIN FAMILY.

He became a champion of the Aboriginal cause, one of the first white Australians to refer to the Aborigine as 'my dark brother', in 1925. Leandro died in obscurity as a labourer in Australia in 1946, but some of his descendants, who number over two hundred, are at the forefront of the struggle for Aboriginal rights and welfare in twenty-first-century Australia.[13]

Nicholas Illin had not, however, gone straight to North Queensland: he had first taken his family to another outpost of 'civilization', and settled in Patagonia, in the foothills of the Andes. Here they scratched out a living for nearly fifteen years before moving on. They arrived in Queensland in 1910, the year of Tolstoi's death. Soon they were clearing land in the rainforest of the Atherton Tablelands, near Cairns, and establishing a Russian colony, later known as Little Siberia, conceived as a home for fugitives from Tsarist Russia, doing what Illin had wanted to do, but had been unable to do, in Argentina.

The colony may seem an unlikely aim, but at the time (1910–15) a sizable proportion of the growing Russian population of Queensland was made up of men who had escaped from prison or exile in Siberia, most of them revolutionaries.

---

13   For a more detailed account, see Elena Govor, *My Dark Brother: The Story of the Illins, a Russian-Aboriginal Family*, UNSW Press, Sydney, 2000.

FIGURE 5   The Illins' family farm.
REPRODUCED BY KIND PERMISSION OF THE ILLIN FAMILY.

The idea of an egalitarian colony, serving to help and support those fleeing Russia, remained Nicholas Illin's *idée fixe*, which he carried with him from Patagonia to Queensland and later to Honduras, and leads one to wonder whether he was really as anti-Tolstoian as he purported to be. It may be truer to say that he took the spirit of Tolstoi's teachings more literally than most, more literally perhaps than Tolstoi himself. Illin's view of Tolstoi, in relation to himself, at the end of Tolstoi's life is expressed in an allegorical *causerie* in the Brisbane Russian newspaper *Echo of Australia* (Эхо Австралии): 'Non-resistance before the Highest Court' ('Непротивление перед судом вышним'). A layman (обыватель) and a sage (старец) 'who had called for non-resistance', newly deceased, appear before the Almighty for judgement. The verdict passed on the former is: 'He was a sinner, but he tried to reform ... He recognized his shortcomings and regretted them. Let him return in a new incarnation and atone for his sin'. By contrast, for the sage (that is, Tolstoi) there was no absolution whatsoever.[14]

---

14   N. Il'in, 'Neprotivlenie pered sudom vyshnim', *Ekho Avstralii*, 4, 18 July 1912, pp. 2–3; 5, 25 July 1912, pp. 2–3.

FIGURE 6   Alexander Zuzenko c. 1905.
REPRODUCED BY KIND PERMISSION OF KSENIA ZUZENKO.

The story of Alexander Zuzenko, his global travels and adventures, and his literary connections, has been told elsewhere,[15] so only the briefest summary is needed here.

Born in Riga in 1884, he went to sea at the age of about fifteen, joined the Socialist Revolutionaries (SRs) only a little later, was an active member of the SRs' Combat Organization during the revolution of 1905, when he organized strikes in Riga and took part, he later claimed, in 'terrorist acts', for which he was briefly imprisoned. In 1911 he made his way to Australia, via London, and spent the next seven and a half years in the northern parts of the continent, where he made a name for himself as an anarchist, agitator, pugilist, strike-leader, journalist and ally of Fedor Sergeeff (Artem) – the hero of Tom Keneally's novel *The People's Train*.[16] (Like Sergeeff, he figures in several works

---

15   Kevin Windle, *Undesirable: Captain Zuzenko and the Workers of Australia and the World*, Australian Scholarly, Melbourne, 2012.
16   Tom Keneally, *The People's Train*, Viking, Sydney, 2009. For more detail on Artem, see Tom Poole and Eric Fried, 'A Bolshevik in Brisbane', *Australian Journal of Politics and History*, 1985, XXXI, 2, pp. 244–54, and Kevin Windle, 'Brisbane Prison: Artem Sergeev Describes Boggo Road', *New Zealand Slavonic Journal*, XXXVIII, 2004, pp. 159–80.

FIGURE 7   Alexander Zuzenko in 1921.
REPRODUCED BY KIND PERMISSION OF KSENIA ZUZENKO.

of Russian literature, usually slightly disguised.) After a period of activism on behalf of the Industrial Workers of the World (IWW), in 1918 Zuzenko became the leader of the Brisbane Union of Russian Workers (URW), the focus of 'disloyal' agitation at this time. In April 1919 he was deported to Soviet Russia for leading the 'Red Flag' procession in Brisbane, which resulted in severe rioting and an emergency situation in the city. He returned briefly to Australia as an agent of the Comintern in 1922 (now no longer an anarchist but a Bolshevik), only to be deported a second time, and eventually became a Soviet sea captain on the Leningrad-London route, until Stalin's purges overtook him in 1938.

He was arrested in April, charged with espionage on behalf of the British, and executed in August 1938.

In his later life in the USSR, Zuzenko, though fond of recounting his adventures in Australia, rarely spoke of Illin, but it is clear that at one period they were on close terms, even if contact was infrequent. Illin was viewed by some in the Russian community as a kind of spiritual leader, although he never aspired to exert any practical direction. He lived in the remote fastnesses of the North, a thousand miles from Brisbane, and in his later years travelled little. Zuzenko travelled widely, and was well known in the areas where groups of Russians regularly found work: the sugar-cane plantations of the north-

FIGURE 8   Cane-cutting. Zuzenko seated, centre.
REPRODUCED BY KIND PERMISSION OF KSENIA ZUZENKO.

ern coast, the mining areas of central and north-western Queensland, and scattered railway-construction sites.

His acquaintance with Illin is reflected in an early novel by Konstantin Paustovskii, *The Gleaming Clouds* (*Блистающие облака*). Paustovskii, who was friendly with Zuzenko in 1923–24, made extensive use of him in this and other works. He claimed to have relied exclusively on what he knew of Zuzenko personally and what Zuzenko told him of his past.[17] It is certainly the case that Zuzenko told some tall stories about his own exploits, but much of the incidental detail reported by Paustovskii has the ring of authenticity. In *The Gleaming Clouds*, the character named 'Captain Kravchenko' recalls a visit to an elderly Russian doctor known in the community as 'Lev Tolstoi', in the 'jungle' of northern Australia, 'where the savages have not yet died out'.[18] Here this 'Lev Tolstoi' has cleared some land and farms it with his sons. There

---

17 Konstantin Paustovskii, letter to R.E. Zaborovskii, quoted in Al'bert Izmailov, 'Stroptivyi i dobryi chelovek', in L.P. Krementsov, ed., *K.G. Paustovskii: materialy i soobshcheniia, sbornik*, Vypusk 4, *Personazhi i geroi knig K. Paustovskogo*, Kniga 1, Mir Paustovskogo, Moscow, 2007, p. 89.
18 Konstantin Paustovskii, *Sobranie sochinenii*, Khudozhestvennaia literatura, Moscow, 1957, I, p. 298. 'Kravchenko' (Zuzenko) says of 'Lev Tolstoi' (Illin), 'He was our advisor'.

is scant detail beyond this, and the point of the episode is not really 'Lev Tolstoi' at all, but this figure is clearly based on Illin, and it is noteworthy that although he had long since declared that he had broken free of Tolstoi's influence, others regarded him with great respect, a respect at least partly related to his still being perceived as a Tolstoian. Clearly there was much in his mode of life which marked him as belonging permanently in that category.

There is further evidence of contact between these two men in the writings of Zuzenko's comrade in Brisbane, Herman Bykoff (also known as Rezanoff). Bykoff was a sailor, like Zuzenko, originally from Saratov (like Illin), who arrived in Australia in 1916 and quickly made his mark in the Union of Russian Workers. Like Zuzenko, he was active in journalism, and edited at least one illegal Russian newspaper in Brisbane after Zuzenko had been deported, and before he was deported himself.[19] In his politics he often differed from Zuzenko and at one stage joined a rival Russian workers' group, but at the time of the Red Flag demonstration (23 March 1919) he shared a leadership role with Zuzenko: they marched side by side at the head of the column. Only weeks before that event, Bykoff had written a short play, satirizing the leading personalities in the URW, especially Zuzenko. Never published, it is now held in the National Archives of Australia (NAA), having been seized with Bykoff's other papers at the time of his arrest. It bears the unpromising title *How we are learning self-management and regulation* (О том, как мы учимся самоуправлению и контролю) and purports to depict a farcical meeting of the URW in December 1918. 'Rip-the-Sails', also known as 'the Great Destroyer', speaks of being 'the spiritual son of my spiritual father', and a helpful explanatory footnote identifies 'Rip-the-Sails' as 'A. Z-nko', indicating the source: 'see Z-nko's letter to the counter-revolutionary Illin, whom he regards as his spiritual father'.[20]

The letter to which Illin refers has not been traced, but the background to it is clear from other communications intercepted and translated by the military censor, and it is safe to infer that in that letter Zuzenko stated that in view of Illin's recent public statements he could no longer regard Illin as his 'spiritual father'. Bykoff had contacted Illin to seek details of their earlier association;

---

19 See Kevin Windle, '*Nabat* and its Editors: the 1919 Swansong of the Brisbane Russian Socialist Press', *Australian Slavonic and East European Studies*, XXI, 1–2, 2007, pp. 143–63.

20 National Archives of Australia (NAA): 'Papers relating to miscellaneous events involving the use of a red flag', BP4/1, 66/4/2165, 'O tom, kak my uchimsia samoupravleniiu i kontroliu', p. 360. See also Kevin Windle, '"Unmajestic Bombast": The Brisbane Union of Russian Workers as Shown in a 1919 Play', *Australian Slavonic and East European Studies*, XIX, 1–2, 2005, pp. 29–51.

any evidence of ideological or other affinity between the two men would have served his purpose admirably while he composed his parodic drama. Illin's belated response, written on 24 April 1919, when Bykoff was in Brisbane Prison,[21] confirmed the fact of Zuzenko's visit to his North Queensland home, which figures in Paustovskii's novel: Illin writes that Zuzenko stayed with him for a few days in 1913, and that they talked at length. Soon afterwards, Zuzenko wrote to Illin, saying that he had come to think of him as his 'spiritual father'. Illin formed the opinion that his visitor was far from being a radical revolutionary: 'In our conversation he never appeared to me as an extremist, his ideals were always modest and reasonable'. He added that he was 'very much surprised when he [Zuzenko] joined the extremist crowd whose programme is out of all reason'. Further, since Illin had made plain his revulsion for both Bolshevism and anarchism, Zuzenko 'did very wrong to call me his spiritual father. People who destroy without reconstructing never could be spiritually dear to me'.[22]

A definitive parting of the ways was reached in late 1918. The occasion was the assassination of the Romanov family in Ekaterinburg. Like many others, Illin was appalled by the murders, and said so publicly in a letter to the *Cairns Post*.[23] He expressed his horror, although writing as 'a bitter enemy of Czarism', as one who had rejoiced at the February revolution and supported Kerenskii and the Constituent Assembly. By speaking out in the Australian press he could only incense the hard-line members of the URW. A member in Cairns, G. Tokareff, duly wrote to Zuzenko in Brisbane to report Illin's views and voice his own indignation. By declaring his abhorrence of Bolshevik brutality and the slaughter of innocents, Illin had cut his ties with the revolutionary community in Australia. Tokareff wrote, 'I am writing to you because I can't do anything myself to the dirty dog who wrote this astounding rubbish to the *Cairns Post* ... I could only give him a hiding which I certainly would have done if I had met him immediately after reading'.[24]

Zuzenko, as leader of that community and editor of its newspaper, responded by repudiating Illin's stance and stating categorically that, whatever their

---

21   NAA, A6286, 1/126, QF3859, N. Illin to A. Resanoff, 24 April 1919.
22   A cynical censor (NAA QF3859) commented that in this letter Illin was 'apparently out to save himself' by a letter which he knew would be scrutinized by the authorities. Misreading Illin's innate unworldliness, he describes the letter as 'suspicious in its loftiness of tone', and supposes that the writer must be pretending not to know that 'Resanoff' (Bykoff) is in prison.
23   Nicholas Illin, 'A Russian on Russia', *Cairns Post*, 4 October 1918, p. 2.
24   NAA, A6286, 1/76, QF2277, G. Tokareff to A. Zuzenko, 22 October 1918.

earlier relationship, he and Illin now had nothing in common. The 'spiritual son' and his 'spiritual father' had emphatically disowned each other and disclaimed any philosophical ancestry in Iasnaia Poliana.

What, then, was the ideological position held by Zuzenko at this period? Bykoff, who mocks him as 'the Great Destroyer' and 'His Anarchic Majesty', presents him as the upholder of somewhat confused political principles, contrasting with Bykoff's own unadulterated and orthodox Bolshevism. (Bykoff also appears in his own play as the voice of rational proletarian Bolshevism.) The playwright makes Zuzenko say, 'Tolstoi and Christ were revolutionaries and did not recognize Caesar's Law. And they perished as fighters for the liberation of the Working Class, for anarchic communism'.[25] At about the same time, Bykoff wrote in an article intended for the Russian-language newspaper *Knowledge and Unity* (Знание и единение), but never published, 'Zuzenko and Gorskii tried unsuccessfully to persuade the comrades that Bolshevism was anarchic communism. I demonstrated that that was simply absurd'.[26]

However, if this is an accurate representation of Zuzenko's politics in 1919, it is clear from some of Zuzenko's own writing that within a fairly short time he had moved away from anarchism, having earlier been an admirer of Bakunin and Kropotkin, and from his earlier adherence to Tolstoian principles. He proclaimed his rejection of anarchism in an article published under the name 'Matulichenko' in the New York daily *New Russian Word* (Новое русское слово) in 1921.[27] His rejection of Tolstoi was evident already, but is unmistakably clear from a story written after his return to Soviet Russia. Zuzenko is not known as a writer of fiction, but he did leave one unpublished short story, *The Law of the Fang and the Cudgel* (Закон клыка и дубины, с. 1924), a kind of parable which, he felt, summed up the Australian way of life.[28] The protagonist, Lavrov, is a meek and downtrodden Russian worker at a remote Queensland mining and smelting site, who refuses to stand up for his rights. When brought to see the error of his ways by the more pugnacious narrator, he proceeds to murder his tormentor, an overbearing foreman, with a crowbar – an outcome the nar-

---

25 See NAA BP4/1, 66/4/2165, 'O tom ...' (Bykoff's capitals), p. 360.
26 NAA BP4/1, 66/4/2165. A. Rezanov [Bykoff], 'Rus' avstraliiskaia'. In English in Kevin Windle, 'Hades or Eden? Herman Bykoff's *Russian Australia*', *Australian Slavonic and East European Studies*, XXVI, 1–2, 2012, pp. 1–25.
27 A. Matulichenko [Zuzenko], 'Kak ia, anarkhist, stal lenintsem: neskol'ko slov o teorii i praktike revoliutsii', *Novoe russkoe slovo*, 16–18 February 1921.
28 'Zakon klyka i dubiny'. Typescript kindly provided by the late Ksenia Zuzenko. A copy is held in the Poole-Fried Collection, Fryer Library, University of Queensland, UQFL 336, Box 8, folder 9.

rator had not intended.[29] Zuzenko's message is simple: The Bible, Christian doctrine, and Tolstoi are mistaken! There can be no turning the other cheek. Non-resistance is not the way. The workers must assert themselves and overcome their oppressors. A few years later, when travelling as an agent of the Comintern, Zuzenko encountered a community whose principles would once have held much appeal for him, the Dukhobors, who had established themselves in southern British Columbia largely thanks to material aid provided by Tolstoi. In 1922 Zuzenko was making his way back from Moscow to Australia on Comintern business. The journey was difficult, and a seamen's strike in the USA slowed his progress. Unable to take ship, he devoted much time and effort to raising funds in Russian communities for famine relief in Russia, and promoting societies for technical aid. His aim in visiting the Dukhobors was to urge them to return to Soviet Russia, where their skills as agriculturalists would form the basis of new farming communes and, he thought, 'make a powerful contribution to the communization of the countryside'. He duly visited the community in Brilliant, British Columbia, addressed mass meetings and held an extended public debate with its renowned leader, Petr Verigin. The latter, in Zuzenko's words a 'sly, imperious, proud old man', made a show of interest but speedily alerted the police to the presence of a Soviet agent, compelling him to make a hurried departure to evade capture.[30]

By the time he had embarked on his new career in Soviet Russia, as a sea-captain, Zuzenko thought of himself only as a Communist (Bolshevik). Even in the family he did not, it seems, refer to membership of any other party, although he is known to have been an SR and later a member of the IWW, or to ever being attracted to rival strains of revolutionary thought. Since Australia eventually proved more resistant to all strains than it seemed in 1917–19, his impact in that country was ultimately slight. His efforts as a Comintern agent to foment revolution in 'the Achilles heel of British imperialism' in 1922 were

---

29 The story is based on a case of murder for which a Russian worker, Alek Yakunin, was tried in Cloncurry in 1916. See Kevin Windle, 'Murder at Mount Cuthbert: A Russian Revolutionary Describes Queensland life in 1915–1919', *AUMLA*, CX, 2008, pp. 53–71. The narrator of the story is clearly Zuzenko himself, but he may have exaggerated his own role in the incident.

30 Rossiiskii gosudarstvennyi arkhiv sotsial'no-politicheskoi istorii (RGASPI [Moscow]): Dokumenty Kommunisticheskogo Internatsionala, *fond* 495, *opis'* 94, *delo* 18, pp. 1–17, Aleksandr Mikhailovich Zuzenko to the Executive Committee of the Third Communist International, 28 February 1923. In English in Kevin Windle, '"The Achilles Heel of British Imperialism": A Comintern Agent Reports on His Mission to Australia 1920–1922. An Annotated Translation', *Australian Slavonic and East European Studies*, 2004, XVIII, 1–2, pp. 143–76.

no more successful than the earlier strikes and demonstrations, but he could at least take comfort in having proved a cause of serious concern to the security authorities in Australia and Britain, spoken of several years later in Federal Parliament as a 'very violent agitator'[31] and 'dangerous alien'.[32] By this stage, he had moved far from the ideals propounded by Lev Tolstoi in the last decades of his life.

As for Nicholas Illin, by now in Central America, he was consumed by a deep sense of regret and responsibility for what the revolution had become. The mistakes of his generation, those swept up by the 'noble ideas' circulating in the 1870s and 80s, including *Tolstovstvo*, had produced something very different in the new rulers of Russia. He was powerless to change the situation there, but he could help those seeking refuge from civil war, famine and persecution, by establishing a new Russian colony far from Russia. Australia, which, thanks to the activities of Zuzenko and Bykoff, had witnessed increased animus towards Russians in 1918–19, was no longer a suitable place for his project. Virgin land awaited them, he thought, in Central America. There he could establish a home for thousands of refugee families, now forced to flee from Bolshevik rule. And so, at the age of seventy, he took his family – minus Leandro, who stayed with his Aboriginal wife in Australia – to San Pedro Sula in Honduras,[33] where he died some six months after their arrival. His last words on his deathbed in 1922 were to urge his children to return to Russia and publish his works there. The latter injunction, of course, was even more impractical than the former. His many descendants were in no position to do either. They did, however, do their utmost to preserve his memory in the countries in which they lived – Honduras, Australia and the USA – while upholding his devotion to his ideals, ideals which reflected, in some degree at least, his early devotion to Lev Tolstoi.

Bibliography

Anon., *Severnyi vestnik*, 6, 1892, pp. 75–9.
Gor'kii, M., *Vospominaniia. Rasskazy. Zametki*, Kniga, Berlin, 1925.

---

31 Senator George Foster Pearce in Federal Parliament, *Commonwealth of Australia: Parliamentary Debates*, CXII, 1926, p. 1203ff.
32 John Latham in Federal Parliament. *Commonwealth of Australia: Parliamentary Debates*, CXII, 1926, p. 461ff.
33 'Un poeta ruso, ignorado, descansa para siempre en San Pedro Sula', *Tiempo. El diario de Honduras*, 13 October 1971, p. 18.

Govor, E., and Windle, K., 'Dva neobychnykh tolstovtsa v Avstralii', *Literaturnaia Amerika*, 2, 2016, pp. 375–395.

Govor, Elena, *My Dark Brother: The Story of the Illins, a Russian-Aboriginal Family*, UNSW Press, Sydney, 2000.

Il'in, N., 'Neprotivlenie pered sudom vyshnim', *Ekho Avstralii*, 4, 18 July 1912, pp. 2–3; 5, 25 July 1912, pp. 2–3.

Il'in, N.D., *Dnevnik tolstovtsa*, M. Iants, St Petersburg, 1892.

Il'in, N.D., 'V novom kraiu: roman-khronika iz vremen zavoevaniia Turkestana', *Knizhki 'Nedeli'*, 1–11, St Petersburg, 1886.

Illin, N. to Resanoff, A., NAA, A6286, 1/126, QF3859, to 24 April 1919.

Illin, Nicholas, 'A Russian on Russia', *Cairns Post*, 4 October 1918, p. 2.

Keneally, Tom, *The People's Train*, Viking, Sydney, 2009.

Latham, John in Federal Parliament. *Commonwealth of Australia: Parliamentary Debates*, CXII, 1926, p. 461ff.

Matulichenko, A. [Zuzenko], 'Kak ia, anarkhist, stal lenintsem: neskol'ko slov o teorii i praktike revoliutsii', *Novoe russkoe slovo*, 16–18 February, 1921.

National Archives of Australia (NAA): 'Papers relating to miscellaneous events involving the use of a red flag', BP4/1, 66/4/2165, 'O tom, kak my uchimsia samoupravleniiu i kontroliu', p. 360.

Paustovskii, Konstantin, letter to Zaborovskii, R.E., quoted in Izmailov, Al'bert, 'Stroptivyi i dobryi chelovek', in Krementsov, L.P., ed., *K.G. Paustovskii: materialy i soobshcheniia, sbornik*, Vypusk 4, *Personazhi i geroi knig K. Paustovskogo*, Kniga 1, Mir Paustovskogo, Moscow, 2007, p. 89.

Paustovskii, Konstantin, *Sobranie sochinenii*, Khudozhestvennaia literatura, Moscow, 1957.

Pearce, Senator George Foster in Federal Parliament, *Commonwealth of Australia: Parliamentary Debates*, CXII, 1926, p. 1203ff.

Poole, Tom and Fried, Eric 'A Bolshevik in Brisbane', *Australian Journal of Politics and History*, 1985, XXXI, 2, pp. 244–54.

Repin, I.E., *Dalekoe blizkoe*, Iskusstvo, Moscow, 1964.

Repin, I.E., *Pis'ma k pisateliam i literaturnym deiateliam*, Iskusstvo, Moscow, 1950.

Rezanov, A. [Bykoff], Rus' avstraliiskaia', NAA BP4/1, 66/4/2165.

Rossiiskii gosudarstvennyi arkhiv sotsial'no-politicheskoi istorii (RGASPI [Moscow]): Dokumenty Kommunisticheskogo Internatsionala, *fond* 495, *opis'* 94, *delo* 18, pp. 1–17, Aleksandr Mikhailovich Zuzenko to the Executive Committee of the Third Communist International, 28 February 1923.

Stasov, V., *Nikolai Nikolaevich Ge*, Posrednik, Moscow, 1904.

Tokareff, G. to Zuzenko, A., NAA, A6286, 1/76, QF2277, 22 October 1918.

Tolstoi, L.N., *Polnoe sobranie sochinenii*, Khudozhestvennaia literatura, LXXXVIII, Moscow, 1950.

'Un poeta ruso, ignorado, descansa para siempre en San Pedro Sula', *Tiempo. El diario de Honduras*, 13 October 1971, p. 18.

Windle, Kevin, '"The Achilles Heel of British Imperialism": A Comintern Agent Reports on His Mission to Australia 1920–1922. An Annotated Translation', *Australian Slavonic and East European Studies*, 2004, XVIII, 1–2, pp. 143–76.

Windle, Kevin, 'Brisbane Prison: Artem Sergeev Describes Boggo Road', *New Zealand Slavonic Journal*, XXXVIII, 2004, pp. 159–80.

Windle, Kevin, '"Unmajestic Bombast": The Brisbane Union of Russian Workers as Shown in a 1919 Play', *Australian Slavonic and East European Studies*, XIX, 1–2, 2005, pp. 29–51.

Windle, Kevin, '*Nabat* and Its Editors: The 1919 Swansong of the Brisbane Russian Socialist Press', *Australian Slavonic and East European Studies*, XXI, 1–2, 2007, pp. 143–63.

Windle, Kevin, 'Murder at Mount Cuthbert: a Russian Revolutionary Describes Queensland Life in 1915–1919', *AUMLA*, CX, 2008, pp. 53–71.

Windle, Kevin, 'Hades or Eden? Herman Bykoff's *Russian Australia*', *Australian Slavonic and East European Studies*, XXVI, 1–2, 2012, pp. 1–25.

Windle, Kevin, *Undesirable: Captain Zuzenko and the Workers of Australia and the World*, Australian Scholarly, Melbourne, 2012.

Zuzenko, A., 'Zakon klyka i dubiny'. Typescript held in the Poole-Fried Collection, Fryer Library, University of Queensland, UQFL 336, Box 8, folder 9.

CHAPTER 9

Reconfiguring the Empire through Performance: Petr Fomenko's 2001 Production of Tolstoi's *War and Peace*

Alexandra Smith

Abstract

In his stage adaptation of *War and Peace* Petr Fomenko was seeking to break out of the creative fetters of the past and produce a version of *War and Peace* which spoke to the post-Soviet condition. A connection can be identified between Tolstoi's search for a cohesive vision of the Russian empire, via his novel, in the 1860s and Fomenko's search, via its adaptation, for a cohesive narrative of continuity at the beginning of the twenty-first century. Because of the canonical status of *War and Peace* the theatre audience is invited to engage in a dialogue between the innovative performance and their established ideas of Russian history, derived from the novel itself. In Fomenko's view, therefore, theatre has the power to transform established beliefs. In the case of adaptations he seeks to bridge the gap between source and performed texts, and indeed to lay this process bare: thus, actors periodically read from a copy of *War and Peace* placed on a table on stage. The optimistic tone of the novel's ending survives the transposition: Fomenko's production celebrates the notion of youthful optimism, the vision of family happiness and the resilience of Russians to survive any corruptive influences from the west.

Keywords

Staging Tolstoi's *War and Peace* – Petr Fomenko – attitudes to Russian history and empire

In the Soviet period many experimental theatrical forms associated with such names as Bertolt Brecht, Vsevolod Meierkhold and Mikhail Chekhov were scorned by the authorities or banned altogether. Since the collapse of the Soviet Union in 1991, it is not unsurprising that we have seen a boost in dramatic productions and an exciting range of theatrical experiments that have drawn on Russian and western twentieth-century innovations. According to Birgit Beumers and Mark Lipovetsky, Soviet theatre

> remained somewhat on one side of the conventional divide of the theatre as illusion of reality (verisimilitude, or *dostovernost'*) by developing the notion of emotional experience (*perezhivanie*) in order to stimulate the spectator emotionally; and the theatre of demonstration (*predstavlenie*), of conditionality (*uslovnost'*) that opposes these principles and seeks instead to push the spectator towards a rational response to the stage events, to make him aware of the spectacle and to use attractions to enhance theatricality.[1]

In their study of the use of violence in contemporary Russian theatre – a hallmark of many contemporary productions – Beumers and Lipovetsky talk primarily about the emergence of the New Drama and its focus on the representation of violence. Their analysis of the New Drama overshadows other theatrical developments of the 1990s and 2000s, including the revival of many experiments and ideas associated with the Russian avant-garde theatre of the 1910s and 1920s. Several famous productions by Vsevolod Meierkhold, Evgenii Vakhtangov and Sergei Tretiakov were resurrected by prominent post-Soviet directors, including Valerii Fokin,[2] Grigorii Aredakov[3] and Yurii Liubimov.[4] Together with Liubimov, Petr Naumovich Fomenko (1932–2012) is considered to be an heir to the Russian avant-garde tradition rediscovered by Soviet theatre and film directors during the Thaw period of the 1960s. The present chapter will discuss Fomenko's 2001 production of Tolstoi's novel *War and Peace*, both in the context of theatrical experiments of the post-Soviet

---

1 Beumers, Birgit and Lipovetsky, Mark, eds, *Performing Violence: Literary and Theatrical Experiments of New Russian Drama*, Intellect Books, Bristol, 2009, p. 106.
2 Fokin's production of Meierkhold's 1926 version of Gogol's play *The Inspector General* took place in the Aleksanrinskii Theatre in St Petersburg on 5 October 2002. See: https://alexandrinsky.ru/afisha-i-bilety/revizor/ (accessed 5 August 2020).
3 Grigorii Aredakov's production of Sergei Tretiakov's 1926 play 'I want a baby!' (banned during the Soviet period) took place in Saratov on 18 June 2005: it was undertaken by the final-year students of the L. Sobinov Saratov State Conservatoire. See: http://sati-sgk.ru/index.php/id-2006-xochu-rebjonka.html (accessed: 21 October 2022).
4 On 30 September 2007 Liubimov's play inspired by Meierkhold's production of Griboedov's comedy *Woe from Wit* was produced by the Taganka Theatre. Although Liubimov denies any influence of Meierkhold's art on his play *Woe from Wit*, Zhanna Filatova sees it as a homage to Meierkhold and his production of Griboedov's play. See Zhanna Filatova, 'Rezhisser dolzhen byt' kak razvedchik', *Teatral'naia afisha*, August-September 2007; the electronic version is available here: https://mxat.ru/authors/directors/mashkov/10737/ (accessed 5 August 2020).

period and the intellectual debates about the legacy of the imperial past that inform many post-Soviet cultural developments.[5] Fomenko, anticipating films imbued with nostalgic overtones (such as Sokurov's 2002 film *The Russian Ark* and Vladimir Khotinenko's 2004 TV series *Death of the Empire*), interpreted Tolstoi's masterpiece in a way that raises questions about the growing role of literature and theatre in the formation of an 'imagined community' searching for a new collective identity.[6] Undoubtedly, the collapse of the Soviet Union in 1991 traumatized many among the older generation of the Russian intelligentsia and affected their perception of history. For example, Nancy Condee, in her analysis of Mikhalkov's films produced during the post-Soviet period, suggests that Mikhalkov's 'narrative of imperial continuity' might be seen as a reaction to the extreme discontinuity 'to which his imaginative project reacts by revealing its anxieties and ambitions'.[7] Condee's assessment of Mikhalkov's fascination with the notion of imperial continuity is fully applicable to Fomenko's employment of Tolstoi's novel for the purpose of creating the illusion of a bond existing between Tolstoi's vision of the Russian empire of the 1860s and Fomenko's own search for a cohesive narrative of continuity at the beginning of the twenty-first century.

We could say that the audience could have perceived Fomenko's production of *War and Peace, the Beginning of the Novel* (Война и мир. Начало романа) as a veiled commemoration of the tenth anniversary of the Soviet empire's collapse. As Mark R. Beissinger noted, 'The general consensus now appears to be that the Soviet Union was an empire and therefore it broke up. However, it is also routinely referred to as an empire precisely because it did break up'.[8] In many ways, the chaotic representation of life in Fomenko's play based on Tolstoi's novel invites the audience to compare the state of post-Soviet Russia with the representation of the divided society described in the first part of Tolstoi's epic. The use of French language in Fomenko's play also brings to the fore an analogy between unpatriotically minded members of Moscow high society during the Napoleonic wars and the post-Soviet elite. The latter also confuses the notion of Russian identity with imperial collapse. Just as Sokurov

---

5 See, for example, the discussion of this trend in K. Ravetto-Biagoli, 'Floating on the Borders of Europe: Sokurov's *Russian Ark*', *Film Quarterly*, LIX, 1, 2005, pp. 18–26; Nancy Condee, *Imperial Trace: Recent Russian Cinema*, Oxford University Press, New York, 2009.
6 This concept is developed by Benedict Anderson: *Imagined Communities: Reflections on the Origin and Spread of Nationalism* Verso, London, 2006, pp. 6–7.
7 Condee, p. 239.
8 Mark R. Beissinger, 'The Persisting Ambiguity of Empire', *Post-Soviet Affairs*, XI, 2, 1995, pp. 149–84, (155).

conveyed imperial collapse through 'the elegies, the drama of British imperial catastrophe, and the recurrent tales of death',[9] so Fomenko creates a spectacle that focuses on the theme of death. Thus the portraits of Napoleon and Alexander I are mocked as disempowered embodiments of the Romantic notion of hero; the death of Pierre Bezukhov's father is presented as the symbolic death of the old order; the recurrent question about the justification of war and personal sacrifice is a leitmotif for the whole play that alludes to the disintegration of the existing values and beliefs shaped by the imperial consciousness. 'When empires come crashing down', asserts Jack Snyder, 'they leave hunks of institutional wreckage scattered across the landscape: pieces of bureaucracies, military units, economic networks, administrative districts, as well as demographic and cultural patterns that bear the marks of the imperial past'.[10] If we were to view Fomenko's play as a creative response to the post-Soviet condition associated with the wreckage and the remnants of the Soviet empire, how then could we reconcile the post-Soviet melancholy and lament for an imagined community embedded in Fomenko's production with the optimistic and mythopoetic overtones of Tolstoi's novel? As Ewa Thompson points out, Tolstoi's *War and Peace* is both 'largely responsible for improving the image of Russia in the West' and for creating a mythologized account of Russia at war with Napoleon. More importantly, Thompson states that 'the novel is replete with vitality and optimism' and its author seems to share Pierre Bezukhov's belief that 'all is right with the world'.[11]

As will be demonstrated below, Fomenko's interest in Tolstoi's novel, as a repository of memory about loyalty, kinship and communal ties, results in the creation of a spectacle that brings Tolstoi's characters closer to post-Soviet subjects who are ill prepared to face the challenges of the new social order and are impeded by naïveté about their present life and their future. Undoubtedly, a trace of the utopian thinking of the Thaw generation seems to have become entwined, in Fomenko's interpretation of Tolstoi's novel, with the re-affirmation of the vitality of Russian culture. Given that *War and Peace* is a canonical novel and an integral part of the Russian school curriculum and collective memory, Fomenko also appears to advocate the idea that a theatrical adaptation is a kind of intertextuality that engages the audience in ongoing

---

9   Condee, p. 240.
10 Jack Snyder, 'Introduction: Reconstructing Politics amidst the Wreckage of Empire', in *Post-Soviet Political Order: Conflict and State Building*, Barnett R. Rubin and Jack Snyder, eds, Routledge, London, 1998, pp. 1–13 (1).
11 Ewa Thompson, 'Leo Tolstoy and the Idea of Good Life', in *Kultura rosyjska w ojczyznie i diasporz*, Lidia Liburska, ed., Jagiellonian University Press, Krakow, 2007, pp. 231–8 (231).

dialogue in which the audience compares the work it already knows with the one that it is experiencing. Drawing on Bakhtin's notion of dialogic consciousness which presupposes that every artistic utterance is a hybrid construction, Robert Stam suggests that Bakhtin's vision of the dialogic nature of literary works is even more applicable to film which relies on a collaborative effort and makes complete originality impossible, even undesirable.[12] As an experienced director who has produced numerous film and theatre adaptations of Russian and Soviet literary works in the post-Soviet period, Fomenko presented himself as a liberal director, with a strong belief in collective creative effort and intertextuality as an immersive and interactive mode of engagement in the style of Bakhtinian carnivalesque performance. Yet, through carnivalizing Tolstoi's masterpiece and celebrating the libidinal forces of laughter, Fomenko managed to demonstrate that carnival could comprise both utopian and dystopian traits.

In order to understand Fomenko's strategy of carnivalizing Tolstoi's epic, we should first outline the biographical and contextual setting of Fomenko's adaptation that can shed light on his directing style and his artistic outlook. After the opening of his theatre (known usually as 'Fomenko's Studio') in 1993, Fomenko became known as a leading theatre director of the post-Soviet period with experimental productions which were often deemed provocative and controversial. Yet Fomenko's popularity was not comparable to that of Lev Dodin and Mark Zakharov whose plays attracted mass audiences in the late Soviet and post-Soviet periods. According to Beumers, Fomenko, together with Fokin, 'made an important contribution in one way or another to the development of theatre and acting in the period of transition'.[13] In spite of the many structural changes and financial pressures affecting theatres in post-Soviet times, Fomenko did not really need to cater to the mass audience. Although Beumers praises Fomenko's productions for 'masterful accomplishment of a fine psychological analysis of the play in the best traditions of the Moscow Art Theatre',[14] Fomenko had a difficult relationship with some established Moscow Art Theatre (MKhAT) actors and directors: in 1953 he was expelled from the MKhAT theatre training college for subversive behaviour and was accused of being a living embodiment of everything fundamentally alien to the traditions of Russian drama. After his expulsion from the

---

12   Robert Stam, *Literature through Film: Realism, Magic and the Art of Adaptation*, Blackwell Publishing, Malden, MA and Oxford, 2005, p. 4.
13   Birgit Beumers, *Pop Culture Russia!: Media, Arts, and Lifestyle*, ABC-Clio, Santa Barbara, California, 2005, p. 152.
14   Ibid., pp. 152–3.

MKhAT, where he had briefly trained with Boris Vershilov, a former associate of Vakhtangov, Fomenko studied in the Department of Philology at Moscow Pedagogical University and in the Department of Directing at the State Institute for Theatre Arts (GITIS): he graduated from these institutions in 1955 and 1961 respectively. In the 1960s two of Fomenko's experimental productions were banned for ideological reasons: his 1966 production in the Maiakovskii theatre of Sukhovo-Kobylin's play *Tarelkin's Death* (*Смерть Тарелкина*) was taken off after 50 shows and his 1967 production by the Lensovet Theatre of *The New Mystery Bouffe* (*Новая Мистерия-Буфф*) was also banned for censorship reasons.[15] Fomenko's controversial production – performed in the style of European 1920s political cabaret performances – was supposed to mark the fiftieth anniversary of the October Revolution but the authorities and censors interpreted it as a form of veiled criticism of the Soviet censors and of authors such as Evgenii Evtushenko and Andrei Voznesenskii. In truly Maiakovskian manner, the introductory part of Fomenko's play questioned the ability of Soviet poets of the 1960s to meet Maiakovskii's challenge and add contemporary content to his play *Mystery Bouffe*. The original *Mystery Bouffe* combined medieval mystery play technique with propaganda art that preached a gospel of proletarian revolution compatible with the Expressionist eclectic, mixing social philosophy and Christian symbolism. Fomenko's play had more in common with German Expressionism and Russian Futurism than with the primitive agit literature of the 1920s or the socialist realist aesthetic of the late Soviet period. The unsuccessful attempt to revive the avant-garde aesthetic of the 1920s did not preclude Fomenko from trying to revolutionize Russian theatre in the late Soviet period. His 1980 production of the play *Terkin-Terkin* (*Теркин-Теркин*), based on Tvardovskii's controversial poem *Terkin in the Otherworld* (*Теркин на том свете*), staged by the Theatre of Comedy in Leningrad, was also banned after severe criticism from Soviet critics and censors. As Anatolii Smelianskii rightly notes, Fomenko's excessive liking for grotesque manifestations of human emotions, and for existential and metaphysical matters in the style of the subversive satirical spectacle *bouffonade*, were out of place in a period dominated by 'grand style' Soviet theatre.[16] Although Fomenko's flirtation with experiments in the Soviet period ended unsatisfactorily, the

---

15   Marina Dmitrievskaia, 'Novaia Misteriia-Buff Petra Fomenko. Istoriia zapreshchennogo spektaklia', *Peterburgskii teatral'nyi zhurnal*, III, 33, 2003: http://ptj.spb.ru/archive/33/historical-novel-33/novaya-misteriya-buff-petra-fomenko/ (accessed 16 August, 2020).
16   Anatoly Smeliansky, 'Pyotr Fomenko's "three cards"', in id., *The Russian Theatre after Stalin*, trans. Patrick Miles, Cambridge University Press, Cambridge, 1999, pp. 202–11.

post-Soviet theatrical world has nevertheless put the previously marginalized director at the very hub of the new Russian theatre.

The collapse of the grand style of Soviet theatre associated with the master narrative of the 1990s Soviet utopia enabled Fomenko to move to a more philosophical mode of artistic expression that explored the heritage of Silver Age theatrical and artistic thought. In Smelianskii's opinion, Fomenko's interpretation of Tolstoi's novel *War and Peace* as collective therapy reveals his fundamental belief in the role of theatre in the contemporary world. According to Fomenko, the role of theatre is to transform one's beliefs and experiences. It is akin to the role of ritual or performance that enables the audience and the director to restore a lost sense of unity through a shared experience of reading transformed on stage into an event. In addition to theatre's therapeutic function, identified by Smelianskii as the hallmark of Fomenko's aesthetic, the critic also notes Fomenko's strong interest in the rhythm of his productions and in a poetic theatre entwined with a rich visuality of spectacles that highlight the materiality of words. Smelianskii lists among Fomenko's main achievements as a teacher the fact that his disciples have a strong interest in poetic theatre and feel at ease with the notion of polystylistics, freely mixing Faulkner and Blok. Their artistic sensibility favouring free improvisation and an associative mode of thinking stands close to poetic forms of expression reliant upon metaphor and metonymy. Clearly, Fomenko's mode of training his actors and directors is subordinated to breaking the mould of the didactic style of performance and melodramatic forms of social engagement in theatre that enjoyed a considerable popularity in the Soviet period.[17]

Furthermore, Smelianskii's book illustrates how the straight-jacket mentality of Soviet theatre directors and critics stood in stark contrast to western artistic experiments. Although Soviet theatres after Stalin's death revived interest in those works of Tolstoi and Dostoevskii that might be suitable for theatrical transposition, most directors and actors lacked the courage to deviate from the norms of socialist realist theatre. For example, Smelianskii cites Iosif Iuzovskii who, as with many other Soviet theatre critics of his generation, was totally smitten by the production of Shakespeare's *Hamlet* by Peter Brook and Paul Scofield that stunned the Moscow theatre world in December 1955. As Smelianskii puts it, 'This was one of those productions that made an indelible impression on all who were to decide the course of Russian theatre for decades to come'.[18] It appears that Soviet artistic imagination

---

17   Ibid., p. 210.
18   Ibid., p. 7.

differed markedly from the European when it came to treatment of the classics. This can be exemplified by Soviet critics' responses to Brook's production of *Hamlet*. They were amazed by Brook's relaxed approach to the tradition, his innovative use of space, and the sense of freedom of the director and actors that gave the impression of their complete contempt for stage clichés and conventions.

Undoubtedly, the post-Soviet theatre world boasts many productions that draw on Brook's imaginative rendering of *Hamlet*. Beumers' survey of Russian contemporary theatre identifies several theatre directors who turned to Russian classical literature in search of new theatrical forms of expression. Beumers especially praises Anatolii Vasilev whose 2000 production of Pushkin's tragedy *Mozart and Salieri: Requiem* (*Моцарт и Сальери: реквием*) is considered to be one of the most significant achievements of contemporary theatre, aspiring to adopt the conceptual and metaphysical language of Brook's productions. In her review of Vasilev's play in the *Petersburg Theatre Journal*, Elena Fomina proudly states that Brook would have found it truly sacred.[19]

Yet it is obvious that Nikolai Evreinov's notions of the theatricalization of everyday life and theatrical instinct, Voloshin's definition of modern theatre as the theatre of dreams, Viacheslav Ivanov's call for the rebirth of Dionysian theatre, and Meierkhold's aspiration to contemporize the classics, had a considerable impact on the artistic imagination of post-Soviet directors who began to rebel against the legacy of Stanislavskii's stage realism that the Moscow Art Theatre had canonized. Embodying the revolt against Stanislavskii's stage realism at its best, Fomenko's 2002 play *Egyptian Nights* (*Египетские ночи*) was performed in the style of montage, including several Pushkin works: the unfinished tale *Egyptian Nights*; fragments from 'We Spent an Evening at the Dacha …' ('Мы проводили вечер на даче …') and 'The Guests gathered at the Countess' Dacha …' ('Гости съезжались на дачу ***'); then, various passages from Briusov's poem, also entitled *Egyptian Nights*; and music by Paganini and Rossini. The use of Paganini's *Caprice in A minor No. 24*, which inspired many variations and imitations, is a leitmotif of the whole production and highlights the central theme of Fomenko's play. It communicates Fomenko's very Meierkholdian message to the audience, suggesting that all artefacts and canonical narratives of the past should be read in a creative manner. For Fomenko any production of literary texts should result in the

---

[19] Elena Fomina, 'Pravila ottorzheniia "ia". (O shkole dramaticheskogo iskusstva Anatoliia Vasil'eva)', *Peterburgskii teatral'nyi zhurnal*, XX, 2000, pp. 53–60, (60).

unique shared experience of theatrical performance that brings together actors and spectators.

In contrast to many enthusiastic reviews for such directors as Dodin and Fomenko, the prominent post-Soviet film and theatre director Kirill Serebrennikov points out that no new aesthetic and philosophical approaches to performance were produced in the post-Soviet period. Most post-Soviet directors failed to replace the format of socially engaged theatre or to surpass the experiments of the 1960s. 'Instead,' asserts Serebrennikov, 'old philosophies prevail, which announce the decline of Europe along the lines of the French existentialists and French theatre of the 1960s and 1970s, emphasizing man's solitude and his isolation, a total lack of understanding and the resulting violence and despair'.[20]

In many ways, Fomenko's productions stem from preoccupation with the civic spirit (гражданственность) that permeated literary and theatrical experiments of the Thaw period.[21] A striking feature of this theatre is the cult of collective discussion and shared experiences in the style of Vakhtangov's studio and the amateur theatres of the 1950s-70s.[22] Like Liubimov's Taganka theatre in the late Soviet period, Fomenko's studio-like theatre created a sense of community and 'family' atmosphere in the post-Soviet era. It stood in striking contrast to the aspirations of some post-Soviet directors to create a new grand-narrative that would pivot either around the notion of Eurasianist identity or new Russian patriotism. The collapse of the Soviet Union in 1991 triggered many debates about Russia's imperial past and its impact on the artistic imagination of Russian writers, artists and filmmakers. These debates often focus on the notion of Russian national identity and Russia's need to come to terms with her past.

The most important cultural trends of the 1990s reflect a search for a usable past that could revive a sense of nationhood. Yet Boris Yeltsin's 1996 call for a new Russian idea that could build unity did not result in many significant achievements, because Yeltsin chose to focus upon the negative aspects of Soviet history. In Kathleen Smith's opinion, 'pride in nation and state typically

---

20 Kirill Serebrennikov, 'Foreword' in Beumers and Lipovetsky, pp. 9–12, (9).
21 Thus, for example, Vladimir Valutskii characterized Iurii Liubimov's Taganka theatre productions as performances permeated with a lofty note of civic spirit. See Vladimir Valutskii, 'K voprosu o teatre na Taganke', *Sovetskaia kul'tura*, 30 March, 1965, pp. 2-3 (2).
22 An excellent survey of Soviet post-Stalin amateur theatres and their role in the subversion of socialist realist aesthetic and censorship is offered in Susan Costanzo's article: 'Amateur Theatres and Amateur Publics in the Russian Republic, 1958–71', *The Slavonic and East European Review*, LXXX, 2, April 2008, pp. 372–94.

rests on narratives of achievement, not on expressions of remorse and apology'.[23] In contrast with Yeltsin, Vladimir Putin, who was also preoccupied with the need for a new form of social cohesion, decided to create a revived sense of nationhood around the one achievement many Russians could still remember with pride – the victory over Nazi Germany. On Victory Day 2000 (9 May), Putin declared that memories of the war 'will help to build a strong and prosperous country'.[24] Putin also expressed his wholehearted support for the August 2000 plan for the 'Culture of Russia, 2001–2005', proposed by Mikhail Shvydkoi (then Minister of Culture) and agreed to provide 20 billion rubles for cultural products that would help to revive Russian patriotism.[25] As Rosalind Marsh has aptly remarked, 'By 2006 it has become evident [...] that Russian society's confrontation with its past has remained one of the main themes of Russian culture throughout the 1990s and the early twenty-first century, and that Russian writers' and readers' interest in history has by no means diminished, but simply developed and changed'.[26] Marsh's insightful observation – that the gradual decline of literature of sensational quality gave rise to a more rigorous investigation of Russian and Soviet history, an explosion of autobiographical narratives and an increased preoccupation with the philosophy of history – provides an important contextual setting for Fomenko's 2001 production of *War and Peace* which challenges the canonical adaptations of the novel produced during the Soviet period. As will be argued below, Fomenko's interpretation of the novel might be seen as an attempt to offer a critique of politicized readings of Tolstoi's epic (as expressed in Soviet textbooks, films and musical adaptations of the novel) and its use for ideological purposes as a text suitable for a patriotic upbringing during World War II and in the post-Soviet period.

Viewed in the light of those post-Soviet cultural developments that pivot around the notion of patriotism, Fomenko's interest in Tolstoi's *War and Peace* and the Russian war with Napoleon might appear to be at odds with the revival of interest in Putin's Russia in World War II and its presentation in the mass media as the major event of Russian twentieth-century history. According to Geoffrey Hosking, 'Russians today are divided about many things, including

---

23   Kathleen Smith, *Mythmaking in the New Russia: Politics and Memory in the Yeltsin Era*, Cornell University Press, Ithaca, NY, 2002, p. 172.
24   Quoted in S.M. Norris, 'Guiding Stars: The Comet-like Rise of the War Film in Putin's Russia: Recent World War II Films and Historical Memories', *Studies in Russian and Soviet Cinema*, I, 2, 2007, pp. 163–189 (165).
25   Loc. cit.
26   Rosalind Marsh, *Literature, History and Identity in Post-Soviet Russia, 1991–2006*, Peter Lang, Oxford, New York, 2007, p. 13.

their own imperial past, as was demonstrated by the controversies surrounding the funeral of Nicholas II and his family in July 1998' but 'one achievement that Russians can unite around and remember with pride is their victory over Nazi Germany in the Second World War'.[27] In this vein many scholars have noted that the myth of the Great Patriotic War created in the USSR and appropriated in the 2000s offered the chance to perform the past, including parades and rituals, and to present collective and individual memories as a usable past that can be relived and re-experienced through their performances.[28]

However, Hosking has argued convincingly that 'Russian empire-building from the sixteenth century onwards had impeded Russian nation building' to the effect that the imperial notion 'Russian [*rossiiskii*] citizen' has stunted the ethnic aspect of the Russian [*russkii*] identity.[29] More importantly, Hosking suggests that in modern times ordinary Russians felt alienated from the imperial ruling class, and that the split between ethnic and imperial identities was a major cause of Russia's disintegration and division effected by World War I and the October 1917 revolution. According to Hosking, the notion of Russian identity has often been interpreted in a paradoxical manner. Hosking notes that Russian national feeling itself often takes universalistic and messianic forms. As a result of this trend, expressions of popular messianism, which were suppressed during the period of modernization started by Peter the Great, re-emerged in the early twentieth century in the form of Marxism. In Hosking's opinion, it was 'a new kind of universalist and messianic movement promising to create a better society throughout the world'.[30] This factor explains why, even though at its very beginning the Soviet Union was envisaged as a resolutely internationalist state, in 1941–45 the notion of 'Russianness' was constructed as an amalgam of ethnic and imperial elements.[31]

The logic of Hosking's argument suggests that the USSR in 1945 had the chance to develop into a fully-fledged nation state, but the political regime made several major mistakes that undermined the newly created national cohesion and led to the collapse of the Soviet Union in 1991. Hosking says

---

27 Geoffrey Hosking, 'The Second World War and Russian National Consciousness', *Past and Present*, CLXXV, 1, May 2002, pp. 162–87 (162).

28 See, for example, Jay Winter, *Remembering War: The Great War Between Memory and History in the Twentieth Century*, Yale University Press, New Haven, 2006; Thomas C. Wolfe, 'Past as Present, Myth, or History? Discourses of Time and the Great Fatherland War' in *The Politics of Memory in Postwar Europe*, Richard Ned Lebow, Wulf Kansteiner, and Claudio Fogu, ed, Duke University Press, Durham, NC, 2006, pp. 249–83.

29 Hosking, p. 162.

30 Loc. cit.

31 Ibid., p. 172.

that the truth about the war was suppressed for many years because in 1946 Stalin had prohibited the publication of war narratives and in subsequent years war memories were tailored and censored in order to serve the purposes of the political regime. In other words, existing memories were not articulated coherently as part of an authentic collective memory. This development led to considerable fragmentation and falsification of truth. Hosking writes:

> Where memory is not validated in the public media, when it cannot be periodically reinforced by the spontaneous exchange of personal recollections in the community, then it becomes fragmented, insubstantial and cannot function as an underpinning of national identity. In one sense, the outcome of the war did confirm the millennial outlook of the Communist Party's convinced believers. It is true that the perfect society had not been built, and there was no prospect of its being built, but on the other hand, the Soviet Union had averted the apocalypse, in the form of Nazi victory, and had saved Europe from it, too.[32]

It could be added, though, that the experiences and the policies related to World War II provided the Soviet authorities with the chance to foster further links between the Russian imperial past and the Soviet vision of modernity, since many references to the war with Napoleon, the 1812 Battle of Borodino and Tolstoi's epic *War and Peace* were used successfully for nation-building purposes. Thus, for example, in 1943 the Soviet government reinstated the full range of military ranks as they had been in the tsarist army, with gold braid and shoulder straps to match. Soviet officials also created a series of new decorations for officers, including those of Aleksandr Nevskii and Mikhail Kutuzov.[33] Given the strong 1940s tendency to amalgamate nation building and empire building, it is not a coincidence that the list of the most popular radio broadcasts of that decade included a series of programmes based on Tolstoi's novel *War and Peace*. Narrated by D.N. Orlov, the first part of this cycle was broadcast on 6 August 1940. Another popular radio programme featured the recital of passages from Aleksandr Tvardovskii's long poem *Vasilii Terkin* (broadcast on 30 April 1944).[34] Lisa Kirschenbaum identifies notions of motherland, home and family as key constituents of Soviet patriotism that emerged

---

32   Ibid., p. 187.
33   Alexander Werth, *Russia at War, 1941–1945*, Barrie and Rockliff, London, 1964, pp. 415–16.
34   A.A. Sherel', ed., *Radiozhurnalistika*, Izdatel'stvo Moskovskogo universiteta, Moscow, 2000.

during World War II.[35] In this context the popularity of Tvardovskii's character Terkin among soldiers alongside *War and Peace* might be seen as odd. As Hosking puts it: 'Viewed in the light of pre-war proletarian internationalism, even in its neo-rossiiskii phase, Terkin is a strange and archaic figure, closer to the fantasies of the nineteenth-century narodniki than to anything Lenin or Stalin might have conceived'.[36] Nevertheless, despite some mythologized and apolitical overtones, Tvardovskii's poem was not anti-Soviet. Hosking thinks that its strong appeal to Soviet readers was due to its successful re-emphasis of aspects of Russian national identity obscured or downplayed in the public discourse of the inter-war years.

Yet, as Hosking's article on Russian national consciousness during World War II demonstrates, successful policies to merge nation building and empire building during the 1940s did not develop into a new strategy of social cohesion owing to ideological constraints. Hosking argues that the conclusion of World War II had an unusual effect on Soviet millenarianism:

> The centre of gravity of the symbolic life of the Soviet state, and therefore of Soviet society too, shifted from the future to the past, from expectation of the distant and somewhat ghostly anticipated triumph of socialism to remembrance of the very real and undeniable victory of Soviet arms in what everyone could agree in calling 'the Great Patriotic War'. This fixation on the past combined with the fracturing of national identity, both russkii and sovetskii, generated by the regime's own policies, to hollow out the spiritual life of the Soviet peoples and to undermine their sense of community. In that way the Soviet regime gradually negated its own greatest triumph and prepared the way for its own eventual downfall'.[37]

This inward-looking trend was replaced in the post-Soviet period by a new search for a usable past. Several critics have characterized the fixation on the past in post-Soviet times as a special form of nostalgia either for the Russian imperial past or for the Soviet period.[38] Similarly to Sokurov's film *The Russian Ark*, Fomenko's rendering of *War and Peace* dwells on the anxiety caused by

---

35   Lisa Kirschenbaum, '"Our City, Our Hearths, Our Families": Local Loyalties and Private Life in Soviet World War II Propaganda', *Slavic Review*, LIX, 4, 2000, pp. 825–47 (828).
36   Hosking, p. 178.
37   Ibid., p. 187.
38   See, for example, Svetlana Boym, *The Future of Nostalgia*, Basic Books, New York, 2001; Ravetto-Biagioli, pp. 18–26; Nancy Condy, 'Perezhivaia chuzhuiu katastrofu: Imperiia smotrit *Gibel' imperii*', *Pro et Contra*, July-August, 2006, pp. 29–37.

a sense of disorientation and demonstrates how nostalgia lends itself to the production of new myths and historical amnesia, presenting history as a poetic construction that has drifted in and out of Europe via allusion and myth.

In her assessment of Russian twenty-first century theatre, Monika Greenleaf identifies Moscow as one of the most important post-Soviet theatrical centres and highlights the growing popularity of directors' studio theatres, suggesting that their previously marginal formats overshadowed many established theatrical companies sponsored by the government.[39] Greenleaf's list of exciting productions of the last decade include several plays directed by Fomenko. Greenleaf finds Fomenko's adaptation of Boris Vakhtin's novella *One Absolutely Happy Village* (*Одна абсолютно счастливая деревня* [1965]) especially exciting and successful, because of its effective use of minimalist stage design and the remarkable bond between actors and audience. 'In *One Absolutely Happy Village*,' writes Greenleaf, 'a wooden box, a stringy hammock, and a few boards over a blue cloth "stream" suffice to articulate the places of common labour and passionate individual bonding in the village'.[40] More importantly, Fomenko's ability to create magic out of minimalist setting creates a special sense of intimacy and shared creative experience that brings together spectators and actors. Greenleaf writes: 'Here the audience members, split into two groups by the simple stage, have to look over their shoulders at actors behind them, as though sharing the enormous scattered Russian space and the single sky above'.[41] Greenleaf emphasizes that Fomenko masterfully creates a sense of social cohesion through clever use of space and imaginary landscape that bypasses temporal and spatial boundaries. According to Greenleaf, 'animated by a choreography of light and darting motion, Fomenko's characters, like his spaces, convey at once individual impulsiveness and overall harmonization'. In addition to this observation on Fomenko's ability to render the flow of life in a Tolstoian manner on stage, Greenleaf identifies the director's ability to use audio effects effectively: 'The atmosphere is also a skein of sounds, musical motifs interweaving with the melodic rise and fall of characters' voices as they summon each other's hidden thoughts and dreams into external expression, dangerous exposure, contact, and evolution'.[42] Greenleaf's observations on the style and subject matter of Fomenko's post-Soviet productions testify to the growing interest in the revival of nationalist trends of the 1960s-70s

---

39 Monika Greenleaf, 'In medias res: A Diary of the Moscow Theatre Season, 2007–2008', *Slavic Review*, LXVII, 2, 2008, pp. 422–36 (423).
40 Greenleaf, p. 432.
41 Loc. cit.
42 Loc. cit.

exemplified by the village prose writers. The search for a new national identity in post-Soviet times is often associated with the revival of the notion of the nation-state. Yet, as Benedict Anderson and Stathis Gourgouris remind us, any return to the nation-state should be viewed as a product of the imagination and dreams rather than the return of history, because the process of employing a usable past triggers the forgetting of the recent past (and even of the present) not the recollection of a distant history.[43]

Commenting on Fomenko's staging of *War and Peace, the Beginning of the Novel* Greenleaf observes that all four locations featured in the production, including 'the Petersburg soirée of Anna Scherer, the Rostovs' rambunctious Moscow household, old Count Bezukhov's Catherinian mansion, and the Bolkonskii estate with its strictly defined male and female sectors' slide 'into a constantly mutating two story frame, making Lev Tolstoi's temporal and atmospheric counterpoint visible'.[44] Greenleaf rightly indicates that Fomenko's rendering of Tolstoi's novel creates a sense of duality and fragmentation, suggesting irrevocable loss of unity. It appears that Fomenko treats the many themes embedded in Tolstoi's novel as highly relevant to a post-Soviet audience. It is not a coincidence that Fomenko draws attention to the notion of framing and mirroring throughout the whole four-hour performance. Greenleaf describes the dynamic use of space thus:

> Two rotating pier-glass frames set up at either side serve now as doors, now as mirrors, now as playful or imprisoning enclosures (Natasha watches Sonia trap Nikolai for a kiss; an implacably smiling Prince Andrei traps his fearfully smiling wife in its rotation and his condescending conversation; characters dart back and forth trying to make choices for the future, or cling to the past, through its vertiginously spinning frame).[45]

I would argue that such a minimalist and highly crafted use of space reinforces the sense of fragmentation of society and destabilizes both the space of Tolstoi's narrative and the very notion of historical truth. It emphasizes the point that recollection of events and any artistic depiction of real life depends upon the narrator's individual point of view or the editorial framing of this or that report. In other words, in a postmodernist vein, Fomenko suggests

---

43   See Benedict Anderson, *Imagined Communities*, Verso, New York, 1983; Stathis Gourgouris, *Dream Nation*, Stanford University Press, Stanford, CA, 1996.
44   Greenleaf, p. 432.
45   Loc. cit.

that attempts to revive empire or nation-building strategies in a contemporary world are problematic.

It appears that Fomenko's aim for his *War and Peace* is twofold. On the one hand, it presents Russian literature as a museum-like space in the style of Andrei Bitov's novel *Pushkin House* (*Пушкинский дом*) implying that the museum provides the observer with the opportunity to reassess it as a repository of historical and cultural memory. On the other hand, Fomenko focuses his attention on the crisis of the imperial sublime and the notion of the empire in a postmodern world, questioning the relationship between war and modernity. To this end, it is not a coincidence that some critics view Fomenko's version of *War and Peace* as an embodiment of a 'pure Tolstoian philosophy of non-violence' ('толстовство в чистом виде'),[46] invoking parallels between Fomenko, seen for the most part of his career as an outcast and a severe critic of Soviet totalitarian ideology, and Tolstoi who towards the end of his life became a Christian anarchist and pacifist. Viktoriia Nikiforova, for example, considers Fomenko's production of *War and Peace* to be an expression of a new sentimentality, suggesting that the use of associative and impressionistic narration is based on female logic.[47]

While viewing Fomenko's play as a light-hearted representation of everyday life in the style of Oscar Wilde, another Moscow critic, Roman Dolzhanskii, says that the main theme permeating Fomenko's production is philosophical meditation on the role of military conflicts in contemporary Europe. Dolzhanskii thinks that it is about the purpose of war *per se*. Dolzhanskii especially admires Fomenko's production for its lyricism and enchantment, which show the absurdity of everyday life and paradoxes of human behaviour highlighted by the references to the Napoleonic wars, the map of Europe and the portraits of Napoleon and Alexander I. Dolzhanskii rightly observes that the director's aim, conveyed vividly through the performance, is to depict a world about to be shattered by war and world catastrophes. Indeed, Fomenko's decision to omit the war scenes from the play creates a powerful effect upon the audience. Furthermore, the tragi-comic elements of the production are reinforced by the ephemeral atmosphere of the play that features Pierre's father's death; the minimalist decorations including ladders that serve hardly any purpose; the portraits of Napoleon and Alexander I that sometimes turn

---

46 Roman Dolzhanskii, 'Tolstovstvo v chistom vide. Petr Fomenko postavil kusok *Voiny i mira*', *Kommersant*, 30, 20.02.2001, p. 13; http://www.kommersant.ru/doc-y.aspx?DocsID=168867 (accessed 3 August 2020).

47 Viktoriia Nikiforova, 'Mezhdu mirom i voinoi', *Ekspert*, 10 (270), Moscow, 12.03. 2001; https://fomenki.ru/performance/warandpeace/3841/ (accessed 21 October 2022).

into doors; and the incongruity between Bolkonskii's desire to go to war and his wife's pregnancy.

Despite the overall impressionistic and playful narration, the play's structure is well organized. Fomenko draws the audience's attention only to the first part of Tolstoi's novel and presents scenes from the novel that precede Andrei Bolkonskii's departure for the war with Napoleon in a mosaic-like manner. The overall impression is that the three families who feature most prominently in the play — those of Pierre Bezukhov, Natasha Rostova and Andrei Bolkonskii — represent the three worlds in which the notion of happiness has been threatened by the social and historical developments beyond their control and comprehension. The play is in three acts: the first presents Petersburg and its high society, including Anna Scherer's salon and the party of drunken youths, including Dolokhov. The highlight of this act is the performance of the French eighteenth-century nursery song 'Marlborough went to war' ('Malbrouck s'en va-t-en guerre') which was very popular in Europe in the eighteenth and nineteenth centuries and was sung to different verbalizations, including the English version titled 'For He's a Jolly Good Fellow'. In this context, all discussions about the war appear linked to the notion of masculinity and Romantic fantasies of heroic deeds. Andrei Bolkonskii is presented as an escapist driven to war partly because of his profound disillusionment with aristocratic lifestyle and the everyday humdrum. The use of the French nursery song in this act highlights the infantile outlook of Russian aristocrats estranged both from their selves and from Russian society. The satirical overtones of Tolstoi's novel are mimicked and hyperbolized in Fomenko's play to the extent that the absurdity of everyday life on the verge of catastrophe is even more clearly articulated than in Tolstoi's novel. Such an emphasis on the infantile outlook of Tolstoi's characters evokes the escapist behaviour of the characters featured in Chekhov's 1904 play *The Cherry Orchard*, well recognized by audiences in Russia and abroad. It is difficult not to agree with Svetlana Evdokimova's compelling argument that Chekhov's play 'focuses on the universal childishness of Russian society' to the effect that 'the comic nature of the characters stems to a large extent from their infantilism'.[48]

Recalling Greenleaf's observation on Fomenko's ability to enchant the audience, I would like to suggest that the Chekhovian trait of his personality as director enables Fomenko to identify himself with Pierre Bezukhov who appears in the beginning of the play as a philosopher and at the same time

---

[48] Svetlana Evdokimova, 'What's so funny about losing one's estate, or Infantilism in *The Cherry Orchard*', *The Slavic and East European Journal*, XLIV, 4, 2000, pp. 623–48 (625).

a confused teenager. In playful manner, he pronounces a long monologue on the nature of historical events and historical memory standing on a ladder in front of excessively large portraits of Napoleon and Alexander I that appear to be durable. The comic appearance of Pierre Bezukhov (played by Andrei Kazakov) in this elevated position at the start of the play has the effect of framing the whole performance, enabling the director to stress the importance of the youthful gaze with its implied sense of optimism in the representation of everyday life; this despite the uncontrollable forces of history embodied by the references to the war with Napoleon. As with Chekhov, Fomenko aspires to render the universal childishness of Russian society and the sense of historical amnesia associated with this trait.

In light of the above observations, we may note that the most comical part of the production is linked to the play's second act, which features several Moscow scenes. It seems especially significant that in this act Fomenko gives artistic expression to the notion of simultaneity embedded in Tolstoi's novel. The stage is divided into two levels for the audience to observe two spatial and temporal dimensions simultaneously. The upper level features the dying figure of Pierre Bezukhov's father, his doctors and various relatives eager to obtain his will and secure their inheritance rights, while the lower level depicts Natasha Rostova's household. The contrast between the images of the two households highlights the director's preoccupation with the satirical and comic devices that foreground the importance of a communal bond and humanist values based on trust, mutual respect and love. The third act depicts Andrei Bolkonskii's visit to his father's estate in Lysye Gory. It is fair to say that Galina Tiunina's performance as Princess Mary to a great extent steals the show and contributes to another set of binary oppositions featured in the play such as piety and pride, feminine and masculine, Russian and European outlooks, collective and individualistic, Christian and profane. Undoubtedly, Fomenko's production gives the impression that the image of war exists only in the imagination of Tolstoi's characters. The dual perspective on everyday life enables Fomenko to highlight the notion that its theatricality and fluidity is threatened by external forces beyond the control of individuals.

According to Dolzhanskii, Fomenko's framing of the narration is highly effective: it makes the audience realize that the life of individuals is precarious and subordinated to the irrational forces of history.[49] In this respect, Fomenko alerts the audience to how the philosophical and aesthetic doctrines in *War and Peace* were largely influenced by the debates of the 1860s over evolution,

---

49   Dolzhanskii, op. cit.

individual freedom, the essence of the soul and the laws of history. It seems that Fomenko's aesthetic sensibility derives from Tolstoi's own brand of realism as expressed in *War and Peace*. As Ilya Vinitsky compellingly argues, the psychological and spiritualist aspects of the novel are entwined with the historical and stem from the 1860s debates that question the essence of the soul and immortality. Drawing on Leskov's and Ginzburg's observations, Vinitsky suggests labelling Tolstoi's mode of writing in *War and Peace* as transcendental realism or realistic spiritualism. In Vinitsky's view, Pierre Leroux's 1840 philosophical tract *De l'humanité* had influenced Tolstoi's optimistic vision of history: 'According to Leroux's optimistic philosophy, death is a dream that results in a "reawakening" to an eternal life on earth. Past generations reawaken as today's living, and the total evolution of humanity will be the triumph of all those who lived before'.[50]

Vinitsky's observation sheds a new light on Tolstoi's philosophical concerns that were omitted from Soviet textbooks, rendering Tolstoi as a great patriot and a passionate critic of European empires. The metaphysical and spiritual dimension of the novel discussed in Vinitsky's article seems of particular interest to Fomenko, the ageing post-Soviet director, searching for a cohesive narrative that could bring together different generations of Russian readers of Tolstoi's novel.

Fomenko's reluctance to depict scenes of war with graphic violence might be seen as a polemical touch that questions the unprecedented popularity of the New Drama with its revival of the naturalistic gloomy depiction of the everyday (*chernukha*). As Eliot Borenstein observes, the *chernukha* of the perestroika period 'functioned like satire without being satirical', exposing flaws and social ills to the effect that violence and horror became associated with the act of truth telling.[51] By contrast with the use of naturalism during the perestroika period, the *chernukha* of the 1990s was shaped by a flourishing Russian popular culture, including thrillers, pulp fiction and daily television programmes that focused on the sensationalist representation of violence. Borenstein writes: 'Instead, in a world in which the private has been made public for the first time, and in which the publicly owned has been privatized, the rhetoric of neo-chernukha is, if anything, that of *overexposure:* let us

---

[50] Ilya Vinitsky, 'The Worm of Doubt: Prince Andrei's Death and Russian Spiritual Awakening of the 1860s' in *Anniversary Essays on Tolstoy*, Donna Tussing Orwin, ed., Cambridge University Press, New York, London, 2010, pp. 120–37 (126).

[51] Eliot Borenstein, *Overkill. Sex and Violence in Contemporary Russian Popular Culture*, Cornell University Press, Ithaca and London, 2008, p. 11.

see once again what horrifies us every day [...] Chernukha functioned discursively as an unhealthy habit widely enjoyed even as it was derided'.[52] According to Lipovetsky and Beumers, while the New Drama revived the traditions of the *chernukha* of the late 1980s, it lacked the moral pathos of the perestroika period: 'The authors of New Drama do not trust the cleansing force of the truth, because this belief had already crashed in the 1990s. Moreover, they represent violence as social norm, and thus they continue on the one hand the *chernukha*-based entertainment of the 1990s, while on the other hand they diverge from "In-Yer-Face-Theatre"'.[53] In contrast to the alienating effect of the New Drama, Fomenko's ability to produce intimate dialogue with the audience is reflected in his 2001 adaptation of Tolstoi's *War and Peace*. It was well received by critics who welcomed Fomenko's adaptation of Tolstoi's novel as 'an epic in the format of cabaret theatre' ('эпопея в камерном формате').[54]

Some critics also liked the open-ended nature of Fomenko's production. Oleg Zintsov suggests that the effect of indeterminacy and the open-ended nature of the play is achieved with the help of the impressionistic étude-like style of Fomenko's production. Indeed, the subtitle – 'scenes from the novel' – points to the importance of collage in Fomenko's adaptation: it is subordinated to the principle of subversion of the grand style prevalent during the Soviet period. The use of collage evokes the revival of monodrama in Russia and Europe in the 1910s-20s, especially the type of monodrama that features several characters. The goal of monodrama is to align the spectator as closely as possible to the protagonist so that the viewer would relate to the protagonist's experience as it was unfolding on stage. In Evreinov's theoretical works, for example, monodrama was a form concerned with the external expression of the internal experience of a single protagonist. To this end, Fomenko presents Pierre Bezukhov as a mouthpiece for Tolstoi's views on history and the role of individuals in history. However, Pierre's monologue at the beginning of the play downplays the monumental quality of Tolstoi's epic. The intimate atmosphere achieved by Fomenko's play recreates many features of modern monodrama that might be seen as a manifestation of high-spirited revolt against the grandiosity that gave rise to a new theatrical language. According to Senelick, 'The playwrights featured at André Antoine's *Théâtre Libre* in Paris claimed

---

52 Ibid., pp. 9–10.
53 Beumers and Lipovetsky, p. 35.
54 Oleg Zintsov, 'Epopeia v kamernom formate: *Voina i mir* v Teatre Petra Fomenko', *Vedomosti*, 20 February, 2001.

they were presenting "slices of life", best exposed in short, striking format'.[55] Indeed, the spirit of revolt against grand narratives and monumental styles is manifested in Fomenko's production vividly.

Fomenko's impressionistic style, the minimalist use of decorations, the use of playfulness and parody oriented towards engagement with the audience also evokes many features embedded in the Russian modernist theatre of ideas and in European monodrama. The studio-like format of the theatre of ideas was often seen as an artistic form that could unite actors and directors sharing a vision of the art of acting and methods of that particular theatre. As Vera Komissarzhevskaia points out, 'every such theatre must be like a community, following a "master", something like what in painting is called a "school", in which all the disciples carry out freely and enthusiastically the ideas of their leader and are able to work together on the same picture'.[56] One of the living examples of such a community of kindred spirits was Vakhtangov's studio. Fomenko is well aware of this tradition, especially because in the 1950s he was trained by two of Vakhtangov's disciples. One was Boris Vershilov (orthonym: Veisterman, 1893–1957), his teacher at the MKhAT Training College. Nikolai Gorchakov, Fomenko's supervisor of studies at GITIS, was also trained by Vakhtangov and wrote a book of memoirs explaining Vakhtangov's ideas on acting and directing. Since Fomenko himself had been working in the Vakhtangov theatre as a director since 1989, his own outlook as director was largely shaped by his involvement with the actors and directors of the Vakhtangovian mould. It is not coincidental that famous practitioners of the Vakhtangov school of acting and directing define Fomenko's studio as a living embodiment of Vakhtangov's principles of playfulness and the collective spirit of creative process.[57]

A feature of Fomenko's production of *War and Peace* strikingly reminiscent of Vakhtangov is that Fomenko and his group of actors spent seven years reading the whole novel before staging the first part of book one. The act of reading is an important part of spectacle, too: during the performance several actors pick up an antique-looking volume of Tolstoi's novel from the table and read

---

[55] Laurence Senelick, 'Boris Geyer and Cabaretic Playwriting' in *Russian Theatre in the Age of Modernism*, Robert Russell and Andrew Barratt, eds, Macmillan, Houndmills, 1990, pp. 34–5.

[56] Vera Komissarzhevskaia, quoted in James Roose-Evans, *Experimental Theatre: From Stanislavsky to Peter Brook*, Routledge, London, New York, 1989, p. 13.

[57] From a personal interview with Olga Partan (née Simonova) who interviewed several actors and directors associated with the Vakhtangov theatre in Moscow for her book on the Vakhtangov theatre (date of interview: 25.07.2010). See: Olga Simonova-Partan. *Ty prava, Filumena! Vakhtangovtsy za kulisami teatra*, Prozaik, Moscow, 2012.

aloud from it, as if they are reminding the audience what should be happening next. This gesture enables the actors to interweave Tolstoi's own words as narrator into the play, but the monologic style is presented from different viewpoints and through different voices, which highlights the notion of subjectivity.

At the same time, it creates an impression of being faithful to Tolstoi's text and sensitive to his style. It can be also viewed as a parodic touch that resembles Mikhail Shveitser and Sofia Milkina's direction of the 1987 film *The Kreutzer Sonata*. As Philip Strick writes, 'While a satirical intention could be argued from the use of Offenbach's familiar "can-can" theme on the soundtrack for a brothel sequence, and of "O Sole Mio" for scenes by the Trevi Fountain and other Roman landmarks [...] Tolstoy's text is closely observed'.[58] More importantly, the playful use of one of the first editions of Tolstoi's novel throughout the play might be seen as an ironic device that reminds the audience about the boundary between literature and theatre that mocks any expectations of a literal reading of Tolstoi's novel. As with Vakhtangov, Fomenko advocates the notion of creative reading and improvization and shies away from the tradition of naturalist theatre. 'Vakhtangov', says W.L. Turner, 'attempted to teach, not merely technique, nor even a consistent theatrical style and theory, but a method of artistic creativity that would outlast both his directorial genius and his times'.[59] Vakhtangov developed Stanislavskii's principles of acting in his own way but, just like Stanislavskii, Vakhtangov believed that the art of acting should lie at the heart of theatrical form. He also advocated the principle of realist detail, suggesting that every action be realistically justified and stem from emotional memory. 'On the stage,' Vakhtangov wrote, 'the actor works in an atmosphere of untruths. [...] He calls a comrade father, he makes the words of others his own, he pretends the scenery is a real landscape. The moments when he makes this untruth truth are moments of creation and art'.[60] Vakhtangov insisted that emotion should arise from the action and encouraged his actors to break the mould of acting clichés by concentrating on the essence of each character in order to impart to his body the feeling of plasticity found in Nature. Vakhtangov's ironic style – defined usually either as fantastic realism or imaginative

---

58   Philip Strick, '*The Kreutzer Sonata*', *Monthly Film Bulletin*, LVI, 660, January, 1989, pp. 16–17 (16).
59   W.L. Turner, 'Vakhtangov: The Director as Teacher', *Educational Theatre Journal*, XV, 4, 1963, pp. 318–26 (319).
60   Quoted in Turner, loc. cit.

realism – was built, not from commonplace naturalistic detail, but from elements of the grotesque. According to Vakhtangov, grotesque is 'the height of expressiveness, the most appropriate form of the scenic presentation of the content' because it is 'a method which enables the actor and the director to justify inwardly the vivid, condensed content of a given play'.[61]

Fomenko's adaptation of *War and Peace* is full of examples of the grotesque, especially in relation to the representation of real historical figures such as Napoleon and Alexander I. The play starts with Tolstoi's monologue on history and the role of individuals in history. As has been mentioned above, the speech on history is delivered by Pierre Bezukhov standing on a ladder. His appearance, as well as the initial stage setting, imitate the atmosphere of a library. The two portraits depicting Napoleon and Alexander I reinforce the atmosphere of a library and museum setting, alluding to Bitov's 1978 novel *Pushkin House* which presents the Institute of Russian literature of the Academy of Sciences in a highly critical manner. It symbolizes the end of Russian history and presents Russian literary space as a museum. The museum-like space serves as a site of memory that ironically evokes the Stalinist archive of high culture. Sven Spieker explains:

> Bitov based his novel on Modest Platonovich's inference that Russian history came to an end with the Bolshevik revolution. As a result, the subsequent Stalinist period represents the culmination of all history, a period in which the notion of history has in itself become historical. Under Stalin, the past is replaced by the school curriculum, a pantheon of canonical names and texts.[62]

The Stalinist curriculum plays an important role in the novel, shaping the main protagonist's education. Furthermore, Bitov's parodic use throughout the novel of references to the school curriculum, in the form of the many chapter headings and epigraphs, subverts the Soviet textbook account of the canon of nineteenth-century Russian literature. 'Unable to come to terms either with the past or with the present,' notes Spieker, 'Leva and his intellectual friends cultivate the kind of "alcoholic" lifestyle that is a hallmark of Russian prose in the 1960s and 1970s'.[63] Bitov's satirical depiction of the self-presentation of 1960s and 1970s Soviet intellectuals as the guardians of Russian

---

61   Loc. cit.
62   Sven Spieker, 'Pushkin House', in *Reference Guide to Russian Literature*, Neil Cornwell, ed., Fitzroy Dearborn Publishers, London and Chicago, 1998, pp. 171–2 (171).
63   Loc. cit.

pre-revolutionary culture, and their assumption that education and knowledge could make them free and independent from ideological constraints, demonstrates that they were unable to realize that the pre-revolutionary past and its culture might not be continued. Greenleaf's description of post-Soviet Moscow theatre-going practice utilizes the metaposition of Russian intellectuals *vis-à-vis* official culture exposed in Bitov's novel. According to Bitov, Soviet textbooks are permeated with a deceptive worldview that confuses the school curriculum with history, and the sign with its reference. It is interesting that Greenleaf senses the existence of the same paradigm in twenty-first-century Moscow's theatres:

> Theater is the force that frees the story from its nineteenth-century binding or its 'school-program' incarnation and represents it to a Russian audience who may be leading adult lives of comparable bewilderment and media-saturated fantasy, tucked away behind Moscow's regilded commercial facades. Theatergoing offers a traditional locus of resistance to the new regime of privatized spaces and bodies.[64]

Undoubtedly, the aim of Fomenko's rendering of *War and Peace* is to make the audience shift away from the deceptive views on history and culture offered by Soviet and post-Soviet textbooks.

More importantly, Fomenko's rendering of *War and Peace* makes a mockery of Sergei Bondarchuk's lavish 1965 film adaptation of the novel that embodies the monumental style of socialist realist art at its best. It became the first Soviet film to win the Oscar for Best Foreign Picture. Bondarchuk not only directed the film, but also co-wrote the screenplay and acted in the lead role of Pierre. The film took seven years to produce and cost over US$100 million; according to the *Guinness Book of World Records*, the depiction of the Borodino Battle featured 120,000 soldiers, making it one of the largest battle scenes ever made. It is clear that Fomenko shies away from the grand style adopted by Bondarchuk's film, well-known for its spectacular battle scenes (one of which runs for 45 minutes) and graphic depiction of Napoleon's invasion, featuring scenes of violence that led to many horses being killed. In the words of American critic Roger Ebert, Bondarchuk's film strikes the right balance between the spectacular, the human, and the intellectual: 'Even in the longest, bloodiest, battle scenes there are vignettes that stand out. Bondarchuk is able to bring his epic events down to comprehensible scale without losing his sense

---

64   Greenleaf, p. 432.

of the spectacular. And always he returns to Tolstoy's theme of men in the grip of history'.[65]

In some ways, Fomenko's production stands closer to Prokofiev's opera *War and Peace*, the first revision of which was completed on 3 April 1943. Despite subsequent revisions, Prokofiev never saw a full-scale performance of his opera. Critics praised Prokofiev's opera for its lyricism, suggesting that it successfully combined traditional and modern opera. In many ways, Prokofiev wanted to give his audience a sense of social cohesion and patriotism. The use of two choruses in the opera, especially in scene eight – 'Thus our Kutuzov came to the people' – and scene nine -'Just see how she burns' – featuring a Russian militiamen chorus and a mixed chorus of Muscovites, was meant to underscore and emphasize the role of the Russian people in the war with Napoleon.[66] Despite Prokofiev's attempts to re-fashion his opera according to the demands of the socialist realist canon and official watchdogs, many officials, including Stalin and Zhdanov, were scornful of Prokofiev's depiction of war scenes, fearing perhaps that it might inspire participants of World War II to reveal their personal accounts of war experiences. According to Denis Wakeling's 1990 review of Prokofiev's opera, it might be defined as a 'work that contains a series of scenes and tableaux taken from the novel, rather than a well-made dramaturgical totality'. Nevertheless, Wakeling finds it comparable to other masterpieces of a uniquely Russian tradition, including *Boris Godunov*, that exemplify a distinct historical national style.[67]

It is clear that Fomenko's production develops the approach to Tolstoi's epic undertaken by Prokofiev. However, by omitting any graphic depiction of war scenes and focusing on the representation of the everyday and human psychology, Fomenko poses an important question about the impossibility of the application of the nineteenth-century European and Russian grand narratives about empire-building strategies to the contemporary world without critical assessment of the ideas that shaped them. Furthermore, Fomenko's staging of *War and Peace* might be better understood as a symbolic illustration of Hosking's thesis expressed in his 1997 book *Russia, Empire and People* suggesting that Russian tsars after Alexander II implemented Russifying policies. Yet Hosking highlights the fact that their 'national imperialism' did not attempt to nurture a Russian nation. It was directed toward the preservation of the

---

65 Roger Ebert, 'Reviews': '*War and Peace*', 22 June, 1969, https://www.rogerebert.com/reviews/war-and-peace-1969 (accessed 3 August 2020).
66 Malcolm H. Brown, 'Prokofiev's *War and Peace*: A Chronicle', *The Musical Quarterly*, LXIII, 3, 1977, pp. 297–326 (304).
67 Denis W. Wakeling, *Opera Quarterly*, VII, 1, 1990, pp. 227–30 (230).

government 'through greater administrative unity and coordination'.[68] To this end, Fomenko, who often presented himself as an outsider and a director who preferred to live on the margins of official culture, stands out as a true disciple of Vakhtangov's tradition aimed at the subversion of the official culture. In contrast to the most popular trends, Fomenko, in a manner reminiscent of Vakhtangov, relies on preserving community and cultural traditions through the community spirit of studio-like theatres.

One can also sense an anti-state resistance in Fomenko's reading of Tolstoi's *War and Peace* that draws the audience's gaze away from terrorist violence turned into spectacle by the mass media, in which terrorists, victims and audience play out their respective roles, both consciously and unconsciously. Fomenko is acutely aware that images of real violence, as news event or performance, lose meaning through repetition. It can be argued that the artistic goal and the structure of Fomenko's adaptation of Tolstoi's *War and Peace* are subordinated to the expression of postmodernist ethics. In his assessment of modernist and postmodernist representations of terror, Anthony Kubiak writes:

> The great critique of social disintegration that begins the modern period in the work of Ibsen is effectively neutralized in the incessant repetitions of terrorist violence in the video image, until modernist disintegration itself now seems to dissolve into self-parody. This, as I see it, is more and more the ethos of the postmodern.[69]

Yet, in spite of the layers of intertextual references embedded in Fomenko's production, his message remains clear. In Tolstoian fashion, Fomenko's production celebrates the notion of youthful optimism, the vision of family happiness and the resilience of Russians to survive any corruptive influences from the west. Thompson elucidates Tolstoi's vision of the good life conveyed in *War and Peace* thus: 'Tolstoy began his life and career by equating good life with success [...]. In *War and Peace* Tolstoy added another ingredient of the happy life: the ability to enjoy existence per se, enjoy being alive and understand that physical existence in itself is a great blessing'.[70] Undoubtedly, the reinforcement of Tolstoi's message about the good life in Fomenko's produc-

---

68 Geoffrey Hosking, *Russia, Empire and People*, Harvard University Press, Cambridge, MA, 1997, p. 397.
69 Anthony Kubiak, *Stages of Terror: Terrorism, Ideology, and Coercion as Theatre History*, Indiana University Press, Bloomington and Indianapolis, 1991, pp. 149–50.
70 Thompson, p. 238.

tion of *War and Peace* testifies to the rise of certain nationalistic trends in post-Soviet Russia and in the former Soviet Union that manifest themselves in a form of post-Communist and post-dissident art. According to Boris Groys, this new type of artistic expression 'clings to peaceful universalism as an idyllic utopia beyond any struggle'.[71]

Bibliography

http://sati-sgk.ru/index.php/id-2006-xochu-rebjonka.html (accessed: 21 October 2022).
https://alexandrinsky.ru/afisha-i-bilety/revizor/ (accessed 5 August 2020).
https://mxat.ru/authors/directors/mashkov/10737/ (accessed 5 August 2020).
Anderson, Benedict, *Imagined Communities: Reflections on the Origin and Spread of Nationalism* Verso, London, 2006.
Beissinger, Mark R., 'The Persisting Ambiguity of Empire', *Post-Soviet Affairs*, XI, 2, 1995, pp. 149–84.
Beumers, Birgit and Lipovetsky, Mark, eds, *Performing Violence: Literary and Theatrical Experiments of New Russian Drama*, Intellect Books, Bristol, 2009.
Beumers, Birgit, *Pop Culture Russia!: Media, Arts, and Lifestyle*, ABC-Clio, Santa Barbara, California, 2005.
Borenstein, Eliot, *Overkill. Sex and Violence in Contemporary Russian Popular Culture*, Cornell University Press, Ithaca and London, 2008.
Boym, Svetlana, *The Future of Nostalgia*, Basic Books, New York, 2001.
Brown, Malcolm H,. 'Prokofiev's *War and Peace*: A Chronicle', *The Musical Quarterly*, LXIII, 3, 1977, pp. 297–326.
Condee, Nancy 'Perezhivaia chuzhuiu katastrofu: Imperiia smotrit *Gibel' imperii*', *Pro et Contra*, July-August, 2006, pp. 29–37.
Condee, Nancy, *Imperial Trace: Recent Russian Cinema*, Oxford University Press, New York, 2009.
Costanzo, Susan, 'Amateur Theatres and Amateur Publics in the Russian Republic, 1958–71', *The Slavonic and East European Review*, LXXX, 2, April 2008, pp. 372–94.
Dmitrievskaia, Marina 'Novaia Misteriia-Buff Petra Fomenko. Istoriia zapreshchennogo spektaklia', *Peterburgskii teatral'nyi zhurnal*, III, 33, 2003: http://ptj.spb.ru/archive/33/historical-novel-33/novaya-misteriya-buff-petra-fomenko/ (accessed 16 August, 2020).
Dolzhanskii, Roman, 'Tolstovstvo v chistom vide. Petr Fomenko postavil kusok *Voiny i mira*', *Kommersant*, XXX, 20.02.2001, p. 13; http://www.kommersant.ru/doc-y.aspx?DocsID=168867 (accessed 3 August 2020).

---

71   Boris Groys, *Art Power*, The MIT Press, Cambridge, MA and London, 2008, p. 172.

Ebert, Roger, 'Reviews': '*War and Peace*', 22 June, 1969, https://www.rogerebert.com/reviews/war-and-peace-1969 (accessed 3 August 2020).

Evdokimova, Svetlana, 'What's so funny about losing one's estate, or Infantilism in *The Cherry Orchard*', *The Slavic and East European Journal*, XLIV, 4, 2000, pp. 623–48.

Fomina, Elena, 'Pravila ottorzheniia "ia". (O shkole dramaticheskogo iskusstva Anatoliia Vasil'eva)', *Peterburgskii teatral'nyi zhurnal*, XX, 2000, pp. 53–60.

Gourgouris, Stathis, *Dream Nation*, Stanford University Press, Stanford, CA, 1996.

Greenleaf, Monika, 'In medias res: A Diary of the Moscow Theatre Season, 2007–2008', *Slavic Review*, LXVII, 2, 2008, pp. 422–36.

Groys, Boris, *Art Power*, The MIT Press, Cambridge, MA and London, 2008.

Hosking, Geoffrey, 'The Second World War and Russian National Consciousness', *Past and Present*, CLXXV, 1, May 2002, pp. 162–87.

Hosking, Geoffrey, *Russia, Empire and People*, Harvard University Press, Cambridge, MA, 1997.

Kirschenbaum, Lisa, '"Our City, Our Hearths, Our Families": Local Loyalties and Private Life in Soviet World War II Propaganda', *Slavic Review*, LIX, 4, 2000, pp. 825–47.

Kubiak, Anthony, *Stages of Terror: Terrorism, Ideology, and Coercion as Theatre History*, Indiana University Press, Bloomington and Indianapolis, 1991.

Marsh, Rosalind, *Literature, History and Identity in Post-Soviet Russia, 1991–2006*, Peter Lang, Oxford, New York, 2007.

Nikiforova, Viktoriia, 'Mezhdu mirom i voinoi', *Ekspert*, 10 (270), Moscow, 12.03. 2001; https://fomenki.ru/performance/warandpeace/3841/ (accessed 21 October 2022).

Norris, S.M., 'Guiding Stars: The Comet-like Rise of the War Film in Putin's Russia: Recent World War II Films and Historical Memories', *Studies in Russian and Soviet Cinema*, I, 2, 2007, pp. 163–189.

Ravetto-Biagioli, Kriss, 'Floating on the Borders of Europe: Sokurov's *Russian Ark*', *Film Quarterly*, LIX, 1, 2005, pp. 18–26.

Roose-Evans, James, *Experimental Theatre: From Stanislavsky to Peter Brook*, Routledge, London, New York, 1989.

Senelick, Laurence 'Boris Geyer and Cabaretic Playwriting', in *Russian Theatre in the Age of Modernism*, Russell, Robert and Barratt, eds, Andrew, Macmillan, Houndmills, 1990, pp. 34–5.

Sherel', A.A., ed., *Radiozhurnalistika*, Izdatel'stvo Moskovskogo universiteta, Moscow, 2000.

Simonova-Partan, Olga, *Ty prava, Filumena! Vakhtangovtsy za kulisami teatra*, Prozaik, Moscow, 2012.

Smeliansky, Anatoly *The Russian Theatre after Stalin*, Miles, Patrick, trans., Cambridge University Press, Cambridge, 1999.

Smith, Kathleen, *Mythmaking in the New Russia: Politics and Memory in the Yeltsin Era*, Cornell University Press, Ithaca, NY, 2002.

Snyder, Jack, 'Introduction: Reconstructing Politics amidst the Wreckage of Empire' in *Post-Soviet Political Order: Conflict and State Building*, Rubin, Barnett R. and Snyder, Jack, eds, Routledge, London, 1998, pp. 1–13.

Spieker, Sven, 'Pushkin House', in *Reference Guide to Russian Literature*, Cornwell, Neil, ed., Fitzroy Dearborn Publishers, London and Chicago, 1998, pp. 171–2.

Stam, Robert, *Literature through Film: Realism, Magic and the Art of Adaptation*, Blackwell Publishing, Malden, MA and Oxford, 2005.

Strick, Philip, 'The Kreutzer Sonata', *Monthly Film Bulletin*, LVI, 660, January, 1989, pp. 16–17 (16).

Thompson, Ewa, 'Leo Tolstoy and the Idea of Good Life', in *Kultura rosyjska w ojczyznie i diasporz*, Liburska, Lidia, ed., Jagiellonian University Press, Krakow, 2007, pp. 231–8.

Turner, W.L., 'Vakhtangov: The Director as Teacher', *Educational Theatre Journal*, XV, 4, 1963, pp. 318–26.

Valutskii, Vladimir, 'K voprosu o teatre na Taganke', *Sovetskaia kul'tura*, 30 March 1965, pp. 2–3.

Vinitsky, Ilya, 'The Worm of Doubt: Prince Andrei's Death and Russian Spiritual Awakening of the 1860s' in *Anniversary Essays on Tolstoy*, Orwin, Donna Tussing, ed., Cambridge University Press, New York, London, 2010, pp. 120–37.

Wakeling, Denis W., *Opera Quarterly*, VII, 1, 1990, pp. 227–30.

Werth, Alexander, *Russia at War, 1941–1945*, Barrie and Rockliff, London, 1964.

Winter, Jay, *Remembering War: The Great War Between Memory and History in the Twentieth Century*, Yale University Press, New Haven, 2006.

Wolfe, Thomas C., 'Past as Present, Myth, or History? Discourses of Time and the Great Fatherland War' in *The Politics of Memory in Postwar Europe*, Lebow, Richard Ned, Kansteiner, Wulf and Fogu, Claudio, eds, Duke University Press, Durham, NC, 2006, pp. 249–83.

Zintsov, Oleg, 'Epopeia v kamernom formate: *Voina i mir* v Teatre Petra Fomenko', *Vedomosti*, 20 February 2001.

CHAPTER 10

Bridging Cultures?
John McGahern's *The Power of Darkness*

Cynthia Marsh

Abstract

Stage adaptations of Tolstoi's novels considerably outnumber performances of his drama in the UK. However, his best known play, *The Power of Darkness*, received a particularly interesting reception when it was performed at the Abbey Theatre in Dublin in 1991. John McGahern had initially adapted it as a play for Radio 3 as long ago as 1972, significantly using Irish English (at the BBC's request) as a way of distancing itself from the language of the English target audience and, more controversially, relying upon certain assumptions about the nature of rural Irish culture. This chapter also notes the erasure of Tolstoi's authorship in credits for the stage adaptation of the play in favour of the adapter, an interesting inversion of the anonymization of the translator. Indeed, so hibernicized was the play and its performance, that heated critical discussion followed about the legitimacy of such a harsh representation of Irish life and morals. The critical furore engendered by the Irish version of the play in many way replicated the outrage provoked by the Russian original.

Keywords

Relation of translation to version – Tolstoi's drama – performance and reception of *The Power of Darkness* in Ireland – John McGahern

The title of John McGahern's *The Power of Darkness* has an immediate Tolstoian resonance[1] for those who engage with Russian culture. However, on the published version[2] of the script there is no indication of Tolstoi as source, either on the front or back cover, or on the internal title pages. The cover illustration is not notably Russian either. It shows a dark house in close-up, and

1 L.N. Tolstoi, *The Power of Darkness* (*Vlast' t'my*, 1886).
2 John McGahern, *The Power of Darkness*, Faber and Faber, London and Boston, 1991.

two tiny dark figures standing by a hay barn below it, against a sunlit view of patchwork fields with green hills in the distance and dark mountains beyond. It was the incongruity of this picture with a Russian landscape which drew me to investigate further: was it Tolstoi or not? The conclusion reached after the investigation is a surprising one.

The first clues come in the short Introduction to the published 1991 text where John McGahern acknowledges a lifelong interest in Tolstoi's works.[3] Many years previously he had been commissioned by the BBC 'to adapt Tolstoi's melodrama into Irish speech for radio'.[4] Subsequent research showed that it was broadcast by Radio 3 on 15 October 1972.[5] The feeling had been that the play was better suited to Irish country speech and to the Irish set-up, whereas in English, McGahern wrote, 'it could sound merely quaint or antiquated and even ridiculous'.[6] This statement may not be surprising: a recent article suggests he had worked from the Louise Maude translation first performed in 1904.[7] McGahern continued to work on his adaptation after 1972; he subsequently defended his position as follows, in the process identifying two issues which drew him to Tolstoi's play and so, to his mind, aspects of both cultures:

> I had come to realise that the language I used for the adaptation had been too colourful and idiomatic and that it skimmed over what was at the heart of the play. *The Power of Darkness* is a perfect description of that heart and is uncannily close to the moral climate in which I grew up. The old fear of famine was confused with terror and damnation. The confusion and guilt and plain ignorance that surrounded sex turned men and women into exploiters and adversaries.[8]

---

[3] Ibid., p. vii.
[4] Loc. cit.
[5] Christopher Murray, 'The "Fallen World" of *The Power of Darkness*' in *John McGahern Yearbook*, John Kenny, ed., NUI Galway, Galway, 2009, pp. 78–92 (82–3).
[6] McGahern, loc. cit.
[7] Murray, loc. cit. The edition was that published by World Classics in 1929. On p. 79, Murray refers to the first British production as 1902, but in other sources this production, by the Stage Society in London, is given as 1904: see W. Gareth Jones: 'Tolstoy Staged in Paris, Berlin, and London' in *The Cambridge Companion to Tolstoy*, Donna Tussing Orwin, ed., Cambridge University Press, 2002, pp. 142–57.
[8] McGahern, loc. cit.

In fact, the McGahern archive, housed at the University of Galway,[9] has documents that suggest McGahern returned to the play 39 times between 1972 and his death in 2006.[10] By 1991, he was advised that the final version was very far from the original, far enough to 'abandon the Tolstoy frame altogether and approach it as a new work'.[11] From the points of view of translation studies, particularly of drama translation, and of 'bridging cultures', there are already a number of issues here calling for comment. However, a brief account of McGahern's play will narrow the range of possible approaches.

McGahern's *The Power of Darkness* is set in Ireland and, as far as can be surmised from the script, could be contemporary to its production date of 1991. One critic wrote, 'This is a play in serious danger of being "relevant" to the enclosed moral environment of 1990s Ireland',[12] while another wrote of 'a terrifying picture of poverty-stricken rural life shot through with Catholic guilt and oppression'.[13]

Peter King is dying. He is a wealthy smallholder, a breeder and trader of horses, but still lives in the manner of the impoverished farming stock of his origins. He has a daughter from his first marriage, Maggie, and a second wife Eileen who is half his age, both of whom are expected to work on the farm. Since becoming ill, Peter has hired in a young workman, Paul, to help. The son of a neighbour, Paul is handsome, a bit feckless but pleased to be away from his father Oliver, a religious man. His mother, Baby, is a schemer. The parents have a part-time worker, Paddy, a former soldier in the British army who becomes the drama's 'moral voice', as the opening plot summary to the 1991 script points out.[14] The play revolves around the death of Peter, the passing on of his wealth, the marriage of Paul and Eileen and the miscarriage of Maggie's baby by Paul, which coincides with her wedding to someone else. In fact, event-wise, this plot is not very different from the Tolstoi original.

At this point, it is appropriate to make my approach clear. First of all, it is important to clarify what this present exploration will not cover. There is no detailed and direct comparison between the two texts, the Russian and the English; nor is there a comparison between the original 1972 McGahern text

---

9   'The John McGahern Papers', James Hardiman Library, National University of Ireland Galway (ref code: p. 71 [c. 1958–2006]).
10 Murray, p. 82.
11 McGahern, p. viii.
12 John Waters, 'Into the Dark', *The Irish Times*, 12 October, 1991, p. 29.
13 Michael Coveney, 'Mortality and a Sock in the Face', *The Observer*, 20 October, 1991, reprinted in *The Irish Times* on 22 October, 1991, p. 20.
14 McGahern, p. ix.

and the 1991 text, though there are strong arguments for approaching this topic on their basis, but my aim is not to castigate or laud the author for his particular approach; nor is a discourse on translation ethics or practices particularly revealing, though there will be some reference to these concerns.

To investigate the cultural role of the two texts, and whether or not a palpable bridge between cultures has been erected, a context for each text is required. Therefore, the history of staging *The Power of Darkness* in English, Russian, and Irish English will be examined. Some information about the author of this Irish version along with some analysis of the different roles of Irish English and English will be included, as well as an exploration of the reception of the 1991 production. In addition, there will be a brief focus on copyright. Finally, we shall investigate what conclusions can be drawn about the transfer of Tolstoi's play to Irish and British English targets which may have implications for the transfer and reception of Tolstoi's work and, indeed, foreign works in general. In fact, in what ways might this work be regarded as 'bridging' cultures, more than 100 years after Tolstoi's death?

Tolstoi is well-known on the British stage, but principally for adaptations of his novels: of the 20 productions in British theatre located between 1945 and 2005, 15 are adaptations of his prose. Some reviewers even express surprise that Tolstoi wrote plays at all. His work written for the theatre ranges from short moral pieces directed at educating the peasants to full-length plays.[15] Two of his longer efforts have reached the British stage in the post-war period: *The Power of Darkness* in 1949, 1984 and 1997, and *The Fruits of Enlightenment* (*плоды просвещения* [1889]) in 1979 and, at the Royal Academy of Dramatic Art (RADA), in 1957. So, these two plays have only relatively rarely been seen in Britain, but the reviews indicate they have attracted attention because of the classic 'awe-inspiring'[16] other works by their author.

Banned when it was first written, Tolstoi's uncomfortable play, *The Power of Darkness*, about the evils of village life and the power of Orthodox Christianity as a redemptive force, had a chequered early history in the Russian theatre. Murder, poisoning, sexual abuse, exploitation and jealousy are rife in the extended peasant family at the heart of this piece. These aspects ensured it had a difficult path through the censorship of late nineteenth-century Russia.

---

15   As well as the two plays discussed here, Tolstoi wrote *The Living Corpse* (*Zhivoi trup*, 1900), a full-length play, focusing on the disappearance of a husband from a loveless marriage by faking his own suicide. The short plays include a piece against drunkenness, *The First Distiller* (*Pervyi vinokur*, 1886).

16   Felix Barker, 'Strange Fruits but Very Ripe', *Evening News*, 15 March, 1979 (Royal National Theatre [hereafter RNT] Archive. Review materials are filed under production names).

The play was published through some adroit networking by Tolstoi's associate V.G. Chertkov, among others, which secured words of approval from the Tsar. The key censoring figure E.M. Feoktistov remained sceptical, however, and lobbied for the piece to be banned from performance. His view was that 'nerves of steel are necessary to sit through all this'.[17] Finally K.P. Pobedonostsev, then serving as Minister of the Interior, was drawn in and used his direct access to the Tsar to raise his concerns. He wrote in February 1887, in fact echoing Feoktistov's original report: 'I have not come across anything like this in any literature [...] the skill of the writer is remarkable, but what a degradation of art! What a lack – no, more than that – *negation* of the ideal, what a degradation of moral sense, what an insult to good taste'.[18] He emphasized the, to his view, appalling fact that the play had been published in a very cheap edition aimed at mass circulation. In fact, by the time Pobedonostsev was writing this letter the play had come out in at least three editions for different markets, totalling 100,000 copies.[19] However, such opposition as Pobedonostsev's prevailed and, despite the fact that the play was already in rehearsal at the Aleksandrinskii theatre in Petersburg, the production was cancelled.[20] It was premièred by Antoine at his *Théâtre libre* in Paris in 1888 as part of the new wave of challenging drama surging across Europe. It was then seen in Berlin and London.[21] It took Stanislavskii to give it its first thorough, naturalistic production in Russian in the repertoire of the Moscow Art Theatre in 1902.

Tolstoi's *The Power of Darkness* draws on a provocative blend of genres. It is written in the style of naturalism which supports its apparent agenda of demonstrating the negative effect upon human beings of a deprived environment. None of the harsh details and their outcomes are spared, whether of an economic or sexual kind: be that the toll of continual daily labour in a peasant smallholding, or the claustrophobic conditions imposed by difficult family relationships involving abuse, jealousy, family ties, and the preservation of family wealth. In its engagement with these darker sides of human existence Tolstoi's play also skirts melodrama and contains an occasional grim and pessimistic humour. Finally, the play, in its assertion of a Christian ethic of confession, appears to change course completely and offers hope of salvation

---

17 N. Gudzii, 'Vlast' t'my', Istoriia pisaniia, pechataniia i postanovok na stsene *Vlasti t'my*' in *L.N. Tolstoi, Polnoe sobranie sochinenii*, XXVI, V.G. Chertkov, ed., Moscow, 1936, pp. 705–37 (715 [my translation]).
18 Ibid., p. 722.
19 Ibid., p. 719.
20 Ibid., p. 723.
21 See Jones, passim.

from these devastating conditions. In their different ways the majority of these themes are reflected in the response of the reviewers to British productions, demonstrating another truism: that no one production will ever encompass the potentials of a text, and that interpretation will change with the social conditions of a play's reception context.

As mentioned above, there have been three professional productions in Britain of *The Power of Darkness* in the post-war period. The first in 1949, in a translation by Peter Glenville at the Lyric Theatre, was condemned by the anonymous *Times* reviewer for the acting style which 'lacks the peasant quality'.[22] Refreshingly frank, the critic maintained that the actors of the 1940s were too civilized and so 'were bound to be outside the characters they were playing', and the leading lady's accent 'would become a Kensington drawing room'.[23] Here is an interesting example of a play from another culture serving as a catalyst to expose the incapacity for stylistic variety among British actors of the period.

The other two productions in 1984 and 1997 were staged in the same translation (by Anthony Clark) in the same theatre, the Orange Tree in Richmond. This commonality of translation, performance space and audience expectation in the knowledge of this particular theatre's reputation, provides a rare opportunity for a comparison between the two sets of responses.

The 1984 production caused a stir. It was a 'dramatic landmark', 'its capacity to handle great themes ... dwarfs any other play currently to be seen in London'[24] and it made 'shattering viewing';[25] its assertion of a 'holy order'[26] and ability to show 'how human nature is governed by economic necessity'[27] were noted. It was compared to opera in the power of its 'climactic sequence, brutally cathartic',[28] when a new-born baby is crushed to death.

By contrast a repeated comment on the 1997 production was that 'the cumulative power is tremendous' but Tolstoi's point was 'hammered home' and the production leaves you 'emotionally bludgeoned and spiritually scourged'.[29] Seen in the earlier production as a marriage of the 'minute' and 'majestic', and

---

22   *The Times*, 29 April, 1949, p. 6.
23   Loc. cit.
24   Michael Billington, *The Guardian*, 6 March, 1984 (*London Theatre Record* [hereafter LTR], IV, 1984, p. 167).
25   Giles Gordon, *The Spectator*, 17 March, 1984 (LTR, IV, 1984, p. 162).
26   Loc. cit.
27   Billington, loc. cit.
28   Martin Hoyle, *The Financial Times*, 5 March, 1984 (LTR, IV, 1984, p. 167).
29   Charles Spencer, *Daily Telegraph*, 14 April, 1997 (*Theatre Record* [hereafter TR] 9–22 April, 1997, p. 445).

as 'great', this play was now regarded by more than one viewer as didactic,[30] and showing a 'humour' which 'sits awkwardly' with Tolstoi's 'melodramatics'.[31] With the same givens of translator, performance space and audience expectations, such different interpretations indicate the weight of responsibility carried by directors, performers and designers. Furthermore, the importance of continuing production and translation is imperative to enable the play to transcend time and place and produce relevance for new generations.

Bearing in mind that McGahern's version was staged in 1991 in between the two Orange Tree productions, three points which will be key to reception of the McGahern play have been made here. Firstly, the ability of an imported text to highlight difference in target-language acting styles and cultures; secondly, that the relations between the text and an individual production, and the social conditions of the reception context, cause changes in interpretation; and thirdly, recognition of the weight of responsibility carried by the agents of the performance (directors, designers, performers) in constructing interpretations.

Best known as a novelist, McGahern was born in 1934 in rural Ireland and died in 2006. He wrote intense works about life in Ireland, drawing on his none-too-happy childhood experiences. Two early works were banned for what was called pornography (exposing child abuse), which lost him his job as a school-teacher. He went on to a string of successes, including *Amongst Women* (1990) which was shortlisted for the Booker Prize, and *That They May Face the Rising Sun* (2002) confronting Republican issues. He also produced a collection of short stories. His plays were mostly written for radio, and much less attention was afforded them; they are often unfortunately now not considered alongside his prose work. Tolstoi was an important early, and continuing, model for McGahern in his prose writing as well as for the play under discussion. McGahern was awarded many honours and fellowships for his work and spent periods teaching in America and Britain as well as in Ireland.[32]

A comparison between an Irish and British version of a text highlights the tensions between Irish English and British English. We began with the BBC

---

30 Paul Taylor, *The Independent*, 14 April, 1997 (TR, loc. cit.); Dominic Cavendish, *Time Out*, 16 April, 1997 (TR, 9–22 April, 1997, p. 446).
31 Douglas McPherson, *What's On*, 16 April 1997 (TR, 9–22 April, 1997, p. 446).
32 As yet there is no full-length biography of John McGahern, but see sites such as https://aran.library.nuigalway.ie/handle/10379/15 (accessed 27 July 2020) and studies such as Terence Brown, *The Literature of Ireland: Culture and Criticism*, Cambridge University Press, Cambridge, 2010; David Malcolm, *Understanding John McGahern*, University of South Carolina Press, Columbia, 2007.

idea that British English was not suited to Tolstoi's play, perhaps echoing the inappropriateness of the 'Kensington drawing room accents' referred to earlier. However, why should Irish English be considered more appropriate to Tolstoi's play? McGahern explained this opinion as a cultural concept with reference to similarities in moral climate, but I am not entirely sure this is what the BBC had in mind. Under BBC 'Irish' came both backwardness and, for the radio listener, less sensitivity to regional difference than might have been the case had Northern English or Somerset accents been used. And would not such a choice also have conveniently distanced a text designed to shock?

A further point is that some Irish writers have reclaimed texts imported into British English for their own culture, quite rightly feeling that imposing Britishness on a Russian text has little relevance to the Irish context. It was also a fertile means for scoring points against the imposition of British culture. An industry has sprung out of this particular point of view. It is pertinent to note that McGahern submitted a version of his play in 1988 to the Field Day Theatre Company founded by Brian Friel and Stephen Rea. This company was noted for its focus on the problems of Northern Ireland and desire to distance it from British culture. Friel's interest in the Russian classics was well known; and Thomas Kilroy, another writer keen to claim translated classics into an Irish idiom, was also on the Board. He supported the production of McGahern's *Power of Darkness*, despite or maybe even because the play's critique of Irish society was clear. However, the play, with its large cast at that time, was an uneconomic prospect for Field Day's touring programme. McGahern was advised by Kilroy to re-write. McGahern's adoption of this strategy led to further distancing from the Russian source.[33]

The first production was eventually part of the debut season of a new director, Garry Hynes, at the Abbey in Dublin in 1991. McGahern's *The Power of Darkness* was preceded by two other shows in the season. The new director staged a 'controversial reworking'[34] of Sean O'Casey's classic, *The Plough and the Stars*, to negative reviews. It was followed by an Irish disaster, a new play by Niall Williams, *The Murphy Initiative*, an embarrassing production of a 'script so naïve and unpolished' that the reviewer 'winced at the recollection'.[35] Then came McGahern's adaptation. The reputation that it was the novelist's first staged play (not entirely true, it seems, to judge from the Galway archive listings) 'evoked a certain excitement, tempered by the knowledge that not many novelists have also become successful playwrights'. This same critic,

---

[33] Murray, pp. 82–3.
[34] Gerry Colgan, 'A Tough Act to Follow', *The Irish Times*, 26 October, 1991, p. 33.
[35] Loc. cit.

Gerry Colgan of *The Irish Times*, went on: 'It was a debacle, a melodrama of crude simplicities that left one stunned and incredulous that lightning could strike again, and yet again'.[36] The reception context, in this case the none-too-happy debut of a new artistic director at the Abbey Theatre, intensified the disastrous response to McGahern's play. His *The Power of Darkness* was regarded as aggressively negative. The lack of acknowledgement of the Tolstoi source text made McGahern's criticisms directed at Ireland seem all the more pointed. Equally, the importance of directors and other agents of the production to the reception is clearly seen. Hynes' reputation for 'in your face theatre', on what was considered the Irish national theatre stage, hardly provided the grounds for a positive reception; and McGahern's play was seen as highly critical of Irish rural life. Had Tolstoi's framework, now almost completely denied (certainly in the marketing material) been still in place,[37] the reception might have been different.

There are marked similarities between the original controversial reception of Tolstoi's play in Russia, particularly the negative reaction from the censorship and the fact that it was initially banned from the stage, and the controversy which flared in Dublin. Tolstoi, I thought, had really bridged the cultures, but not in a way that I would have expected. Further investigation of the reception accorded this Irish production quickly began to provoke a number of questions.

The extremely negative review by *The Irish Times* critic ('debacle', 'lightning could strike again') spurred the Abbey into reproducing a positive one from the English newspapers, by Michael Coveney of *The Observer*.[38] The Abbey published the review in full in the *Irish Times* on its advertisement page for entertainment in Dublin. Coveney regarded this 'adaptation of Tolstoi's play' as a 'sock-in-the-face' and described it, as already quoted, as 'a terrifying picture', and praised the 'tremendous' production by Garry Hynes. The British critic had taken the play at face value as a condemnation of Catholic rural Ireland. Some Irish reviewers responded in kind, suggesting that the play in no way reflected Irish rural attitudes and should not have been staged in their national theatre.

This controversy sparked off a month's correspondence on *The Irish Times* letters page. Here, I thought, would be rich material for the reception of Tolstoi's play, and maybe statements about how important it was that the Russian

---

36 Loc. cit.
37 The current Abbey Theatre Website cites the play as 'After Tolstoy'. See https://www.abbeytheatre.ie/archives/production_detail/531/ (accessed 27 July 2020).
38 See note 13: Coveney, 'Mortality and a Sock in the Face', republished in *The Irish Times*, 22 October, 1991, p. 20.

classic writer had been claimed from the British for Ireland. I could not have been more wrong. Not once was Tolstoi's name or Russia mentioned.[39] In the view of these theatre goers the play was entirely about Ireland. Some saw it as a wrongful condemnation of their country; others thought it a penetrating picture. On the one hand, nowhere was there any recourse to the fact that it was an adaptation and so, in the last resort, might be regarded as strictly not generic to Ireland; on the other hand, the tricks and turns of the play were all ascribed to McGahern, though most of them derived in fact from the original Tolstoi. The comedy of the final act – whether a rope is a tether or a means of hanging oneself and so escaping – is pure Tolstoi, but was admiringly ascribed to the Irish author: for example, '[...] McGahern's introduction of a comical element in the final scene is quite masterful'.[40]

McGahern had so utterly 'Irishized' the play that its transition from Russian culture was complete. In many ways the result was a splendid one, in that there was no escape from the power and shocking nature of the piece; and the controversy matched that accompanying Tolstoi's original play, both in its subject matter on the one hand, and its ethic of Christian / Orthodox salvation on the other. McGahern's Paul admits his guilt and feels a need to confess within the Catholic tradition just as Nikita does within the Orthodox. But the result is that Tolstoi all but ceases to exist in the Irish context.

Copyright is a tricky element here too. Should Tolstoi's text not be allowed to assert its rights in cultural transition? Or indeed the rights of the original translator, Louise Maude? McGahern's estate can claim royalties for almost the next 60 years (from his death in 2006) on a text which he had borrowed not only from Tolstoi, but also from a translator or translators. In the end does it matter? What matters most of all here is an underlying process which may make a controversial principle: complete suppression of the source text is a means of increasing a play's impact on its receiving culture. Idealistically we might want that to happen so that the force of the Russian Tolstoi text might be felt, but can we condone it ideologically, or indeed, morally?

There is another point, and it is an ironic one: complete suppression of the Russianness in transition and adoption of new cultural tactics where necessary actually point up for those in the know the essential *differences* between the cultures, rather than the bridges and moments of communication between

---

39   Tolstoi was mentioned in the piece by John Waters above (note 12), but only to be rejected, as McGahern felt he had moved so far from the original play in his adaptation, though Waters acknowledged the play was rooted in Tolstoi and 'religious undercurrents were still potent elements'('Into the Dark' p. 29).
40   Letter from Jeananne Crowley, *The Irish Times*, 8 November, 1991, p. 13.

them. For example (a small one but indicative of many other things) the murder of the baby is given in blood-curdling detail in Tolstoi's version.[41] In McGahern's version the baby is already dead when handed over to be disposed of in a ditch by the hapless father.[42] Are we to conclude that Russians are by nature more violent, capable of greater evil than their Western counterparts? Equally, Nikita's complete capitulation in his public admission of guilt at the end of the Russian play, even to the point where he takes on his wife's and his mistress' guilt, is transformed in the Irish play into an *off-stage* confrontation between Paul and his family and the new family of his about-to-be-wed mistress. Are the Russians also able, at the other end of the scale, as it were, to repent to a degree of intensity unknown in Irish Catholicism?

So, in conclusion it might be as well to look, against expectation, for new aspects of the original culture in imported works, precipitated by their very difference from their adapted target-culture texts, rather than only judge translations / adaptations by the degree to which they have been acculturated in transference. In this way the true nature of Tolstoi's work as a bridge might be reached: bridges can, it seems still go both ways, even 100 years and more on, between cultures.

---

[41] See close of act four in Tolstoi's play. In a harrowing scene, the baby is seen alive briefly on stage, and then the sound of its bones being crushed under a board placed on it by Nikita in the cellar is described in detail by him and the women. His last-minute panic and certainty the baby is still crying suggest that the murder is finally completed by Matrena, Nikita's mother. In 1895, on the orders of the censors, Tolstoi supplied an alternative version of this scene. The description of the action is first channelled through the 10-year-old Aniutka, who is with Mitrich (the farm labourer and retired soldier) in the peasant hut, while Nikita, his wife and mother are in the cellar. This version allows, among other things, for a mitigating discussion of the fate of children after physical death (they go straight to God), and for Mitrich's story of a child who was saved from slaughter by soldiers, who subsequently looked after her. It also allows for Nikita's reactions to be more distanced from the actual murder, which is now firmly placed off-stage, and is thus potentially less disturbing. Mitrich, however, lets fly against women in his responses to Aniutka's troubling questions.

[42] See McGahern, act four, p. 42. Baby responds to Paul's question whether the baby is alive with a countering question of her own: 'How could it be alive the way it came into the world?', the implication being that Maggie has had a miscarriage. There is still room for ambiguity, but there are no references to the baby still crying. Moreover, the beginning of act five (p. 45) seems to confirm the baby was dead, given the comparison with calves found dead in the fields.

Bibliography

https://aran.library.nuigalway.ie/handle/10379/15 (accessed 27 July 2020).
https://www.abbeytheatre.ie/archives/production_detail/531/ (accessed 27 July 2020).
Anon., *The Times*, 29 April, 1949, p. 6.
Barker, Felix, 'Strange Fruits but Very Ripe', *The Evening News*, 15 March, 1979 (Royal National Theatre [RNT] Archive. Review materials are filed under production names).
Billington, Michael, *The Guardian*, 6 March, 1984 (*London Theatre Record*, [LTR], IV, 1984, p. 167).
Brown, Terence, *The Literature of Ireland: Culture and Criticism*, Cambridge University Press, Cambridge, 2010.
Cavendish, Dominic, *Time Out*, 16 April, 1997 (TR, 9–22 April, 1997, p. 446).
Colgan, Gerry, 'A Tough Act to Follow', *The Irish Times*, 26 October, 1991, p. 33.
Coveney, Michael, 'Mortality and a Sock in the Face', *The Observer*, 20 October, 1991, reprinted in *The Irish Times* on 22 October, 1991, p. 20.
Crowley, Jeananne, *The Irish Times*, 8 November, 1991, p. 13.
Gordon, Giles, *The Spectator*, 17 March, 1984 (LTR, IV, 1984, p. 162).
Gudzii, N., *'Vlast' t'my*, Istoriia pisaniia, pechataniia i postanovok na stsene *Vlasti t'my*' in *Tolstoi, L.N., Polnoe sobranie sochinenii*, XXVI, Chertkov, V.G., ed., Moscow, 1936, pp. 705–37.
Hoyle, Martin, *The Financial Times*, 5 March, 1984 (LTR, IV, 1984, p. 167).
Jones, W. Gareth, 'Tolstoy Staged in Paris, Berlin, and London' in *The Cambridge Companion to Tolstoy*, Tussing Orwin, ed., Donna, Cambridge University Press, Cambridge, 2002, pp. 142–57.
Malcolm, David, *Understanding John McGahern*, University of South Carolina Press, Columbia, 2007.
McGahern, John, *The Power of Darkness*, Faber and Faber, London and Boston, 1991.
McPherson, Douglas, *What's On*, 16 April 1997 (TR, 9–22 April,1997, p. 446).
Murray, Christopher, 'The "Fallen World" of *The Power of Darkness*' in *The John McGahern Yearbook*, Kenny, John, ed., NUI Galway, Galway, 2009, pp. 78–92.
Spencer, Charles, *The Daily Telegraph*, 14 April, 1997 (*Theatre Record* [TR] 9–22 April, 1997, p. 445).
Taylor, Paul, *The Independent*, 14 April,1997 (TR, 9–22 April, 1997, pp. 445).
'The John McGahern Papers', James Hardiman Library, National University of Ireland Galway (ref code: p. 71 [c. 1958–2006]).
Waters, John, 'Into the Dark', *The Irish Times*, 12 October, 1991, p. 29.

CHAPTER 11

Elizabeth Gaskell, Tolstoi and Dostoevskii

Katherine Jane Briggs

Abstract

This chapter reviews and compares the creative paths of two great European writers in the wake of, in Gaskell's case, the bicentenary of her birth in 1810 and, in Tolstoi's, the centenary of his death. Gaskell was first introduced to a Russian readership by the serialization of *Mary Barton* in *Vremia* in 1861; Dostoevskii used his preface to its publication to favourably compare Russia's treatment of the poor with England's. A strong sense of social justice is a feature common to both Tolstoi's and Gaskell's works, as is an interest in moral and religious questions. Trollope is also relevant to this discussion. Although overtly clerical themes are not as prominent in Russian literature as they are in English, Trollope's exploration of the conflict between Christian poverty, humility and service, on the one hand, and the craving for power, preferment and authority on the other is certainly applicable to Tolstoi's *Father Sergius*. The similarities between *Anna Karenina* and *North and South* are explored, particularly in the characterization of John Thornton and Levin; also discussed is the degree to which both writers portray themselves in their novels (Gaskell as Margaret Hale and Tolstoi as Levin).

Keywords

Tolstoi and Dostoevskii compared with Elizabeth Gaskell – social issues in literary works – clerical themes in literature

The centenary of the death of Tolstoi stimulated new interest in his life and work; and prompted us to consider the significance of his work for the twenty-first century, as well as his relationships with other writers. The same year, 2010, also marked the bicentenary of the birth of Elizabeth Gaskell, and a memorial to her was dedicated in Poets' Corner in Westminster Abbey, as a tribute to her work as a novelist and social reformer. In prospect, at least, the celebrations for Tolstoi might have been more problematic, especially in his own country, because of his troubled relationship with the Orthodox Church.[1]

Tolstoi's long life made him a contemporary of many distinguished writers. He was born at Iasnaia Poliana in 1828, and died at Astapovo railway station in 1910. Elizabeth Gaskell was born in 1810, and died in 1865, so they were contemporaries for 37 years. The links between these two novelists may be explored through reference to a number of works, which include those of Dostoevskii, Charles Dickens and Charlotte Brontë. Tolstoi read Gaskell's *Life of Charlotte Brontë*[2] on his 'Grand Tour' of Europe in 1857.

Tolstoi and Dostoevskii led rather colourful lives, while Gaskell's experiences were somewhat different.[3] However, all three writers sustained long marriages with supportive spouses; and, in their novels, all portray many different aspects of marriage, with particular reference to their impact on women in all classes of society. Christian theological concepts with regard to marriage and family life are also introduced, with particular reference to the care and nurture of children. There is evidence to show that Gaskell used many real-life examples in her novels, as did the two Russian writers; so, the relationship between life and art remains a subject for discussion.

In this chapter I will explore various connections, including letters and questions of translation, in the context of nineteenth-century English and European literatures. The novels of Tolstoi and Dostoevskii will be considered in relation to those of Elizabeth Gaskell; in turn, this will offer an interesting perspective on feminist theology and the role of women, in the light of both the Russian view and English evangelical literature of the time. These discussions will also be contextualized by reference to, *inter alia*, Austen, Charlotte Brontë and George Eliot.

For a long time, the works of Elizabeth Gaskell were considered outdated and irrelevant to contemporary society.[4] However, the huge popularity of tele-

---

1 For further information on this see the newspaper articles: Lisa Grainger, 'On the Trail of Tolstoy', *The Sunday Telegraph*, 7 March, 2010; Andrew Osborn, 'Russia abandons literary past, ignoring Tolstoy's centenary', *The Daily Telegraph*, 25 March, 2010.
2 Gaskell's *Life of Charlotte Brontë* was first published in 1857: the edition for Everyman Paperbacks was published in 1997, by J.M. Dent, London, with an introduction by Jenny Uglow (Series Editor for the Everyman Elizabeth Gaskell: Graham Handley).
3 K.J. Briggs, *How Dostoevsky Portrays Women in his Novels: A Feminist Analysis*, Edwin Mellen Press, Lewiston, New York, 2009. Links between Dostoevskii and Gaskell are explored in detail, pp. 16–17, 20–1, 110, 125, 265, 278–9, 283, 290 and 307.
4 I know from personal experience that British GCE Ordinary level students in the 1960s were required to study the works of Jane Austen and Anthony Trollope, but we never heard of Elizabeth Gaskell. However, my father read Tolstoy's *Anna Karenina* at a council secondary school in the 1920s.

vision costume drama series has given her work a welcome boost for modern audiences, and secured her many modern readers. Films, stage presentations, and television adaptations of the novels of Brontë, Dickens, Dostoevskii, and Tolstoi have stimulated interest in the works of these nineteenth-century writers, and prompted re-issue of their books in new translations, and in the paperback format which is available to everyone. In the nineteenth century itself, people bought and read the literary journals: today, they buy and read paperback novels. The links between Russian and English writers are both literary and international in their social and cultural influence; and also have significant religious and moral connotations for modern society, as observed by critics such as the former Archbishop of Canterbury in his recent work on Dostoevskii.[5]

It was, in fact, Dostoevskii who was responsible for introducing Gaskell to a Russian readership. The first issue of Dostoevskii's journal *Time* came out in April 1861, following the Emancipation of the Serfs in February of that year. He chose Elizabeth Gaskell's novel, *Mary Barton* (1848), for the serial, and wrote the Introduction himself – albeit to express his view that Russian society was superior to England in its care for the poorest people. He wrote:

> We publish this interesting novel because it vividly illustrates to us the way of life and the sufferings of the working class in England. Of all the European states, perhaps Russia alone can view this distress with brotherly sympathy – as this class hatred is, by the mercy of God, unknown to her. For us, the allotment of land to the peasant works for good everywhere today, and protects us from this terrible harm – which is known as pauperism or proletarianism (19 April 1861).[6]

With the benefit of hindsight, we might consider this a bit rich – but even a 'prophet'[7] like Dostoevskii cannot always foresee everything. It does, however, reflect a typically Slavophile position with respect to social solidarity, even if the Emancipation ultimately did not have the effect that he envisages. In *War and Peace*, Tolstoi describes the hostility of the peasants to Princess Maria, on their country estate, before she was rescued by Prince Nikolai. Dostoevskii also

---

5   See Rowan Williams, *Dostoevsky: Language, Faith and Fiction*, Continuum, London, 2008.
6   See F.M. Dostoevskii, *Polnoe sobranie sochinenii v tridsati tomakh*, Nauka, Leningrad, 1972–90, XIX, pp. 211–12 (my translation).
7   For discussion of this concept, see P.T. Kroeker and B.K. Ward, *Remembering the End: Dostoevsky as Prophet to Modernity*, SCM Press, London, 2002.

had to deal with the rumours that his father had been murdered by his own serfs on his estate.[8]

Like Tolstoi, Elizabeth Gaskell was a country child. However, following her marriage to William, she was plunged into the maelstrom of life in an industrial city. William Gaskell was a Unitarian minister who preached at Cross Street Chapel in Manchester. He ministered to the mill hands and cotton weavers – some of the poorest and most deprived people in England at the time. Elizabeth supported William in his ministry, visited his parishioners, and portrayed their lives in her novel, *Mary Barton*. Her depiction of their sufferings is continued in probably her greatest novel, *North and South* of 1855, which contrasts the lives of the rural and urban poor in nineteenth-century England. She used many of her personal experiences and real-life examples in these novels. Gaskell also found time to bring up her children and to continue her own literary career as journalist, novelist and prolific letter-writer. She also, eventually, earned enough money to buy a house of her own – a fact which ought to be of great encouragement to women writers, from Virginia Woolf onwards – not just a room, but a whole house of one's own!

Dostoevskii published *Mary Barton* in a specially commissioned translation by Elizaveta Grigorevna Beketova, maternal grandmother of the poet, Alexander Blok. Blok writes in his memoirs: 'I treasure that copy of the English novel which Dostoevsky gave to my grandmother personally to translate. This translation was published in *Time* in 1861'.[9] Blok adds that his grandmother was 'well-read and commanded several languages ... her translations are the best there are even now'.

Elizaveta Beketova lived from 1836–1902, so she and Elizabeth Gaskell were contemporaries for 29 years. Dostoevskii became acquainted with Andrei Nikolaevich Beketov (Blok's maternal grandfather) and his brothers while they were students together at the Academy of Engineers in St Petersburg, and through their involvement in a progressive literary society which came to be known as the 'Petrashevskii Circle'. The young Dostoevskii wrote to his brother, Mikhail, that 'they are people of sense, clever, with excellent hearts, nobility of character and determination'.[10]

---

8   For discussion of this, see Joseph Frank, *Dostoevsky: The Seeds of Revolt 1821–49*, Robson Books, London, 1979, pp. 81–91.
9   Quoted in C.A. Johnson, 'Russian Gaskelliana', in *A Review of English Literature*, VII, 3, July 1966, pp. 39–51 (44).
10 Quoted in Avril Pyman, *The Life of Aleksandr Blok: Vol 1, The Distant Thunder 1880–1908*, Oxford University Press, Oxford, 1979, p. 4.

Their father, Nikolai Beketov, managed to remove his sons from harm's way, before other members of the Petrashevskii Circle, including Dostoevskii, were arrested for alleged subversive activities against the state, condemned to death, and then reprieved by the Tsar, their sentences being commuted to exile and hard labour in Siberia. In Dostoevskii's case, this was followed by six years' service in a convict army regiment – and all for belonging to a literary society. The reason was that political discussion in those days was, as we know, largely proscribed, and that literary societies were suspected as offering a forum for intelligent people to discuss rather more than the latest novels.

Dostoevskii returned to mainstream Russian society in 1859, and in 1861 he started his literary journal, *Time*, and, as we noted earlier, chose Elizabeth Gaskell's novel for the serial. He needed a sympathetic translator, and it seems natural that, on his return to St Petersburg, he would have renewed his acquaintance with old friends. Andrei Beketov was by now a distinguished and enlightened Rector of St Petersburg University, who pioneered the cause of higher education for women. He married Elizaveta Grigorevna Karelina, who came from a family where all the daughters grew up 'fluent in German and French, and well-read in all the classics'.[11] Their father, Grigorii Karelin (like Nikolai Beketov) was a member of the old Russian intelligentsia in St Petersburg. Blok's recollections of his grandmother are as follows:

> She was extremely well-read and spoke several languages; her personal philosophy was astonishingly lively and original, her style vivid, her use of language – precise and bold. I remember her voice, her embroidery frame on which flowers blossomed with astonishing speed, bright patchwork quilts sewn of carefully hoarded scraps that were of no use to anyone – and, over all this, a kind of irretrievable health and merriment.[12]

She certainly sounds like a lovely person – and, more importantly for our present purposes – a sympathetic translator for the works of Elizabeth Gaskell. Elizaveta's favourite contemporary author was Anton Chekhov – and she treasured a letter of thanks from him following the appearance of her translations of two of his stories into French. Between them, she and her husband had some personal acquaintance with almost all the distinguished Russian writers of their day.[13]

---

11   Ibid., p. 6.
12   Quoted ibid., p. 7.
13   See ibid., pp. 4–10.

So, how did she feel about Dostoevskii? Contemporary accounts suggest that she did not like him. Her husband disapproved of Dostoevskii's politics post-exile, but could not bring himself to condemn the great novelist as a man or as an artist. However, Elizaveta viewed him as an 'odious figure' and his work as 'obscurantist' – and we have to consider that Dostoevskii's inferior social status and chequered political career might have had something to do with it. If you reside in the upper échelons of St Petersburg social and intellectual society, how do you receive a marginally disreputable character like Dostoevskii – who has just been released from prison, and is trying to scratch a living as a literary journalist? However, something happened to change her mind, and numerous questions arise. What was it that prompted Elizaveta to take on the job of making a Russian translation of an English novel to be serialized in the first issue of Dostoevskii's new journal – in 1860 when she was occupied with preparing for the birth of her third child – and why did she preserve the copy of the novel he gave to her, and pass it on to her grandson? As we mentioned earlier, Blok himself treasured this heirloom. Was this 'English novel' a copy in English (in which case, how did he come by it) or was it a French translation? It would be nice to think that the Russian lady in St Petersburg felt some connection to the English lady in Cheshire, and thought it worthwhile to translate her novels.

We now move on to consider Gaskell's links with Tolstoi. According to Simmons,[14] on his 'Grand Tour' of Europe in 1857,[15] Tolstoi read such works as 'related to the questioning in his mind'. As well as the four Gospels, these included Gaskell's newly published *Life of Charlotte Brontë* – although, as ever, he had little time for fiction or poetry. This is the only specific and definite link between Tolstoi and Gaskell that I have been able to unearth; and this work is also the subject of Gaskell's correspondence with a 'Russian girl'. In 1858, in a letter to Charles Eliot Norton, Gaskell wrote: 'Speaking of letters from distant places, I am receiving *such* nice letters in *English* – from a Russian girl with an unpronounceable name – living many leagues South East of Odessa. She wrote to me about Miss Brontë's life'.[16]

These letters have not survived, so we have no way of establishing the identity of this 'Russian girl'. However, the Tauchnitz editions of English authors

---

14   Ernest J. Simmons, *Leo Tolstoy*, John Lehmann, London, 1946, p. 182.
15   If Tolstoy was 29, this would have been the summer of 1857.
16   See Johnson, p. 40, letter from Gaskell to Charles Eliot Norton, 25 July 1858. Johnson adds that 'the Tauchnitz editions of English authors were widespread in Europe' and there is 'no reason to suppose that they were not also well known in Russia' at this time. Tauchnitz published all Elizabeth Gaskell's major novels, beginning with *Mary Barton* in 1841.

were widespread in Europe at the time, and there is no reason to suppose that they were not also known in Russia. Tauchnitz published all Gaskell's major novels, beginning with *Mary Barton* in 1849. English literature usually came to Russia through French translations, but, as we have seen, Blok says that Dostoevskii gave his grandmother 'the English novel' to translate. It is thought that Dostoevskii was unlikely to have known English well enough to have read the novel in the original – it seems more likely that he would have read the French translation.[17]

Simmons also records that Tolstoi (as did Dostoevskii, of course, having had his first works in the 1840s published there) read *The Contemporary*, which published serial versions of many novels, including in translation. Moreover, *The Daily Telegraph* had a correspondent in St Petersburg at the time. So, there are numerous ways in which Russian writers could have become acquainted with the works of the English novelists. Tolstoi could read English well enough; and in London, he attended a lecture on education given by Charles Dickens (though he was less proficient in spoken English). Dickens' links with Gaskell and other writers are many and various. Gaskell's notes about her life in an English country town were first published in Dickens' journal, *Household Words*.[18] Tolstoi describes Dickens as having 'a great influence' on his work;[19] and Dostoevskii says the same: he refers to Dickens as 'that great Christian' who portrays 'humble people – the just but pliant, the eccentric and the downtrodden' in all his novels.[20] In their different ways, both Tolstoi and Dostoevskii broke new ground in their depiction of the lives of poor people, and also in their portrayal of the lives of women in different classes of society. Both men sustained long marriages with devoted wives who acted as copyists and critics – and what we owe to their insights may never be known. However, both women left detailed diaries about their lives; and there is also much to be learned from their letters.[21]

---

17   See Michael H. Futrell: 'Dostoevskii and Dickens', pp. 83–121 in W.J. Leatherbarrow, ed., *Dostoevskii and Britain*, Berg, Oxford, Providence, RI, 1995, especially p. 89.
18   Elizabeth Gaskell met Dickens and was invited to contribute to his journal, *Household Words*, in 1850: 'From this year on, Dickens became the chief publisher of Gaskell's shorter works'. See Jenny Uglow, *Elizabeth Gaskell: A Habit of Stories*, Faber and Faber, London, 1993, p. 254.
19   For discussions of this, see: R.F. Christian, *Tolstoy: A Critical Introduction*, Cambridge University Press, Cambridge, 1969, pp. 28–9, 160 and 250.
20   See Fyodor Dostoevsky, *A Writer's Diary*, I, Kenneth Lanz, trans., Northwestern University Press, Evanston, Illinois, 1994, p. 514.
21   See various chapters on women's reading and writing, in Wendy Rosslyn, ed., *Women and Gender in Eighteenth-Century Russia*, Ashgate, Aldershot, 2003, especially the chapter by

In many ways, Gaskell was Tolstoi's equal in the range and depth of character, at this stage in his career. One thing she could not do, of course, was to portray army life and the experience of warfare as he could, because this lay outside her experience. Tolstoi, having been a soldier, could do this very well. In turn, Dostoevskii's novels are mainly centred on life in the city; but the characters of both Gaskell and Tolstoi move between the country and the city with ease. In Gaskell's best-known novels, *Mary Barton, Cranford, Wives and Daughters* and *North and South*, she portrays the lives of people in all classes of English society – from the gentry on a country estate, to the poorest workers in Manchester, taking in Squire Hamley and Molly Gibson, and the ladies of 'Cranford' (Knutsford), on the way. One of her most sympathetic heroines, Margaret Hale in *North and South*, experiences the whole range – from her childhood as the daughter of a country Rector, through London society in the home of her wealthy aunt, to an impoverished life, with her dying mother, in the industrial city of Manchester – and her character undergoes significant development, emotional, intellectual and spiritual.

It is thought[22] that Tolstoi could have read the translation of *Mary Barton* in *Time*, in 1861, which may have stimulated his interest in her novels, as well as her biographical works. Gaskell's *North and South* was published in 1855 (serialized in Dickens' journal, *Household Words*) – and Tolstoi's *Anna Karenina* appeared 20 years later (1873–7). Numerous points of correspondence emerge. Gaskell's John Thornton and Tolstoi's Levin are both men of integrity and substance, but lonely and of a melancholic disposition. Both work hard, but experience difficulties with their workforce, who do not share or even understand their aspirations. Both fall in love with beautiful young women; but their initial proposals of marriage are rejected. Both Margaret and Kitty refuse these first proposals, but accept them later on. In the interim, these women experience great personal loss; and learn to mix with people from different backgrounds and to offer help to those less fortunate than themselves. Through this kind of suffering and significant character development, they learn to appreciate the sterling qualities of the men who love them, their kindness, patience and integrity. At the same time, the men come to appreciate the qualities of their future wives. They are not just 'girls with pretty faces', but strong, intelligent and sympathetic women, from whom their husbands

---

Olga Glagoleva, 'Imaginary World: Reading in the Lives of Russian Provincial Noblewomen, 1720–1825', pp 129–46.

[22] This is based on the consensus of opinion among delegates at the Neo-Formalist Conference, Mansfield College, Oxford, 13–15 September, 2010: Professor Deborah Martinsen said, 'Tolstoy read *everything* – if it was there, he would have read it!'

have much to learn. Their creators offer these two couples a real chance of happiness and success in their lives together.

Rosemary Edmonds suggests that 'Tolstoy produced no novel which did not contain a portrait of himself'.[23] Robin Milner-Gulland modifies this assertion, saying that Tolstoi took aspects of his own character and pushed them to the limit in his fictional heroes.[24] However, it is easy for the reader to see Tolstoi's identification with the character of Levin, a country landowner, struggling against life-long depression, and harbouring suicidal thoughts. He married a younger woman, but found that marriage and the birth of children did not necessarily solve all his problems.

Gaskell too may have identified with her character, Margaret Hale, who enjoyed an idyllic childhood in the country. Like her heroine, she suffered great personal loss and saw her journey north to a great industrial city as symbolic of the transition from childhood to maturity. She viewed the opportunity for marriage as a source of happiness and fulfilment. But, for Gaskell, it was also the source of great suffering, through the loss of her infant children – with which Dostoevskii and his wife, Anna, would have been able to sympathize. These 'correspondences' reinforce an age-old question: should we focus exclusively on the 'stand-alone' qualities of the novels – or also take into account the life experiences of the writers? This partly depends on how the novelists themselves relate to such experiences: Josie Billington, in her comparative study of Gaskell and Tolstoi, regards Gaskell as 'inhabit[ing] an impersonal view which goes beyond the scope of any first person' [...] whereas 'Tolstoy starts from his incapacity [...] ever to get outside a single first-person view'.[25]

A common theme that emerges from the works of both Tolstoi and Dostoevskii at this time concerns the female suicide. Flaubert's *Madame Bovary* (1857), which was well known to them as well as Turgenev, is written from the point of view of a woman trapped in a disappointing marriage, who entertains various lovers, and overspends her income on pretty clothes and furnishings for her home. She eventually commits suicide, because she can see no other way out of the personal problems and debts in which she has become enmeshed. Dostoevskii's Matresha in *The Devils* (1872) is an example

---

23   See Rosemary Edmonds, trans. and ed., Introduction to *Childhood, Boyhood, Youth*. Penguin Books, London, 1964, p. 7.
24   Comment made at the Neo-Formalist Conference, Mansfield College, Oxford, 13–15 September, 2010, during the Collective Analysis on 'Tolstoy and Music'.
25   Josie Billington, *Faithful Realism. Elizabeth Gaskell and Leo Tolstoy: A Comparative Study*, Bucknell University Press, Lewisburg and Associated University Presses, London, 2002, p. 117.

of a girl, abused by an older man, who believes she has committed a mortal sin by entering into a sexual relationship with him. She receives no support from her parents, and perceives suicide as her only means of escape. *Anna Karenina* appeared in serial form from 1873–7; and the final chapters, where Anna commits suicide, would have been published around the time when Dostoevskii's mind was exercised by the news reports of a young seamstress who killed herself because she was unable to find work, in order to support herself in a respectable manner. He discusses this in *Diary of a Writer*, October 1876; and presents his fictional story, *The Meek One*, in the same publication the following month, November 1876.

None of Gaskell's female characters actually commits suicide, although some of them come pretty close. They die in childbirth, from poverty and starvation, from infectious diseases, or from industrial diseases such as those caused by inhaling cotton fibres in the mills. In 1855, Gaskell wrote her novel *North and South*, depicting the conflict between the masters and mill hands in Manchester; and raises questions about whether the ideal of union solidarity makes things better or worse for its poorest members. Is it preferable for your family to starve at the behest of the masters or the union bosses – and what will the consequences be if you break ranks? There are close links between Gaskell and Dostoevskii in depicting the lives of the poorest seamstresses and governesses in their novels; and in their examination of why it was so difficult for poorly educated women to earn an honest living.

Although there is no doubt that contemporary social issues are prominent in the works of both Gaskell and Tolstoi, it is in Tolstoi's work that we find the more graphic, even melodramatic consequences of it: suicide, uxoricide and infanticide. One may debate whether this contrast reflects a difference in Russian and English cultural norms or whether, particularly in the case of Tolstoi, it is a matter of individual creative choice. It can be argued that, whereas Gaskell reaches some accommodation with the social issues she describes,[26] Tolstoi cannot rest until his plot has pushed matters to their shockingly tragic conclusion. In *Anna Karenina*, however, the architecture of the novel allows us to see, in Levin's plot, a counterbalance to the tragedy of Anna. 'The contrast between Anna and Levin is left [...] to speak for itself [...] Tolstoy is here applying Gaskell's own acceptance and tolerance to the sheer fact of good and bad, right and wrong thus (separatedly) existing side by side'.[27]

Following the publication of *Mary Barton* in 1848, Gaskell visited London, met Charles Dickens, and began to write for his journal, *Household Words*

---

26 On this see Billington, passim.
27 Billington, p. 139.

(1850). These articles were later published in the form of her novel, *Cranford*, which depicts ladies in impoverished circumstances trying to keep up appearances. However, their genteel poverty is nothing in comparison with the families who suffer complete destitution; and the responsibilities of bank shareholders are touchingly described in relation to Miss Matty, who never thought she would have to face such a moral dilemma.

In her novel *Ruth* (1853) Gaskell boldly deals with the controversial subject of the unmarried mother, and the hypocrisy and lack of compassion in a nominally Christian society. Mr Bradshaw employs Ruth as governess to his daughters, and while he believes she is a widow, he is happy to do so. However, when he learns that she is a 'fallen woman', he casts her out – despite the commendation from his minister of religion, and despite the protestations of his girls who love her. Elizabeth Gaskell knew whereof she wrote. As the wife of a Unitarian minister in Manchester, and an untiring worker in support of his Christian ministry to the poorest and most destitute people, she used real-life examples in her novels – as did Dostoevskii, especially in *The Meek One*.

Literary critiques of the lives of women by male authors like Dostoevskii and Tolstoi appeared to have excited little controversy among their readers at the time. However, the same could not be said of the reaction to Gaskell's *Ruth*. Her letters offer a moving testimony to her suffering at the hands of her husband's Christian congregation. She says: 'I am in a quiver of pain about it ... crying all night at the unkind things people are saying'.[28]

What appeared to excite this criticism was her portrayal of the Christian minister, Mr Benson, and his sister (aptly named Faith) promoting the illusion that Ruth was a widow, rather than a 'fallen woman'. Their maidservant, Sally, guesses the true state of affairs immediately; but despite her initial disapproval, she colludes with her employers out of love and loyalty, and also out of her sympathy for Ruth, a poor seamstress who has been cruelly deceived by a 'gentleman'. This raises questions as to whether Mr Benson's version of the truth is actually more Christian, more moral, and more compassionate than the facts; and also as to whether male writers like Dickens, Dostoevskii or Tolstoi would have been subjected to the kind of censure which Elizabeth Gaskell endured.[29] (Indeed, it would seem that there was a double standard for women writers as well as for women in terms of their sexual behaviour.)

---

28   J.A.V. Chapple and A. Pollard, eds, *The Letters of Mrs Gaskell*, Manchester University Press, Manchester, 1966, letter No. 148, p. 221. See also Uglow, 1993, p. 338.

29   The attack on Gaskell is local and personal, in response to one particular novel, in which her husband's congregation may have perceived criticism of their own way of life – the charge of hypocrisy. Tolstoi, in contrast, was involved at the national and political level. His criticisms of the Orthodox Church led to excommunication – the most serious rejec-

This was a subject for correspondence between Gaskell and George Eliot (Marian Evans) at the time. It is also worth noting, in this context, that Eliot's partner, George Henry Lewes, wrote to Elizabeth Gaskell to congratulate her on her *Life of Charlotte Brontë*: 'The early part is a triumph for you; the rest a monument to your friend'.[30] Although Gaskell's Ruth does not actually commit suicide, her fearless nursing of the sick may be viewed as an invitation to death from one of the most dreaded infectious diseases of the time; and she may have been driven to this by the cruelty and lack of charity in her church congregation. This pursuit of a self-destructive way of life may be compared to that of Nastasia Filippovna in Dostoevsky's *Idiot* – both women had suffered from deception and abuse by men when they were very young, and this damage cannot be rectified by the kindness and support of others when they are older. *Ruth*, was serialized by Dickens in *Household Words*; and Dostoevskii began to publish the translation in *Time* – as a follow-up to *Mary Barton* – but his journal folded after the first instalment. In the same year, the Reverend Patrick Brontë asked Elizabeth Gaskell to write his daughter, Charlotte's, biography, which appeared in 1857 – so Tolstoi read it in England when it was newly published.

Despite the presence of a religious theme in *Ruth* there is an 'absence in Gaskell's work of such spiritual questions as are strenuously and explicitly urged in Tolstoy's writings'.[31] Although Tolstoi's religious sensibility was in many ways unique, it may also be attributable to the considerable differences in the nature of religious belief in England and Russia.[32]

The works of Anthony Trollope might offer evidence of this. Many of his novels contribute to what George Eliot called 'Scenes from Clerical Life'. He wrote about the influence of the Church in England – both the lust for power

---

tion of a Christian soul from his church, following what Jesus called 'blasphemy against the Holy Spirit' (cited in all three Synoptic Gospels). Gaskell's critique is directed at what Jesus called the 'hard-heartedness' of men towards women (in Matthew and Mark; and in John 8).

[30] George Henry Lewes to Elizabeth Gaskell, 15 April 1857. See Gordon S. Haight, ed., *The George Eliot Letters*, 9 volumes, Yale University Press, London, New Haven, 1954, II, pp. 315–16. Gaskell records that, towards the end of her life, Charlotte married one of her father's curates, the Reverend Arthur Nicholls, on 29 June 1854. She died on 31 March 1855, from an illness almost certainly associated with pregnancy; and on her deathbed, she whispered: 'I am not going to die, am I? God would not separate us, we have been so happy!' See Gaskell's *Life*, p. 434. It is comforting to know that Charlotte did eventually experience some happiness in marriage, albeit for such a tragically short time.

[31] Billington, p. 131.

[32] On this see loc. cit.

and preferment among senior clerics; and the problems facing the poor clergymen in caring for their families and their parishioners.[33] In many Russian novels, Orthodox priests are either wholly absent or do not seem to be involved in the lives of ordinary people in the same way as English parish priests – in the education of poor children; or in the fabric of country society which was held together by the priest, the squire, the doctor, and the schoolteacher, as the best educated members of the community. This was in part due to the poor education of many of the Russian rural clergy, who had little in common with the Russian landowning class, many of whom entertained sceptical Western attitudes towards religious belief and practice. In this context, however, Tolstoi's *Father Sergius* is instructive. Its aristocratic hero leaves his privileged life to become a monk, thus attempting to cross the divide between his class and the clergy. Although set in the austere surroundings of a Russian monastery, the story does show us that personal ambition thrives here as well as in the Anglican close.

The coming of the railways changed English country life irrevocably; and the inevitability of change is portrayed in various ways by both Gaskell and Tolstoi in their novels. For Tolstoi railways often provide ominous settings, as in *Anna Karenina* and *The Kreutzer Sonata*, and his death at Astapovo railway station may seem to partake of the same trope. In 2010 a newspaper article, entitled 'Notes from Underground', describes travellers' reactions to a new metro station in Moscow named after Dostoevskii. It was feared that the murals on the 'gloomy' Dostoevskii station might 'push travellers to suicide'. However, the artist, Ivan Nikolaev, said: 'What do you want? Scenes of dancing? Dostoevsky does not have them'. Nikolaev also denied that the scenes were gloomy: 'I think that people who say so do not fully understand the tragedy in Fyodor Dostoevsky's novels'.[34]

This is true. Readers who understand the tragedy in *Hamlet* and *Macbeth* do not criticize Shakespeare for being 'gloomy'. The Christian message in Dostoevskii's novels offers hope for the future through reconciliation and redemption. Tolstoi's novels offer many 'scenes of dancing' but he died away from home at a railway station, his wife prevented from seeing him until he had slipped into unconsciousness. Dostoevskii, by contrast, died in his own bed,

---

[33] In England, the role of the clergy wives and daughters was significant, both in the founding of schools for village children, and through their offerings of food for the sick and destitute, and their care for women in childbirth through the provision of linen and clothing, as we see in Charlotte Brontë's *Jane Eyre*, for example.

[34] See Andrew Osborn, *The Daily Telegraph*, 22 June 2010, 'Notes from Underground: Gloomy Dostoevsky station may push travellers to suicide', p. 14.

with his wife reading his chosen passages from the Gospel. A memorial window to Elizabeth Gaskell was dedicated in Poets' Corner in Westminster Abbey on 25 September 2010, to celebrate the bicentenary of her birth, and to confirm her place in English literary memory as a novelist and social reformer. This is *the* accolade for any English writer, and she takes her place beside such luminaries as Fanny Burney and George Eliot, as well as poets like Tennyson and Keats. The celebrations were further continued in her home town of Knutsford, Cheshire, with a lecture in Brook Street Chapel, and the ringing of a special peal on the church bells to mark her birthday on 29 September 1810.

As regards Tolstoi, the more muted response to the centenary of his death seems to illustrate the words of Jesus: 'a prophet is not without honour – except in his own country'. (Mark 6). Near the end of his life, Tolstoi became a 'spiritual anarchist', a stance that resulted in his formal excommunication by the Orthodox Church in 1901. According to Tolstoi's great-grandson: 'The subject of the Church is complicated. The authorities are feeling the attitude of the Church to Tolstoy, so although they (the State) support our family celebrations, they cannot take part'. Given the current power of the Orthodox Church – described by some Russians as 'not unlike that of the Communist Party 30 years ago' – being seen as actively pro-Tolstoi today might be seen as being not only anti-Government, but anti-Russian.[35]

With regard to the character traits of Tolstoi and Gaskell, questions may be raised, once again, about the relationship between life and art – do readers expect their great writers to be consistent and to set an example? There is a marked contrast between the personality of Lev Tolstoi, considering the unpleasant characters he chose as his mentors and friends, and the way he treated his long-suffering wife,[36] and the exemplary life of Elizabeth Gaskell as a wife and mother, and Christian social reformer who engaged with the poorest people in her husband's parish. In her personal life, and in the love and allegiance she received, first from her husband and family, and later from her readers, Gaskell would seem to have more in common with Dostoevskii than with Tolstoi.[37]

---

35 See Grainger, loc. cit.
36 See A.D.P. Briggs, *Brief Lives: Leo Tolstoy*, Hesperus Press, London, 2010, pp. 57–8, 101–2, and 103–4.
37 On the other hand, it is interesting to consider how far this affinity to Dostoevskii accords with Isaiah Berlin's celebrated 'hedgehog / fox' dichotomy, whereby Dostoevskii belongs among the hedgehogs whose creativity revolves around one unifying idea, as opposed to the foxes whose inspirations are diverse. Tolstoi, Berlin argues, is a fox who tries to

In an article on the modern concept of 'social mobility', Simon Parke[38] suggests that the latter should include not only economic, but also emotional mobility. By the age of 50, Tolstoi was 'very rich, very famous, and very depressed, with thoughts of suicide'. What he lacked was 'emotional mobility, which is concerned with internal circumstances'; and which takes us from 'the anger, anxiety and fear of undigested childhood' to 'the freedom, spontaneity and courage of aware adulthood'.[39]

It is significant that Tolstoi's conflicts with the Orthodox Church led to excommunication in his own life-time; that his work was promoted during the years of the Communist suppression of the Church;[40] and that now the Church is experiencing a resurgence, Tolstoi is once more in the doldrums. To say that being pro-Tolstoi would be anti-Russian is like saying that to be pro-Shakespeare or pro-Gaskell would be anti-English. The celebrations for the bicentenary of the birth of Elizabeth Gaskell indicate that she has come home, and established her place in the English literary consciousness. The place of Tolstoi in the Russian psyche, which was thought to be firmly and irrevocably established, appears open to question at home, if not abroad, where readers still retain a passion for his works.

Bibliography

Billington, Josie, *Faithful Realism. Elizabeth Gaskell and Leo Tolstoy: A Comparative Study*, Bucknell University Press, Lewisburg and Associated University Presses, 2002.

Briggs, A.D.P., *Brief Lives: Leo Tolstoy*, Hesperus Press, London, 2010.

Briggs, K.J., *How Dostoevsky Portrays Women in his Novels: A Feminist Analysis*, Edwin Mellen Press, Lewiston, New York, 2009.

Chapple, J.A.V. and Pollard, A., eds, *The Letters of Mrs Gaskell*, Manchester University Press, Manchester, 1966.

Christian, R.F., *Tolstoy: A Critical Introduction*, Cambridge University Press, Cambridge, 1969.

---

be a hedgehog. See Isaiah Berlin, *The Hedgehog and the Fox*, Weidenfeld and Nicolson, London, 1979 (first published 1953).

38   Simon Parke, 'The Ups and Downs of Life' in *Church Times*, 29 October 2010, p. 14.
39   Loc.cit.
40   See Jonathan Luxmore, 'Atheism Was Vital to Communists', *Church Times*, 22 October 2010, p. 16. Tolstoi's excommunication from the Russian Orthodox Church led to his theological view of Christianity being claimed as 'atheism' by the Communist regime.

Dostoevskii, F.M., *Polnoe sobranie sochinenii v tridsati tomakh*, ed. Bazanov, V.G. et al., Nauka, Leningrad, 1972–90.

Dostoevsky, Fyodor, *A Writer's Diary*, I, Lanz, Kenneth, trans., Northwestern University Press, Evanston, Illinois, 1994.

Frank, Joseph, *Dostoevsky: The Seeds of Revolt 1821–49*, Robson Books, London, 1979.

Futrell, Michael H., 'Dostoevskii and Dickens', in Leatherbarrow, W.J., ed., *Dostoevskii and Britain*, Berg, Oxford, Providence, RI, 1995, pp. 83–121.

Gaskell, Elizabeth, *The Life of Charlotte Brontë*, J.M. Dent, London, 1997 (first published 1857).

Grainger, Lisa, 'On the Trail of Tolstoy', *The Sunday Telegraph*, 7 March 2010.

Haight, Gordon S., ed., *The George Eliot Letters, 9 volumes*, Yale University Press, London, New Haven, 1954.

Johnson, C.A., 'Russian Gaskelliana', in *A Review of English Literature*, VII, 3, July 1966, pp. 39–51.

Kroeker, P.T., and Ward, B.K., *Remembering the End: Dostoevsky as Prophet to Modernity*, SCM Press, London, 2002.

Luxmore, Jonathan, 'Atheism Was Vital to Communists', *Church Times*, 22 October 2010, p. 16.

Osborn, Andrew, 'Russia abandons literary past, ignoring Tolstoy's centenary', *The Daily Telegraph*, 25 March 2010.

Osborn, Andrew, *The Daily Telegraph*, 22 June 2010, 'Notes from Underground: Gloomy Dostoevsky station may push travellers to suicide', p. 14.

Parke, Simon 'The Ups and Downs of Life' in *Church Times*, 29 October 2010, p. 14.

Pyman, Avril, *The Life of Aleksandr Blok, I, The Distant Thunder 1880–1908*, Oxford University Press, Oxford, 1979.

Rosslyn, Wendy, ed., *Women and Gender in Eighteenth-Century Russia*, Ashgate, Aldershot, 2003.

Simmons, Ernest J., *Leo Tolstoy*, John Lehmann, London, 1946.

Tolstoy, Leo, *Childhood, Boyhood, Youth*, Edmonds, Rosemary, trans., Penguin Books, London, 1964.

Uglow, Jenny, *Elizabeth Gaskell: A Habit of Stories*, Faber and Faber, London, 1993.

Williams, Rowan, *Dostoevsky: Language, Faith and Fiction*, Continuum, London, 2008.

Index

Alexander I 8, 182, 194, 196, 201
Amvrosii, *Starets* 93, 94
Aredakov, Grigorii 180
Arnold, Matthew 11–13
Austen, Jane 221, 221*n*

Bakhtin, Mikhail 102, 183
Belyi, Andrei 154
    Petersburg 154
Berlin, Isaiah 15
    Hedgehog and the Fox, The 15*n*, 233*n*
Bitov, Andrei 194
    Pushkin House 194, 201–2
Blok, Aleksandr 88, 185, 223–6 *passim*
Bloomsbury Group, The 12
Bonaparte, Napoleon 8, 79, 84, 89, 181, 182, 188, 194, 196, 201, 202
Bondarchuk, Sergei 202
    War and Peace (film) 202
Brecht, Bertolt 37, 179
Briggs, Anthony 38, 43, 44, 45, 47, 49, 53, 58, 63, 65, 66
Bromfield, Andrew 38, 40, 43, 44, 47, 58, 63, 66
Brontë, Charlotte 83, 221, 222, 225, 231, 231*n*, 232*n*
    Jane Eyre 83
Bulgakov, Mikhail 154
    Days of the Turbins, The 154, 159

Chekhov, Anton 13, 37, 148, 151, 224
    Cherry Orchard, The 195
    Lady with the Little Dog, The 121*n*, 122*n*
    Three Sisters 153, 158*n*
Chekhov, Mikhail 179
Chernyshevskii, Nikolai 69–70
    What Is to Be Done? 137
Chesterton, G.K. 2, 13
Covid-19 23

Dickens, Charles 222, 226, 226*n*, 227, 229, 230, 231
    Household Words 221, 231
Dobroliubov, Nikolai 69–70

Dole, Nathan Haskell 38, 43, 45, 47, 49, 53, 59, 62, 64, 66
Dostoevskii, Fedor 84, 94, 102, 107, 112, 143, 185, 222
    Elizabeth Gaskell and 220–34
    Brothers Karamazov, The 94, 98, 102, 108, 137, 153, 154–5
    Crime and Punishment 8, 79
    Devils, The 153, 228
    Diary of a Writer 229
    Idiot, The 231
    Meek One, The 229, 230
    Notes from Underground 84
    Compared to Tolstoi 15–16, 21, 79, 92–110
    Stage adaptations of novels 153, 155, 185
    Village of Stepanchikovo, The 153*n*
    Zosima 92–109 *passim*, 143
Dukhobors 98, 175
Dunnigan, Ann 35, 36, 38, 43, 47, 49, 53, 58, 62, 65, 66

Edmonds, Rosemary 36, 38, 43, 45, 47, 49, 53, 58, 61, 62, 65, 66, 228
Eliot, George 83, 86, 221, 231, 233
    Scenes of Clerical Life 83

Flaubert, Gustave 228
    Madame Bovary 113, 113*n*, 125*n*, 228
Fokin, Valerii 180, 180*n*, 183
Fomenko, Petr 180–204
    Aesthetics 197
    Early productions 184
    Expulsion from MKhAT 183–4
    Impressionism 199
    Optimism 204
    Training of actors 185
    Use of collage 198

Gardin, Vladimir 151
Garnett, Constance 36, 38, 43, 45, 47, 49, 53, 58, 61, 62, 64, 66
Gaskell, Elizabeth 220–34
    Cranford 227, 230
    Compared to Tolstoi 220–34

Gaskell, Elizabeth (*cont.*)
  Life of Charlotte Brontë, The 221, 221*n*, 225, 231
  Mary Barton 222, 225*n*, 226, 227, 229, 231
  North and South 223, 227, 229
  Ruth 230
  Wives and Daughters 227
Ge, Nikolai 164, 165
  What Is Truth? 164, 166
Genette, Gérard 85
George, Henry 159
Gogol, Nikolai 4*n*, 36, 93, 95*n*, 122*n*
  Diary of a Madman 122*n*
Goncharov, Ivan 4*n*, 136
  Oblomov 4*n*, 136
Gorkii, Maksim 19, 156, 165
  Enemies 157*n*
Grossman, Edith 36, 37

Heidegger, Martin 16
Herzen, Alexandr 100
Historical author 83–9

Illin, Nicholas 162–76
  Attitude to Tolstoi 164, 168
  Diary of a Tolstoian, The 164–5
  In the New Land 163
  Portrayal by Paustovskii 171–2
  Relations with Zuzenko 172–4
Implied author 86, 86*n*, 87, 88, 89
Ivanov, Vsevolod 152
Ivanovskii, Aleksandr 151

James, Henry 85
James, William 14

Kennan, George 159
Khotinenko, Vladimir 181
  Death of the Empire 181
Kireevskii, Ivan 93
Kollontai, Aleksandra 157–8
  Love of Worker Bees 158
Kropotkin, Princess Alexandra 36, 37, 38, 40, 43, 45, 49, 63

Lawrence, D.H. 13–14
Lenin, Vladimir 19, 41, 65, 71*n*, 156
Leonid, *Starets* 93

Lermontov, Mikhail 10, 114, 123
  Hero of Our Time, A 10, 22, 114
  *Pechorin's Journa*l 4
  Princess Mary 26, 114, 124
Leskov, Nikolai 100
Li, Yiyun 23–4
Liubimov, Iurii 180, 180*n*, 187

Maiakovskii, Vladimir 184
  Mystery Bouffe 184
Makarii, *Starets* 93
Markov, P.A. 152*n*, 153*n*, 154
Maude, Aylmer and Louise 38, 43, 47, 49, 53, 58, 62, 63, 64, 65, 66
Maude, Aylmer 16*n*, 20
Maude, Louise 209, 217
McGahern, John 208–18
  Amongst Women 214
  Power of Darkness, The 208–18
  Reception of *The Power of Darkness* 216–17
  Relation of *The Power of Darkness* to source text 216–18
  Stage history of *The Power of Darkness* 211–12
  That They May Face the Rising Sun 214
  Use of Irish speech 209, 214–15
Meierkhold, Vsevolod 179, 186
Melville, Herman 86–7
  White Jacket 86
Mikhalkov, Nikita 181
Mikulich, V. *See* Veselitskaia, Lidiia
Moscow Art Theatre (MKhAT) 149, 151, 154, 155, 156, 159, 184, 199

Nemirovich-Danchenko, Vladimir 153, 153*n*, 154, 157
New Testament, The 136, 137, 138, 144, 145
Nicholas II 189
  Execution of Royal family 178
Nietzsche, Friedrich 79

O'Casey, Sean 215
  The Plough and the Stars 215
October Revolution, The 13, 19, 20, 21, 71, 138, 143, 149, 150, 158, 162, 184, 189
Old Testament, The 136, 137, 138, 139, 143, 144, 145, 146

INDEX

Orwell, George 18
   Tolstoi and 18
Ostrovskii, Aleksandr 153*n*, 158*n*

Paustovskii, Konstantin 171
   Gleaming Clouds, The 171–2
Pevear, Richard and Volokhonsky, Larissa
   37, 38, 43, 44, 45, 49, 58, 65, 66
Pisarev, Dmitrii 69–70
Prokofiev, Sergei 203
   War and Peace (opera) 203
Protazanov, Iakov 151
Pushkin, Aleksandr 8–11, 15, 70, 79, 136, 151, 186
   Boris Godunov 203
   Bronze Horseman, The 9
   Captain's Daughter, The 9
   Dubrovskii 9
   Egyptian Nights 186
   Eugene Onegin 8, 10, 27, 125*n*, 136
   Gypsies, The 11
   Mozart and Salieri 186
   Queen of Spades, The 8
   Station Master, The 151*n*
Putin, Vladimir 188

Queensland 166–7, 173

RAPP (Russian Association of Proletarian Writers) 150, 151
Repin, Ilia 164–5
Rousseau, Jean-Jacques 3–5, 77, 78
   Confessions, The 4
Rozanov, Vasilii 109, 135–46
   Views on family 134, 136, 137, 142
   Relations with Tolstoi 135–46
   Views on illegitimacy 139–40

Schopenhauer, Arthur 5–7, 16, 146
Shakespeare, William 82, 87, 185, 232, 234
   Hamlet 185–6, 232
   Macbeth 232
Shklovskii, Viktor 75*n*, 135, 136, 145, 149*n*
Socialist Realism 21, 27, 28, 157
Sokurov, Aleksandr 181–2
   Russian Ark, The 181, 191
Solovev, Vladimir 94

Stalin, Joseph 71, 79, 150, 157, 185, 190, 201, 203
Stanislavskii, Konstantin 152, 153, 153*n*, 155, 212
Starchestvo 93–109 *passim*, 143
   Revival of 99
   Tolstoi's attitude to 97

Tolstoi, Lev *passim*
   About Art 1889 68
   Anna Karenina 9–10, 11, 12, 13, 14, 22, 23, 74, 85, 88–9, 95, 95*n*, 114, 115, 117, 118, 119, 121, 122, 124, 125*n*, 126–7, 143, 144, 145, 157*n*, 159, 221*n*, 227, 229, 232
   Autobiographical themes in 73, 82
   Childhood 4, 69, 78
   Compared to Elizabeth Gaskell 220–34
   Cossacks, The 9
   Death of Ivan Ilich, The 2, 7, 9, 16, 17
   Family Happiness 115
   Father Sergius 92–109
   First Distiller, The 149, 159
   Fruits of Enlightenment, The 153*n*
   Influence of Rousseau and Schopenhauer on 3–7
   Influence of Pushkin on 8–11
   Influence on Wittgenstein 16–17
   In post-revolutionary Russia 19–22
   Kreutzer Sonata, The 4, 13, 77, 85*n*, 89, 114, 119, 122, 134, 163, 200, 232
   Landscape, use of 49–53
   Living Corpse, The 152
   Metaphors, use of 58–9
   My Confession 4, 88*n*, 146
   Ostranenie, use of 17, 55–8, 75*n*
   Philosophy and 14–19, 53–5
   Popularity of 149
   Power of Darkness, The 142, 152, 208–18
   Prisoner of the Caucasus The 69
   Reception in England 11–14
   Religious themes in 76, 92–109
   Resurrection 4, 11, 13, 74, 138, 141, 145, 148–59
   Sentimentalism in 75
   Sex, views on 77
   Shakespeare, view of 17–18, 70*n*
   Tolstoianism 161–2, 163, 164, 174

Tolstoi, Lev *passim (cont.)*
   Translations of   34–67
   Use of French by   58–9, 64–6, 181
   War and Peace   34–67, 74, 79, 84, 85, 89, 145, 152, 179–207
   What Is Art?   68–80
Trenev, Konstantin   151
Tretiakov, Sergei   180
Trollope, Anthony   221*n*, 231
Turgenev, Ivan   11, 70, 78, 97, 136
   Home of the Gentry   136
Tvardovskii, Alesandr
   Terkin in the Otherworld   184

Vacation, concepts of   111, 113, 114–17, 120–9
Vakhtangov, Evgenii   180, 187, 199–201, 204
Vakhtin, Boris   192
   One Absolutely Happy Village   192
Venuti, Lawrence   35
Veselitskaia, Lidiia   111–29
   Mimi the Bride   112, 116, 126
   Mimi at the Spa   111–29
   Mimi Has Taken Poison   112, 127, 128

Treatment of fashion by   115, 116, 118–22, 124, 124*n*, 126

Wagner, Richard   75
Wellek, René and Warren, Austen   82
   Theory of Literature   82*n*
Wiener, Leo   35, 37, 38, 43, 44, 45, 49, 62, 64, 66
Wilde, Oscar   194
Winfrey, Oprah   23
Wittgenstein, Ludwig   7*n*, 16–17

Yeltsin, Boris   187–8

Zhitiia   100–4, 105*n*, 108
Zuzenko, Alexander   162–76
   Execution   170
   Law of the Fang and the Cudgel, The   174
   Membership of SRs   170
   Portrayal by Paustovskii   171–2
   Rejection of Tolstoianism   174
   Relations with Illin   172–4
   Service as sea captain   170
   Union activism   170

Printed in the United States
by Baker & Taylor Publisher Services